I0816739

EXPECTATION OF VALOR

Planning for the Iraq War

COLONEL KEVIN C. M. BENSON, US ARMY (Ret.)

CASEMATE

Pennsylvania & Yorkshire

Published in the United States of America and Great Britain in 2024 by
CASEMATE PUBLISHERS
1950 Lawrence Road, Havertown, PA 19083
and
47 Church Street, Barnsley, S70 2AS, UK

Hardback Edition: ISBN 978-1-63624-426-6
Digital Edition: ISBN 978-1-63624-427-3

A CIP record for this book is available from the British Library

Typeset in India by Lapiz Digital Services, Chennai.

For a complete list of Casemate titles, please contact:

CASEMATE PUBLISHERS (US)
Telephone (610) 853-9131
Fax (610) 853-9146
Email: casemate@casematepublishers.com
www.casematepublishers.com

CASEMATE PUBLISHERS (UK)
Telephone (0)1226 734350
Email: casemate@casemateuk.com
www.casemateuk.com

Contents

Foreword		v
Acknowledgements		viii
US Military Ranks		ix
Glossary		x
Introduction: Cold War, Hot Wars, Peace Dividends, Wars on "The Periphery"		xvi
1	Planning for War	1
2	Planning the Invasion Until D-Day	25
3	Build-up to D-Day	55
4	Planning While Fighting, March 2003	87
5	April in Iraq	111
6	Off-ramps and Phase IV	139
7	Building the Coalition, May 2003	171
8	A Bad Feeling	199
9	My Last Month in Theater, June 2003	221
10	Final Thoughts	241
Bibliography		247
Index		249

On D-Day, June 6, 1944, General Patton wrote a letter to his son:

"TAKE CALCULATED RISKS. That is quite different from being rash. My personal belief is that if you have a 50% chance take it because the superior fighting qualities of American soldiers led by me will surely give you the extra 1% necessary."

This is the expectation of valor.

Foreword

History involves the study of the Great Captains and decisive battles to glean lessons about the art of war, strategic decisions, and seminal inflections in international relations. The recent wars of the United States—Grenada, Panama, Somalia, Iraq (*Desert Shield/Desert Storm*), the Balkans, Afghanistan, Iraq (*Iraqi Freedom*), even the proxy wars in Ukraine and Gaza—are fresh in the memory of the nation but are not fully evaluated for historic purposes.

It is rare to get the perspective of one whose position on the field of battle was the formulation of the plans that were implemented or not implemented; the discussions that happened before the war started and throughout the course of the war, as well as the considerations for termination of a given conflict.

In retrospect, the outcome of such formulations may seem to be the result of clear choices and unambiguous circumstances such that everything falls into alignment, from the grand strategic level to the tactical action level. But this is a sanitary evaluation of what is instead an extraordinarily unsanitary matter, a matter driven by human personality and ego dynamics and shrouded in fog, friction, uncertainty, and chance; fraught with miscalculations, missed opportunities, grossly incorrect self-awareness relative to the actual circumstances, and untimely decision-making.

In my experience after graduating with a Master of Military Art and Science degree from the US Army School of Advanced Military Studies, I was privileged to serve the United States as a plans officer within the staffs of many prominent military commanders, and as a commander of very large, complex, multi-nation military commands during periods of war and in contested deterrence in several regions of the world. Serving "in the arena" in policy and military advisory roles at the highest levels of governments undertaking international relations, I learned firsthand that theory and practice are routinely discordant.

Colonel Kevin C. M. Benson, a colleague from my class at the School of Advanced Military Studies and the author of *Expectation of Valor: Planning for the Iraq War*, has captured the inner workings of a high command at war, with all the warts, blemishes, and scars that the real experience of such a thing delivers, and theory cannot. COL Benson's work is a "must read" for any serious study of civil–military relations and national security decision making. The book serves to dispel the worn myth that the military had not planned beyond the initial attack to eliminate the Ba'ath Party regime of strongman Saddam Hussein.

Indeed, there was planning. There was planning for the deployment and receiving of forces from multiple countries with unique caveats and limitations, connected to each country's sense of national honor and appetite for risk which could not be known in advance. There was planning for the conduct of combat operations to achieve strategic goals, but the goals were inadequately described, leaving plans in the wrong place. There was planning for what comes after major combat operations to establish conditions of stability in a country that was not ready for self-determination and a non-occupational touch, leaving the plans out of alignment with the realities that emerged and widely off the mark in terms of policies required to consolidate the gains made by military action. The reality of the limits of military action to create lasting gains is evident and on display.

Victory does not come from the plan, not even from planning which is necessary but not sufficient. Victory comes from clear vision, perseverance, unity of effort, and continuous applications of instruments available to a nation to generate its power. The opening acts of Operation *Iraqi Freedom* was characterized by blurred vision, hastiness, discordance between decisions and actions and haphazard application of the nation's instruments.

Considering stark evidence provided by Colonel Benson from his position on the field, there can be no lasting gains without clear policy aims and the correlated commitments of the many powers, beyond military power, of the United States and others who join with the United States. In the Iraq War, such clear aims did not emerge. Such correlation could not be manifested.

This work is well-fitted to the intersecting lattice of military history, political history, international relations, and civil military affairs. Colonel Benson's perspective is certainly not the only perspective of what happened in the period leading up to the invasion of Iraq in 2003, and the ultimate reduction of forces and handover to civilian leadership concurrent with an accelerated descent into a deadly period of counterinsurgency.

Yet, his perspective must be included to see the nuances of the finished tapestry, which is not yet complete. How did things go so brilliantly, according to expectations, only to fall so short of requirements and end up being sourly dissatisfying in their costly outcome. This book may open the reader's eyes in a way that facilitates deeper learning about what it takes to win militarily and strategically. Without seriously considering these insights, the foreign adventures of the United States and like-minded countries will likely find the future to be as dissatisfying as the relatively recent past from 1950 to the present.

General Vincent K. Brooks, US Army (Ret.)

General Brooks served over 42 years, from his entry into the United States Military Academy in 1976 until his retirement from active duty on the first day of 2019. He served as a general officer from 2002 to 2019 in key positions in the Pentagon with the Joint Staff and the Department of the Army. He was field commander conducting operations in the Balkans, in Iraq, throughout the Middle East and Central Asia, throughout the Indo-Pacific region, and in Korea and Japan. He was also a plans and policy officer in several commands. Serving as the operations spokesperson for US CENTCOM at the start of the invasion into Iraq in 2003, he was a witness to the story told in this book.

Acknowledgements

This book is dedicated to the superb team of men and women I had the honor of leading during the planning for and early execution of Operation *Iraqi Freedom/COBRA II*. I mention them by name in this book: officers such as Tom Reilly, Evan Huelfer, Frank Jones, Mike Hendricks, Willie Davis, Joe Whitlock, Winston Gaines, Glenn Patten, Bill Innocenti, Wayne Grieme, Bryan Sparling, Chris Field, and Nick Elliot. The people of our operational plans group worked through the challenges of putting together a plan that worked, at the outset at least. Their song must be sung.

I worked with the "dream team" of general officers: General Dave McKiernan (Ret.), General J. D. Thurman (Ret.), Lieutenant General Chris Christianson (Ret.), Lieutenant General "Fuzzy" Webster (Ret.), Lieutenant General Robert R. "Rusty" Blackman, USMC (ret.), Major General James "Spider" Marks (Ret.), Major General Hank Stratman (Ret.), and UK Major General Albert Whitley (Ret.). Our corps and MEF commanders—General Scott Wallace (Ret.) and General James Conway, USMC (Ret.)—commanded their units from the front, and with distinction.

The wonderful editors at Casemate Publishers, Ruth Sheppard, Tracey Mills, Elke Morice-Atkinson and Lizzy Hammond helped me produce a book of quality. I must add any factual errors, typos, or other errors are solely my fault. As I explain in the introduction, this book is based on my daily reports and personal journal.

I must also add this book could not have been completed without the support of my wife, Kate, my daughter, Sharon, and my mother-in-law, Marion Stevens. These three ladies kept me humble.

US Military Ranks

US Army

2LT	Second lieutenant
1LT	First lieutenant
CPT	Captain
MAJ	Major
LTC	Lieutenant colonel
COL	Colonel
BG	Brigadier general (one star)
MG	Major general (two stars)
LTG	Lieutenant general (three stars)
GEN	General (four stars)

US Navy

RDML	Rear admiral (lower half), equivalent of a BG
RADM	Rear admiral, equivalent of a MG
VADM	Vice admiral, equivalent of an LTG

For clarity, I used US Army rank throughout the book when referring to USAF and USMC general officers.

Glossary

AAMDC	Army air and missile defense command
AASLT	Air assault, the designation of a unit going into battle via helicopter
AC or A/C	Active component, a generic term for the standing force of the US Army
A-Day	The day on which air operations begin
AFB	Air force base
Ansar al Islam	An Iraq-based Sunni terror group
AOR	Area of responsibility
APS	Army Pre-positioned Stocks, either Army equipment stored in warehouses in particular regions or on a group of contracted cargo ships carrying equipment for Army units
APOE/D	Aerial port of embarkation/debarkation
ARCENT	Army Forces Central Command
ARRC	Allied rapid reaction corps, a NATO three-star general led headquarters
ATACMS	Army tactical missile system
C4ISR	Command, control, communications, computers, intelligence, surveillance and reconnaissance
CCIR	Commander's critical information requirement
C-Day	The day on which official movement of forces to the theater of operations begins
CENTAF	US Air Forces Central Command
CENTCOM	United States Central Command
CFACC	Combined Force Air Component Command
CFLCC	Combined Force Land Component Command
CFMCC	Combined Force Maritime Component Command
CFSOCC	Combined Force Special Operations Component Command
CG	Commanding General
CGSC	Command and General Staff College

CINC	Commander in chief
CJSOTF	Combined Joint Special Operations Task Force
CJTF	Combined Joint Task Force
CLC	Coalition liaison center
CMATT	Coalition Military Assistance Training Team
CMO	Civil–military operations refers to operations supporting US and host nation civil governance
CofS	Chief of staff
COMCENT	Commander, US Central Command
COMCFLCC	Commander, Combined Forces Land Component Command
CONPLAN	Contingency plan
CONUS	Continental United States
CPA	Coalition Provisional Authority
CS	Combat support, generally Army units like engineers and chemical decontamination units
CSA	Chief of staff, Army
CSM	Command Sergeant Major
CSR	Controlled supply rate, the rate at which selected munitions will be resupplied
CSS	Combat service support, generally Army units that sustain combat forces such as transportation truck units, ordnance, and maintenance
DA	Refers either to Department of the Army or to direct action, a Special Operations Forces task
DART	Disaster Assistance Response Team
DCG	Deputy Commanding General, (O) means Operations and (S) means Support
D/CofS	Deputy chief of staff
D-Day	The day a major operation begins
DEPORD	Deployment order
DOD/DoD	Department of Defense
DTRA	Defense Threat Reduction Agency
EAC	Echelon above corps, refers to logistical support units
EAD	Early arrival date, also echelon above division which are logistical support units
ENCOM	Engineer Command
EPW	Enemy prisoner of war
eSB	Enhanced separate brigades, selected Army National Guard brigades kept at a higher level of readiness
EUCOM	US European Command

FDO	Force deterrent option
FIF	Free Iraqi Forces
FLOT	Forward line of troops (used to identify the general line of advance of friendly troop units
FORSCOM	US Army Forces Command
FRAGO	Fragmentary order—a shorter form of an official order, usually directing an immediate upcoming change to the flow of an operation
FUOPS	Future operations
G-Day	The day on which a major operation's ground operations begin
HET	Heavy equipment transport
HMMWV	High-mobility multipurpose wheeled vehicle
HOC	Humanitarian Operations Center
HQDA	Headquarters, department of the Army
HUMINT	Human intelligence, reports from a network of agents
ID	Infantry division
IO	Information operations
ISG	Iraq Survey Group
ITO	Iraq Theater of Operations
JDAM	Joint direct attack munition, a precision-guided bomb
JMD	Joint Manning Document
JOPES	Joint Operations Planning and Execution System
JSOC	Joint Special Operations Command
JSOTF	Joint Special Operations Task Force
JTF	Joint Task Force
KAZ	Kurdish autonomous zone
KDP	Kurdistan Democratic Party
LAD	Latest arrival date—the latest date a deploying unit can arrive without disrupting an operation
LD	Line of departure—the line on the ground that establishes, when crossed, that an operation had begun
LNO	Liaison officer
MARCENT	Marine Forces Central Command
MarDiv	Marine division
MEDEVAC	Medical evacuation, mostly referring to helicopters
MEF	Marine expeditionary force
MeK	Mujahedin-e-Khalq—an anti-Iranian government group sponsored by Saddam Hussein
MEU/ARG	Marine expeditionary unit/amphibious ready group

MLRS	Multiple-launch rocket system
MND	Multi-national Division
MOPP	Mission oriented protective posture that uses a scale ranging from one to four to indicate the level protective clothing needed to protect from chemical weapons. Level one indicates a protective suit should be one, and level four indicates that a completely closed protective suit and mask should be worn
MPRI	Military Professional Resources, Inc.
MPSRON	Maritime pre-positioned squadron—a group of ships carrying equipment for a Marine Corps unit
NAVCENT	Naval Forces Central Command
NCO	Non-commissioned officer—generic reference to sergeants of any rank from Sergeant (E5) to Command Sergeant Major (E9)
NGB	National Guard Bureau
NIC	New Iraqi Corps
Non-resident CSC/CGSC	Used to describe Army officers who were not selected to attend the Command and General Staff College course, but who elect to take the course of instruction as a non-resident
OGA	Other government agency, the CIA
OPCON	Operational Control
OPG	Operational plans group
OPLAN	Operations plan
OPSDEPS	Operations deputies
ORHA	Organization for Reconstruction and Humanitarian Assistance
OSD	Office of the Secretary of Defense
PJHQ	Permanent Joint Headquarters, a British headquarters
POTUS	President of the United States
Profis	Professional filler system, used to place called to active duty reserve doctors into US Army battalions
RC	Reserve component, generic term for the reserve forces of the US Army
RFF	Request for forces
RFI	Request for information
RGFC	The Iraqi Republican Guard Forces Command
ROE	Rules of engagement
ROK	Republic of Korea

RSR	Required supply rate, the derived rate of resupply of munitions based upon historical data
SAMS	School of Advanced Military Studies
SCIRI	Supreme Council for the Islamic Revolution in Iraq—an anti-Saddam Shia group
SECDEF	Secretary of Defense
SETAF	Southern European Task Force
SIGINT	Signals intelligence
SPOD	Sea port of debarkation
SPOE	Sea port of embarkation
SSE	Sensitive site exploitation
STO	Special technical operations
SOCCENT	Special Operations Component Central Command
SOF	Special Operations Forces
STARTEX	Start of the exercise—the conditions at the beginning of an exercise
SVTC	Secure video teleconference
TACON	Tactical control
Task Organize	The US Army defines a task organization as "A temporary grouping of forces designed to accomplish a particular mission" and defines task-organizing as "The process of allocating available assets to subordinate commanders and establishing their command and support relationships." (Army Doctrinal Reference Publication 1–02).
TBM	Tactical ballistic missile
TLAM	Tomahawk Land Attack Missile
TOA	Transfer of Authority
TPFDD	Time phased force deployment data
TPFDL	Time phased force deployment list
TRADOC	US Army Training and Doctrine Command
TRANSCOM	United States Transportation Command
TSC	Theater Support Command
TTP	Tactics, techniques, and procedures
USARC	US Army Reserve Command
USAREUR	US Army Europe
USDA	United States Department of Agriculture
UNHCR	United Nations High Commission on Human Rights
UNSCR	United Nations Security Council resolution
USNS	United States naval ship
VCSA	Vice chief of staff, Army

VOCO	Verbal order of the commander
VTC	Video teleconference
WG	Working group
WMD	Weapon of mass destruction
XO	Executive Officer

Plans Referenced

Operations Plan 1003

The first plan that was the basis for Central Command planning on a war with Iraq, written in 1998.

Operations Plan 1003V

A revised plan based on Plan 1003 that reflected an invasion of Iraq in accordance with the 2002 presidential directives. This plan was the basis for all CENTCOM component-level plans.

Operations Plan Cobra II

The Third Army/CFLCC plan for the land force's role in the invasion of Iraq. The first COBRA plan was executed in July 1944 when Patton's Third Army was introduced into combat in Europe. We chose the name Cobra as a link to the history of Third Army.

Operations Plan Eclipse II

The plan developed by Allied and Third Army planners for the occupation of Iraq. The first Eclipse plan was executed in 1945 for the occupation of Germany. Again, we chose the name Eclipse as a link to the history of Third Army.

Phases

US Army and US Joint Forces doctrine makes use of phases to describe the flow of the execution of a plan. There are four phases to a plan: I–IV. Phase I focuses on the alerting, mobilization, and deployment of units to the theater of war. Phase II focuses on the initial air operations and the roles of other components (land, sea, special operations) in support of air operations. Phase III focuses on the conduct of land operations designed to accomplish the main objectives given to the senior theater commander. Phase IV broadly encompasses the completion of the operation, from restoring order in the theater, reestablishing civil authority, and the return of forces to home station.

Introduction

Cold War, Hot Wars, Peace Dividends, Wars on "The Periphery"

"So, there I was." All war stories start with that phrase, or some variation of it. My purpose in writing this book is to tell my "war story," and to take on the common narrative told about the Iraq War, which is the Army did not plan how to conclude the war. Though some American general officers have stated this case, it is simply untrue. I know it is not true because in 2002 and 2003 I was assigned to Third Army and responsible for directing the development of the plans for the invasion of Iraq.

Before I start to tell my story, I offer the following framework for it to aid the reader's analysis. In my education as an Army officer I learned war is an instrument of policy. Military strategy is derived from policy because the political objective of the war determines the amount of force available for use during the war. This was not the approach used to develop strategy during the Iraq War. I believe that prior to the beginning of the war, policy making staffs and policy makers—civilian as well as military—conflated strategy and policy. The result was we ended up with neither, and this materially affected the planning for the campaign and supporting major operations. Bear this in mind as I tell my story of the development of the plans for the invasion of Iraq and for what was to happen once we arrived in Baghdad. My story starts at the beginning of my planning efforts at Third Army, though I will highlight a few notable events in my career leading up to arriving at Third Army in July 2002.

I went to war for the first time as a staff colonel. In my first experiences of war, I was guided by my education, institutional and personal, as well as the experience I had gained during my professional career up to that point.

The Cold War was in full swing when I graduated from the US Military Academy in June 1977. During my senior year, the Supreme Allied Commander, Europe, General Alexander Haig, addressed my class. General Haig asked the assembly of my classmates who was going to Germany on their first assignments. About one third of my class raised hands. Haig told us that when our war came it would not be in the central region of Europe. Our war, he stated, would be on the periphery.

I often reflected on this prophetic comment over the course of my career. I was commissioned in 1977 as an Armor officer and went to Fort Knox for the Armor Officer Basic Course. Over the years I had a normal pattern of assignments in the United States and Germany. I was fortunate to attend the Marine Corps Amphibious Warfare School after company command, and when I returned from Germany in 1989, I attended the US Army Command and General Staff College course, as well as attending the School of Advanced Military Studies, SAMS. After SAMS I served as a planner for the XVIII Airborne Corps. Following my planner assignment, I was sent to be the executive officer of the 2nd Cavalry Regiment.

I served as the regimental executive officer for two years, and worked for Colonel Walter "Skip" Sharp. I also served as the chief of staff for US Forces-Haiti before arriving at the Third Army staff for my second tour as a planner, which spanned 1996–98. There, in Atlanta and Kuwait, I worked for two outstanding leaders: Lieutenant General Steve Arnold and Lieutenant General Tommy Franks. When LTGs Arnold and Franks wanted things to get done to a high standard, they called on the planners: the SAMS graduates on the staff. I learned a great deal from LTG Arnold. He was a gentleman and a superb Soldier. Arnold was the G3 operations officer of Third Army during the First Gulf War, and commanded the 10th Mountain Division in Florida during the aftermath of Hurricane Andrew, as well as in operations in Somalia. Early in my tour of duty, Saddam Hussein rattled his sabers and Arnold sent the Third Army advanced command post and staff to Kuwait for 100 days. I accompanied the staff as the G3 Plans section leader. During this period, our commander on the scene was Major General Robert Ivany. MG Ivany was a sound tactician and, having served as President Reagan's aide-de-camp, was well versed in the nuances of policy and strategy. LTG Tommy Franks assumed command of Third Army upon LTG Arnold's retirement. Working for Franks was exciting.

I was in charge of LTG Franks's introduction to Third Army and the regional war plans, specifically the main war plan, 1003-96. This was the major "on the shelf" plan to counter an Iraqi invasion of Kuwait. I accompanied LTG Franks to Kuwait and took him to my favorite observation point on the anti-tank berm that defined the Kuwait–Iraq border at the time.[1] Before this trip I had only imagined breaching those berms to go north to Baghdad.

So, we were standing on top of the berm in the summer of 1997. It was hot as a firecracker and I was explaining the flow of the operation and the assumptions we were making to Franks, and he put his hand on his shoulder and said, "Kevin, when this happens again, we're never giving up Kuwait. I want you to start thinking about how we would start from here to go north." Franks had exciting ideas, along with the gift of provoking intense loyalty. You simply did not want to let the old man down.

---

1 The berm around Kuwait was 10 feet high and 20 feet wide. This berm was part of the border defense the Kuwaiti Government built after the first Gulf War in 1991.

Now perhaps I was lucky, because he was also one of those senior leaders who only gave a staff officer one chance to earn his spurs, and you never really knew when the test would come. If you passed his test, you were on his team. I did not know what the test was or when it would be, but I met his unstated standard and he treated me exceptionally well. We had a really tremendous relationship. I did not abuse it, but I never wanted to let LTG Franks down.

There was a dark side to LTG Franks as well. If you did not pass the test, you were marginalized; he did not have time for you. You were not moving at his speed. At the time I was a lieutenant colonel, and I saw how some colonels on his staff were ignored. These officers were not fired but just dismissed from important decisions. To Franks, these men were simply placeholders.

After battalion command the Army sent me to MIT (the Massachusetts Institute of Technology) from 2001–02. The superb MIT security studies program really prepared me for my next assignment as the Director of War Plans, J5, for Third Army. Oddly enough though, when I arrived at MIT I did not have a follow-on assignment. I actually had to look for my own assignment, and this did not make much sense to me. The Army had invested a great deal of money in sending me to live in the Boston area for a year, as well as attending the amazing security studies program at MIT, and I had to look for my own assignment? But again, here I was extremely lucky. LTG PT Mikolashek, then commanding Third Army, called me in August 2001 and asked if I would come back to Third Army as the chief of plans. I said "Yes" because I knew the headquarters and what they did, and because of the region it was in, and with it being the Army component of Central Command, it was always an exciting place to be. Then 9/11 happened.

I called LTG Mikolashek on the afternoon of 12 September 2001, and asked him if he wanted me to report immediately. His response was very interesting. We were not on a secure telephone line, but Mikolashek said "No, stay in school. You know what's coming next." I knew immediately what he was talking about—Iraq—and it really struck me. So I said, "Okay, Sir." I spent the rest of that year really digging into strategy, policy development, and reading all I could on the so-called "Neocon" movement and what all that meant.

I was very much interested in Secretary Donald Rumsfeld, Deputy Secretary Paul Wolfowitz, Dr. Stephen Cambone, and Mr. Douglas Feith. I read about where they were coming from politically, where were they coming from a policy point of view, their world views, etc. Even in September and October of 2001 there were news reports saying the administration was thinking about invading Iraq as a means to strike back at Al Qaeda. There was turmoil on the MIT campus and among the faculty as these people came to grips with the attack on the US and the nation going to war. It was a very interesting time to be at MIT. It was quite useful to talk to the faculty, especially as I considered where I would be heading after graduation.

I asked to be "read on" (meaning allowed to read the highly classified initial planning documents related to Iraq) to the planning effort before I reported in to Third Army. LTG Mikolashek agreed to this request and funded a trip for me. In late April and early May of 2002, I went to MacDill Air Force Base and CENTCOM headquarters, and then to Washington, D.C. and the Pentagon. While I was in Tampa, I met Colonels Mike Fitzgerald and Dave Halverson. Dave Halverson and I had first met in the summer of 1996 when we spent 100 days in Kuwait during my first tour at Third Army. I did not yet know COL Fitzgerald, but I formed an immediate and positive impression of him. When Franks wrote his memoirs, Dave and Mike were the only staff colonels he mentioned by name. They were truly heroes in this effort. I also asked about Phase IV planning, basically what were we going to do after we got to Baghdad and removed Saddam, while I was in Tampa.[2] I was told that as of April 2002, the planning for mission analysis had just started. I was puzzled by this and asked some questions as to why the effort was only just beginning. I received tired looks from COLs Fitzgerald and Halverson. They were so involved with getting the combat operations portion of the plan approved by the secretary of defense that there had been no time to even put together a plans team for the total campaign plan. The day in May 2002 I left Central Command, LTC John Agoglia convened the first Central Command-level plans team meeting on the fourth phase of the campaign plan.[3]

My education in the developmental process of this campaign continued when I went to Washington, D.C. and the Pentagon. I used the network of SAMS graduates to get access to the planning effort as well as a personal connection to the Deputy J5, who at the time was Major General Walter "Skip" Sharp, my former regimental commander. My SAMS classmate, Colonel Bob Drumm, met me inside the Pentagon and brought me up to speed on "the building's" efforts, as experienced Pentagon staffers called it. Bob Drumm took me to his office where he worked for a deputy assistant secretary of defense for policy, and I saw former Speaker of the House, Newt Gingrich and another man entering the Deputy Secretary of Defense Office. I asked COL Drumm who the fellow with Gingrich was. Bob told me it was Ahmed Chalabi of the Iraqi National Congress.

---

2 As mentioned in the glossary, US Army doctrine calls for the use of phases when developing complex operations plans. Phases lay out the anticipated logical flow of events during the execution of an operation. Phase IV covers post-hostilities actions, as well as the departure of forces from the theater of war.

3 Dave Halverson went on to promotion and service as the ADC (S) of the 4th Infantry Division, and so went back to Iraq in the fall of 2005. He retired as a lieutenant general. Mike Fitzgerald retired as a colonel. He received a Defense Superior Service Medal for all of his work, which is a travesty in my mind. He and Dave should have both received the Distinguished Service Medal for all the work they did for LTG Franks.

Bob Drumm had a really hard time inside the Pentagon. He had not, as he called it, "drunk the Kool-Aid." Drumm was convinced the decision to go to war had already been taken, and he was worried about the kind of forces we would be allowed to have to start the war. He was concerned Chalabi was telling everyone American forces would be met with open arms and Saddam's regime was a "house of cards." Drumm had not seen any intelligence to indicate that this was true. The trip to Tampa and the Pentagon was sobering.

War is a human endeavor. The first lesson any planner learns is that, just as the Coalition forces enter a war planning on being victorious, so too does the enemy enter a war with the thought of victory, and they will do just about anything to gain that victory. Did we planners in the land forces expect the sort of opposition that arose in the aftermath of the handover of Iraq operations in 2011? The answer is no. In 2003 we felt there would be a continued resistance to our forces, but we also assumed that the Iraqi Army would be recalled, the Iraqi police would return to duty, and Coalition forces could begin a withdrawal from the country over some time schedule linked to the ability of the Iraqi Army and security forces. Our planning group figured that there would be remnants of former regime loyalists who would be left with no option but to fight. We did consider an insurgency, but it was rated as less likely.

We also expected that fanatics (Al Qaeda, Ansar al Islam, Wahabi sects, etc.) would also try to come into Iraq to kill Americans. We could not have foreseen, in my mind, the depth of the resistance we ended up facing. We expected to be able to recall the Iraqi Army. Once the Coalition Provisional Authority (CPA) and Ambassador Bremer took the decision to disband the Iraqi Army as it stood and establish a completely new Iraqi Army, that particular assumption became invalid.

The great Chief of the Imperial German General Staff Helmut von Moltke, known as "Moltke the Elder," stated that no plan could look with certainty beyond initial contact with the enemy's main body. This dictum remains true today. A great deal of planning took place before, during, and after the conclusion of Phase III of the CENTCOM Campaign Plan 1003V and the CFLCC supporting major operations Plan Cobra II. I have already mentioned that war, as planners know, is an extension of policy by other means. The enemy gets a vote and policy will change as a result of that interaction with the enemy. And so, war is and will remain a human endeavor. It is a contest of wills, and the side with the stronger will, as well as the best weapons for the task, will ultimately prevail.

During Phase III, in the face of continuous questions from the Office of the Secretary of Defense (OSD) and the White House on various facets of the campaign, the serious work of thinking through potential decision points, transitions, branches, and sequels continued. The key result of the continuous questioning was that the senior leadership of the land forces and CENTCOM, despite their best efforts, were drawn into the current fight and the effort to keep Washington informed.

It is a planner's job to think about the "How" and "What If" of unfolding plans, but planners are not empowered to take decisions. That privilege is reserved for commanders. Based on that experience, and my own personal reflections on what I did and didn't do well, I feel I, too, can offer reflection on Iraq, and cautions on the next war.

Our Army exists to defend the Republic by waging war in its name. Of course, the Army will do many other things for our Republic—from firefighting to disaster relief—but its primary purpose is preparing for war and, when directed, fighting and winning war. We started out in Iraq with a doctrine that guided action, and it was incredibly successful. The conduct of the war began to change and, recognizing the change, the Army and Marine Corps adjusted its doctrine while fighting, trained units in new methods, and delivered them to the war. This is an astounding accomplishment. The Armed Forces of the United States also concluded the Iraq War in a manner that must be considered victorious: these forces were never defeated in battle and accomplished objectives that led to attaining the policy objective of handing the security challenge over to the Iraqis and departing in accordance with a nation-to-nation agreement in December 2011. This is something that had never been done before in that region of the world: an Army leaving in accordance with conditions of an inter-governmental agreement, and not remaining indefinitely as an occupying power.

The main contributor in all the decision making was, again in my view, a seeming inability to be able to communicate with policy makers what a force could, and more importantly could not, do. Could we have gotten to Baghdad with one brigade? I suppose we could have, but the real question was, what would we do once we got there? This was the issue I could not get into the fore; the policy objectives were straight forward enough, but I could not get a hearing on possible ways to attain the necessary military conditions linked to attaining policy success. For reasons I am still not clear on, we could not get around an initial expectation (from policy makers: Rumsfeld, Feith, Wolfowitz, Cambone, etc.) that Iraq in 2003 would be a replay of Kuwait in 1991, and Jeffersonian–Jacksonian democracy would simply break out, as if there was a little American inside every Iraqi yearning to breathe free. But at this point in time, these reflections belonged to the future. When the efforts that would result in the development of major operations plan Cobra II began, I had served as a planner at the corps, joint task force, and field army levels. During these assignments I participated in the planning and execution of stability and support operations in Somalia and Florida, major operations planning for Bosnia, the defense of Kuwait, the invasion of Iraq, and other planning efforts. I worked with Air Force, Navy, Marine Corps, and special operations planners. I briefed ambassadors, US Senators, foreign chiefs of defense staff, and US regional commanders in chief. I also commanded a tank battalion.

My professional education introduced me to military theory, international relations theory, critical thinking, and familiarized me with alternative perspectives on deterrence. I was now about to enter a new level of planning, as I was going to be the planner for a field army; and it would be more than a field army à la World War II. I would be an operational-level planner writing directions for two corps formations whose objective was the defeat of an opposing army and associated irregular troops, all of which would lead to the replacement of a regime. I felt I was ready for the challenge. I was a SAMS guy, so I would figure it out.

Some context for the reader: my account covers the period of time from roughly June 2002 to July 2003. At the beginning of this timeframe, my plans team and I had been working at Fort McPherson in Atlanta, Georgia. We then went into the theater of war, initially based in Kuwait City, Kuwait, and then in Baghdad, Iraq. While we were in these locations, many of us travelled to destinations like the United States, Great Britain, and Poland, to name a few. We attended conferences related to the planning and execution of the Iraq War.

We made use of the technology of the time. We communicated using secure telephones and secure email. We also made use of secure video teleconferences, especially when interacting with officials in the Pentagon. By secure, I mean the signals used to transmit messages and live video were encoded to prevent enemies and adversaries from easily "reading our mail," so to speak.

Our entire headquarters staff deployed from Fort McPherson to Kuwait. Thus, the plans team, the people working directly for me, and the planners from other staff sections, were committed to the process. Once deployed we worked 7 days a week, 16–18 hours a day. When the war commenced in March 2003, we wore our chemical protective suits almost constantly. We took this precaution because we really believed the Iraqis would use chemical weapons.

I based this account on the daily reports I rendered via email to my commanding general, as well as in my daily journal. I wrote the reports myself, drawing on other reports I received from my planners, talks with them, what I had understood of their impressions of the effort. I also included my assessment of intelligence reports and how these would influence our planning for future events. With this context, on to the story of planning for the war in Iraq.

CHAPTER ONE

Planning for War

In a theoretical world, planning proceeds in parallel with higher-level headquarters, as well as in collaboration with subordinate headquarters. The planning for what would become Operation *Iraqi Freedom* did not take place in the theoretical world (an understatement to be sure). I confirmed—for myself at least—that the Prussian philosopher of war, Carl von Clausewitz, was correct: war is a continuation of policy by other means. True planning at the level I served at takes place in the space between military and policy requirements. My challenge was to sustain the energy required to complete a total major operations plan supporting the CENTCOM campaign plan while dealing with the demands of policy and policy makers from above, and commanders and staffs below our headquarters.

These demands from policy makers came in the form of email, phone calls, and the famous Rumsfeld "snowflakes." Secretary Rumsfeld sent numerous memos to the joint staff in Washington and to Central Command headquarters. These contained questions and comments all requiring immediate replies, and came out of the secretary's office so frequently they were termed snowflakes. The situation was best summed up by my SAMS classmate and friend, then Colonel (Brigadier General select) Vince Brooks. Colonel Brooks wrote to me on 19 July 2002, saying that there was great impatience in Washington and we'd be asked to do things on the cheap, "well beyond the scope of military logic."

Brooks did not elaborate on what he meant by the scope of military logic. I inferred he meant I would need to think through the theory learned in SAMS and recognize everything would be controlled in Washington (even if it was not controllable). He told me I would earn my pay as a planner when I could offer plans that got the impossible done, and which defied the odds and overcame extraordinary risk. This was wise counsel, and something I kept to myself.

In the coming pages, I will relate the story of the effort to produce a major operations plan that would link the battles and engagements fought by the Army's V Corps and I Marine Expeditionary Force to the strategic objectives established by Central Command, the Joint Chiefs of Staff, and the policy goals of the Office of the Secretary of Defense, and the White House.

The planning began with a review of the standing war plan, Plan 1003, which was rejected by Secretary Rumsfeld as "old think." This was the so-called "generated start" plan. The generated start was based on a lengthy period of deployments of Army and Marine Corps units from the United States and Europe to Kuwait. There was an equally lengthy period of time for the conduct of extensive bombing of Iraqi defensive positions before ground forces entered Iraq and engaged Iraqi Army units en route to Baghdad. "Old think," from Secretary Rumsfeld's perspective, meant unchallenged assumptions, a lack of understanding of the effect of combining new technology and special operations forces on the conduct of battles, and insufficient speed to shock the Iraqi leadership.

The rejection of the standing war plan led to the frenetic development, at first in PowerPoint only, of the "running start" plan which envisioned starting the war with a small force and deploying follow-on forces while the battle was joined. My arrival at Third Army coincided with the start of the development of the "running start" planning effort. The challenge of "running start" was getting enough forces into Kuwait before the decision to start the war. This challenge was not easy to overcome.

We had to explain the necessity of bringing conventional forces into Kuwait in advance of a presidential decision to begin the war. At the time, Secretary Rumsfeld's

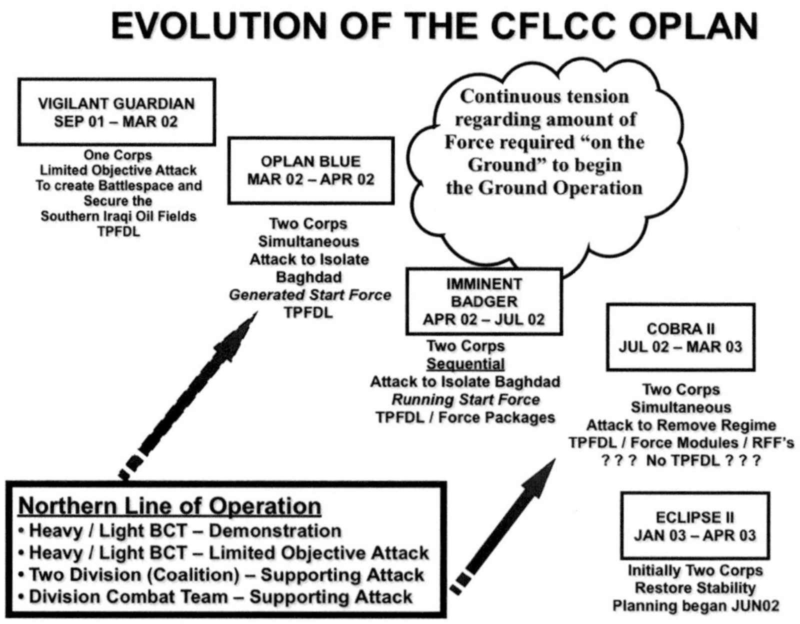

Chart 1. This chart was developed to outline the evolution of the overall planning effort and the versions of the plans made for the invasion as policy and senior commander guidance changed over time. (From the author's personal files, and prepared in 2003 by officers working for the author.)

experience of war consisted of watching Special Forces teams in Afghanistan riding horses, and calling in bombs dropped by airplanes. A war in Iraq would be far different to the ongoing war in Afghanistan. In addition to this major planning and educational effort, we also faced a number of other planning requirements, ranging from how to conduct the expected city-based fight inside Baghdad to the handling of the anticipated evidence of weapons of mass destruction our intelligence indicated we would find throughout Iraq. The first challenge, indicative of these tensions, was waiting for me when I arrived at Fort McPherson, Georgia, on a hot day in late June 2002.

US Central Command had organized for war with subordinate commands for all assigned US and Coalition land, sea, air, and special operations forces. Ninth US Air Force was designated the Combined Forces Air Component Command (CFACC, pronounced "See-Fac"). CFACC controlled all air operations in the Central Command theater of operations. The US Navy's Fifth Fleet was designated the Combined Forces Maritime Component Command (CFMCC, pronounced "Sif Mick"). CFMCC controlled all naval operations in the theater. A Special Operations headquarters assigned to Central Command was designated Combined Forces Special Operations Component Command (CFSOCC, pronounced "Sif-Sock"). CFSOCC controlled most special operations forces in the theater. I arrived at Third US Army/Combined Forces Land Component Command (CFLCC, pronounced "See-Flick") in late June 2002. CFLCC controlled all conventional land forces in the theater.

When I arrived, I met the Deputy Commanding General, Major General Hank Stratman. He and I had never served together before, and the initial interview between us was somewhat abrupt, as MG Stratman was used to getting people assigned to Third Army who'd never served above the battalion-level. I do not think he knew

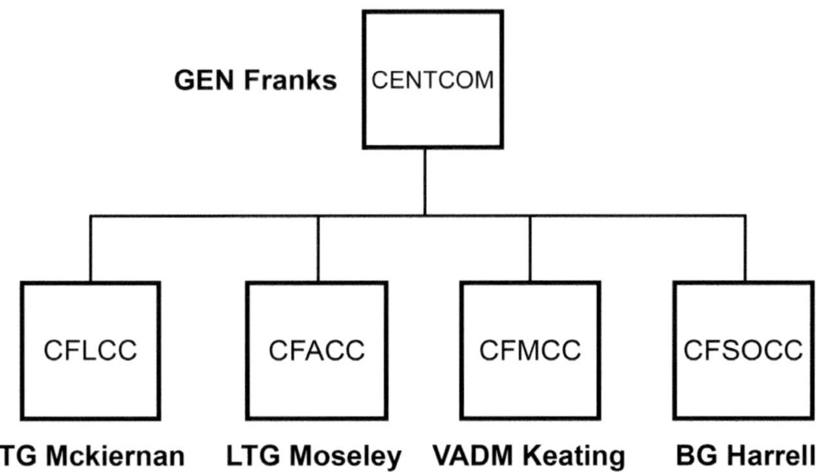

Chart 2. This chart depicts the major subordinate elements of CENTCOM.

anything about my previous Army experiences. When Stratman rather tiredly asked if I had any experience above battalion I told him this was my second tour at Third Army, I had a tour of duty at the XVIII Airborne Corps plans section, and I was a SAMS graduate, as well as coming from the MIT Security Studies program. Stratman was surprised I was assigned to Third Army. He approved of my assignment as the director of plans for CFLCC. He did not know LTG Mikolashek asked for me by name for that exact position. I went to a familiar place: the plans office in the former warehouse that housed Third Army headquarters.

First "Snowflake"

I was the first new arrival into the office in some time. The plans section was in tough shape. The planners were already very tired as the entire plans team had started work on the afternoon of 11 September 2001, and had not yet stopped for a breather. I asked my predecessor, Colonel Rich Kaiura, for all of the written work done thus far, especially with a view towards the final portion of the campaign: what was to be done after we got to Baghdad. Kaiura sent me to the senior planner, LTC Tom Reilly, a SAMS graduate and veteran of the 2nd Cavalry Regiment in which he had been decorated for valor in the First Gulf War. Reilly reported to the office to meet me; he had deep bags under his eyes. He was leading the effort to develop the time-phased force deployment list, TPFDL (pronounced "Tip-fiddle," more on this later). I asked Reilly how the planning for what we would do after we got to Baghdad, Phase IV, was going. He looked at me with very tired eyes.

LTC Reilly told me the team was currently working on a "snowflake." I was unfamiliar with the term at the time. I asked him what the task was, and he handed me a copy of an interoffice memo which read, "We have a brigade on the ground. Why can't we go now?" The note was signed by the Deputy Secretary of Defense, Paul Wolfowitz. I laughed.

I thought this was a terrific indicator of the real morale of the section. Tom Reilly was actually busting my fanny on the first day I was in the office. This had to be an example of "planner humor." After I finished chuckling, I told Reilly that while I appreciated a good joke, I was the colonel after all, and so to please stop the joking and let me know what's going on. Tom Reilly just shook his head and assured me this, in fact, was a legitimate task from the Office of the Secretary of Defense.

The task we received along with the note was to answer Wolfowitz's question as to why we could not go to Baghdad right then, June 2002, as we had a brigade combat team on the ground in Kuwait. It was an amazing question, and was answered only after we did the math on the amount of fuel, ammunition, water, and food it would take to move one M1A1 Abrams tank and its four-man crew from Kuwait to Baghdad, and the support structure required to move that much fuel, ammunition, water, and food. It also made me wonder why the Army officers within the Office of the Secretary Defense or on the joint staff had not answered this note. This was my first snowflake. There were many others to come. We had to deal with such questions that took time and effort away from the hard-thinking required to develop a major land operations plan that fit inside the larger picture of a campaign plan.

At this time, June/July 2002, it appeared GEN Franks, the regional commander in chief, CINC, was engaged in a process of responding to questions from people in the Office of the Secretary of Defense, not to mention the Secretary himself, on what it was going to take to replace a regime in a sovereign country and then provide enough security to ensure a follow-on government that was friendly to our own.[1] Why else would the operational-level command staff need to spend the time answering the snowflake from the Office of the Secretary of Defense? It seemed the lack of military experience within the office was contributing to drawing the wrong conclusions from operations conducted in Afghanistan.

Also around this time, there was a book published by Eliot Cohen titled *Supreme Command: Soldiers, Statesmen, and Leadership in Wartime*. This was the book du jour in Washington.[2] I cannot say for sure how many people actually read Cohen's book, but I did. I concluded some staff officer read the book, then gave a briefing to the senior people in the Office of the Secretary of Defense. My guess was that incorrect conclusions or interpretations were drawn based on this briefing. Simply put, I came to believe these people concluded a lack of military education was not enough reason to preclude them from interfering in military planning. There was an idea to press the military into thinking "outside the box" because the military mind could not do this. My "box" was the planet Earth and bounded by Newtonian physics, where it took time to move mass over distance.

Based on this conclusion and my interpretation of the constant briefings GEN Franks had to send to Washington, I came to believe he *was* involved in a very important process of education. He was educating the secretary of defense and the people in the Office of the Secretary of Defense on just what CENTCOM and CENTCOM's subordinate commands were engaged in, as hasty decisions taken by the Office of the Secretary of Defense could lead to beginning the campaign too early, and without sufficient structure to sustain the campaign. The downside of this effort was that CENTCOM's very best officers were drawn into this process.

In every headquarters, there are a handful of really good officers, a large group of average officers, and some less than capable officers. The handful of really good officers at CENTCOM, those who could really understand the mind of the commander, focused exclusively on the problem of educating people in the Office of the Secretary

---

1 Shortly after I arrived, the Secretary of Defense changed the titles of the regional CINCs to regional commanders, as there is only one Commander in Chief.

2 On the dust jacket of the book, William Kristol was quoted thus: "If I could ask President Bush to read one book, this would be it."

of Defense. While average officers are good, the effort to develop a campaign plan involving an unspecified number of Coalition troops that need to be organized to defeat a large land army and remove and then replace a regime which had been in power for 30 years was daunting to say the least.

Thinking about "What to do after we get to Baghdad"

I knew I had to get a separate group up and running to look at Phase IV, post-hostilities. To that end, I put LTC Mike Hendricks, a SAMS graduate and my executive officer, and three other officers—LTC Glen Patten, an engineer, LTC Winston Gaines, US Army Reserve, and MAJ Willie Davis, Signal Corps—to the task. Patten had a Corps of Engineers background, thus giving us an edge in thinking through the inevitable challenges of reconstruction and the contracting efforts. Gaines had been called to active duty specifically to join the Third Army staff. He was an Adjutant General's Corps officer, but his best quality was he was a really thoughtful guy. Davis, an active duty officer, was really looking forward to planning the communications system required for an invasion. I told the three of them, "You're going to be part of the Phase Four team. You guys start digging into the details, and even if it's just a skeleton you've got to give us something to build on. You guys build me the skeleton."

I put LTC Hendricks in overall charge to keep the group focused because our operational plans group, all of the planners on the Third Army staff who nominally worked for me, were so tied up with developing TPFDL and the following series of plans: Generated Start, Running Start, and Hybrid. Under LTG Mikolashek, all of the CFLCC plans began with I Marine Expeditionary Force as the tactical-level headquarters in command of all ground forces. Later on, our plans brought V Corps Headquarters in as more divisions entered the fight. This was done in accordance with directives from CENTCOM and the Pentagon to speed up the execution and deployment cycle. Later on, LTG McKiernan took command of Third Army and directed that CFLCC would begin the war with two corps headquarters: V Corps and I MEF. Our efforts at the time took advantage of an expedited request for forces process which brought over all of the 3rd Infantry Division and the 1st Marine Division. This change entailed another major rewrite of the concept of the operation. During all of this effort, we were laboring under the impression the decision to go to war would be sometime after the secretary of defense's approval of the TPFDL and the movement of forces to Kuwait.

The Decision to go to War

The decision to begin the preparation for the invasion was taken at the CENTCOM Commanders' Conference in August 2002. This was the first commanders' conference I attended as the Director of Plans. From start to finish this conference was auspicious, both for me personally and for the future planning and execution effort.

I sat directly behind LTG Mikolashek, the commanding general of Third US Army/CFLCC. Mikolashek brought me and COL Mike Hawrylak, the lead Operations Officer, J3, with him to the conference. I had not served with Hawrylak prior to this assignment but I knew of him. He served at CENTCOM in the operations directorate and had extensive experience with planning the use of air power as a response to Iraqi antiaircraft and missile fire incidents. As the lead Operations Officer, J3, Mike Hawrylak was pushing for a large land forces zone of operations for the invasion and control of air-delivered fires. This push quickly became a "Franks's decision."

We all stood when GEN Franks entered that room in a secure facility on MacDill Air Force Base. Aside from him now wearing a fourth star, Franks looked about the same as the last time I'd served as his planner. His earthy sense of humor and Texan accent masked an incisive mind and a deep understanding of policy, strategy, and the operational art. His eye took in the room as he walked in, slapping backs and calling his component commanders and senior staff by their nicknames. He sat at the head of the conference table and then I caught his eye. Franks nodded and then said, "PT, now that I see Kevin Benson has joined your team, I expect great things of your planning effort." I was very flattered by that comment, and I also noticed that many other folks were now looking around trying to figure out who Benson was, and where he was sitting.

The conversation quickly turned to the current situation in Iraq. LTG Mike "Buzz" Moseley, US Air Force, dominated the room. His Ninth Air Force was the basis of the CFACC. His pilots were flying increasingly dangerous missions up to the limits of the UN-mandated no-fly zone over southern Iraq. At this conference, Moseley made a pitch for an even more aggressive scope of operations. He wanted to begin attacking the Iraqi air defense command and control system in the west of the country, starting from the conference's conclusion. Attacking the command and control nodes above the no-fly zone in Iraqi-controlled airspace really was an act of war, not covered by UN mandate but in keeping with the aggressive series of actions CENTCOM was taking in preparation for war.

General Franks leaned back in his chair after LTG Moseley's presentation. He looked around the room and just said, "Approved." In my journal entry for that day, I noted this was the day the decision for war was taken. It appeared that so long as our actions remained below a certain level, they'd essentially be invisible to the media, which was exactly the intended effect. In August 2002, Franks put into effect a pattern of activity consisting of peaks of action and then troughs of inaction which were ever so gently increased. The intended effect was to acclimatize both the media and the Iraqis to patterns of activity and attacks which would appear "normal" over a period of time.

This was quite a brilliant decision, and we did in fact establish an increasing pace of activity in theater which was not picked up by either the media or the Iraqis, not even when we moved prepositioned sets of equipment for both Army and Marine Corps units ashore and manned them with more and more Soldiers and Marines. At the time this was all in the future though, as Franks had only just taken the decision to pick up the pace and ferocity of our air attacks on the Iraqis.

General Franks then spoke about the conduct of the campaign. He looked at LTG Mikolashek and told him he expected his ground force commander to think broadly, boldly, and ask for a range of forces.

The good fortune of having a previous tour at Third Army would pay off for me at this conference. I knew what forces were apportioned to CENTCOM through the Joint Strategic Capabilities plan, JSCP. During the August component commander's conference, Franks said that we, the Third Army, should think about how to get to Baghdad as rapidly as possible and what other kinds of forces we might need. Franks said, "PT, I expect you'll come to me and ask for the 82nd Airborne Division." Mikolashek looked over his shoulder at me to see if I caught the remark. I had. I then nodded at Mikolashek and started thinking about how we might be able to use the 82nd to extend the range of attack helicopters when we started land operations. I wrote LTG Mikolashek a note saying, "I know exactly how to use them, Sir. Let's go for them right now. We've got a license to steal." This would require coordination with the Ninth Air Force/CFACC. We would certainly need a number of C-130 Hercules cargo planes. My time at the XVIII Airborne Corps, and associated airborne operation planning factors, were rolling around my head. I was looking forward to the break so I could introduce myself to my air planner counterparts.

First Encounter with the CFACC Planners

Just before the first break in the conference, LTG Mikolashek leaned over to LTG Moseley and passed him a sheet of paper. I had no idea what was on the paper and did not really pay attention until I saw LTG Moseley go red from the nape of his neck to the top of his head. When GEN Franks called for a break, LTG Moseley pushed his chair back, turned around, fixed an angry glare at me, and growled to his chief air planner, Colonel Al Wickman, US Air Force, to "look at this bullshit from CFLCC." He stomped past me to the general officer break area.

COL Wickman and the other air planners huddled together, reading the paper and muttering expletives about the Army. Finally, I went up to the group and asked if something was wrong. Wickman turned on me, thrust the paper into my hands, and asked to me explain the credentials I had in air planning which gave me the temerity to tell LTG Moseley how to conduct air operations. I had no idea what he was talking about, so I read the paper. It was a copy of an email from our J3, COL Hawrylak, to our commander, LTG Mikolashek. The email set out how LTG

Mikolashek should control the sequencing of air strikes on the ground force zone of operation, from specifying bomb loads to the number of strikes assigned to Army ground forces. My name was not on the paper at all.

I looked at COL Wickman and held the paper up with my finger on the address line. I announced in a loud voice, "Hey, look at this," and pointing to the name line I said, "Hawrylak, Mikolashek," then pointed to my name tag and spelled out "B-E-N-S-O-N." Then I asked the folks on the air plans staff of CFACC to give me a chance to see the totality of what was going on in my own headquarters. My deal with my fellow planners, made right on the spot, was that I would aggressively maintain my position as commander, but I would never surprise them. I would share information, since this would be a joint campaign, and we would all have a hand in winning the fights ahead. Our fellow Marine and Navy planners wandered over to enjoy the Army–Air Force skirmish, but all joined in the laughs when I was done. We were off to a good start among the planners based on the paper LTG Mikolashek passed to LTG Moseley. It was not quite over though, as I then turned around and bumped right into LTG Moseley.

Moseley looked right at me, started poking me in the chest with his finger, and said, "Who the FUCK do you think you are, telling me how to run an air battle? Do I tell you how to check the air pressure on Hum-Vee tires? GODDAM Army sonofa----!" I stopped him right there and repeated my Hawrylak–Mikolashek–B-E-N-S-O-N spiel. Moseley looked at the paper, looked back at me, smiled, laughed loudly, and said, "Goddammit Benson, you are okay, but you bastard, don't ever tell me how to run the air war, okay!" He then walked away from me. Later on in the planning effort, I'd re-visit the execution of the air operations.

This first exposure to the planning atmosphere of CENTCOM and the component commands was a clear indicator of the pressure under which we were operating. It was going to take enormous effort to defend our commanders' positions while keeping lines of communication open among planners and working towards a common goal. Maintaining lines of communication to all the component planners was terribly important given the snowflakes, and the efforts required in answering those notes. The time needed to answer these notes took time away from collaborative planning and wargaming. I was worried about this diffusion of our planning efforts.

Finding the "Smoking Gun" of WMD

The CENTCOM campaign plan, the one that would be called 1003V, Ten-O-Three Victor, tasked the land component, Third US Army, with the responsibility of finding so-called "sensitive sites" and removing weapons of mass destruction. While we were trying to focus the efforts of the plans team on the broad outline of the Third Army/CFLCC major operations plan, these tasks diverted the focus of the entire team towards supporting and secondary planning efforts.

The effort to develop the entirety of the major operations plan for all land forces demanded our continued focus. For example, even though I briefed the new J3, Major General J. D. Thurman, on the scope of the planning effort shortly after he arrived at headquarters, Thurman directed the J35, future operations section, to begin work on a branch plan for sensitive site exploitation (SSE).[3] The Pentagon wanted to know how CFLCC would cover the discovery and exploitation of sensitive Iraqi sites and expected weapons of mass destruction, SSE/WMD. The exploitation of discovered sites was intended to present evidence of Iraqi violations of UN sanctions in international information efforts to support the administration's policy objectives. In support of the effort to answer the question from the Pentagon, our planners met with scientists from the Defense Threat Reduction Agency. This effort began in October 2002, when we received a tasking from the secretary of defense. The secretary of defense tasking included a timeline. We had less than 10 days to provide Secretary Rumsfeld with a response. The response was due by 8 November 2002. At this time, the overall campaign plan was incomplete.

The components—land, air, sea, and special forces—were all working on supporting plans without a complete campaign plan. According to my notes from the time, MG Gene Renuart, US Air Force, the CENTCOM Director of Operations, told his planners that CENTCOM had received a tasking from the Secretary via the Joint Chiefs of Staff to develop a plan to exploit, via the media, the finding of any Iraqi WMDs.

MG Renuart reported that Secretary Rumsfeld said, "You are going to have a team of people ready to get very hard information on WMDs, so that it can be made available to the public. It has to be overwhelming." While Renuart directed the CENTCOM information operations section to coordinate the media operations part of the overall exploitation effort, the bulk of the effort fell to the operational plans group directed by my CFLCC J5 section. CFLCC, the ground component of CENTCOM, ultimately received the task of finding and exploiting Iraqi WMDs in the CENTCOM campaign plan. Given the short response timeline, our planning group ran through a course of action analysis to make a recommendation on how to exploit sensitive sites within the Iraq theater of operations. To do this we developed a purpose, tasks, and mission statement and from there came up with the requirements.

We determined a specialized task force was required to accomplish the mission of finding and exploiting sites suspected of holding weapons of mass destruction

3 The future operations section, together with the operations staff, was responsible for the development of fragmentary orders that refined the tasks of subordinate units based on changing battlefield conditions. The future operations section also developed branch plans that answered the "what if" questions that arise during combat, such as "what if" enemy forces commit their reserves.

and relevant materials. The task force needed a colonel-level headquarters to direct the operation to find and analyze "sensitive sites" possibly containing WMDs. The unit would need an infantry battalion augmented with intelligence analysts, and nuclear, chemical, and biological weapons specialists. The task force would also need bomb disposal specialists and criminal investigation detachments to secure evidence. The security force/entry teams would need special training on building entry so they could minimize the destruction of evidence as they cleared buildings to avoid harming the US government's ability to use data and material as evidence in the court of public opinion, or in an actual court. The task force would be split into southern Iraq—the priority effort—and northern Iraq elements.

GEN Franks's intent for this force was to have the unit available for work as soon as ground forces crossed the border in response to the pressure from Washington to find evidence of weapons of mass destruction that hadn't been declared to the United Nations Security Council, the "Smoking Gun." This meant the exploitation task force had to be among the first forces in theater. Since the secretary of defense had to personally approve requests for forces, we had to dedicate huge amounts of time and effort to alert units, form the task force, and get the unit deployed to Kuwait in time for the start of the operation.

Adding this new task force to our organization did assist in establishing a process that our land forces could use when they uncovered sites suspected of containing WMDs. We also wrote "on order" tasks for V Corps and I MEF to exploit opportunities to uncover evidence of undeclared WMD sites. Major Andy Stein, one of the chemical officers on the staff, led a group that developed what they called the "In-Stride Concept" of dealing with WMD sites that the corps and MEF might encounter in their respective zones after we crossed into Iraq.

MAJ Stein and his group developed tasks to maneuver units, attached chemical units, military police, and public affairs sections. These tasks provided precise details for dealing with known and discovered WMD sites. The "In-Stride Concept" bridged the time in between a unit discovering a WMD site and the arrival of the exploitation task force. They thought through the necessity of detaining personnel from an encountered site based on information provided by the CIA. The group noted that the CENTCOM intelligence fusion cell would direct which sites, outside the CFLCC zone of operations, would be exploited, and in what priority.

The operations group developed a really thorough plan of action for both corps and MEF exploitation. CFLCC would still retain responsibility for the operational planning and development of fragmentary orders, FRAGOs, directing site exploitation as WMD caches were encountered. Complicating this effort was the fact that CFLCC received a list of potential WMD sites throughout Iraq that numbered well over three hundred. There was no ranking or prioritization of these sites from the intelligence community. All of the sites were "important," but no one agency could tell us which might be more important than the others.

All of this work was well done and clearly thought through, and resulted in exceptionally clear tasks being incorporated in the base plan. The work also reflected the reflex comfort zone of the majority of our staff members—the tactical level. While our planners were wrestling with trying to link CFLCC actions to the accomplishment of strategic objectives due to demands for detailed information, we had to divert efforts to figure out: how many protection squads would be needed; the number of chemical sections per exploitation team needed; the necessary laws that might govern the gathering of evidence; and so on. This was vital work.

It also diverted effort from developing the main plan and troop deployment list. We were trying to determine the sequencing of the arrival of forces into Kuwait for operations in Iraq, and how the sequence would support the yet-to-be-finalized operational concept. I struggled to understand the need for so much manpower to be dedicated to a task that really should have been assigned to a subordinate headquarters.

Determining Conditions for D-Day and the CENTCOM "Main Effort"

In addition to the planning efforts caused by intermittent taskings and OSD snowflakes, we also faced questions from our commanding general regarding the effort by CENTCOM to produce a campaign plan while dealing with Secretary Rumsfeld and White House inquiries. A major concern of our commander, LTG McKiernan, was the timings of D- and G-Day, the start of operations and the start of ground operations respectively. (See Chart 3.)

Associated with timing the start of ground operations was the shift of the CENTCOM main effort, that being the component that received the greatest level of support from all components, and most especially priority in terms of air support from the air component command. The definition of these days, and associated designation of the CENTCOM main effort, was a proper concern for my commander. On 29 December 2002, LTG McKiernan noted that in the draft CENTCOM campaign plan, G-Day was set to occur almost a month after the president's decision to begin moving large numbers of forces to the Gulf, but G-Day, when our conventional ground forces would cross into Iraq, was four days after the air attacks began. This timing indicated the air operations would continue to be the main effort of CENTCOM until at least twenty days had passed. This did not make sense to LTG McKiernan, who wanted to call GEN Franks personally. He wanted to ensure GEN Franks would order that, once ground operations began, regardless of a specified date, the main effort of the entire campaign would be concentrated on the ground forces.

I would continue to engage with the CENTCOM planners to ensure they completely understood LTG McKiernan's concern, and I would recommend a definitive statement be placed into the campaign plan that made it clear the CENTCOM main effort would shift to the ground forces once ground forces entered Iraq. I also recommended that McKiernan allow me to continue work on this point, and keep his call to GEN Franks as an option. McKiernan agreed to this, and of course I kept him informed of my progress. Ultimately, GEN Franks made it clear the ground forces would be his main effort once ground forces crossed into Iraq.

As this indicates, we were all well into the details of ground combat and the expected decisive phase of the campaign, the operational maneuvers to isolate and then seize Baghdad. The designation of G-Day was important to the ground portion of the campaign as this meant that the ground commander, LTG McKiernan, would lead the main effort. In practical terms, this meant that ground forces would have the priority on air-delivered fires and air support, and thus LTG Moseley would dedicate the preponderance of his forces to the support of the ground forces. The planning effort also focused on how to seize Baghdad, as this became a major topic of discussion within OSD and the White House. On Christmas Day 2002, I MEF commanders also gathered for a "Baghdad discussion."

The Marines

I sent Lieutenant Colonel Chris Field—the Australian officer assigned to the J5—to be our observer at this meeting. LTC Field was an infantry officer and a graduate of the Marine Corps equivalent of SAMS, the School of Advanced Warfighting, or SAW. As some of Field's SAW classmates had been assigned to the MEF staff, I was depending on his association with them to break down any barriers to information sharing as well as to access to the Marines' planning effort. Chris Field did not disappoint.[4]

The Marine meeting took place on 25 December 2002, at Camp Commando, the facility that the Kuwaitis allowed I MEF to use for its headquarters. The key presentations were given by Major General James Mattis, Commanding General of the 1st Marine Division, 1 MARDIV, and Major General James Amos, Commanding General of 3rd Marine Air Wing, 3rd MAW. The Marine senior leaders were concerned about the fight that would develop in Baghdad because LTG McKiernan had decided that there would be one commander in charge of the battle, and that commander would be LTG Scott Wallace of V Corps.

LTC Field reported that the commanders of I MEF had a different view of how the Baghdad fight would develop. While they accepted LTG McKiernan's decision,

4 We called LTC Field "High Yield Field," such was the energy he brought to our efforts. Lieutenant Colonel Field was awarded a Conspicuous Service Cross by the Australian Army for his service with CFLCC. Additionally, he was awarded an American Bronze Star. At time of writing (2022), LTC Field is a major general and serves on the staff of the Australian Chief of Defence Forces.

they believed the conditions on the battlefield at the time might lead to another decision needing to be made concerning how the fight in Baghdad would unfold. There were practical considerations to be taken into account as the march to Baghdad unfolded. The primary of these considerations was air–ground coordination. The fight in Baghdad would challenge existing US military operations in urban terrain paradigms.

Both the senior commanders within the MEF, MG Amos and MG Mattis, spoke of the air–ground coordination required in Baghdad, in particular the methods to coordinate ground assaults and air support, as these differed somewhat between Marine, Navy and US Air Force air units in support of Army and Marine ground units, issues of collateral damage, joint on-call aircraft outside Baghdad, air command and control with CFLCC/V Corps, and the distinction between rotary-wing and fixed-wing close air support (CAS), and the designation of clearly definable boundaries within Baghdad in order to support the coordination of air–ground attacks. Finally, the Marines recommended CFACC consider declaring Baghdad Sector 10 as an NFZ. According to how CFLCC had proposed Baghdad should be divided, Sector 10 was in the heart of the city at the bend of the Tigris River.

The Marines also discussed other topics, but the fight in and around Baghdad dominated the discourse. The issue of clearly definable boundaries for ground units would come up again as forces closed on Baghdad.

The Marines' conference ended with the recommendation that CFLCC chair a Baghdad wargame to ensure a synchronized Baghdad fight. The wargame should consider the issues of: the allocation of dismounted infantry; the allocation of CAS, both fixed- and rotary-wing; the coordination of air command and control, C2; and the allocation of forward air control, FAC, assets.

Focus on Baghdad

Baghdad was the real prize of the campaign and its center of gravity. There were all manner of pressures on us as we planned and war-gamed this major campaign fight. The White House in particular did not want the fight for Baghdad to resemble the urban fighting in Berlin or Manila in 1945. This would not play out well with international media. In January 2003, General Jack Keane, US Army, vice chief of staff, adamantly directed that the Army better beat the Marines to the city. I MEF planners and commanders were getting the same "guidance" from the commandant—Marines better be in on the final fight. Our Baghdad wargame, which we had run many times, was never conclusive. No matter how we weighted the main effort, Army and Marine forces would reach the city at nearly the same time. This would complicate matters of command and control in the city fight. The Marines would insist on retaining control of their forces, as the MEF was under the tactical control (TACON) of CFLCC. This meant that LTG McKiernan could not task organize Marine forces. For example, he could not direct the MEF to place a Marine regiment under the control of V Corps; this was not allowed by joint doctrine and would remain a point of contention until we actually reached Baghdad. Planning continued apace.

The planning for the campaign to remove Saddam's regime and defeat his forces focused on what we called Phase III: Decisive Maneuver. While I kept a small group of officers looking at what to do after we got to Baghdad, the majority of our planners were kept hopping in having to deal with answering questions from the White House and the Office of the Secretary of Defense. The guidance from the Joint Staff regarding the future of Iraq was limited to a single line in a message that went to all regional combatant commands. The regional combatant commands were told to be prepared to support interagency efforts and Coalition nations in responding to stabilization and support requirements as a result from decisive combat operations against Iraq, these included Phase IV tasks, humanitarian assistance, and civil–military operations.

Cobra II included stability tasks to V Corps and I MEF.[5] The rolling (or blurred) transition to Phase IV post-hostilities tasks demanded that CFLCC forces control the zone of advance. The best way to do this was the simultaneous execution of combat and stability tasks. The plan also envisioned the possibility of regime collapse. But regardless of the outcome, the stability tasks were to stay the same during all Phase III operations. These were:

- Maintaining unity of military command;
- Maintaining unity of effort with Coalition government agencies, international organizations, and non-governmental organizations through our civil–military operations center structure;
- Utilization of existing Iraqi organizations and administration;
- V Corps and I MEF exercising military authority in the wake of combat operations prior to regime collapse. V Corps and I MEF engage with and utilize existing Iraqi provincial administration;
- Following regime collapse, establishing an interim authority which interacts with Iraqi ministries;
- Initially, stability operations were to be conducted within CFLCC zones. After regime removal, the battle space should be reorganized to include the whole of Iraq.[6]

5 US Army doctrine defined stability tasks as those tasks that would establish conditions for a return of governance to civil authority. These ranged from the repair of civil infrastructure to the re-establishment of local governmental services: trash pick-up, schools and local police. Stability tasks differ from combat related tasks but are key to setting the military conditions on the ground for attaining the policy objectives set by the US Government.

6 The complete range of documents from the development of the plans, orders, and presentations related to the opening of the Iraq War were declassified and can be found at https://ahec.armywarcollege.edu/CENTCOM-IRAQ-papers/index.cfm.

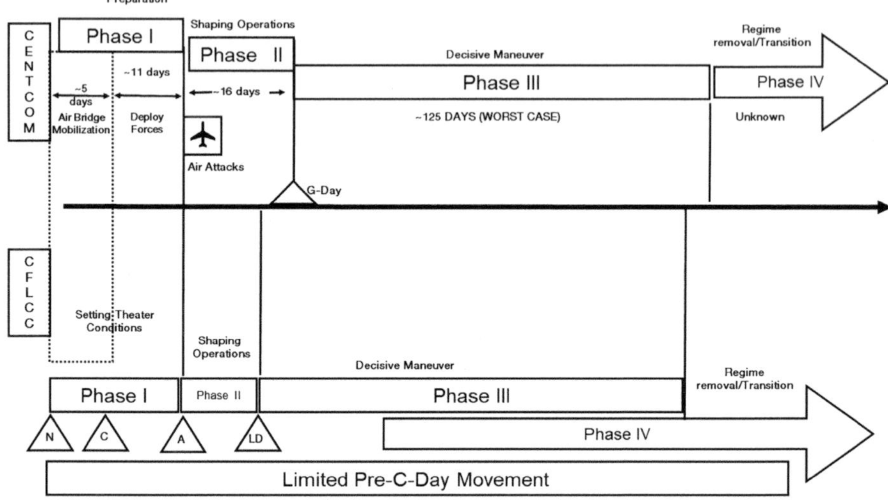

Chart 3. This chart was developed to highlight the different points of view of how Operation *Iraqi Freedom* would shift from phase to phase. Called the "5-11-16-125" chart the top half of this chart was used to brief President Bush. We, CFLCC, put our timeline underneath it. We used this chart to make the point that when ground forces crossed the line of departure this was phase III and the ground forces were the main effort of the campaign. (From the author's personal files, and prepared in 2003 by officers working for the author.)

Chart 3 above is a graphic representation of the CFLCC appreciation of the flow of the campaign juxtaposed with the CENTCOM perspective.[7] The CFLCC appreciation was sent to CENTCOM, but our view never made it out of CENTCOM headquarters. We presented our view of the flow of the campaign and major operations to our higher headquarters.

The CENTCOM Phase III transition to Phase IV was to occur at the completion of the removal of the Saddam regime. CFLCC chose to end its Phase III when Baghdad was isolated. The CFLCC assessment of the regime was all the means of control emanated from Baghdad. Once the city and thus the regime apparatus were isolated in the city, transition to Phase IV could begin throughout the country, and with it the completion of regime removal. A good start to this regime removal would depend upon the phased arrival in Iraq of forces from the United States, mostly reserve forces. The sequenced arrival of forces was to be done in accordance

7 General Franks referred to this as the 5-11-16-125 Chart, and used it to brief President Bush.

with another so-called "relic" of the Cold War: the time-phased force deployment list, or TPFDL.

Going TO the War

In the preceding section I delineated the various lines of effort involved in the process of planning for this complex campaign. The education of the people in OSD and the White House in matters of war, and the competing pressures—growing pains really—between subordinate components within Central Command were challenges that all planners faced. The major challenge in going to war, however, is *going* to the war.

In SAMS, we read a lot of material written by what we called "dead Germans." Professor Jim Schneider, the SAMS theoretician at the time I was a student there, not only guided us through the intricacies of Carl von Clausewitz, but also the dicta of the Prussian officer and chief of the Great German General Staff, Helmuth von Moltke or Moltke the Elder. One of the sayings of Moltke the Elder was that an error in the initial placement of forces cannot be corrected throughout the course of a campaign. Schneider intended this dictum to remind us planners that a great deal of thought must be put into the design of the flow of forces into a theater of war and operations: thought as to which unit would arrive at which time; why it would arrive at that time; and how it would enter into battle.

The sequencing and sustaining of operations was a key element in our instruction as SAMS students. This orderly and complex process was called the development of the time passed force deployment list, TPFDL, based on time-phased force deployment data. The *art* of war could only be practiced through an understanding of the *science* of war. The science of warfare was based on getting to the theater of war with the right equipment at the right time and in the right order.

Secretary Rumsfeld looked down on the process of developing a TPFDL, believing it was too archaic for 21st-century warfare. This may have some truth, but it was the only system we had at the time which attempted to bring order into the process of alerting, mobilizing, and moving military units into a distant theater of operations. Of all our armed forces, the reserve components depended most on a relatively smooth system of alerts for mobilization. The disruption caused by throwing this system out while we were trying to execute a complex campaign only made its execution even more complex.

The purpose of a TPFDL is to coordinate the movement of large numbers of troops and equipment in unit sets from their home stations in the United States or forward deployed locations—in our case Europe—to an air or seaport of embarkation. The TPFDL also coordinates the arrival of sealift ships and airplanes to move the troops and equipment to an air and seaport of debarkation in the theater of operations. The starting point for the development of the TPFDL is the establishment of the required delivery date of the unit equipment in the theater of operation, or in other words, of when the commander wants a unit to arrive. Working backwards in time from this date, planners estimate a time of transit from the US air and seaport to the in-theater air and seaport, the movement time from home station to the ports of embarkation, and the time required to load the ships while in port.

As I wrote earlier, the time we all spent at Scott Air Force Base—the headquarters of US Transportation Command—was valuable as it was the only time the planners were together and away from the pull of other demands. We attempted to maximize our use of this time for focused wargaming of some of the most important areas of the campaign plan. Getting to the conferences was time-consuming in and of itself, as can be seen from the events of the TPFDL conference on 1 and 2 October 2002.

The following text, from my field notes and journal, is a description of the conference and the hurdles we had to overcome just getting to the conference. I sent a note to LTG McKiernan giving him an update on a meeting I had with British Major General Fry, a representative of the British Army's Permanent Joint Headquarters. At the time, although the British had a large liaison element with Third Army, the UK Government not yet taken the decision to commit forces to operations in Iraq.

I spent the day of 1 October 2002, with Brigadier Adrian Bradshaw, giving a series of presentations to MG Fry.[8] The briefings went very well. We made MG Fry a believer in our effort. He confessed that before he came to Atlanta he had been a bit skeptical of how serious we really about the northern axis through Turkey into Iraq. The northern axis had been integrated into our planning as a result of the CENTCOM commanders' conference in August, but drew on planning the CFLCC J5 had already done in 2002. The CFLCC J5 anticipated and had done preliminary planning for the inclusion of an attack from the north. As a result of our presentations, MG Fry knew the north axis was a vital part of our planning effort. Major Evan Huelfer, one of the superb planners assigned to my section, gave the presentation on the overall land scheme of maneuver.

I stressed throughout the day that the north was not an add-on to the plan, and LTG McKiernan was serious about having a force come from the north. MG Fry, his principal deputy (an RAF Air Commodore), and his political advisor asked good questions about the history of the effort, the level of analysis, and the support we were prepared to give to the effort. I explained in some detail the combat power, armor, infantry, artillery, and logistical units that would accompany the 3rd Armored Cavalry Regiment, the force the US would contribute to the force in the north if the UK were to commit a division to the north.

8 Brigadier Bradshaw was the initial British liaison officer assigned to Third US Army. He went on to command a UK brigade, to serve as director of UK Special Forces, and as the deputy commanding general in Afghanistan serving as a lieutenant general, he retired as a general.

MG Fry's last words to me were that he now really believed we were serious, that this was a vital part of our plan, that British contribution would be vital to the overall plan, and that he would alert the commanding general of the British armoured division to come over to Atlanta to meet with LTG McKiernan. He also said he would push the policy side of the UK's Ministry of Defense (MoD) to take a decision as quickly as possible, and he would stress that the people in MoD were wasting valuable time. From the Third Army/CFLCC perspective, it was a very good effort. I then traveled to Scott Air Force Base for the TPFDL conference.

At this time, the work at Scott was also going very well. LTC Tom Reilly of the J5 and Terry Moran (a retired officer and a civilian contractor), LTG McKiernan's personal initiative group, were doing great things for CFLCC. I remained at Scott Air Force Base and the US Transportation Command (TRANSCOM) sponsored TPFDL conference until the conclusion of the CENTCOM J5 wargame, after which I went back to Atlanta to update LTG McKiernan. McKiernan was alerted that he was expected in Tampa on 7 October 2002, to brief GEN Franks on our plans for seizing Baghdad. I had my executive officer, LTC Hendricks, collect slides for the presentation McKiernan wanted to give to our senior staff prior to his departure. Once again, in the absence of a coordinating campaign plan from CENTCOM, we were planning for portions of our major operations plan focused on the latest area of interest within the White House and OSD. We had yet to hear if the UK had decided to participate in the campaign, and had to spend time convincing British leadership that we intended that their forces play a vital role in the effort.

Almost simultaneously, we were engaged in planning for the part of the campaign which seized Baghdad, as this was the focus of interest in the White House. Of course, given this dispersed effort, only the planners were concerned there was no definitive mission statement for the CENTCOM campaign plan or a well-thought-through concept of the campaign, the heart of maneuvering joint forces.

LTC Reilly and Moran really worked hard on the TPFDL effort, as well as on communicating with the corps and MEF planners. LTG McKiernan was conducting his own estimate of the situation and envisioning the flow of the CFLCC major land operations. The CFLCC message concerned the sequencing of efforts in the south, namely to block Iraqi forces in and around Basrah and focus the initial attacks to the northwest toward An Nasiriyah. The line CFLCC took with the CENTCOM and component air, naval, Marine, and special operations planners was that Baghdad was central, and that we must have our operations set up with this line of effort in mind. There were still questions about how the Iraqis might use the water held behind dams on the Euphrates, about how to preempt this possibility, whether the use of airborne forces could be used to seize these dams, or perhaps to seize just one—Milh—which would stop or mitigate the use of water higher on the Euphrates.

The more we studied how the Iraqis might potentially make use of these waters, the more we were convinced we must have forces in place, or within C130 range, capable of seizing these dams. I was sure CFLCC forces could link up with them within the planning factor times for the relief of an airhead. I was equally sure the proposed airborne force would never really be in serious jeopardy, given the ability of our Air Force to control the skies and deliver fire from the air. I presented this work to LTG McKiernan on 6 October 2002.

We planners never really considered a parachute assault as a major part of the operation, although we planned for one on Saddam International Airport. We wanted to have a well-thought-out plan in case the opportunity presented itself, but there really wasn't any enthusiasm for this kind of assault in our headquarters or at CENTCOM. We continued the hard work of developing the TPFDL.

The refinement of the early TPFDL continued to be relatively good news. We learned we could close tactically significant forces earlier than anticipated: 7th Marines Regimental Combat Team, RCT, and 5th Marines RCT by C+30, and the rest of the 3rd Infantry Division at nearly the same time, C+32/33. The forces were also logistically sustainable, a major consideration given the "Why can't we go now?" note I had to deal with upon arrival, enough to justify some risk if the opportunity to exploit a weakness in the Iraqi regular army or Republican Guards Forces Command, or even regime collapse, arose, both of which were extremely interesting considerations to people in OSD and CENTCOM.

The approach I took at the wargame with the CENTCOM planners—coordinated with Reilly and Moran—was a modification of the CENTCOM J5 tasks to CFLCC in Phase II of the skeleton of a campaign plan. Phase II concerned mainly air operations, with the caveat to CFLCC to be prepared to take advantage of opportunities to attack significant objectives, e.g., oil fields and the Basrah International Airport. The arrival of the tactically significant forces would allow CFLCC leeway to attack toward Jalibah, Iraq (the site of a good air base), and initially block Basrah until the arrival in theater of the 7th Marines RCT. This closure would give CFLCC enough force to seize the oilfields and Basrah International Airport without distracting from operations toward Baghdad. There was also a discussion of the expected level of Iraqi resistance.

I pressed for the CENTCOM planners' estimate of the level of enemy resistance, and where the CENTCOM J3 and J5 planners believed we could and *would* accept risk. From my long experience as a planner, I never asked an open question of higher headquarters; I also provided higher headquarters with what I thought the answer should be. I told my fellow planner and friend, COL Mike Fitzgerald of the CENTCOM J5, that I thought there would be very little fight from the Iraqi regular army and only limited resistance from the Republican Guard Forces Command, RGFC, divisions, and corps. This resistance would diminish in proportion to the closure of Coalition ground forces and the application of fires (lethal and non-lethal).

I expected moderate to heavy resistance from the range of the fanatical Special Republican Guard, SRG, units we would face. This meant I thought we would face some fighting in Baghdad itself. I based my answers on talks I had with the deputy CFLCC J2, COL Steve Rotkoff, and some CENTCOM J2 people, COL Carol Stewart for one. At the time, I felt we planners needed a definitive statement regarding expected enemy resistance from the CENTCOM J5. During a CFLCC Joint Target Coordination Board, JTCB, LTG McKiernan stated that his assessment was that the degree of risk was cross-component, meaning land, sea, air, and special operations forces needed to share a common estimate of risk at the beginning of the campaign.

Mitigating the risk to our forces and the expected level of resistance we could face played a large role in crafting the information operations messages tailored to Iraqi forces. While at Scott Air Force Base, I also held talks with our information operations experts to make sure they understood what LTG McKiernan expected from them and the Joint Psychological Operations Task Force.

I left Scott AFB feeling very confident that the experts in information operations understood what my commander wanted them to prepare in terms of messages to the Iraqi regular army. We wanted the Iraqi regular army to stay out of the fight and join us in establishing the post-Saddam Iraq. Messages laying out how the Iraqi regular army could display the intent *not* to fight were prepared for approval, as were the means of delivery, and the specific targets—units and people. I explained the application of fires, lethal and non-lethal, on the Iraqi Republican Guards Forces Command as well.

However, I told LTG McKiernan I was concerned by a "throwaway" line I picked up while at the Scott conference, as these "throwaway" lines were indicative of our ad hoc approach to the planning process required for a joint campaign. A discussion of base operating support[9] for a Jordanian air base, Al Jafr, came up, and the CFACC/ Ninth Air Force planners allegedly said they could not sustain the effort to run the base, but since some Army intelligence-gathering units were operating there as well—a Guardrail outfit—CFLCC could pick up the mission.[10] The Central Command J5 planners agreed and without much discussion took the decision that CFLCC would have the task of base support. I informed LTG McKiernan I would handle this situation colonel-to-colonel, holding the deputy commanding general, MG Webster, in reserve if I could not get this casual yet significant situation corrected.

I felt that our CFLCC J5 section was earning its pay. My notes from 5 October 2002, record that there was a CENTCOM video teleconference which was indicative of the many uses made of the transportation conferences at Scott Air Force Base. It also highlights the importance of having competent liaison officers at the higher headquarters as the CFLCC was not present on the Scott AFB end

9 Base operating support ranged from guard forces to contracted mess hall, laundry, maintenance for common use vehicles and the like.

10 Guardrail is an electronic warfare aircraft, an RC-12, that is used to intercept and monitor enemy radio communications.

of the video teleconference. COL Fitzgerald reported to the senior CENTCOM staff that conference participants now had a good handle on the total personnel requirements. The next step was working to "smooth" the flow to account for force module movements.

Base operating support for forces using Al Jafra Air Base in Jordan became an issue as CENTCOM did not direct a service component to take the lead for this base. As such, neither the Air Force nor the Army had taken any action to determine support requirements, or made any assessment of what could be contracted within Jordan. MG Renuart decided he would task the CFLCC to provide base operating support. The discussion centered on the force mix at Al Jafra, which would be primarily US Army forces, but which would also include British and Australian Special Operating Forces, Guardrail, and some support units.

The USAF was running out of the type of Air Force units organized to run air bases, and the fact the CFACC had three other bases to support in Jordan played a role in assigning this base in Jordan to CFLCC. MG Renuart believed there was available capability in Jordan for contracting much of the required support, although how he knew this I did not know. He said he was aware that CFLCC had other competing demands, however unless we made a strong objection, which could result in a Franks's decision, we got the mission.

This meant CFLCC had to work with the Army staff to identify an unapportioned unit from US Army Forces Command for the mission, get it alerted, and send this as-yet-unidentified unit all the information we had at the time. This unit then had to get clearance to conduct a reconnaissance of the Jordanian base to survey requirements, as well as coordinate with Army Special Forces, the Combined Forces Special Operations Component Command, CFSOCC, and the Joint Special Operations Command, JSOC, to determine requirements for possible impacts on the deployment schedule. The list of requirements was constantly being updated, as every time another force requirement came up, we had to determine when the unit needed to arrive in the theater, how it would get there, how many ships and airplanes were required to move the unit, and so on. On that day, the conference also covered operational planning topics, points that were raised during our wargaming sessions.

Part of the CFLCC operational maneuver toward Baghdad involved the seizure of the dams along the Tigris River by special operations forces, the CFSOCC. The purpose of seizing control of the dams was to prevent a controlled or catastrophic release of water that would disrupt the downstream crossing sites CFLCC intended to use en route to Baghdad. The timing of the operations to seize the dams had a direct relationship to the length of time CFSOCC had to sustain the special operating forces and light infantry at these sites.

CFSOCC did not have the means to sustain its forces for great lengths of time. These units would be supplied by air until CFLCC ground forces could link up with them, thus opening a ground line of supply. In order to determine sourcing for ammunition and other supplies for special operating forces, we in CFLCC had to determine how long it would take us to relieve the units that seized the dams and then justify the length of time. The staff update also touched on the use of Turkey for conventional and special forces.

There were indications that planning challenges for the early deployment of SOF units into Turkey might not be as significant as first perceived. There were some indicators of some positive movement on this by Turkey, primarily the Turkish Armed Forces. The use of conventional forces remained problematic for both Turkish and American headquarters.

Based on our wargaming and analysis of the lines of communication at Scott AFB, we were concerned about sustaining the northern force in Turkey: both the 4th Infantry Division and the 173rd ABN. The port of Iskenderun could not berth our large, medium-speed, roll-on, roll-off ships. Transportation Command would have to activate ships from the ready reserve fleet of transports to move the 4th Infantry Division. CFLCC planners really did not have a clear understanding of the mission for the 173rd ABN, so it was difficult for CFLCC and European Command planners to determine the type of support infrastructure European Command needed to provide in Turkey. The state of the development of the northern axis of advance included Coalition concerns as well.

The British planners at Scott suggested the possibility of a British corps-level headquarters in command of the northern forces, and raised the issue of whether the British would also send a division through Turkey and attack into northern Iraq. This headquarters would command British and US forces in the north. We felt the British wanted to press the issue and play a larger role in the operation. The issue seemed to focus on the UK not wanting to be seen in a role of follow and support.

CENTCOM J3 raised the point that CFLCC needed to be prepared to deal with the possibility that the French or some other Coalition partner may be willing to offer forces—like two brigades or a division—which could have a major impact on the force flow. MG Renuart requested that CFLCC planners think about how we would use additional Coalition forces for Phase III, and how we would sequence them into the campaign.

The conference notes concluded with information passed on by MG Renuart to keep the planning community informed. Renuart said GEN Franks wanted to start a series of no-notice readiness tests akin to a *Desert Spring* exercise near the Kuwait–Iraq border. Franks expected a CFLCC branch plan briefing on exploiting success. Renuart told us that GEN Franks would request the Joint Chiefs of Staff to pass him control of Operation *Northern Watch*. The secretary of defense, Renuart told us, had tasked Central Command to determine how to put us on a war footing. GEN Franks expected his staff to brief him on the status of deception planning. Renuart reported that GEN Franks and Secretary Rumsfeld would start working with the State Department on building the Coalition (this on 5 October 2002). Franks would travel to Turkey at the end of October and his staff was preparing the presentations he would give the Turks on: Fortress Baghdad; humanitarian assistance and civil affairs; operational information operations; and WMD.

Lastly, GEN Franks directed all of us planners to take a look at thoughts on "speed" versus "collateral damage" effects. He wanted to know at what point we should cross the threshold or overcome the balance between speed, violence, shock, and increasingly unacceptable collateral damage estimates. The TPFDD conferences at Scott AFB covered a great deal of ground. We were taking advantage of every opportunity for planner cross talk and brainstorming. The requests for information and requirements to brief OSD never stopped.

Concern over the size of the force was never far from the mind of the secretary of defense. On 7 January 2003, I received a note from COL Mike Fitzgerald, the principal planner in the CENTCOM J5. He wrote there was a great deal of excitement about the size of Army forces going to the theater. At the moment, based on a TPFDD "pull" Fitzgerald had completed, the force was two hundred and eighty thousand strong, not including Marines. Fitzgerald actually wrote, "SECDEF had a cow" when he was briefed on the size of this force.

Mike needed help in answering two questions coming from the Secretary: "Is your timeline in Phase III still valid: are we still looking at 125 days in Phase III? Does the UK division (which I am told is coming) substitute for an Army Div such as 1st Cav?" My response was that the number "125" came from CENTCOM, and I really had no idea if Phase III would last that long, and no, a UK division would not take the place of a US Army division. This was the first indication of the tension we would face regarding the means of strategy, specifically the number of Soldiers we would need to conclude the upcoming fight. Going to war, and going *to* the war, grew more and more complex.

Going to the war—more specifically to air and seaports in Kuwait, Turkey, and other countries—was vital in establishing what LTG McKiernan would call our "stance": the initial placement of forces, the manner in which we prepared them for combat, and how we would sustain them on the march to Baghdad. There was no time to focus on just one thing, for example developing the TPFDL, wargaming the concept of the operation, or thinking through the requirements of Phase IV. We were constantly answering questions from the secretary of defense, from GEN Franks, and even from within our own staffs. The pressure was on us to develop an operational-level plan linking the tactical tasks given to V Corps and I MEF with the strategic objectives of CENTCOM and the policy objectives given us by the Secretary and the White House. Time spent in planning, like time spent on reconnaissance, is not wasted.

CHAPTER TWO

Planning the Invasion Until D-Day

It would be an understatement to say that planning at the operational level is difficult. Our military education system focuses on the tactical level: battalions, brigades, and to a lesser extent, divisions. The operational level of war involves the movement of divisions and corps along with supporting formations. This is sequencing and sustaining battles. Key to operational-level planning is linking these tactical actions to attaining the conditions needed to ensure strategic and policy-based success. Given our tactical focus, I really had to work with our plans team to ensure we were envisioning large scale movements, figuring out how a division would fight so we could write tasks to V Corps and I MEF.

There again is another difficulty in operating at the operational level of war. In our military schools, officers are taught to wargame at the tactical or small-unit level, envisioning how the fighting will develop two levels of command below their present level. Given the usual level of battle staff experience in our officer corps, this meant the majority of our officers war-gamed company-level (units of one hundred Soldiers) fights while serving at a brigade, a unit of around five thousand Soldiers. At the field army level, two echelons of command below us was a division, a unit of roughly fifteen thousand Soldiers. Wargaming at our level of command meant I had to ensure the planners were viewing the campaign in terms of how a division would fight en route to Baghdad in order to write appropriately worded tasks to the corps and MEF commanders—three-star generals. This effort was exacerbated by the fact that Central Command—being a joint headquarters—had Navy and Air Force officers involved in planning the campaign, the centerpiece of which was land operations. This is not a small point, as all officers are educated differently in the methods of planning.

I recorded a note in my journal on 22 August 2002, which I felt (then and to this day) truly illustrated how an operational decision was made in a very unorthodox manner. The note I recorded detailed how we officially included a "northern option" of at least a division-sized force attacking into Iraq from Turkey. I wrote that this was an amazing occurrence. Colonel Fitzgerald, of CENTCOM J5, admitted to me he included reference to a division attacking from the north in his briefing chart on assumptions to the Central Command J3, MG Renuart. He did this to press for the J3 to make a decision on whether to include the "northern option" as an integral part of the scheme of maneuver for the campaign.

Apparently we would no longer follow any form of doctrinal decision making. The more detailed thinking would go into the preparation of briefing slides, as our decision makers were not reading the actual plan or order, but they *would* see the slides, so this was the planners' assured method of getting information in front of the key Central Command staff officer decision makers. So, on 22 August 2002, CFLCC had to revise its major operation scheme of maneuver to incorporate a force attacking from the north. This decision, based on a line from a PowerPoint chart, caused the CFLCC planners to: revise the TPFDL; look into Turkish air and seaports; and develop a line of communication that could sustain at least a division-sized force through Turkey and into Iraq. My note concluded I had to write this down so I would not forget it.

In late August 2002, LTG Mikolashek handed over command of Third US Army and CFLCC to LTG McKiernan. I had served in Germany with LTG McKiernan, and he was my division commander at Fort Hood. He was a highly regarded officer and had a real sense for warfare at the tactical and operational level. He was also coming out of the Army staff G3 position, so he had a sense for the state of the Army and, I gathered, the politics of the impending invasion. McKiernan's arrival also heralded the arrival of the so-called "dream team" of general officers who would lead our staff sections.

On 7 October 2002, the dream team assembled in our top-secret briefing area within the headquarters in Atlanta. Major Generals Thurman, the new J3, Marks, the J2, along with MG Christianson, J4, and MG Webster, the deputy commander for operations, were all present. This was a very instructive session.

LTG McKiernan talked a great deal on his views, nothing we had not heard before, but great interaction with the new general officers. All—no surprise—bought into the operating principles which he suggested, and how he wanted to fight. McKiernan said he was thinking about our CFLCC mission statement and would "write out" his thoughts on it, as well as the intent I gave him to think about. The intent I proposed was this:

> The purpose of this operation is to isolate/control Baghdad with combined arms forces and the effects of operational fires, IO, and SOF to attain the strategic objectives of the campaign; regime change and control/elimination of Iraqi WMD. The calibrated application of fire and maneuver, coupled with the full acceptance of calculated risk at the tactical and operational level, will effect the rapid destruction or neutralization of actively opposing forces, while preserving infrastructure and selected civil–military institutions to support an efficient and short-term post-hostilities transition. At the end of Phase III, Decisive Operations, CFLCC forces will control Baghdad and be postured to transition to post-hostility stabilization operations throughout Iraq and ultimately to JTF-Iraq.

I was not sure what LTG McKiernan would write in response to the intent, but I wanted to make sure he had been made aware of the thoughts of my planning section. I merged the comments of all of my planners into my proposal.

Before I gave the presentation on the invasion plan at that time, LTG McKiernan told the assembled generals that, "Kevin is my planner, I am not asking for a general officer to come in and replace him." This was a great moment for me, as LTG McKiernan empowered me in front of his generals. I was a staff principal, the J5. From that moment on there was nothing I would not have done for him.

I presented the plan as it was at the time. We would begin the attack with I MEF commanding both 1st Marine Division and 3rd Infantry Division. V Corps would enter the battle after we crossed the Euphrates near An Nasiriyah, at which time V Corps would become the main effort during our advance on Baghdad, with I MEF on the right as the supporting effort. It was clear to me that McKiernan did not like this part of the plan, so I knew my planners would be in for some work as he made the plan his own.

Following my presentation, LTG McKiernan gave some initial planning guidance to let us in on the direction of his thinking about the campaign. Regarding fires, he said he wanted CFACC to strike the Republican Guards divisions around Baghdad "starting on A-Day." MGs Thurman and Webster noted this and would begin talking with their counterparts on the CENTCOM staff. McKiernan indicated his understanding of "fixing" the Republican Guards divisions to mean that CFACC would hit Republican Guard Forces Command command and control, C2, nodes, and logistics units on A-Day, and afterwards to prevent large unit movements into Baghdad. McKiernan told us that his position and CFACC's position were becoming more aligned, indicating he'd been talking to LTG Moseley. I took note as the topic of control vs. destruction, bombing and information operations would come up again at GEN Franks next component commanders' conference, which would be LTG McKiernan's first.

I raised three points: the CFLCC zone; the staging of the 173rd Airborne Brigade; and regime collapse/exploitation. The CFLCC zone was still a point requiring resolution, as I felt that establishing the zone would assist McKiernan in making this plan his own. The zone would allow him to have the major directive authority on the use of air-delivered fires, thus shaping the operational battle for V Corps and I MEF.

I suggested to LTG McKiernan that we should think about basing/staging the 173rd ABN in either Italy or Cyprus for use in dam seizure or exploitation. This would put those operations under our command vice relying on CFSOCC or JSOC to conduct the operations. McKiernan decisively nixed this suggestion, and told us he wanted the 173rd attached to the 4th Infantry Division when it attacked from the north. He also informed us he was certain that if CFLCC needed paratroopers for dam seizure or exploitation, we would go to the Army for the 82nd Airborne

Division, which I'd done earlier as per LTG Mikolashek's guidance. I did not get a chance to discuss this further with him as it was near the end of the session, but he was pretty clear to me.

On the topic of the exploitation of an anticipated regime collapse, I proposed giving these related tasks to V Corps for planning, along with the projected forces available at those times. I wanted my planners to do some more work on this, though. Exploiting a scenario involving regime collapse was definitely a branch plan to our major operations plan. As such, there were more details to refine through wargaming. We could announce this effort in more detail in another warning order.

At the end of this session, LTG McKiernan said, "The Army will not come out of this with a black eye." He explained this meant he would not let the Army be subject to criticism like Task Force Hawk was during the Kosovo air campaign, in which critics called the Army too slow and not mobile enough. Further, he said we would not give ammunition to those who thought that all the Army needs is special operating forces, some light troops, engineers, aviation, military intelligence, and logistics units. Cutting divisions was still being considered in some offices in the Pentagon. This was an informative and energizing session.

In spite of this declaration by LTG McKiernan that I would remain his planner, it was not easy being the only colonel and staff principal when the other primary staff officers were generals. MG J. D. Thurman was our J3, and a powerful man, and he never could figure out why I was not working for him. For example, in December 2002 we were working on the maneuver graphics for our operation, the control measures we would draw on our map overlays that divided our army-level battle space. These established zones of action for subordinate units. Thurman looked over my shoulder and asked why the V Corps zone was so small, and who owned the open area on the corps' left flank, the area of Iraq south to the Saudi Arabian border. I told him the area on the V Corps left was CFLCC's area. Thurman was outraged at this, and demanded I give the area to V Corps. He then launched into rather personal attacks, poking his finger into my chest and asking me in his Southern accent, "Where the fuck did you learn that bullshit, huh? In SAMS? What if the enemy comes into that area, what do we do then? Are you going to teach that shit in SAMS?"

I stood chest-to-chest with him and answered, "No J. D., I learned how to weight the main effort of the attack in the Armor Officer Basic Course: narrow sector, priority of fires, placement of the reserve, and placement of the commander. And if the enemy should happen to attack in the open desert on the V Corps' left flank, I propose we alert the fucking band and the fucking Air Force because it will be a turkey shoot!"

MG Thurman started to breathe rapidly, go red in the face, and then smiled, put me in a head lock, and gave me a Dutch rub, saying "Aw Kevin, you know I'm just funning with you." I wasn't sure if he really understood what I was driving at, but he never raised the graphics with me save one more time.[1]

Once we determined the operational maneuver graphics of V Corps and I MEF, MG Thurman went on another tirade. He had previously served as the Commanding General of the National Training Center. From this experience gained in this role dealing with brigades and battalions, Thurman was determined to have precise operational overlays at all headquarters. In the age of grease pencils and acetate overlays this was a vital and appropriate concern. In the electronic age, when we were using devices called Blue Force Tracker and could transmit operational graphics electronically to precise, 12-digit grid coordinates which would not change when we changed the scale of the map electronically, zooming in and out to see small-unit detail to large-unit maneuver, it made no sense to waste time writing out grease pencil graphics.

Nonetheless, MG Thurman was the J3 and demanded this level of effort from the G3s of V Corps and I MEF. When the day of the meeting arrived and we posted the overlays one on top of the other, Thurman looked triumphant when, as we all knew would happen, there were discrepancies in them. He was convinced that he'd saved lives. It took until we actually reached Baghdad for him to realize that we were transmitting operational graphics and changes to them via the electronic communications means we had at the time. Thurman wasn't the only staff principal who felt he had to establish a dominant position vis-à-vis me as the J5.

MG Marks was our senior intelligence officer, J2. He was a superb intelligence officer with a great range of experience. In the main we got along very well, but for reasons still unknown to me there was one instance when he felt he had to make sure I knew I was just a colonel and he was, as he put it, "a major fucking general." Following a briefing in early November 2002 I was talking to Marks, taking notes as he was talking and answering his questions about if I was getting what he was saying with, "Roger ... Roger." Suddenly he got red in the face, poked his finger into my chest repeatedly, and said, "Throw a SIR in there any time you feel like it, goddamn it. I'm a major fucking general." Marks then walked away. Later on, I asked my classmate and the deputy J2, COL Steve Rotkoff, if I could see MG Marks to set things straight. Rotkoff told me MG Marks didn't know what I was talking about and there was nothing to set straight.[2] It was a crazy place to work.

When LTG McKiernan took command, our Third Army headquarters was split between Fort McPherson, Georgia, and Kuwait. On 5 September 2002—our first full day with LTG McKiernan—I wrote a note to MG Stratman, our deputy

1 Major General Thurman went on to four stars and retired as the commanding general of US forces in Korea.

2 Marks retired as a major general and is a consultant for CNN. We remain great friends.

commanding general for support, to keep him informed of was going on, from my perspective. Stratman was forward in Kuwait.

That day, headquarters faced an immediate request from the Central Command J5 for more input into the GEN Franks briefing to the "tank," the Joint Chiefs of Staff, which was to be presented to the secretary of defense the afternoon of that same day. We also learned that GEN Franks was going to Camp David over the coming weekend to talk to President Bush and British Prime Minister Tony Blair.

LTG McKiernan wanted some changes made to the slides we provided to the J5. I mentioned this to MG Stratman, as the set of charts I'd sent to Major Frank Jones did not have the latest updates. MAJ Jones was in Kuwait and did not know about the changes. McKiernan was taking steps to demonstrate he was putting his stamp on what our headquarters would execute during planning and operations.

The first response we received was from the CCJ3, MG Renuart. He thought we were being too aggressive for our first presentation to GEN Franks. This news came to us on the day of the change of command. McKiernan directed us to respond by articulating to the CCJ5 planners that we would present on tasks we were not truly sure we could execute AND sustain. McKiernan also directed us to not show deep-attack helicopter operations—the attack helicopters we have would be in support of the close fight. He didn't want either Third Army or CENTCOM making tactical level decisions based on slide reviews and templates.

The presentation that went forward showed aggressive actions from A-Day to A+3—when air operations opened—these ranged from ground reconnaissance into Iraq, artillery fires to kill Iraqi listening and observation posts, and air strikes to destroy command and control headquarters and integrated air defense nodes. On A+4, we proposed limited objective attacks to establish the security zone from Um Qasr to Az Zubayr to Jalibah Airfield. From A+4 on, we indicated "ON ORDER," meaning if conditions were right we would exploit to Tallil—with the attendant risk of stretching the Marine Expeditionary Unit, MEU's zone of operations—to remain in contact with the remnants of the Iraqi 51st Mech. If conditions did indicate exploitation, then on G-Day we would attack from our security zone to Tallil/An Nasiriyah and proceed with bridgeheads over the Euphrates, awaiting more force closure for Phase IIIB operations.

This thinking took place early in the planning stage and under the assumption we would only have limited forces on the ground when operations began: the conditions of Secretary Rumsfeld's thoughts on a "running start." The tenor of the operational planning would change as LTG McKiernan became more familiar with the planning effort and came to see that once we crossed the line of departure, the war was on, and there really couldn't be any sub-phases within Phase III.

LTG McKiernan told us if the Saddam regime truly collapsed, the necessity of getting to Baghdad quickly would really require generating strategic lift to get a brigade of the 82nd Airborne or 101st AASLT into Baghdad International. We would also require a rapid advance up the highways to Baghdad, while ensuring key pieces of ground were occupied, ranging from the locks on the Milh dam on the Euphrates to suspected WMD storage sites.

I told MG Stratman that I'd communicated all of LTG McKiernan's thoughts to the CENTCOM J5 planners, and if something hot broke overnight from GEN Franks's talk with Secretary Rumsfeld, they would call me at home. If nothing broke then I would call them early on the morning of 6 September, to get an update. To keep MG Stratman in the loop, I also let him know LTG McKiernan was going to Washington on 6 September to talk to GEN Franks, and would then go on to Tampa for talks with the CENTCOM staff. I accompanied McKiernan to Washington and then returned to Atlanta.

In a postscript to the note I'd written to MG Stratman, I'd just learned from the CENTCOM J5 planners that GEN Franks went to see Secretary Rumsfeld at 1700hrs, on 5 September, and as of 1955hrs that same day, GEN Franks was still in with the meeting with Secretary Rumsfeld.

This was an important detail, as it was the first directive guidance which we received from LTG McKiernan. I felt it was crucial that as many people as possible received the guidance, especially MG Stratman, as he was forward in Kuwait when the change of command took place, and the key planners from my section.

Our CFLCC planning effort began under the direction of LTG Mikolashek, who hired me to be his planner. I knew LTG Mikolashek was disappointed he had not been appointed as the Land Component Commander for the Iraq invasion. There was a distinct feeling in the Third Army headquarters that the senior leaders in CENTCOM and on the Army staff were not satisfied with LTG Mikolashek and his guidance of the Third Army staff. That said, the only manifestation of dissatisfaction I saw was at the start of a conference of the senior leadership of the entire US Army held in the Pentagon, and this was after LTG McKiernan had taken command of Third Army.

On 16 October 2002, I accompanied LTG McKiernan to the most amazing gathering of Army general officers I'd ever seen. Held in the Pershing Room of the Pentagon, the conference was attended by every three-star staff principal on the Army staff, the chief and vice chief, every Army four-star general officer (except GEN Franks), our US-based corps commanders, and all of the US-based division commanders.

LTG McKiernan presented our Third Army war plan to the senior leaders of the Army. My planners and I had worked very hard on this presentation. McKiernan also presented a detailed overview of the land component command plan for the invasion of Iraq. There was only one other colonel present—the chief of staff's executive officer—and one civilian, Terry Moran, who was McKiernan's note taker.

My role in this presentation was in the audio-visual room, advancing the charts for LTG McKiernan. I was also taking notes as I could. The only senior Army general not in the room was LTG Mikolashek. He was the Army Inspector General at the time. I heard GEN Keane, the vice chief of staff, express some displeasure with LTG Mikolashek and his relations with GEN Franks. General Franks was also not in the room because he already knew about the CFLCC plan.

When LTG McKiernan took command of Third Army/CFLCC, the plan was we would start with I MEF as the controlling headquarters of both Marine and Army forces under CFLCC, and after we got beyond Nasiriyah, V Corps would be introduced (again the "running start" concept apparently favored by Rumsfeld and people in the Office of the Secretary of Defense). Under this concept, once additional forces arrived, we would press on to Baghdad: an attack on two axes of advance, V Corps, and I MEF. McKiernan came into the headquarters knowing this plan included a surprising level of complexity. We were telling the Army staff we needed help in moving the headquarters of V Corps into theater earlier than previously stated. This briefing was the first time he proposed starting the operation with two headquarters on the ground. The general officers on the Army staff were surprised.

How did the Army staff respond to the presentation? General Shinseki led off the presentation by saying, "Gentlemen, we are not here to check Dave's work. We are here to understand his plan and figure out how to support it." With GEN Shinseki having set this tone, the questions were never on operational art or tactics, they were all: "Dave, what do you need? Dave, how can we help?" This was a powerful meeting.

There was a break about halfway through the presentation. The small audio-visual room had a passageway to the private latrine for the use of the chief of staff and the vice chief. Of course, never having served in the Pentagon, I did not know this. I was in a swivel chair and turned away from the computer keyboards. As I began to stand up, the door swung open. The doorknob hit me square in the forehead and knocked me down. As the stars cleared from my eyes, I saw GEN Keane, the vice chief of staff, standing over me. "Benson," he said, "Get off your ass! Who told you, you could take a break!" He walked on, chuckling, and was followed by GEN Shinseki, who just smiled at me. McKiernan gave me a quizzical look, and all I could do was shrug. The presentation concluded with GEN Shinseki giving a directive to ensure "Dave's plan" would work.

For the rest of the day, I sat in a meeting chaired by the Army G3, Lieutenant General Richard Cody. He would be in charge of shifting money to coffers that would support the invasion of Iraq. He also piled tasks on me until someone mentioned to him that I did not work in the Army G3, but for LTG McKiernan. Then Cody looked at me, scoffed, and said, "Benson's a SAMS guy, he knows what I mean." The Army staff assigned tasks to my section. We were also visited by the British, as the British government considered joining the coalition of the willing.

The British visited CFLCC at Camp Doha in November and December of 2002 developing a plan which involved the British providing the command-and-control headquarters for the force invading Iraq from the north. UK Colonel Richard Irons would lead the team of officers arriving in Kuwait for this effort. The main proposal was the use of the British portion of the Allied Command Europe Rapid Reaction Corps Headquarters to form the nucleus of a British corps. This corps would have under its command the British 1st Armoured Division and the US 4th Infantry Division, as well as associated corps-level forces. This effort got underway before the British formally decided to commit forces to the invasion of Iraq.

We had a rather robust British liaison element headed by a Brigadier Adrian Bradshaw. Brigadier Bradshaw was a really good man, and his team of officers was truly first rate. They were frustrated that the British government had not yet committed to supporting the action. We saw Major General Robin Brims, commanding general of the 1st Armoured Division, in the fall of 2002. He came to Kuwait with a small planning staff to check on the work Irons and Bradshaw were doing.

We met in Kuwait prior to the UK government making the decision to commit forces. We had a remarkable planning drill. The first employment option we considered was the British 1st Armoured in the south with the Marines. Next, we really started to look at coming from the north through Turkey. The thinking was that the British would pull their element out of Allied Rapid Reaction Corps and have a three-star command in the north, and the British 1st Armoured and the 4th US Infantry Division would come from the north as part of the northern axis of advance, at least to the northern part of the concept of the operation. So, we did a 15-day-long planning drill on what the concept of the operation would look like. MG Brims took it back to the London to present to the British Ministry of Defence and some of the senior leaders in the British Army.

These were pretty well-worked plans, although I was still concerned about the logistical feasibility as it relied on a really dodgy (a British term) line of communication. This was down to the effort from the north having to come over a barely adequate two-lane highway and a one-line railroad in Turkey. At the end of that effort, Brigadier Bradshaw told me he was going to recommend the British look at bringing the British 1st Armoured Division to the south, because he wasn't sure the Turks would let the US and UK forces enter their country. Even if the Turks let the Americans in, he wasn't sure that they would do the same for the British.

Of course, Brigadier Bradshaw ended up being correct, but at the time planning and developing the deployment list was quite confusing. The British finally showed up on the ground in January 2003. The final element of the British 1st Armoured Division, 7th Armoured Brigade, was completely closed on D-Day. The entire division completely closed theater a couple of days after D-Day, on 22 or 23 March. The British went into action with the Commando Brigade, 16 Air Assault Brigade, and one battle group—a battalion task force—from the 7th Armoured Brigade. While the planning efforts continued apace, I tried to keep LTG McKiernan informed of everything we were doing in his name. One note I wrote him on 31 October 2002, stands out as a prime example.

I mentioned I'd learned of an upcoming briefing to the President which might be of interest to LTG McKiernan, a briefing which was being presented later in the month of November, no specific date being known at the time. McKiernan wanted to make sure CFLCC got to see the "final cut" of the presentation before it went to GEN Franks to ensure that the presentation was in line with our CFLCC concept. If it was not in line, he wanted time to "shape" the presentation.

I told LTG McKiernan that GEN Franks was going on leave until 7 November, and based on what I gleaned from COL Fitzgerald of the J5, there would be time to shape the effort. On 30 October, COL Fitzgerald informed me that he would speak with the J3 that day and get a feel for the presentation from him. He also told me he'd learned that the POTUS brief had shifted to the following week (13–14 November). I assured LTG McKiernan I would remain in contact with the CENTCOM J5, as I understood how critical this presentation was for our overall planning and execution effort.

LTG McKiernan was interested in the construct of an upcoming wargame/plan rehearsal called Internal Look. This was the final CENTCOM exercise wherein the component commands rehearsed war-gamed events that might occur during the opening of the invasion of Iraq.

There were three vignettes within the construct of the exercise. The first and second vignettes were built around the current "Hybrid" campaign plan, though first vignette was centered on actions on C+27–C+29, the three days covering the opening of operations after 26 days of force flow, that is, starting from C-Day. McKiernan understood the exercise construct but wanted me to ensure the CFLCC perspective especially, as it related to the start of ground operations.

He wrote, "Okay, but ensure all know that BUT C+27 is not really G-DAY; ground attack starts on C+15! So if first vignette starts O/A C+27 STARTEX set will be somewhere around/north of river crossing." This was a point of contention not only with CENTCOM but with CFACC as well. We at CFLCC maintained that when the 3rd Infantry Division and 1st Marine Division crossed into Iraq, this was by definition G-Day, not what was on a chart presented to the President. I assured McKiernan I understood what he wanted and would remain engaged with the CENTCOM J5 and the exercise developers. I would keep him informed.

He asked a third question about the construct of the exercise. The exercise was modeled so that after 60 days of force flow, air operations began, and four days after air operations started, ground operations began. The vignette itself began on C+70, with V Corps and I MEF in place in the game construct. McKiernan wanted to know about the flow of the 4th Infantry Division, 4ID, and about how we would "play" the entry of that powerful division. He wrote, "And 4ID? Will a separate TPFDD be locked for the Generated Start? Impact is different base scheme of maneuver, e.g. both V Corps and MEF start attack in respective zones. Does this mean we should work Generated Start as a major branch plan to COBRA II?" I replied that I had raised a number of questions on this same point with the CENTCOM and exercise planners over the course of the preceding days, but had received no answers. I told McKiernan I did not think this wargame vignette was an indication of a separate plan with a separate TPFDL. However, given the state of CENTCOM planning and information flow, I did not have any more information on the vignette. I would keep digging.

Indicative of the range of planning we engaged in, a question about the rapidly unhinging mobilization process by which US Army Reserve and National Guard units prepared for war had been raised by the US Army G3 in the last few days. During the exercise conference I attended, the Forces Command G3 representative—a friend of mine from XVIII Airborne Corps days, Colonel Gordon Bonham—stated that there needed to be a pre-mobilization in order to get the mobilization stations ready to process the National Guard and US Army Reserve units called-up for the campaign. The opinions of senior officers in the Forces Command G3 was considered to be that if mobilization was ordered without some preliminary efforts and call ups, the units we needed would not be available in time to meet our desired LADs for employment in the theater of operations.

LTG McKiernan wrote that this information needed, "To be relayed to CSA, not only me … FORSCOM/USARC/NGB need to now tell him [GEN Shinseki] they cannot do—they didn't say that at HQDA Conference we both attended." This was not the point Forces Command was raising; it was not about personnel strength. Instead, it was all about having time enough to alert, mobilize, and do pre-deployment preparatory training, etc., while packing out unit equipment and linking up with airplanes for transport to Kuwait. This challenge was only exacerbated when the decision was taken not to use the TPFDL, but to generate a series of requests for forces which would break up the alert–mobilize–deploy process. This was a few months in the future, but it was certainly complicating planning for the arrival of forces we would need once combat operations began. The range of issues we confronted was staggering.

McKiernan was concerned about the deployment flow and how it related to the required/controlled supply rate (RSR and CSR) of critical supplies of ammunition. This ranged from tank main guns (120mm) to small arms (for infantry rifles and machine guns), and Patriot missiles to multiple launch rocket system missiles. McKiernan's major point was that HE would propose the required supply rate to GEN Franks, as it was his prerogative as the land component commander and Army service component commander. McKiernan wrote, "Explain to FORSCOM that CSR FOLLOWS RSR, i.e., a sequential, not simultaneous, development. We have to do some good modeling of our "Hybrid" base plan to give RSR input to CENTCOM, who determines the RSR."

The modeling required was to build a case for consumption rates of ammunition as well as supplies. The operational level of war ranged from linking tactical actions to attaining strategic objectives and sequencing and sustaining the land battles that were the means of strategy. LTG McKiernan had other tasks to accomplish, as the Army service component commander was providing and sustaining guard forces for Patriot units and special operations forces throughout the CENTCOM theater.

The Forces Command operations section reviewed our requirements for guard forces throughout the theater. The total requirement came up to five battalions of infantry, scattered from Jordan to Qatar and Kuwait to Turkey. The Forces Command operations directorate, G3, proposed to take the needed infantry battalions from enhanced readiness brigades from the National Guard for the immediate security force needs. The brigade headquarters would deploy later on in the deployment flow for necessary command and control, with an eye toward operations in Phase IV.

This proposal was the only way the activation/mobilization timeline needs could be met. It was only a proposal however, and needed further development and discussion between the Army Reserve, National Guard Bureau and the Army staff in Washington. Further, tough as it would be to enact, there was no intention to provide reserve component infantry for the special operating force guard requirements. McKiernan stressed this last point to me, and asked about the ability of the reserve and National Guard to meet the required arrival dates in theater. This reflected growing pressure to start the fight with the forces at hand. He wrote, "The SOF infantry rqmts are not firm at this point (and won't be sourced by RC…NO WAY!). PAT site security could be; however, can eSB(s) be ready soon enough to meet TPFDD LADs?? If not must be A/C."

At this time there was very little we could be certain of. In addition to these necessary points related to building a complete plan, we were also reviewing other concepts that came from Washington. One such concept of note was regarding the so-called Free Iraqi Forces being raised from expatriate Iraqis.

Via email, I informed LTG McKiernan that the deputy Forces Command operations officer, BG Tom Goedkoop, had shown me a classified paper from the Defense Intelligence Agency. The subject of the paper was the development and potential use of Free Iraqi Forces, FIF. This paper made me think the FIF notion was an indirect means of putting pressure on Saddam, and was never really intended for execution. McKiernan replied, "Interesting, but are you telling me that FIF is only a deception OP and not to worry about liaison, employment, etc?" He had gotten this impression due to my error; I only meant to convey a thought I had, based on nothing but a gut feeling and my instinctual reaction to the report. At the time, I had no concrete knowledge of a deception effort using FIF as an indirect means to pressure Saddam.

What McKiernan was most interested in was completing our major operations plan. He wrote, "Tomorrow is 1 NOV—when will I see final base plan draft for me to approve (that has been reviewed by staff/DCGs)??" I replied that I had talked to Major Joe Whitlock, one of the two authors of the plan (the other being MAJ

Huelfer) the previous night. MAJ Whitlock had spent a long time working with the C3, MG Thurman, on the order. I reported that I was positive McKiernan would see a completed plan for his review and approval by 1 November 2002. We did meet that deadline.

Indicative of the range of pressures on us to produce plans, the other developing plan was based on notion GEN Franks's notion of "catastrophic success" and how would we handle it. McKiernan wanted to see the force list for this developing branch plan. Again, I reported he that would see another copy of the plan, with his comments incorporated and reviewed by the staff, on 1 November.

LTG McKiernan wrote, "I must see/approve an early Baghdad entry force list for 'Branch TPFDD' build. When will that come to me?" On 2 November I briefed McKiernan on the Pre-TPFDL conference and our Baghdad entry force list, as well as on my thoughts on the points in time when collapse might occur. Planning is more than groups tackling problems and applying doctrine. It is also highly personal, and involves dealing with personalities.

In addition to these actions, I was also engaged in trying to get some planner reinforcements from our Army. Our Third Army was going to war, and yet it took a long time to get across to the greater Army staff that planning and execution of the invasion of a country and the ultimate replacement of a regime was going to be difficult, perhaps more difficult than we could even imagine. My personal stake in this effort was convincing a key general on the Army staff that I needed reinforcements in the form of SAMS-educated planners.

On 4 December 2002, the Army's Deputy G3, operations officer, MG Pete Chiarelli, wrote to our J3, MG Thurman. The CFLCC J3 was the clearing house for official messages and requests to the Army staff. MG Chiarelli worked on filling the personnel requests for our staff. The question of the moment was my request for SAMS-educated planners. Chiarelli wrote, "JD: As of tonight, we have sourced 3 of the 4 SAMS planners you asked for on this latest set of IAs. With the five you already have, three will give you eight. Do you really need nine SAMS-qualified planners? This is hard." He was struggling because just like during the First Gulf War, the demand for SAMS-educated planners was high. Adding to the difficulty of finding graduates of SAMS it seemed that the only person in the entire Army who knew all the SAMS graduates was Ms. Candi Hamm, the office manager at the school.

MG Thurman supported my request. He replied that we had analyzed our situation and truly did need all four of the requested officers, telling Chiarelli "The CG has the folks focused on continuing to finalize the CFLCC 1003 V OPLAN, the early collapse option, northern attack option and the Phase IV piece which is probably the most difficult." Reinforcing the assessment, Thurman also wrote, "Additionally for what it is worth, I own future operations I only have one CGSC graduate. I am not wringing hands or complaining. That is just a statement of fact." Thurman also forwarded a note I had written wherein I outlined who the SAMS graduates were and where they were working:

> MG Thurman,
>
> There are five SAMS grads in C5: me, LTC Tom Reilly, lead planner/TPFDDer, LTC Mike Hendricks, my XO who leads the PH IV effort, MAJ Joe Whitlock, exercises for now and PH III, and LTC Stan Stewart our plans LNO at CCJ5, had to send a horse to CCJ5. Leaves me three guys to do the heavy lifting, in addition to MAJ Frank Jones (resident CSC and a 59 strategic planner) and MAJ Evan Huelfer (resident CSC, 59) neither of whom are SAMS but both smart guys.
>
> My other folks are: MAJ Willie Davis, Signal, a super star, non-resident CSC, LTC Glen Patten, EN, a facilities engineer, smart guy, not a planner, and LTC Winston Gaines, a reservist on a one year active duty stint, another smart guy.
>
> I am playing the hand I was dealt and maximizing everyone's effectiveness by playing to their strengths, but that is it in the C5. The advantage I have is the OPG but these nine officers are the ones leading the planning effort for the land component. Yes, I really think I need four SAMS guys, I'll use anyone I am sent.
>
> Kevin

There was another internal actor on our staff. All throughout this planning effort, I—along with the general officer staff principals—was learning how to work with Terry Moran. Moran had come from the Pentagon with LTG McKiernan, who referred to Moran more than once as his "alter ego." Moran was very close to McKiernan, traveling with him everywhere, including going forward into the combat zone once the war began.

Moran was included in almost all of the general officer meetings at CFLCC, even to the point of clarifying LTG McKiernan's words to the other general officers on the staff. The note below highlights the extent of the role he played. Moran was responding to our Third Army liaison officer at CENTCOM, letting him know that "we have made clear to British Contingent here that 3Star Hqs is not in the cards for 'the North.'" The "we" here was Moran, who clearly got this from LTG McKiernan, as I never had this conversation with the British.

> Howard,
>
> Good roll-up ...we out at TRANSCOM have a pretty good handle on the issues. We expect to eat [cover with forces on hand] the Al Jafra requirement, the Dams issue will be revisited following an updated assessment by CENTCOM o/a 14 October, CFLCC/DA hosted today a WG on CFLCC ammunition requirements, we have made clear to British Contingent here that 3Star Hqs is not in the cards for 'the North,' will work further clarity on 173d (we know what we want to do with it), we are thinking thru the exploitation piece. Thanks for the summary. T

Our relationship came to a head in early December 2002.

I had overslept, and missed a morning senior staff session with LTG McKiernan. Usually my executive officer, LTC Hendricks, would have stepped in to cover me, but at this particular meeting he was not allowed into the room. I arrived at our office and Moran came walking in, very businesslike. In tow were all the planners who worked for me, looking quizzically from Moran to me. Moran proceeded to give instructions to the planners, being very directive and concluding with words to the effect of, "Okay, we have our orders, move out team."

None of my folks moved. They all looked at me. I said something along the lines of "let's get after it as Terry got this from the CG." Moran walked out of my office and did not talk to me at all. I was somewhat upset by this, as were my planners, LTCs Hendricks and Reilly in particular. I knew at that moment I could not let my temper get the better of me and tried to joke that this would teach me to set two alarms to ensure I was never late to a CG morning session. Once LTCs Hendricks and Reilly had calmed down, I wrote a letter to MG Webster and Major General Blackman. It was not as acidic as I felt at the time.

MG Webster and MajGen Blackman, 11DEC02

I'd like to ask you both for some guidance. It has to do with getting the CG to clarify my position as C5 vis-à-vis Terry Moran.

I am at the point of wondering if I have lost the confidence of the CG to be his planner. The planners I have are confused. Our higher headquarters planners communicate directly with Terry as do component planners and I am left out of the information cycle. I feel that the CG's reflex response for planning advice is Terry, not me.

First of all, Terry and I get along famously. We are both old and experienced enough to know that we are both working toward getting our CG the products he needs to make sound decisions and to present our, CFLCC, position on campaign plan issues. Terry and I get along well and have no personal problems between us.

I believe though that our CG has put both of us in a difficult situation. Terry, in his own sense of urgency to move out on CG tasks, gives direct tasks to the planners who work for me. CENTCOM planners are sending Terry notes and information that I do not know about. The guys at CCJ5, CFSOCC and CFACC are communicating directly with Terry and not letting me know what is going on. When I send notes back to the components and CCJ5 requesting that both of us be considered co-equal the effect lasts but a short time. Terry does a good job at trying to keep me informed of his activities, but our fellow components are confused. I freely admit this could be an exaggeration.

I know the CG is comfortable with Terry. I also appreciate that the CG empowered me in the presence of his general officers to be his planner. Terry sees the CG more than I do and I appreciate the information conduit when Terry tells me what is going on in the CG's mind.

I recommend that the CG more formally or informally at least state the relationship and scope of responsibility with Terry, planning, and me. I ask this not for me, but for my planners who are really wondering who is in charge and for whom they work. The situation is undermining my authority as C5.

I did talk to Terry about this but we were interrupted by the CG who I might add was clearly expecting to just talk to Terry when he came into Terry's office.

If you think I am griping over nothing I will shut up and soldier.

KEVIN C.M. BENSON
COL, Cavalry
ACofS, C5
CFLCC

To elaborate on what I wrote, I did attempt to talk to Moran. Actually, I did get to say to him in private what I did not say in front of my planners. In Moran's office, I told him I was committed to victory and to the best way of getting our plan completed. I said that he was never to give direct tasks to my planners. I also told him to never do this to me again, period.

I tried to speak as unemotionally as possible and in the calmest and coldest voice I could muster. Just as Moran was apologizing and promising never to do this again, LTG McKiernan walked in, and from all appearances he expected to just be talking to Moran. I think this incident marked my losing standing with LTG McKiernan. I continued to work as hard as I could for the CFLCC, LTG McKiernan, and for victory, but there was a *feeling*.

McKiernan directed we prepare an extensive briefing for the chiefs of staff of the Army and Air Force, the chief of naval operations, and the commandant of the Marine Corps. He went back to D.C. on 3 January 2003, and while my team worked very hard on this effort, McKiernan took Moran with him. This made sense, as Moran knew a great deal about the Pentagon, but it also raised questions of authority and responsibility among the members of the CFLCC staff. Moran was making changes to the written plan, likely in accord with McKiernan's wishes, but the rest of us learned about these changes in interesting ways.

I wrote Terry a note on 3 January 2003. I told him I was certain the presentation would go well, but I also wanted to check one thing. I mentioned that while going over the draft OPLAN and the additions he put into the ongoing OPLAN briefing, I had noticed that the wording of the CFLCC mission statement below had changed (see the chart text below the mission statement). I wanted to know when LTG McKiernan made the change shown in bold:

> 2. <u>MISSION</u>. When directed, CFLCC attacks to defeat IRAQI forces and control the zone of action, **secures WMD sites for exploitation**, and removes the current IRAQI regime. On order, CFLCC conducts post-hostilities stability and support operations.
>
> [statement on the briefing chart]
> WHEN DIRECTED, CFLCC ATTACKS TO DEFEAT IRAQI FORCES AND CONTROL THE ZONE OF ACTION; SECURE AND EXPLOIT DESIGNATED SITES; AND, REMOVES THE CURRENT IRAQI REGIME. ON ORDER, CFLCC CONDUCTS POST-HOSTILITIES STABILITY AND SUPPORT OPERATIONS; TRANSITIONS TO CJTF-4.

This was a small change in wording but another example of how fragmented we were becoming as the pressure was building towards the execution of this operation.

Moran did have extensive contacts in the intelligence community. For example, on 28 December 2002, he asked a contact in the CIA for feedback based on the first indication we had that the Turks would not allow us to conduct major conventional operations from their country. Moran asked his contact if he could confirm the decision regarding the Turks and their denying us transit through their country. He also asked for information on the feasibility of putting the 173rd Airborne Brigade into northern Iraq to co-locate with Turkish forces and use the same land supply routes the Turks used to sustain themselves from Turkey. This would mean our combat forces were not "in Turkey," so would this to be acceptable to the Turks?

Moran could get information from a range of sources. I was not privy to all of this information, save when Moran felt I had a "need to know." It made being the J5 difficult at times, but in this instance, since I did not know about this proposed placement of the 173rd, it was not a distracter. It was an indicator that, for some reason, McKiernan must have felt he was not getting all he needed from the plans section, or for that matter from the rest of the staff.

Most components, save CFLCC, appeared to stop writing their plans in late November 2002 to await final CENTCOM decision. CFLCC subordinate headquarters, I Marine Expeditionary Force, and V Corps also slowed down their planning efforts in an attempt to avoid excess work. I could not blame them for this. In an attempt to keep all CFLCC subordinate headquarters informed of the planning efforts, I had started sending out warning orders via our classified email network. We could not use regular message traffic, as messages went to everyone in the system. CENTCOM had lowered the classification of the planning effort from TOP SECRET/POLO STEP to SECRET/ORCON, or originator controlled.

This was in essence an attempt to keep top secret-type control over a larger group of people as everyone "read on" to the SECRET/ORCON plan had to be registered, But it took a massive effort on the part of all headquarters. Despite this, the system of warning orders sent to specific addressees worked very well. It was a practice I continued until McKiernan told me I could not send out warning orders as the C5. I could send planning guidance, but not warning orders. By the time he issued this guidance, we were all in-theater, and the primary means of communication became the classified email network anyway. I continued to write my daily notes to McKiernan as a means of keeping him informed of the ongoing plans work.

On 25 December 2002, McKiernan signed our major operations plan, Cobra II. Upon signing it he looked at me, smiled, and directed the C5 take the day off before beginning to review the plan for update and correction. He further directed that he wanted me to coordinate with the chief of staff and deputy commanders for operations and logistics to convene a panel of the general officer staff principals to completely review the entire plan, including annexes.

The planners working for me actually thought this was rather funny, and were looking forward to observing me lead, as they called it, a "squad of generals" in reviewing the plan. This was an extraordinarily good idea by LTG McKiernan as we all learned a great deal about the level of staff work that was done, and how to refine the plan to make it much better.

On 9 January 2003, as per McKiernan's directive and along with the general officers on the staff, I began the review of Cobra II with an eye toward refining it as well as reducing the size of the entire major operations plan. The OPLAN review began with all the general officer staff principals directing their respective sections to give presentations on the pertinent paragraphs of the plan, as well as the annexes for which the staff section was responsible.

The effort began with MG Marks letting the chief of staff and deputy commanders know that he would personally review the intelligence sections of the plan and oversee the refinement. I admired MG Marks for this move, as through it he established that he would take personal responsibility for the completion of his section's work and keep any flaws within the J2 section. This also reduced (somewhat) the workload of the review panel. We reviewed the major operations paragraphs, my section's responsibility, and Annex C—operations—the purview of the C3. By the end of the day, we were about halfway through Annex C. I knew MG Webster, the DCG (O), would update LTG McKiernan, although I sent reports as well.

By the end of the first day, the generals and I decided to split operations on 10 January in order to meet the deadline of disseminating our OPLAN on 13 January 2003. MG Stratman, the DCG (Support), and MG Christianson, the C4, convened with the logisticians and continued the review effort of the administration and logistics section of the base operations plan, as well as covering the major logistics annexes. MG Webster, MG Thurman, and I continued on with Annex C appendices. My C5 section was tracking the changes as they were made, and updating the annexes accordingly. My section covered both the operations and logistics review efforts. It was a painful effort, but ultimately it was worthwhile.

On 10 January, I reported the OPLAN review continued. I let LTG McKiernan know that on 11 January we would also cover "re-dos" from Annex C, and review Annexes G (Civil Affairs), K (Command, Control, Communications, Computers, and Intelligence Systems), Q (Medical Services) and W (Resource Management). MG Thurman also insisted on doing a preliminary graphics review on acetate. I assured LTG McKiernan that, at the very least, we would be able to disseminate the base operations plan, all 60 pages of it, on 13 January.

On 11 January I reported that "Between the DCG (O), DCG (S), CofS, C2, C3, C4, C6, and BG Bromberg we reviewed every annex in the OPLAN at least once." The entire staff participated in the effort, and actually completed re-writing or updating all of Annex B (Intelligence) and 12 of the 18 appendices of Annex C (Operations), with eight of the remaining 15 annexes to the operations plan completed.

The remaining seven annexes to the operations plan came up for final review on 12 January. I further noted that, at the J3's insistence, we would review operational graphics, Appendix 22, Annex C. At my insistence this, review would be done on the command and control personal computer system, C2PC, as well as acetate. The officers, sergeants, and enlisted Soldiers of my plans section were involved in this process, along with officers from the future operations section (FUOPS). The FUOPS officers put together and proofed the acetate overlays. Key officers in the plans section were also scattered about the United States, as other work was also continuing in support of putting together the plan and its associated efforts.

I let LTG McKiernan know that my lead planner, LTC Tom Reilly, and Terry Moran checked in from Scott AFB. They were involved with the setup of the TPFDL conference. MAJ Frank Jones, lead planner on GEN Franks's directed "catastrophic success" plan, would meet LTG McKiernan at Fort Bragg, North Carolina, where the latter would speak with the command group of the 82nd Airborne Division on the parachute assault to seize Saddam International Airport in Baghdad, a key element of the catastrophic success plan.

MAJ Jones had put together the presentation, and was ready to update it with LTG McKiernan as directed. MAJ Evan Huelfer was in Atlanta, and in contact with me. MAJ Huelfer was working on the "stance" slides which LTG McKiernan had directed, and would link up with us in Tampa for the upcoming CENTCOM Component Commanders' conference. LTG McKiernan used the term "stance" to indicate not only the physical positioning of units in Kuwait, but also when units were projected to arrive, along with their completion of the pre-combat checks of equipment. These were the charts McKiernan intended to use to brief GEN Franks and his fellow commanders on the overall readiness of the ground maneuver force for the invasion.

I reported to LTG McKiernan that a team of officers selected from the operational plans group—the large group of officers who worked for me as we developed the COBRA II plan—were developing the slides he had requested. The slides would be completed by the morning of 12 January.[3]

Finally, I reported that MAJ Whitlock was putting the finishing touches on the base operations plan, and that we would deliver a clean final copy for McKiernan's signature to the Chief of Staff on the morning of 12 January. My final comment was, "We have a plan that will work."

On 12 January 2003, while we were preparing for a CENTCOM commanders' conference, I reported the status of the plans efforts to LTG McKiernan. I communicated that "We are over 95 percent complete with the cover-to-cover review of the OPLAN." This was an enormous achievement for my small section. There were people in the plans section who had read through every annex and appendix.[4]

The only element of the plan still awaiting completion was the final update of Annex A, Task Organization, from LTC Reilly and the crew at Scott Air Force Base;

---

3 The team consisted of: LTC Field; Major Phil Chandler, I MEF Plans LNO; Major Frank Glang, from Deep Operations Coordination Cell; Lieutenant Colonel Steve Peterson, C2 Plans; and Major Chuck Webber, C4 Plans. These were the "go to" guys in the plans team.

4 The three people who did this were: MAJ Whitlock (who, at the time of writing, is now a retired major general), Captain Max Moore (now a former battalion commander), and Sergeant Trinket Teltoe (a superb NCO who delighted in telling me that I was the lowest-ranking officer she'd ever served with, as she had come to Third Army from General Wes Clark's personal staff).

Appendix 27, Annex C, Branch Plans would be completed upon LTG McKiernan taking the presentation on the seizure of Saddam International/Regime Collapse branch plan at Fort Bragg. Major Jones would return from Bragg with LTG McKiernan's guidance and complete the branch plan. I told LTG McKiernan that I was sure we would add to the branch plans appendix as the campaign planning progressed and we got more clarity on strategic options for the north and west, as well as on potential airborne options.

I laid out the milestones for OPLAN completion. Our focus of main effort on January 13 2003, was completing the final review and assembling the paper and the electronic copies of the OPLAN. We expected to complete Annex A—the task organization, a huge effort—as well as finishing Annex D, the logistics annex. LTC Andy Dreby of future operations (FUOPS) would write the draft dissemination message.

Once this work was completed, my team shifted to the mundane but necessary task of producing electronic copies of the entire plan. We projected that—given the general officer involvement, review, and approval required for the process—everything would be complete, including transmission and delivery of the plan, by January 14, 2003.

We met this target. Of course, this was not the only effort ongoing at the time. LTC Reilly and our movement–planning team were at Scott Air Force Base completing what we anticipated would be a transportation feasible deployment list.

Reilly and the planners engaged with the preparation and review of Level Four data for the force packaging of our units.[5] The planned opening portion of the transportation conference was going to be a review of the northern axis force deployment list. I told LTG McKiernan that I would wait to hear what Reilly and his crew did during this period. The latter was also working on the "on order" boundary shift between CFLCC and European Command, EUCOM.

It seemed at this stage that European Command wanted to enter the fray by proposing that EUCOM provide the command and control of not only US forces in Turkey, but well into Iraq, if the 4th Infantry Division were to actually execute the northern option. This assuredly well-meaning offer would complicate an already complex command situation. I told LTG McKiernan I had sent LTC Reilly the slides which the plans team developed for the very hasty analysis of continuing the MEF in zone to Kirkuk, and reported that we knew I MEF had done some work on this as an "on order" mission. I told LTG McKiernan I trusted Tom Reilly to represent our point of view on this boundary shift. I knew that Reilly would look at this as well, especially as another decision point for both LTG McKiernan and GEN Franks.

---

5 Level Four data concerns the cubic feet of cargo space required for a unit's equipment, as well as the tonnage of the entirety of the equipment (from tanks to space heaters and tents).

Another member of my plans team, MAJ Willie Davis, was to attend a civil–military operations (CMO) conference in Tampa during this same week. Davis was serving as our Plans Advance Team in Tampa. He would meet me and LTC Patten, Phase IV team, at the airport and provide an update on the CMO effort, especially as it related to our Phase IV effort. Davis was a very good man, and I trusted him to attend this conference, capture this work, and incorporate it into our own Phase IV efforts.

MAJ Huelfer was also in Tampa continuing work with the CCJ5 planners on the conference and campaign plan. I would link up with Huelfer there, completing the plans team. This CFLCC plans team would attend preliminary conferences leading up to the component commanders' conference, and essentially prepare the ground for LTG McKiernan; on arrival he would receive complete briefings on the ongoing planning efforts.

I also engaged with the CCJ5 planners writing the campaign plan and developing the proposed GEN Franks decision points. Based on our graphics review, I would also coordinate with the CENTCOM Special Operations Command planners and work out terrain and boundaries. LTC Patten and I would also meet BG Steve Hawkins and talk about Phase IV planning.

Finally, I reported to LTG McKiernan that our four incoming planners had all made electronic contact with us and we were tracking them. The reinforcements—Majors Bill Innocenti, Wayne Grieme, and Bryan Sparling, and Lieutenant Colonel Tom Sutherland—would arrive at Camp Doha, Kuwait, by no later than 24 January 2003.

I reiterated that I was convinced we had a plan we could transform into an order that would work, and that even if the plan could not look with certainty beyond initial contact with the enemy main body, the total planning effort going into the development would serve us well. I succumbed to a bit of hyperbole there.

Of course, I was using my reports to LTG McKiernan to keep him informed on the status of our efforts towards his plan and priorities. I was also using the names of key players in the effort, a sort of mention in dispatches, to highlight these folks' efforts. I wanted my people to have name recognition, as they were doing the hard work of putting together a plan which would send hundreds of thousands of Soldiers, Marines, Sailors, and Airmen into combat. I also used the numerous conferences we were supporting as a means of getting my officers home to see their families before the war began, whenever it was going to start, as at the time we had no real idea when the ground portion of the war would begin.

After we completed the review, update, and dissemination of the plan, our next major events were the plans to operations handover of the plan and our combined arms rehearsal. With regard to our planning effort on Phase IV, post hostilities, and our plan Cobra II, 9 and 10 February were interesting days for me. Brigadier Albert Whitley, soon to be promoted to major general, offered to act as the enabler of our

CFLCC Phase IV planning effort with that of Joint Task Force 4 (JTF-4) and LTG (Ret.) Garner's Office of Post-War Planning at the Organization for Reconstruction and Humanitarian Assistance, (ORHA). Brigadier Whitley insisted this would be best for our efforts as it would result in a seamless transition into Phase IV. McKiernan had introduced Brigadier Whitley as his "British minder," as they'd served together at a previous NATO assignment. I had not yet met Brigadier Whitley. There was supposed to be a meeting of general officers on planning in general. I followed my instincts and forced my way into the meeting. I figured that if Terry Moran could be there, so could I.

Brigadier Whitley started off by saying that our Phase IV planning was "disjointed." He then offered to take over the entire task. I asserted I had a bit of a problem with this, as I viewed this as my task from the CG, since I was the planner. McKiernan did not make a decision at that point in time, but said he would think on it.

When this short session was over, Brigadier Whitley came to my office to talk to me. He said he did not mean to imply my C5 section was disjointed—it was just that, with JTF-4 under BG Hawkins and LTG Garner's ORHA, there were three sections approaching Phase IV from three different perspectives. He wanted to ensure we were all acting in accord with LTG McKiernan's intent.

I had no argument with this point: it was an area of concern for me as well. This discussion was coming on the heels of MG Webster stating he wanted to relieve the C5 of some tasks. He did not specify what he was talking about, at least to me. Perhaps my ego was bruised. My XO, LTC Hendricks, was rather suspicious of Brigadier Whitley's move, though. We were all pretty wound up given the pace of events.

On 10 February, LTG McKiernan let us know how he wanted work divided and coordinated. I was directed to work on how to transition from Phase III to Phase IV. McKiernan wanted me to determine which tasks would lead to the right conditions for a secure and stable environment to achieve a transfer of authority to a follow-on headquarters. JTF-4 planners would focus on integrating their efforts with ours, focused on the handover and beyond. McKiernan further directed soon to be promoted MG Whitley, would act as Deputy Commanding General for Phase IV. He would ensure CFLCC and JTF-4 efforts were shaped and in concert. This would allow MG Webster to focus north for Phase III.

This decision made a great deal of sense, and demonstrated LTG McKiernan's sense of the flow of the campaign. Since we would be handing over responsibility for Cobra II through Phase III to the C3 after the combined arms rehearsal, we in the C5 would focus on the continued refinement of Phase IV. It was important to the overall effort to ensure our vision of the concluding conditions of Phase IV were widely coordinated and understood by V Corps, I MEF, CENTCOM, JTF-4, and ORHA. Our end-state conditions would in turn act as the initial starting conditions, and thus assumptions for, JTF-4 and ORHA's planning for the concluding stages of the CENTCOM campaign plans stages of Phase IV, stages B and C. CFLCC's participation in the campaign, at the time, ended with the completion of CENTCOM Phase IV, Stage A, our Cobra II Phase IV.

The Combined Arms Rehearsal through Phase III

On 14 February 2002, CFLCC conducted a combined arms rehearsal of Cobra II. The combined arms rehearsal was conducted on a huge terrain model constructed by our senior sergeants under the direction of Command Sergeant Major (CSM) Sparks and the faculty of the Sergeants Major Academy. The faculty was at Camp Doha to conduct an operations sergeant course. The terrain model was a fabulous platform for the rehearsal. The sergeants prepared a huge model, covering the terrain from Kuwait to the Turkey–Iraq border in the north, and from the Iran–Iraq border to the Iraq–Syria and Jordan border. All of our major subordinate units made use of this terrain model for rehearsals of operations.

O the day of the rehearsal we were still following up on major supporting efforts for the completion of establishing our base force for the invasion, and attaining the "stance" desired by LTG McKiernan. In my report of 14 and 15 February, I told him that we would continue to provide a daily update on the force flow, working with the CFLCC J4. We were also monitoring the European Command efforts to clear out a backlog of shipments through the port of Antwerp. This effort by European Command would materially speed up the arrival of V Corps and its units. We were also working with FORSCOM on the sequencing of the 2nd Cavalry Regiment into the force flow. The rehearsal was clearly the main event of the day.

The senior commanders used the combined arms rehearsal as a vehicle to present their understanding of our Cobra II plan through the end of Phase III, which concluded at the arrival of V Corps and I MEF in and around Baghdad. We did not talk about Phase IV at all. Nonetheless, the rehearsal served its purpose, which was to talk through the actions delivering major US combat power to Baghdad. and coordinate the actions of such Coalition combat forces: Polish and Australian special operating forces; along with our US Joint Special Operations Task Forces; JSOTFs; and the British 1st Armoured Division.

LTG McKiernan opened the rehearsal with a truly masterful discussion of his intent and the operational-level scheme of maneuver. MG Marks followed McKiernan with an equally superb discussion of how the Iraqis would fight us all the way to Baghdad. He also mentioned the effect of weather, and the expected sandstorm which would affect our operations (although when this might occur, we did not yet know). MG Marks truly presented a deep and insightful understanding of how the range of Iraqi forces would contest our advance.

Marks also presented a coordinated assessment of the effect of air operations on the command and control of Iraqi forces. He stressed that Iraqi higher-level command

and control would be shattered, with the result being that the Iraqis would attempt to execute existing defense plans in accordance with pre-determined schedules. This would lead to uncoordinated Iraqi actions along our lines of communications, which would include irregular forces we knew existed in the cities along our zones, V Corps and I MEF. Marks outlined the three potential areas where the Iraqis might use chemical weapons: near An Nasiriyah; the Karbala area; and finally, in and around Baghdad itself.

The concentration of US forces near the first two sites presented a lucrative target for chemical fires, as well as the greatest potential to disrupt our operations. Use of chemicals in and around Baghdad were seen as an act of desperation. Marks's assessment was that the actual use of chemical weapons would confirm US, UN, and Coalition statements that Saddam did in fact possess weapons of mass destruction. Thus, he concluded that there was a greater potential for use of these weapons when the point of desperation was reached.

MG Marks went into detail on how individual Iraqi units would rely on existing orders and execute them in accord with defense plans. There would not be much freedom of action on the Iraqis' part. He assessed there would be some effect on how the Iraqis fought based on the effectiveness of our psychological operations, although wisely he did not really predict the actual effect. In essence, he cautioned not to expect too much from the psychological operations.

Marks's final assessment was that the Iraqis would take every measure—conventional and unconventional—to contest our advance and delay our arrival in Baghdad. The hope was that the more delayed our arrival in Baghdad, the more international pressure would be brought to bear on the US and Coalition to halt operations and enter into negotiations. It was a brilliant, and in some ways prophetic, assessment of enemy actions. Marks termed the expected Iraqi strategy "Control-Delay-Attrit."

Our J3, MG Thurman, followed MG Marks. Thurman presented a superb and more detailed explanation of the concept of the operations. This was a straightforward presentation of the corps and MEF zones, of how fires would be coordinated and allocated, how the CFACC would support the advance to Baghdad, which CFLCC-level decisions might be made, and when we anticipated they might be taken. The J4, MG Christianson, followed MG Thurman and delivered another brilliant, straightforward presentation on the flow of logistics in support of the advance. The major subordinate commanders followed these CFLCC staff presentations.

LTG Wallace delivered the V Corps concept of the operation and explained how it was nested in the overall CFLCC concept. He also discussed how the corps would apply fire and maneuver to reach Baghdad with the major combat elements of the 3rd Infantry Division. Wallace then spoke of the first major operation which would support the I MEF crossing of the Euphrates River to the west of An Nasiriyah, and of how the corps would expand the bridgehead line, and then hand over the area to I MEF.

LTG Wallace stressed that his corps main effort would be west of the river, but in order to maintain contact with the MEF forces in their zone, Wallace would place the cavalry squadron of the 3rd Infantry Division on the east bank of the river. He then moved on to discuss expected actions in the Karbala Gap, where terrain favored an Iraqi defense in some depth, as well as a possible use of chemical weapons to disrupt our advance, as MG Marks outlined.

Wallace concluded with his appreciation of how he would control operations in Baghdad in accordance with the plan at the time. The plan called for the establishment of so-called "lily-pads," or areas where we would call for Iraqi civilians to assemble as they fled the city. These areas would be supported by non-governmental humanitarian organizations, and coordinated by civil affairs units from the US and Coalition. Combat actions would be in the form of intelligence-driven raids based on where centers of resistance would be inside the city. My assessment was that V Corps would demonstrate 21st-century siege warfare, wherein we would invest the city and then conduct intelligence driven operations at specific targets. I add that, at the time, I was only thinking along these specific lines. The commonly shared feeling was we would take measures to avoid street-by-street fighting which might call to mind images of the Israelis in Jenin in the occupied territories. We wanted to avoid evoking comparisons to Israeli operations. LTG James Conway, USMC, followed LTG Wallace with an equally straightforward presentation on how the MEF would attack in zone and support the V Corps main effort. Conway also talked about the anticipated corps forward passage of lines that would take place near An Nasiriyah, and the opportunities he expected there would be to accelerate that passage of lines by using bridges around the city.

LTG Conway described how I MEF would use the broad zone given him once across the Euphrates river, as well as remaining cognizant of the buffer area in his zone which would keep US ground units well away from the Iran–Iraq border. Conway would rely on Marine air to observe the area and suppress any Iraqi units trying to exploit the buffer area as maneuver space. He stressed that once operations began, his Marines would maintain unrelenting pressure on Iraqi forces in zone, exploiting the shattered Iraqi chain of command and keeping forces in zone off balance. As Conway understood it, the MEF would be making Marine Corps history; this would be the most extended land operation conduct by the Corps. Conway demonstrated a real understanding of how to use this large Marine Air–Ground Task Force. His was another masterful presentation.

The Third Army-level theater air defense and protection, support, signal, engineer and medical commands followed the major ground combat elements discussions. Observing the rehearsal were Generals Gary Luck and Fred Franks (Ret.). These two men, who commanded XVIII Airborne and VII Corps respectively in the First Gulf War, gave short talks near the end of the session.

General Fred Franks said ours was a "bold and imaginative plan." He cautioned us, however, by saying that nothing goes according to plan, thus we must keep on thinking about options. He suggested that the Iraqis were doing reconnaissance by "taking fire." He asked, "Why are the Iraqis moving their Ababil 100 rockets into Basrah?" Could the enemy be sacrificing a pawn to learn about our intelligence gathering and counter-missile defenses? We had to keep thinking.

Earlier in the day, GEN Luck, who remembered me from XVIII Airborne Corps, had come to ask me about *Henry V*, the Shakespeare play. He asked the name of the battle. Agincourt, I told him. "Benny," he said, "I knew a SAMS guy would know that." General Luck began by saying he wished he was going with us. He told us to keep logistics in mind, and keep open the possibility of using the highways as temporary landing strips for intra-theater airlift. He paused, looked at LTG McKiernan, and then reminded us that war is a human endeavor, that this was our Agincourt moment, and all here were brothers. General Luck told us the "tug of war" was about to begin, and we all had to pull together. LTG McKiernan closed the session by telling us that he did not know when D-Day would be, but that we should all be ready to go when directed.

My officers and I collected our notes from the combined arms rehearsal and started to work on refining the CFLCC commander decision points which were raised during the rehearsal and refined based on the commander-to-commander cross talk occurring during the session. Based on the discourse we'd heard, LTG McKiernan reaffirmed his earlier decision—Baghdad was the center of gravity. He approved the regime collapse branch plan, including the acceptance of the proposed indicators for execution. He also confirmed the proposed decision to commitment of the reserve: the 82nd Airborne.

In the report I made on this momentous day, I told LTG McKiernan that we began work on refining the decision points decided on at the combined arms rehearsal, and we were working with C35, future operations section. I also reported that we received a draft Central Command J5, CCJ5 FRAGO to incorporate Coalition units from Europe, ranging from Slovakia to Ukraine. The units were mostly combat support (engineers, military police, and chemical) and combat service support (truck companies, water, and fuel tankers), with some promise for unspecified combat troops. There were NO projected arrival dates. I sent the FRAGO to MGs Thurman and Webster.

This was also the day we received Secretary Rumsfeld's snowflake on who might guard the Muslim holy sites in Iraq. I told LTG McKiernan we would develop an answer through the CCJ5 on the possible use of Muslim troops to secure holy sites in Iraq, even though no Muslim countries had yet indicated that they would join the Coalition. There was also the fact that the holy sites were Shia, and the Muslim countries that had the potential to commit troops—we were thinking of the Gulf Cooperation Council and Pakistan—were Sunni.

In my journal I made two notes. The first was about trying to scratch several itches regarding the identification and tracking of our request for forces, RFF, generated force flow. These key units had to do with establishing enemy prisoner of war camps, and displaced civilian camps. The units involved were in the Army reserve, and the RFF process disrupted any hope of an orderly mobilization process for these units. My scribbled note said this was hard, but if it were easy then someone else would be doing it.

On 14 February 2003, I also learned from my friend and West Point classmate, Colonel Jim Greer the current director of SAMS, that the chief of staff, GEN Shinseki, had approved me to be the next director of SAMS. I wrote that I was honored by this assignment, but I hoped the war would be over and CFLCC would be out of Iraq by the time I had to report to Fort Leavenworth. Hope, as I knew, is not a reliable method, and though I didn't know it at the time, in this case it was misplaced.

The next day, 15 February, was equally momentous. The report I rendered, shown below, indicates it was also rather full. As GEN Luck mentioned, the "tug" of war was already starting.

OPLAN Refinement:

- Continued work on refining the DPs [decision points] decided on today at the Combined Arms Rehearsal. We are working with C35.
- Received a draft planning order from CCJ5 to CFSOCC regarding the 173rd Abn with a request to review and comment. Our response is below:
    - COMCFLCC fully intends to employ the 173d Airborne Brigade into northern Iraq being Task-Organized with the 4th Infantry Division. The brigade will be under Operational Control of the Commander 4th ID from the point of entry into the Area of Operations [Iraq], and will be OPCON to 4 ID for planning purposes effective upon the forthcoming CFLCC Planning Order to the 173d and 4th ID. CFLCC is currently engaged with the commanders to refine the operational details for the brigade's employment with the 4th ID. The details of the method and timings of the 173d deployment from Italy and initial entry to Iraq are underway with good cooperation from the Southern European Task Force and EUCOM staffs.
    - In the event that Turkey will not allow ground forces into their country but will still grant the over-flight employment, COMCFLCC intends to employ the 173d Bde into northern Iraq, OPCON to Commander JSOTF-North to support both CFSOCC and CFLCC operational objectives. CFLCC respects the desire of CFSOCC to conduct branch planning for the employment of the 173d Abn Bde. CFLCC agrees that such planning is prudent to prepare for the event that COMCENT may place the brigade under the operational or tactical control of CFSOCC.
- Reviewed the update work on OPLAN change two, which is in with the DCG [O] and COLs Clay and Hawrylak for review. Pretty good work.
- Will not send out any issues and notes from the CAR [combined arms rehearsal] without your review.
- We rehearsed our plan handover briefing to C35 tonight. We intend to use the terrain model site for the handover briefing. The handover briefing is scheduled for 1900hrs tomorrow.

I informed LTG McKiernan I'd received a note from the CENTCOM J5 regarding a possible VTC with LTG Abizaid, the CENTCOM Deputy Commander. The subject of the conference was an upcoming (18 February) VTC with LTG Garner. We, CFLCC, had given a presentation during the VTC on "The Next 30–60 Days" of our on-going preparation efforts. I wrote that the planners were working on the presentation and would have a draft for review on 16 February. Abizaid wanted a VTC prior to the Garner conference, as he was traveling to Jordan on 18 February and would not be able to sit in if it went ahead as planned. Abizaid, I was told, wanted to talk to McKiernan about the presentation, and review it, as well as the Washington, D.C. post-hostilities "Rock Drill," with him. I reminded McKiernan the Garner VTC was tentatively set for the early evening of 18 February. I closed my note by thanking LTG McKiernan for the extraordinary privilege of allowing me to be present during the CSA briefings.

GEN Shinseki Visit, 15 February 2003

This would be GEN Shinseki's final visit with us, as GEN Franks had asked the Department of Defense to restrict all flying visits so his components could focus on getting ready for war. While GEN Shinseki visited us, he told us about the "tug" of war in Washington. At the time, I do not think I truly understood what he was telling us, but he was indeed warning us about what was in store in the near future.

General Shinseki told us that while the TPFDD process was a "big war system," we (he was referring to OSD here) "constipated the hell out of the process." In effect, reserve component mobilization was shut down in the US We had not yet started to fight, and there was talk in Washington of putting units on the "off ramp." Shinseki told us that in discussions in the Joint Chiefs of Staff "Tank," he had reminded his fellow chiefs of staff we had to be "on the freeway to get to the off ramp."

GEN Shinseki was clearly frustrated by the request for forces/mobilization effort. He warned us to be prepared for Monday morning quarterbacking and charges the Army is slow to react. His fight inside the beltway was in letting people know that when you break the established process and tamper with decisions, these actions cause the highest degree of friction and always have consequences. Shinseki's real message was on leadership.

He told us that, the broken force flow process aside, we had to get it—the impending fight in Iraq—right; that order would not exist unless we put it in place. Washington was hoping that once order was in place in Iraq, this fact would begin the process of changing the order in other places: in essence, the world of "order" was taking on the world of "disorder." He warned us that Muslims could turn this process of change into something it is not and that for every day this disorder existed, consternation—in the US and in the wider world—would grow. He told us we "had no choice, we have to do it all." He told us—and I am pretty sure he was talking to the "dream team" of generals at CFLCC here—"That's why you are here, because it is too important to screw it up."

General Shinseki reminded us to rest and maintain our stamina, as there were long days ahead. He said what distinguishes US Army general officers is the ability to "make good decisions for a bit longer than anyone else." Shinseki stressed we must remember the American Soldier. He paraphrased Maurice de Saxe to remind us that we must not ask a soldier to go to the fount of courage one time too many. The responsibility of leaders is to care for their Soldiers and recognize when this point is coming. He concluded his informal remarks by saying that he knew tough days were ahead, but he had every confidence in us, and finished off with, "I'll see you in Baghdad, if it is before 11 June. I'll be there." After the CSA departed, LTG McKiernan told us that GEN Shinseki was, mentally and physically, the toughest Soldier he'd ever known: a man of vision. I agreed.

Closing my daily report, I recommended to LTG McKiernan that given what we heard from GEN Shinseki, we should suspend work on the effort to portray our stance vis-à-vis the enemy's on 3 March and 20 March and the risk/gain of waiting. Based on what the chief said about the RFF and its effect on the reserve component mobilization process, I offered that we would begin the war when directed, and with what we had at the time. We would have to let arriving units catch up.

CHAPTER THREE

Build-up to D-Day

Phase IV Meeting

The majority of my reports to LTG McKiernan during this period were via email. Because of the demands on his time, I rarely got to actually see McKiernan to get his guidance face to face. I had to rely on British MG Whitley to relay our concerns about Phase IV. During this time, I met with LTG McKiernan on 16 February 2003, and then again on 17 March.

On 16 February, my Phase IV planners and I had a very good meeting with LTG McKiernan and MG Whitley. This was the first exclusively Phase IV-related meeting I had with McKiernan, and I wanted to get as much of his thinking on Phase IV as possible; I knew that the impending invasion would consume more and more of his time.

McKiernan had an extraordinarily clear view on Phase IV as far as the mechanics of putting together a plan went, and more importantly on just who would remain in Baghdad to execute that plan. He began our meeting by stating "no one wants to get a grip on this thing [Phase IV] at CENTCOM." He went on to muse how it appeared that LTG Abizaid, the deputy CENTCOM commander, was worried he would be stuck with running Iraq. McKiernan assessed the newly arrived Task Force IV as lacking both the horsepower to figure out Phase IV and the necessary scope of the operation, and if Rear Admiral James Robb, the CENTCOM J5, was the CENTCOM spokesman for the effort, then we should not expect a firm CENTCOM position. McKiernan's conclusion, and the point of his guidance to me and the planners, was that what CFLCC proposes to CENTCOM must have some serious thought to it, as in all likelihood CFLCC would be in charge for some time.

On establishing a controlling headquarters for the Phase IV effort, LTG McKiernan opined that a combined joint task force built from the ad hoc joint manning document (JMD) process would be risky, as all the other services would "low ball" the requirements, meaning they would send who was available. This meant our headquarters would end up staying in Iraq for longer.

McKiernan naturally favored getting US forces and headquarters out of Iraq as swiftly as possible, and turning over the post-hostilities administration of Iraq to a Coalition headquarters, perhaps built around the Allied Rapid Reaction Corps (ARRC) headquarters. Use of the ARRC headquarters would signal NATO and European support of the effort in Iraq. We would prepare a message for McKiernan to send to GEN Franks outlining the value of this type of Coalition headquarters, and asking GEN Franks to work on getting the Defense Department, and Secretary Rumsfeld, to support the idea.

Realistically though, LTG McKiernan knew that this would be tough. Thus, he directed us to prepare a range of proposals for a post-hostilities headquarters built around existing Army headquarters. He cautioned that I was not to mention V Corps as a possible Phase IV headquarters, stating, "Nothing leaves CFLCC that says V Corps." McKiernan did direct us to look at building the post-hostilities headquarters around a US Army division. We also talked about how to coordinate with LTG Garner's ORHA.

The beginning of March 2003 was filled with the dual effort of monitoring the force flow, adjusting our request for forces to match what we felt we needed to start and finish the war, and refining our Phase IV sequel plan. While the force flow requirement was time consuming, at this stage of our efforts, my superb section—under the leadership of LTC Reilly—had this down to a science. This was important as it left me time to work with the team developing our Phase IV sequel plan.

For the next few weeks, we focused on this operations plan refinement effort. Our efforts ranged from coordinating with the civil affairs, C9 section, on its review of and input for the JTF-4 effort, along with the C9 input to Phase III and early Phase IV stability operations fragmentary orders for subsequent publication by C35, our future operations section. Per LTG McKiernan's guidance, we worked closely with MG Whitley on Phase IV.

The small team focusing on the Iraqi Army "after next" and exploring possible options for reintegration, etc., presented their efforts to that point to MG Whitley during this time.[1] The team incorporated his guidance into the final product of their planning effort, and also continued the informal staffing among CENTCOM action officers. The C5 Phase IV team updated MG Whitley on the total Phase IV effort. Our briefings went very well, and MG Whitley's guidance—usually in the form of suggested improvements—was always well received. Whitley gave considerable thought to the road ahead for Phase IV and coordination for a handover with JTF-4.

---

1 The term Iraqi Army "after next" came from an adaptation of a term US Army officers used during efforts to design the US Army of the future. It was a commonly understood term at the time, thus all who saw the term Iraqi Army after next would understand it referred to the effort to build a post-Saddam army.

I mentioned our Phase IV planning efforts to LTG McKiernan in every report I sent, and I sent them daily. I put a marker down for publishing a Phase IV sequel to Cobra II, including annexes, on 8 March. The C5 team finished compiling the operational plans group input to the base plan for Phase IVA. We got further input from the JTF-4 staff for Phase IVB and C as well. I reported to LTG McKiernan that we would send the assembled Phase IV efforts to MG Blackman, the Chief of Staff, after final review by MG Whitley for another general officer synchronization board review and approval.

In the weeks before the invasion, we received two potential presidential briefings for review. One was in response to a "what if" drill on the complete loss of Turkey as a base for expanded operations. I reported this particular presentation was not the crisis it was upon its earlier receipt. The coordinator of the effort, the Central Command J5 staff, presented its work to one of the deputy CCJ5 flag officers, BG Perkins, on 1 March. My section coordinated the input received from the CFLCC C2 and C4, and sent it to the CFLCC Command Group for review. The second (and longer) presentation was a first cut at a "civilianized" campaign plan briefing of the period from A-2, that is two days prior to the start of air operations, to G-Day, based on the assumption that the ground invasion would begin four days after the start of air operations. I sent our proposed response through MG Webster, the deputy commanding general, before sending it back to MG Renuart, the Central Command J3. Our work did not always consist of Phase IV and force flow.

We also continued to work on refining a draft FRAGO to incorporate Coalition force units into CFLCC operations. I told LTG McKiernan that the CCJ5 effort was good thus far, but it still lacked the detail we needed to accomplish mission analysis, specifically in the area of Coalition unit capabilities. We were having a good dialogue, but required more solid information.

The Coalition was growing, to a certain extent. My impression, which I sent to LTG McKiernan, was that many countries would wait and see what happened during the opening of the campaign before making any definitive commitments, which was understandable. The work on refining our Phase IV efforts continued.

On 2 March 2003, I reported to LTG McKiernan our work on the sequel to Cobra II continued to progress. We had not yet named the sequel, but work was going well. C5 would host an internal Phase IV planning conference on the afternoon of 3 March. In accord with LTG McKiernan's directions MG Whitley was to oversee the Phase IV efforts. He would address V Corps, I MEF, and CFSOCC planners, as well as our own planning group and others.

My intent for this intense session was: refine our specified task list (what we had to do in Phase IV); refine the troop to task list for Phase IV (how many troops we felt we needed to accomplish the tasks); and share information. In retrospect, given the intensity of the efforts and the building pressure toward the invasion date, I can see how it was that I upset LTG McKiernan.

I reported to him that I was exchanging notes with the air component planners. I had gently poked the CFACC planners by telling them we would consider a recommendation to CENTCOM to have 9th Air Force as the centerpiece of Joint Task Force-Iraq, JTF-Iraq. There was a historical precedent here, as the RAF policed Iraq for Great Britain in the 1920s and '30s. The CFACC planners did not see the humor, and clearly neither did McKiernan.

I also reported a growing interest, judging from the volume of email regarding our work, on refining the FRAGO in incorporating Coalition force units into CFLCC operations. The CENTCOM planners in Tampa were working military-to-military efforts and had several small units ready for integration, though mostly with Combined Joint Task Force-Consequence Management (CJTF-CM). Combat units were high on our list of requests for post-hostilities operations, but many potential Coalition nations were not interested in fighting the Iraqis—their focus was on protecting the Kuwaitis and other Gulf States from the effects of chemical weapons.

Our major issue was space for the staging and placement of these forces. I coordinated with BG Howard Bromberg and the Operational Protection Board. I knew at the time that BG Bromberg was looking at placing other chemical reconnaissance and decontamination units in other areas throughout the Gulf region to speed our response to a WMD-related event, if such an event was to occur. My impression continued to be that many countries were going to wait and see before making definitive commitments.

In the C5 Plans Update for 3 March, I covered a series of events related to our Phase IV planning effort. Our continuing focus was on getting forces into theater, and refining our sequel plan for Phase IV. I repeated we were working on a sequel to Cobra II. This was an important point, at least I thought it was at the time.

McKiernan had asked me a question on the effect of Transportation Command moving the late arrival dates (LADs), CFLCC planners worked out during the final TPFDD conference in January. The officers trying to coordinate the large-scale troop and equipment movements were trying to adjust personnel arrival dates to even out the force flow and attempt to match personnel arrivals with equipment arrivals. This was an important area, the nuts and bolts of moving forces around the world. We coordinated our response with CENTCOM. We did not concur with the movement of troop dates. Our experience thus far led us to conclude the dates needed to remain the same. Ships had broken down during transit, planes were delayed by weather, thus adjustments to equalize arrivals before planes and ships were allocated would result in more confusion. There was enough friction in the works.

We hosted an internal Phase IV planning conference on 3 March. MG Whitley gave a short opening address to V Corps, I MEF, and our OPG planners. CFSOCC planners joined us later in the week. As planned we used this intense session to refine our task list, troop to task list for Phase IV, and to share information. It was a great session. We planned on presenting MG Whitley the draft annex/OPLAN for Phase IV.

I reported our answers to MG Renuart's questions from the morning's video teleconference. I'd coordinated these answers with MGs Webster and Thurman. The questions were:

1) Do we want to bring over the remaining Brigade Combat Team, BCT of the 82nd Abn in case of regime collapse? Answer: NO.
2) Given the growing probability Saddam will leave, based on Arab League pressure how will CFLCC respond? The CENTCOM operations section, J3, will write a formal planning order. Answer: we will execute our branch plan for regime collapse.
3) What will we do with the 4th Infantry Division (4ID) if it comes south? Answer: we will place it under the operational control of V Corps.

I informed McKiernan I was waiting for a response from CFSOCC on how we will coordinate the handover of the 173rd Abn Brigade in case the decision was taken to send the 4ID south. I received a request from V Corps, via the G3, for information on the loads of various ships in the 4ID force package 1, FP 1. Specifically, V Corps wanted the multi-role bridge companies, Military Police Battalion, Hunter unmanned aerial vehicle (UAV) platoon, Signal Battalion, fuel trucks, and logistics units, in order, unloaded first. I began coordination with our Joint Movements Center to determine where in the flow of ships these particular loads were and when we might expect the ships to arrive.

In the C5 Plans Update for 4 March, I announced the name of the successive plan to Phase IV: Eclipse II. After trying and failing to find something in Arabic that evoked some unifying theme from Iraqi history, we reached back to US Army history and the name of the plan for post-war Germany. Third Army played a role in that operation, so it was a part of Third Army history as well.

LTG McKiernan had told me earlier in the week that he wanted a presentation on the entirety of the plan by 7 March. Events were moving apace. During our morning staff update, McKiernan explained the opening days of the campaign. He took the decision that the 173rd Airborne Brigade would fall under the operational control of the CFSOCC. This was significant as it indicated we would have an airborne assault into northern Iraq. McKiernan indicated he wanted to sustain the advance on Baghdad with fuel so we would accelerate the establishment of our internal pipeline distribution system through the western breach of the Kuwait–Iraq border. V Corps would remain the CFLCC's main effort. He also told me, as I was going to Qatar and CENTCOM's forward headquarters on 5 March, that he wanted OPCON of SOF during Phase IV.

I strongly agreed with LTG McKiernan on this point. Phase IV was so complex, I felt we really needed one commander in charge of operations throughout Iraq.

It seemed CENTCOM was leaning this way anyway, as I felt CFLCC would be named the overall commander in Iraq: CENTCOM had two wars and an entire region to be concerned about once we reached Baghdad. I had to point out at the time, regarding McKiernan's desire for OPCON, that it would become an emotional issue for SOCCENT. This did not mean our position was any less correct, merely that we would face very strong opposition to this request from SOCCENT. I said I would visit SOCCENT during my trip and explore the topic with the CFSOCC J3.

I attended a colonel-level VTC on Phase IV on 4 March. Representatives from CENTCOM, ORHA, and the Joint Chiefs of Staff J5 attended the conference. It was a pretty good session. We agreed to keep on meeting via VTC to ensure the more senior-level VTCs remained focused on decision making and approval. The small team I had working on the "Iraqi Army after next" was coordinating efforts with the CJTF-4 folks, who were also working on this point as a portion of the Phase IVB total effort. At the time, there was very good work being done on this major task.

I spent 5 March in Qatar attending meetings with the CENTCOM J5. Events were coming to a head in Washington, D.C., and at CENTCOM too. My planners continued to coordinate the arrival of forces in accord with what LTG McKiernan wanted in terms of necessary combat forces, as well as the forces needed to sustain these combat forces. We worked with FORSCOM on mortuary affairs units, the top 20 reserve component priority units, and general force flow. We learned that the 3rd Armored Cavalry Regiment was moving toward the port. While in Qatar, I also learned it was unlikely that GEN Franks would take a decision on the movement of the 4ID before the Turkish government met on or around 11 March. This decision would have an effect on our forces in theater when we finally crossed the line of departure.

Also while in Qatar, I learned more about a soon-to-be-released planning order on "catastrophic success." This planning order would articulate three scenarios for success prior to D-Day. These ranged from the establishment of an Iraqi government which was completely acceptable to the US/Coalition, which would accept all United Nations Security Council resolutions (UNSCR), to a new Iraqi government which was in partial control of the country and which would request US/Coalition assistance, to a Saddam II.

I had some lengthy discussions with the CENTCOM J3 planners working on this planning order. GEN Franks was insistent on the development of this order, and on our preparation for immediate execution. There was no intelligence information I was aware of supporting this planning, but I concluded the general officers knew something I was not cleared for, or any colonel for that matter, as I asked my counterpart colonels at CENTCOM those questions.

There was more Phase IV work in the offing. I was directed to dispatch a few Phase IV planners back to Washington to support the Army staff as it prepared for exercise Prominent Hammer III. This exercise looked at how the US might deal with other contingencies once the war in Iraq began. I reported I intended to send at least one planner from the C5. I was certain JTF-4 would also send a planner. The CFLCC representatives needed to be in the Pentagon on 9 March so they could prepare the Army staff representatives on 10 March. The colonel-level wargame began on 11 March. I recommended LTG McKiernan consider sending MG Whitley back to D.C. to help the senior Army leadership get ready for the flag/general officer wargame to be conducted from 18–19 March.

I wrote to LTG McKiernan that I recognized there were ongoing operations leading some on the CENTCOM staff and in the senior Pentagon leadership to believe the Iraqi "house of cards" might just fall with one good push. I offered that we ought to consider the Iraqi Army and Republican Guard Forces Command (RGFC) might just fight for pride, as well as we would. The Iraqis, I pointed out, were professionals, and we'd seen some rather good operational-level moves on the part of the Army and RGFC against the Iranians, and during the First Gulf War. I wrote that while we possessed advantages the Iraqis did not, there was still the possibility the Iraqis would at least fight as we first thought: to satisfy their honor. They would achieve some standing in the region just for the fact that they were fighting and not rolling over. I told McKiernan that I knew I was not an Arabist, but this conjecture on my part was consistent with the history I had read on the region.

Every day in March something else would come up which indicated we were getting close to a decision on the invasion. I felt pressure building, and no doubt the generals on the CFLCC staff, and LTG McKiernan especially, were feeling it even more than I was. I know I was writing him about our planning efforts, changes to the force flow, and the results of various wargames we were running, as well as ones in Washington, D.C.

In my C5 Plans Update for 6 March, there were several major points which raised the blood pressure among the staff, me included. I reported that I'd received a message asking about the ramifications of reassigning forces from CENTCOM and the Army from 1003V to Korea for two FDOs. The significant forces we discussed were two MLRS battalions and three AH-64D (Longbow) battalions.

I convened our operational plans group on 7 March to craft our response; I'd already sent it out for staff work. The suspense for an answer was 14 March. I assured LTG McKiernan we would be done in advance of that deadline. This was the first in a series of questions coming from the preliminary work on exercise Prominent Hammer. There were more questions concerning the flow of forces to come.

While I was a student in SAMS, I picked up a number of observations on planning, mostly from Prussian general staff officers. During this time, one particular observation continued to roll through my head: it was that an error in the initial placement (or arrival) of forces cannot be corrected in the course of the campaign. Every time another headquarters wanted to adjust the force flow for its benefit, I would argue from the position of being the main effort in Phase III of the campaign, and state the necessity of having the force set prior to the initiation of hostilities.

I reported I was engaged with CFSOCC J3 on the movement of conventional forces in support of CFSOCC and JSOTF-N. CFSOCC went to Forces Command with requests to move forces within the upcoming 96-hour deployment window that had the potential to disrupt the overall force flow. Specifically, the movement by strategic airlift of CH-47s and aviation unit maintenance unit from the United States to Constanta, Romania. The ultimate destination was within Iraq, but since the CH-47s could not self-deploy from Romania to Iraq, another strategic air move would be required. This was not a general officer or commanding general-level issue yet, but I wanted LTG McKiernan to know about this in advance while I was engaging with CFSOCC J3. The final note on force flow pertained to additional shifts in arrival dates of CFLCC forces.

We learned that the EAD and LAD windows for 1st US Armored Division, 2nd Cavalry Regiment, and 1st Cavalry Division were moving right—that is, changing to be later than we wanted—based on TRANSCOM projections of available shipping. There was nothing we could do about this, save adjust the plan and accept the risk. There were only so many ships. We were also concerned about where and when we could plan on using the 4th Infantry Division.

I learned from my CENTCOM J5 counterparts there was no further word as to a decision on the movement of the 4ID from its location in the Mediterranean to Kuwait. TRANSCOM needed a decision by 8 March. This would not happen; as I mentioned earlier, GEN Franks would not take a decision until he learned of the Turkish government's vote, or non-vote, on 11 March. As a result of having to wait to find out this information, there was a delay in the arrival and employment of the 4ID.

Part of our Phase IV planning involved the development of a proclamation intended for distribution at the end of the fighting. I reviewed a reworked proclamation on the end of fighting which had come from CENTCOM. Terry Moran, LTG McKiernan's initiatives man, made a strong case that McKiernan's name should be the one in the proclamation, based on him being the general officer commanding on the ground. I accepted that Moran's case had strong logic, but ultimately I disagreed. I maintained the name on the document should remain that of GEN Franks, as he was the Coalition force commander and we were acting in his name. There was much more on Phase IV work.

My planners and MG Whitley received a briefing from the Combined Force Air Component Command (CFACC) planners on the status of CFACC Phase IV planning. This resulted in a request that LTG McKiernan mention to GEN Franks that he really needed to issue definitive guidance on who would be "in charge" in Iraq after victory conditions were met.

We engaged the CENTCOM planners on a proposal for restructuring the Iraqi military. We intended to propose an answer to a question we asked them regarding two specified tasks in the campaign plan: "Support an interim security force and provisional or permanent government in order to provide a stable environment for the Iraqi population," and, "Be prepared to support the establishment of an Iraqi military in order to enable Iraq to maintain their territorial integrity." Our question was: what needs to be done? I then proposed that we tell CENTCOM the answer was to recall the regular Iraqi Army. The group we were sending to Washington, D.C., for Prominent Hammer would also carry this message, along with covering tasks in the first sixty–ninety days of the campaign and our draft Phase IV plan. In this report, it was the question from our British cousins concerning the use of the British 7th Armoured Brigade which really caused blood pressure to rise.

Dust-up with the British

I reported that I had spoken with MG Whitley on 6 March about a British force offer. MG Whitley had stated that if we asked for the use of British bridges, the British Chemical Regiment, and especially the British 7th Armoured Brigade, both GEN Jackson (British chief of defence staff) and LTG Reith (Commanding General, UK Permanent Joint Headquarters, PJHQ) would accept and approve the request. I recommended that we should ask for all of this and place the 7th Armoured Brigade under the operational control of V Corps. At the time, the plan specified that the entire UK 1st Armoured Division was under operational control of the Marines.

My purpose was to reinforce the CFLCC main effort, V Corps. I did not think a decision on moving the 4ID would be made in time to allow the division to join V Corps early enough for the attack toward Baghdad. The Marines had sufficient armor and fire power to control their zone and contain Iraqi forces in Basra. Given the amount of combat service support units in V Corps, another tank brigade would not overtax V Corps logisticians. Adding one brigade would also not overtax V Corps command and control. This British proposal made a great deal of sense. This move would give the V Corps commander a powerful formation to reinforce his fight against the Iraqi Republican Guard Medina Division.

The note provoked a storm of protest from the Marines and I MEF, but I was acting on a suggestion from MG Whitley. I saw this as a means of reinforcing the CFLCC main effort, V Corps, without taking away a great deal of fire power from I MEF. Since this suggestion came from the British, I felt I was on solid ground in proposing it. The Marines felt as if I was denuding their effort of its combat power.

The British planners immediately backed away from this controversy and professed no knowledge of where it had come from. At the time, I suspected that the British military wanted to get the 7th Armoured Brigade into the fight, but that this fell afoul with the British government's wish to remain in the south and restrict the movement of British forces in the north of the country. I never found out with any certainty why this was raised and when, but we never shifted forces. I felt the main effort was not reinforced as it should have, but given the request for forces process on one hand and the Marines on the other, we never again raised the issue of shifting a force at hand, the UK armoured brigade, from the supporting to the main effort again. I had the feeling that our British cousins were trying to force something, perhaps from Whitehall, but I was never quite sure.

Off-ramps

Around this time of planning and anticipation, I received a tasking from MG Webster which told me a number of people in Washington, D.C., were asking about "off-ramps" for units in the force flow. Specifically, they wanted to know which units we could do without in the coming campaign, and when we could stop them from deploying. I was rather disgusted. The war had not even started yet, and people were wondering about stopping the force flow. Of course our chief of staff, GEN Shinseki, and Deputy Secretary of Defense Wolfowitz presented thoughts to Congress on the number of troops needed for Phase IV operations in February. I wondered if these inquiries were the result of this public pondering.

Between 7 and 11 March, I had a section of planners working on a Joint Chiefs of Staff planning order directing an assessment of the time required for and risk involved in moving forces from theater during the execution of 1003V to the Pacific Command area of responsibility in order to prevent or swiftly defeat a North Korean attack on the Republic of Korea.

I did not know if this was the result of any developing intelligence which was indicating an attack, or if it was simply prudent planning. I put one of our best planners in charge of the effort: MAJ Evan Huelfer. I gave MAJ Huelfer the task of writing a paper for LTG McKiernan's review and approval to be completed prior to 14 March, the delivery date to the Joint Chiefs.

Our response looked at the potential effect of the proposed shift of units and munitions on our ability to execute actions at the operational level of war. The suspense date for our paper kept moving to the left, from 14 to 12 March. Evan completed the work on 9 March and sent it to MG Blackman (our chief of staff) and MGs Webster and Stratman (the deputy commanders) for review. They approved our assessment, and LTG McKiernan approved the response on 11 March. We included an assessment of the potential loss of Army, Navy, and Marine Corps systems and munitions. This was another indicator that events were moving toward D-Day and an invasion of Iraq.

The daily reports of 7 and 8 March covered our parallel efforts to answer the Joint Chiefs of Staff's request to know how our plan might be impacted by a North Korean attack into South Korea might be, and the request to keep LTG

McKiernan informed on the status of preparing our forces stance for combat. This stance and the subsequent attack into Iraq depended in large measure on our ability to sustain the advance with fuel. We developed priority lists of US Army Reserve units to signal our need as clearly as possible, especially given the shift to requests for forces as opposed to the use of the time-phased force deployment process.

Nine of the ten requested petroleum truck companies were on the ground as of 8 March 2003. My section was also analyzing the force packages coming into theater after the arrival of the 3rd Armored Cavalry Regiment to determine what type of engineer and logistics units we would require to complete Phase IV tasks if the secretary of defense opted to stop the force flow of follow-on combat units. We were informed of work on the Joint Staff regarding "off-ramps" for forces. This work prompted many folks to remark, as GEN Shinseki had earlier told us, that we had to be on the expressway before we could talk about off-ramps. Our other effort remained focused on refining our Phase IV plan.

We were scheduled to give LTG McKiernan a Phase IVA presentation at 1900hrs on 7 March, but this did not happen until 8 March. I released our Phase IV plan, Eclipse II, for planning based on LTG McKiernan's approval. I was of course engaged in parallel planning with V Corps, I MEF, and 377th Theater Support Command. I also reported to LTG McKiernan that we were sending two officers back to Washington on the evening of 7 March to provide information to the Army staff, as the Army G3 prepared for Prominent Hammer. The focus was on: 1) addressing the specified tasks in first 60–90 days of the campaign and 2) our draft Phase IV annex/plan. The instruction I gave, which was reinforced by MGs Blackman, Webster, Stratman, and Thurman, was that the presentation should stay away from "how much" Army will be required in Phase IV except to give broad planning parameters. My officers would return by 10/11 March.

We retained a focus on what the Turks might decide regarding the use of their country for a northern axis of advance for the invasion. My earlier recommendation to move the 4ID to the south in time for the invasion was overcome by events. This late in March, any decision would put the 4ID—our Army's most modernized division—into the fight very late, if at all. I agreed with LTG McKiernan that, in all likelihood, the 4ID would ride the waves until a decision was made by the Turkish government on 11 March.

While LTG McKiernan's schedule precluded us from giving him an update on our Phase IV planning efforts to date, MG Webster asked our Phase IV team to analyze force packages which were scheduled to arrive after the 3rd Cavalry. He wanted to determine what combat support and combat service support units we would still need to have for Phase IV if the decision was taken to not flow deployment order (DEPORD) 190 combat units: the 1st Cavalry and 1st Armored Divisions, and the 2nd Cavalry Regiment.

We completed the analysis on 9 March, having carried out work on it while engaged in parallel planning with V Corps, I MEF, and 377th Theater Support Command on Phase IV. Our Phase IV focus assisted the C35, future operations section, and C9, civil affairs section, in answering a very short-fused Commander, CENTCOM paper on humanitarian assistance actions in Basrah, An Nasiriyah, and An Najaf. We had been drawn in because I had fielded a phone call calling for "more detail" after a CENTCOM VTC. I pointed out that the required detail was in the paper. The pressure to produce answers for Washington was causing lots of folks to overlook work which had already been completed, and to instead rely on phone calls for immediate answers.

The C5 was in charge of coordinating with C3 (current operations) C35 (future operations), G3 V Corps, and G3 I MEF on movement control of forces as were to cross the LD. We concluded that Breach Point West—the lane in the Kuwaiti border berm which led to An Nasiriyah and Iraqi Highway 8—would be an operationally decisive point. This meant CFLCC had to maintain control over this vital point to sustain our advance on Baghdad.

The concluding note of the day came from our daily CENTCOM VTC. We learned that the Saudis had granted approval for cross-border operations. GEN Franks directed the deputy commander to work with the Jordanians for similar permission. Franks was concerned about three events which he termed "operational dis-locators." He cautioned the CFACC and air defense coordinators to be aware of the potential of a spoiling attack within the next three to five days. This would be a no-fly zone violation which turned into an air attack on our assembly areas. He cautioned us to be aware of the potential of a terrorist attack. Finally, he warned that we should refine our media broadcast objectives. The embedded media was showing up and he told us to work our message very hard. Though there was no intelligence from any source leading to a conclusion of either an air attack or a terrorist attack, the caution was a good reminder for us, accustomed as we were to operating under the condition of air supremacy. Franks was reminding us that the enemy gets a vote.

March 8 was another full day of preparation for a war that we knew was coming, but for which we did not yet know the specific start date. My officers continued to work closely with the Central Command planners on the JCS planning order directing an assessment of time and risk involved in moving forces from theater during 1003V execution to the Pacific region in order to prevent or swiftly defeat a North Korean attack on the Republic of Korea.

LTC Reilly and our deployment group sent out another force flow chart based on the latest TRANSCOM slides. We were concerned that the EAD/LAD windows for 1st Armored Division, 2nd Cavalry Regiment, and 1st Cavalry Division continued to fluctuate based on TRANSCOM projections of available shipping. While we were working to make the process less confusing—as there were multiple documents from other headquarters regarding the desired dates—I recommended that we continue to press for our EAD/LAD windows for the forces apportioned to us. I informed LTG McKiernan and our command group that I would press this action with Central Command J5 and with US Army Forces Command in Atlanta, Georgia, providing support as well.

LTG McKiernan assessed the situation vis-à-vis the 4ID, and when we could commit that division to the fight, as being on a "wait and see" basis. I agreed: we would simply have to wait and see what the Turkish government would decide. Our earlier recommendation to move the division to Kuwait and use the ships to load out the 1st Cavalry Division had gone unheeded. I felt we'd missed an opportunity to 1) celebrate Turkish democracy by accepting an earlier "no" vote on coming through the north and 2) more importantly, be able to cross the line of departure with two armored forces: 3ID and 4ID. We were also reviewing a CENTCOM planning order on when to move the 4ID from its at-sea location to the Kuwait ports. The right moment for this movement to have an effect for the invasion had passed.

I acknowledged the guidance given to us by LTG McKiernan at our Phase IVA presentation. We continued the effort as a draft plan in parallel with V Corps and I MEF and with our work with V Corps on Task Force Baghdad. I MEF planners would present their work on Phase IV thus far to LTG Conway on 9 March. My planners and I would go out the I MEF camp to attend this presentation. We continued our work on Eclipse II, and rolled our requests for information into suggested updates to the CENTCOM J5 Phase IV planning order. We continued to address joint command and control, C2, Special Operating Forces C2 relationships, and reinforced this with the CENTCOM planners. I also coordinated for a visit to Qatar with the CENTCOM J5 Phase IV plans team and to work on LTG Abizaid's task to define the headquarters transition between CFLCC and CJTF-Iraq.

We sent C5 officers to Washington to update the Army staff on our planning efforts for Phase IV. They got out of Kuwait with no problem, and would report in when they got to the Pentagon on 9 March. These officers were scheduled for a series of briefings to the Army staff on 10 March, and they were to return to Kuwait on 11 March.

I concluded my daily update to LTG McKiernan with an assessment of D-Day, and a request. I told him I believed there would be several critical points on D-Day battlefield: Breach Point West, where elements of V Corps and I MEF would share an axis of advance; the passage point, where 1st Marine Division would cross into the V Corps battle space for the forward passage of lines; and the crossing sites themselves.

I thought there should be CFLCC presence at these points, or at least at one of these points. Our headquarters needed a presence on the ground in contact with our operations section, and a presence possessing knowledge of the plan and the decision points. I recommended that the C5 perform this role at the start of the operation given there would not be too much planning going on otherwise over those few days and given the criticality of getting across the LD in good form. Receiving direct reports would help in confirming situation awareness and understanding. I never got an answer on this request.

The C5 Plans Updates between 9 and 16 March reflected a growing impetus toward war. While the planners working for me continued to focus on CFLCC priorities, getting forces into theater, and refining our sequel plan for Phase IV, other questions still arose as the Joint Staff, the Office of the Secretary of Defense, the Army staff, and the CENTCOM staff all pressed for more and more information. We were all drawn into answering questions from the secretary of defense's office.

Save some of the planners working for me—LTC Reilly, MAJ Innocenti, and LTC Hendricks, to name a few—we were not able to stop, take a breath, or try to see the larger picture. These three great officers acted as SAMS-educated officers ought, and asked how our effort fitted into the larger picture. I was grateful for their efforts, but we never really got a "big picture" answer from DC or CENTCOM. We simply had to continue answering the Secretary's questions.

During those weeks prior to the invasion, we worked on the flow of forces into theater. Secretary Rumsfeld, through his military staff, was pounding us to reduce the numbers of forces heading toward Iraq. This work involved all of us, as it did on the evening of 9 March when the C4, MG Christianson, was personally involved in the analysis of force packages scheduled to arrive after the 3rd Cavalry. This analysis was to determine what logistics units we would still need to have for Phase IV if a decision was taken to not flow DEPORD 190 combat units. The analysis of the CS and CSS led us to conclude the units we needed to flow were primarily civil affairs, Military Police (regular and prison guard units), truck companies (cargo and fuel), and engineers. The total personnel went from 60,148 to 11,594 with the drop of the combat units and other CS/CSS tied to the combat units. I wrote that I still thought we would need the 2nd Cavalry Regiment, but I recognized we might not have the choice.

Washington and the Pentagon were focused on the flow of forces and on questioning indispensability of just about every unit we felt we would need to continue the campaign. Every day we sent out another force flow chart based on the latest TRANSCOM slides to CENTCOM, and through that headquarters to Rumsfeld's office, the Joint Staff, and the Army staff.

We also provided our assessment of DEPORD 190 CS/CSS units to MG Webster. This deployment order set out: the units which would complete the service support structure necessary to sustain the combat units we had on the ground at that time; what was necessary to sustain the combat units to Baghdad and beyond; and the combat units we felt were needed for Phase IV. We provided a number of "top 20" lists of active and reserve component units to the Office of the Secretary of Defense and the supporting staffs, to include US Army Forces Command.

We worked with our C4 (Supply and Logistics) staff section on a review of the "top 20" reserve component units from DEPORD 187—the deployment order which completed the deployments of units associated with V Corps and CFLCC headquarters, as well as completing the flow of units in support of the 101st Air Assault Division. We extended this to a review of DEPORD 190 as well. The "top 20" worked well. The FORSCOM commander and his staff really worked hard to get those forces over to theater for CFLCC. We also received lots of calls for our priority for movement. LTC Reilly and I talked over and proposed the list below, which gives our proposed sequence of flowing remaining Army forces into theater to LTG McKiernan.

- Complete the closure of Force Module 1 (CFLCC and V Corps communications and logistics)
- Complete the closure of Force Modules 5, 6, and 7 (101st AASLT with associated logistics units)
- Close Force Modules 2, 3, and 4 (3 ACR with associated logistics units)
- Then in priority sequence from DEPORD 190:
    - Close Force Module 9 (2nd Cavalry Regiment)
    - Close Force Module 10 (1st Armored Division)
    - Close Force Module 11 (1st Cavalry Division)

Reilly and I felt it was important to bring Force Modules 9, 10, and 11 from DEPORD 190 into Kuwait in sequence as we had designed and built the force modules to close in this priority. We included CS/CSS capabilities which not only supported the particular force module, but also set the stage for the arrival and employment of the follow-on force modules. Changing sequence at this time could lead to the same drill our headquarters went through when GEN Franks shifted the 101st Air Assault Division in front of the 3rd Cavalry Regiment—a last-minute review and redesign of individual force modules to ensure we had the correct units and capabilities. Another of these drills, we felt, would cause a change in the total strategic lift required and therefore a change in US TRANSCOM transportation allocation.

We also believed that by sticking to a schedule, we could "tighten up" the current projected force flow windows, especially for 1st Armored and 1st Cavalry Divisions. Tom Reilly and I provided the assessment of deploying DEPORD 190 CS/CSS units to MGs Webster, deputy commanding general for operations; Stratman, deputy commanding general for support; Thurman, operations officer; and Christianson, supply officer.

The question of the use of the 4th Infantry Division, 4ID, kept coming up in message traffic between Washington, CENTCOM headquarters, and our headquarters. Throughout the week before the invasion, we were repeatedly asked when the 4ID should move to Kuwait. My team sent a proposed response to the question of the movement of the 4ID to senior staff, chief of staff, and DCGs. We believed that 1) 4ID would remain in position until the Turks took a decision; 2) if the decision was made to move the 4ID but there remained the possibility that the Turks would allow a conventional force into Iraq via Turkey then the European Command and US Army Europe ships containing supplies (and equipment to unload and transship those supplies) should remain; 3) if the Turks completely closed the option of a northern attack then we should reload and move selected ships of the European Command and US Army Europe ships to the south. We spent an extraordinary amount of time worrying over the 4ID.

We were not the only headquarters working with the force flow. During the pre-invasion period we reviewed some TRANSCOM slides which showed a different view of force closure (no surprise). We coordinated with the CENTCOM J5 on the topic of force closure/arrival. The following is from a CENTCOM J5 note:

> The TRANSCOM slides show an adjusted picture to test the capability of the fleet. It does not show our force flow because we haven't adjusted the force flow based on the new execution dates. We have resisted telling you all to adjust your EAD/LAD windows until more is known. TRANSCOM commander did not want to wait so they adjusted the EAD/LAD windows to show what was possible. Please ensure your leadership knows this. We will implement your priorities based on your adjusted EADs. We have told the leadership here that the TRANSCOM slides were one excursion. Don't pay attention to the adjusted dates. Pay attention to the final date for closure of the entire force. That is all those slides tested.

I was constantly reminded of Moltke's dictum that an error in the initial placement of forces could not be corrected over the course of a campaign.

Our own headquarters was also working on adjusting the arrival of forces. I received a C3 request to explore the possibility of bringing the 308th Civil Affairs Battalion forward in the flow. This unit was assigned to V Corps and was vital in establishing our wargame-derived conditions for success in Phase IV. My planners worked with the civil affairs planners to determine where the unit stood in the "prepare to move" stage of the overall alert process. Based on our review of the timing of the arrival of the 308th CA Battalion, MG Thurman decided not to move it up in the flow—the movement forward would prove too disruptive. But this did not put an end the work as LTG Wallace, V Corps commander, asked for an earlier arrival of the unit.

My planners and the CFLCC civil affairs planners worked with US Army Civil Affairs and Psychological Operations Command, the headquarters overseeing all such units in the US Army, to accelerate the arrival of the 308th CA and other civil affairs units. I made sure LTGs McKiernan and Wallace knew we would not get any higher priority for movement until certain special operations forces and Joint Special Operations Task Force-North arrived in theater.

Finally, on 17 March, while we were refining our force flow requests and working through the challenges which the shifts in force flow would create for the crafting of Eclipse II, we received a request to review a briefing for the secretary of defense. We worked on a review of a secretary of defense briefing on force flow decisions. We received this from both the Army staff and the CENTCOM J3 and J5, and reviewed the proposed draft briefing, updated or proposed some of the wording of the charts, and made other suggested changes.

We were, I felt, hurtling toward war while we were trying to reduce the number of forces that would actually fight the battles and attain the policy objectives. In Washington, people were constantly talking about "***off-ramps***" even though many of our units were not even on the highway. Amid these efforts, work on refining the invasion plan, Cobra II, did not cease while we were working on the force flow.

I MEF continued to refine its war plans. I went to the MEF course of action decision briefing to LTG Conway on 9 March, and attended the operations plan rehearsal on 10 March. Both of these events were interesting, and LTG Conway was firmly in charge of his planners and the overall planning process.

During the I MEF Phase IV course of action briefing, LTG Conway held a long conversation on the word "defeat" and its use in Phase IV post-hostilities operations. He preferred to start on the low end of violence and ramp up to defeat. These were very interesting points, and I elaborated on them in a longer report to LTG McKiernan. I also carried them to a meeting with the CENTCOM J5. The major points of discussion ranged from the meaning of word "defeat" to the details of occupying the Shia holy sites, and from fiscal guidance on spending for Phase IV emergency repair projects to redeployment.

LTG Conway asked about the task of "Defeat[ing] remaining pockets of resistance in order to establish a safe environment for post-hostility operations," which had been directed to the MEF. He stated he did not think the term "defeat" was consistent with post-hostility operations, and that instead, defeat meant applying all the combat power of the MEF as opposed to a graduated application of fires and maneuver. My response was that the task was a CENTCOM-specified task to CFLCC, and we had conducted similar conversations with the CENTCOM J5. I told LTG Conway that I would raise the issue again during our talks with CENTCOM planners in Qatar.

The Marines held a discussion on how to occupy or deal with the Shia holy sites and cities of Karbala and An Najaf. In my reports, I told LTGs Conway and McKiernan that we would engage with CENTCOM planners and get a clear statement of guidance from CENTCOM on how to deal with these cities. My belief was that the correct guidance was to not occupy at all but to deal with the Iraqi Shia cleric and city mayors, and tell them to maintain order.

Rear Admiral Kubic, commander of the construction battalions (Sea Bees) in support of the MEF, and LTG Conway talked about the need for fiscal guidance on spending for Phase IV essential repair projects. I took the note as this directive had to come from CENTCOM, but I knew CFLCC itself would have to ask the question and propose the correct answer.

I reported to LTG McKiernan that I had taken a note on standards for housing troops during Phase IV. LTG Conway said this would send a message on the expeditionary and temporary nature of our stay in Iraq. He was correct: if we truly wanted to send the message that we were not an occupying force, then we could not, as GEN Keane, the Army vice chief of staff, had said in January, be building any Camp Bondsteels.[2] I told LTG Conway I would ask about this while I was in Qatar meeting with the CENTCOM J5.

RADM Kubic asked about the tasks CFLCC would give to the 416th ENCOM during Phase IV, and whether the ENCOM would be in general support or direct support of the MEF and V Corps. I could not remember the answer at that moment, and had to get an answer back to RADM Kubic later on. The 416th ENCOM remained in general support of CFLCC and reinforced engineering efforts throughout both the MEF and V Corps zones.

At the end of the Phase IV discussion, LTG Conway held a separate discussion on the retrograde of the MEF. I learned that the planning factor for reloading a maritime prepositioned squadron (MPSRON) was four months. This factor played a large role in our CFLCC efforts to write the redeployment portion of the CFLCC Phase IV plan. The Marines had completely unloaded the sets of equipment from the MPS squadrons to equip both MPSRON-based regiments (5th and 7th Marines). Part of our responsibility was to re-set the afloat equipment sets, as well as to re-load the ships. This effort also included the afloat and ashore sets of equipment used to equip the 3rd Infantry Division: Army pre-position set three, APS3 (afloat) and Army pre-position set five, APS 5K (Kuwait) and 5Q (Qatar) for reconstitution. We also continued to refine the command and control relationships for Phase IV. One such key relationship was between CFLCC and CFSOCC.

During this period, my planners received a presentation from a CFSOCC Phase IV planner, LTC Bob Kelley. We had a very good discussion, especially as it revolved around a secretary of defense execution order which laid out what was next for the greater special operations community. Kelley said we must listen to the secretary of defense execution order presentation on what they would do next, as it would be the basis for why CFSOCC repeatedly argued they could not be under the OPCON of CFLCC. I felt this violated the principle of war unity of command and CENTCOM guidance which stated that there would be one commander in Iraq during Phase IV.

Based on my understanding of LTG McKiernan's guidance, I coordinated for a visit to Qatar with the CENTCOM Phase IV plans team. We would also work on a task which had been laid on us by LTG Abizaid, the deputy commander of CENTCOM, to define the headquarters transition between CFLCC and CJTF-Iraq. The C5 team would attend three planning sessions: headquarters transition, Phase IV planning, and Iraqi Army reformation. My team spent a long day in Qatar.

2 Camp Bondsteel was a base camp built for US Army troops in Kosovo. It was ridiculed for having extensive "creature comforts" as opposed to being focused on warfighting and was an embarrassment for the Army.

On 10 March we got the highly classified presentation on the secretary of defense's execution order to the SOF. I also learned that LTG McKiernan, based on his understanding of this directive, would be satisfied with tactical control (TACON) of SOF in Iraq.

In my update for 11 March, I told LTG McKiernan that it had been a "plans" kind of day. By this I meant there was a great deal going on and I had little to no control over anything. Likely I should have realized that my attempts at relieving the pressure of the moment were not playing well with LTG McKiernan. While my section and I were wrestling with factors related to refining the Phase IV plan itself, there was a great deal of action ongoing in order to get the plan approved, inform a range of people about our plan and, importantly, to get the plans section prepared for war.

On 11 March, we sent out our final draft of OPLAN Eclipse II to the CENTCOM J5, our air, naval, Marine, and special operations component headquarters, and our subordinate headquarters, specifically V Corps, I MEF, and the 377th Support Command. MG Whitley also directed that the military planners of JTF-4 should consolidate with the C5 Phase IV planners. This became necessary because MG Blackman, CFLCC chief of staff, directed that the headquarters element called JTF-4 disestablish itself. I still envisioned the JTF-4 portion of my C5 section becoming the J5 of CJTF-Iraq once we closed on Baghdad. This was a tough task as we had to incorporate 12 new planners into our section, welcome them into our functioning group, and re-establish a team as we prepared for war.

On 11 and 12 March, our four Phase IV planners worked in Qatar at CENTCOM headquarters working with the CENTCOM J5 Phase IV planners on a synchronization matrix of stability and Phase IV tasks. MG Whitley told me I needed to go to Qatar on Friday 14 March to assist in a presentation for LTG Abizaid, the deputy commander. I intended to take along some of the newly incorporated planners from JTF-4 to ensure their participation in the CENTCOM Phase IV effort.

We also received a request for assistance from the CENTCOM J5, who wanted us to help with answering a secretary of defense snowflake. The CENTCOM J5 prepared a presentation on planned humanitarian assistance operations for delivery to the Secretary Rumsfeld, General Pace (the vice chairman of the Joint Chiefs of Staff), and Ms. Clark, the Defense Department public affairs director. The purpose of the presentation was to "develop a conviction that the things the President needs to have happen are happening and that we have figured out ways to have them properly communicated." The suspense date for the presentation was close of business 13 March (in time for GEN Franks's review). The planners we sent to Qatar assisted in the development of the presentation. I also ensured our own C9 civil affairs section knew about the effort and contributed to it.

On 12 March I learned that Michael Gordon of the *New York Times* was our CFLCC-embedded reporter. I reminded the staff principals that, along with LTG

Bernard Trainor, USMC (Ret.), Gordon had written *The Generals' War*, a book about First Gulf War. I had been reading through the book again, and I noted that Gordon had used the word "failure" a great deal when speaking of military planning and executing.

Finally, I reported that the C5 section was conducting pre-combat checks. Together with our administration section, our C5 non-commissioned officer in charge (NCOIC) Sergeant First Class Joe Penor refined the C5 SCUD drill reaction plan. Everybody in our section checked the fit of their chemical protective suits. This action alone drove home the deadly seriousness of what we were doing.

In the plans update for 13 March, I reported some really significant events in the refinement of our Phase IV planning effort. My final two Phase IV planners, MAJs Innocenti and Sparling, returned from two days of working with CENTCOM J5 planners in Qatar. These two, along with MAJ Grieme and UK MAJ Nick Elliot, did superb work on refining Eclipse II, and getting it accepted by CENTCOM.

MAJs Innocenti and Sparling gave a working briefing of our Eclipse II plan which resulted in CENTCOM accepting our stability plan for phases III and IVA as the basis for CENTCOM's plan for Phases III and IVA. This would produce unity of effort within CENTCOM's campaign plan, as it stood then, for Phase IV. At the time, CENTCOM had established seven separate operational plans teams within the staff, with each team focused on a single line of stability operations. These teams now focused on 1) supporting CFLCC planning efforts in IVA and 2) developing CENTCOM's Phase IVB and Phase IVC plans.

LTG McKiernan was concerned about joint command and control, C2, in Phase IVA. As a result of the work done by our team, LTG Abizaid stated that CENTCOM headquarters, with all component elements, would remain in place as long as CFLCC was on the ground in Iraq. He further stated that any forces on the ground in Iraq would "belong to CFLCC" in an operational or tactical control (OPCON or TACON) status.

Through VTC, CENTCOM J5 would brief LTG Abizaid on the transition from IVA to IVB on March 15. The definitive event of this transition would be the transfer of authority from CFLCC to CJTF-IZ. Though CENTCOM wanted to have civil primacy established at the start of Phase IVB, the CENTCOM planners agreed they ultimately had no control over the speed at which ORHA ramped up, and therefore should not tie phasing to civil capability.

We also developed a rough concept of operations for the yet-to-be-established CJTF-Iraq. The CENTCOM J5 and his planners were very interested in meeting with ORHA representatives on 14 March, and indicated a preference to have them permanently in Qatar with a minimum of a planning cell.

The planners I sent to the Pentagon debriefed the section on 13 March. These officers briefed Army G3 LTG Cody and his principal deputies, MGs Huntoon and Chiarelli, on our Phase IV planning effort on 10 and 11 March. They reinforced

LTG McKiernan's guidance to the Army G3: the entire force should flow, and if it did not then the force on the ground—3rd Infantry Division, 4th Infantry Division, 101st Air Assault Division, 82nd Airborne Division (-), V Corps and associated combat support and combat service support enablers—would be strategically fixed for 90 to 120 days after we closed on Baghdad.

LTG Cody told the planners that he fully supported our position on the entire force flow and completely understood that our position about forces being fixed for up to 120 days. We learned the Army staff was putting together a team of seven officers as a Phase IV task force. The primary purpose of briefing the Strategy, Plans, and Policy officers was to highlight the need to continue the current force flow, and was also in support of their wargames with the Joint Staff called "Elaborate Crossbow."

We learned that the chief of staff, Army, and the Army staff supported the current force flow into theater and were of the mind that LTG McKiernan had overall control of the force flow. They also believed that GEN Franks supported the current force flow into theater. There were Joint Staff planners working on recommended "off-ramps" once hostilities commenced.

LTG Cody stated that he understood the need for forces to execute Phase IV operations. He wanted to know if anyone was designated CINC Water, Blankets, and Food for humanitarian assistance operations. At the time I surmised this question was probably in relation to the recent snowflake from Secretary Rumsfeld. Our planners told Cody they were not aware of planning to that level of detail, but the C9, civil affairs planners were working over issues with representatives of the US Agency for International Development, the International Committee of the Red Cross, and others.

LTG Cody directed his staff to gain visibility on force flow and on what was actually on the ships. He wanted to provide the ability to prioritize ships with CS/CSS enablers in the event that combat forces were turned back and enablers were still required. Additionally, he did not want the transportation system set to be set on "autopilot," which would lead to it continuing to blindly ship elements which were not required for the obvious reason of tying up strategic lift.

Our C5 and OPG implied task was to retain the ability to prioritize assets still requiring ships and those which already set sail. My planners coordinated with our logistics section, C4. Based on LTG Cody's perspective on the likelihood of an adjusted flow of forces, our C5 and OPG implied task was to determine what CFLCC would need to sustain operations in the coming months. We had to have visibility on what was already embarked on ships and what else required transportation to theater. My planners coordinated with our logistics section, C4. Our developing position, based on indications of further questions on forces, was that we would not need further combat service support forces if DEPORD 190 did not flow.

The final Phase IV deskside presentation was given to MG Chiarelli in his office. He wanted to know how many troops were required to execute Phase IV of the campaign. This briefing was well after GEN Shinseki's statement to the congressional committee and Deputy Secretary of Defense Wolfowitz's counter-statement. Our planners told MG Chiarelli that the final numbers were an unknown, and were based on where we saw ourselves at the end of Phase III and the beginning of Phase IVA. The planners also told him of some preliminary work being done on determining troop levels, but no definitive determinations on required forces and duration were reached.

We learned an Army-level Phase IV cell was standing up within the War Plans Division labeled Stability Operations Planning Cell. An ad hoc group made up the cell. Its purpose: act as a go-between for issues concerning the Joint Staff, ORHA, and other Army agencies. Our planners gave them a Phase IV brief and answered their questions prior to departing.

Finally, I reported about the other major tasks my planners were working on: answering snowflakes from the secretary of defense and Coalition integration. We provided the CENTCOM J5 with the slides LTG McKiernan had approved as input for the response and briefing to Secretary Rumsfeld on the humanitarian effort which would take place during the campaign. MG Whitley, our deputy commander for Phase IV, was involved in the development of these slides.

We also continued to work on Coalition integration with CENTCOM J5. The advanced party of a Romanian chemical detection unit arrived in theater on 13 March. The Marine-led Joint Task Force-Consequence Management accepted tactical control of the Romanians. The challenge of incorporating Coalition units with their various national constraints on employment would continue.

In my journal for 13 March, I wrote that it had been another "interesting day." My wife Kate wrote to me about the return of Elizabeth Smart, the young woman who had been kidnapped for nine months, to her family. I also wrote:

> I think we will be at war soon. My guess is the POTUS will go for a vote [at the Security Council] when he has nine votes and works on the Russians and Chinese to abstain. If only the French vote no and veto then it is more French vs. US Talked to the section today. Gave them the game face talk, war footing. Reminded all we are w/in range of at least two Iraqi SSM [surface-to-surface missile] systems. Be ready. This feels closer to execution now to me, it really does.

On 14 March, we sent a team to Qatar to work with CCJ5 on strategic lines of operations related to Phase IV. One of our teams worked on the reformed Iraqi Army. The briefing which Secretary Rumsfeld had requested in his snowflake of 13 March had not yet been scheduled. We remained in contact with the CENTCOM J5 planners for more information.

All in all, it was a fruitful trip to Qatar. I had spoken with CENTCOM J5 planners on the overall campaign plan approach for Phase IV and reviewed the headquarters transition briefing requested by LTG Abizaid on the basis for building Combined Joint Task Force-Iraq, CJTF-IZ. CENTCOM J5 planners were again considering building the CJTF-IZ headquarters from the CENTCOM forward headquarters and all of the components with JTF-4 as a base. Our planners and some JTF-4 planners remained in Qatar until 16 March to continue work.

Pre-D-Day Meeting, 14 March 2003

When I returned from Qatar, LTG McKiernan held a meeting at 1900hrs. Senior CFLCC staff were in attendance, along with LTGs Wallace and Conway. McKiernan told us about the "12th hour" timeline leading to war, possibly. The President would give a speech on 17 March. The UN Security Council would vote for the use of force. If the French voted yes, the expectation was there would be a 7–14-day window for diplomacy, or for the use of military force. McKiernan believed this was the least likely option.

The belief was that Security Council Resolution 1441 was enough to justify action. The President would give a speech presenting an ultimatum to Saddam, telling him he must leave Iraq. The expected D-Day would be 19 March, A-Day would then be 21 March and G-Day would be 22 March. McKiernan believed this would be the most likely course of action. Ground forces would do nothing indicating a spike in activity between 14 and 18 March. McKiernan informed us that what he was telling us was of limited distribution. I could not tell anyone in the section what he said.

LTG McKiernan reviewed the activities of the air, sea, and special operations components for us. CFACC, the air component, would be consumed with strategic objectives: Baghdad targets and counter-SCUD missions on A-Day. There would be little to no close air support until G-Day. CFMCC, the naval component, would launch aircraft and TLAMS in support of CFACC. CFMCC would also begin clearing the sea approaches to Umm Qasr for humanitarian assistance deliveries which CENTCOM could exploit via the media. CFSOCC, the special operations component, would track the execution of operations by the three joint special operations task forces: JSOTF-West, JSOTF-North, and JSOTF-South. Task Force 20, the direct action special operations force, would move on targets near the Syrian border in western Iraq.

Lieutenant General McKiernan also told us: there hadn't been any good news from Turkey regarding the use of the northern approach; he expected that GEN Franks would take a decision on the 4ID in the next four days; and, the northern force would consist of the 10th Special Forces Group and the 173rd Airborne Brigade. We then followed this with a discussion on the Turks' options and Iraqi counteractions as we had indications Iraqi regular army units were waiting for instructions from Saddam to secure Kirkuk. We also discussed what we knew of potential Turkish operations, ranging from the possibility of a limited incursion to establish a security zone for displaced persons to a deeper incursion to seize Mosul and Kirkuk.

We had an extended conversation on the possibility of Iraqi units and capitulation. This was a focus of our information operations. We tried hard to persuade Iraqi units and commanders to join us in rebuilding Iraq after Saddam had been removed, rather than fight us. MG Thurman asked about which adjustments we should make to our approach towards the Iraqi 11th Infantry and 51st Mechanized Divisions, given the possible timeline. McKiernan told us to continue to refine our messages over the next few days, and shared there were an increasing number of signs that both divisions were ready to "roll over." MG Marks, our J2, reiterated there were "very good" indications both the 11th and 51st Division commanders had received the "capitulate" message.

LTG McKiernan was cautiously optimistic, but offered the following caveat—if our forces could not confirm a unit had capitulated, we should shoot. He recognized our units might make mistakes but directed we err on the side of caution. We were instructed to identify mechanized units and field artillery units which refused to capitulate and "destroy them." This would encourage other units to throw in the towel. MG Marks reminded us there were reports of three GHN 45 (South African-produced 155mm self-propelled artillery units) in south Rumallah, all of which could range well into Kuwait.

MG Webster, the DCG-Operations, asked whether the mission would remain the same. McKiernan's response was that I MEF would secure the oil fields and seize other key oil production nodes in this instance. The theater engineers had been directed to pull in the oil contractors for their expertise. Discussing oil fires raised the issue of crossing the line of departure early. McKiernan decided that if I MEF crossed the line of departure early, V Corps would cross on order. He asked LTG Wallace how long it would take for V Corps to move, and LTG Wallace said he would get back to LTG McKiernan with an answer. McKiernan closed with a short discussion of the Iraqi military and then gave some final guidance which concerned his knowledge that there were increasing contacts from the Iraqi military, including an unnamed corps commander, who did not want to fight us. Before asking for questions, McKiernan set out the following:

1) Get back into the plan;
2) check the commander's critical information requirements (CCIR);
3) look at intelligence sharing, especially concerning the southern oilfields;
4) check our outposts, as there was a higher likelihood of them being targeted by terror attacks;
5) concentrate on maintenance;
6) check on knowledge of the rules of engagement.

He reported that the proclamations we'd been working on were being reproduced for dissemination.

MG David Kratzer, 377th Theater Support Command Commanding General, said he was concerned about the timing of the decision on bringing the 4ID to Kuwait, and about the availability of pier space at the Kuwaiti ports. McKiernan directed the 377th and the staff to look at using both Kuwaiti ports, as well as directing the 377th to prepare for as rapid a reception, staging, and onward movement of the 4ID as possible. He instructed the 377th to "use every HET to deliver formations as fast as possible to V Corps." McKiernan took the decision to prioritize the unloading and preparation of 4ID units and their movement to V Corps upon arrival of the 4ID ships at Kuwaiti ports.

LTG Conway asked about the possibility for a two-day delay of the ground attack in order for the Marine air wing to conduct close air attacks to reduce Iraqi opposition. LTG McKiernan responded with two options that might trigger a delay of some length: 1) someone claims to have killed Saddam, or 2) there was extremely bad weather that would delay CFACC in completing its strategic tasks. McKiernan reiterated that once we had begun, he did not want to stop on the Euphrates. He rounded off by saying we would gather one more time before G-Day.

We were now four days away from D-Day, although we did not know it. In addition to continuing to refine Cobra II, specifically the Phase IV portion of the plan, in response to requests from Washington, the planners started to work on redeployment. At the time this did not seem out of the ordinary.

General Franks's VTC, 15 March 2003

I spoke to the section again on 15 March to go over the timelines for potential D-Days as well as convey what I knew of upcoming operations. I told them, "We are moving closer to war." My journal entry for that day and my daily report to LTG McKiernan reflect the many pressures we were under, as on one hand we were preparing ourselves to go to war and on the other we were responding to questions from Washington about the end of the war, and how we would re-set the Army Prepositioned Sets of equipment as well as bring forces back to home station. The daily VTC with GEN Franks highlighted this tension of tasks.

During the conference we learned there would be large anti-war demonstrations in the US over this weekend of 15–16 March 2003. Intelligence reports let us know that the Iraqi leadership expected the attacks to begin in the coming week. We learned that Grand Ayatollah Sistani, the elder leader of the Shia community in Iraq, had reportedly told Saddam that he was an infidel, and thus Sistani would not support jihad against America. The J3, MG Renuart, reported that Navy TLAM shooters were coming through the Suez, and would be on station within a day. The conference ended with a few words from GEN Franks.

General Franks was himself: gregarious and earthy. He said, "It's a damn good thing we are pros cause we're all ugly!" He then became very serious, and outlined the strategic context: the next few days would be stressful. Franks expected a decision on Monday, 17 March 2003. On that day we would be "beyond ambiguous." He also anticipated we would be close to D-, A-, and G-Days, as briefed earlier, and stated that "there WILL be friction." In comparison to that conference, our daily work had the appearance of the mundane.

Our work on OPLAN refinement continued. We continued refining our draft Phase IV plan and annexes. We still had a C5 team in Qatar working with CENTCOM J5 planners on strategic lines of operations related to Phase IV. One of our teams was working on the reformed Iraqi Army. I expected this team to return on 16 March, and would send LTG McKiernan a report on the combined CFLCC/ CENTCOM Phase IV effort on 17 March.

We received a copy of the CENTCOM CFLCC to CJTF-Iraq transition presentation which had been given to LTG Abizaid. I reported I thought it was pretty good work, although there were some rather quixotic objectives in the briefing stated as the purpose of some tasks.

It was also during this conference that we held our first OPG meeting on redeployment, in which we refined our estimates on the turn-in of the APS. All of the apportioned sets of equipment in APS 5K (Kuwait), APS 5Q (Qatar), and APS3 (afloat) were used to outfit the 3rd Infantry Division and selected corps-level units.

Restoring these equipment sets depended on Army staff decisions on the long-term status of the APS 5 and 3 stores and equipment, as well as the final decision on how CFLCC returned the stores and equipment to standard. I reported my section would develop some recommendations along with the C4, and C8, comptroller. Anticipating at least as much pressure from DC to get US units out of Iraq as we dealt with in getting units to Iraq, I let LTG McKiernan know I'd directed the plans team and OPG to write a message to the CENTCOM requesting that CENTCOM work on getting access to Saudi seaports for redeployment. I'd prepared the ground on this while I was in Qatar earlier in the week.

The OPG also reviewed a CENTCOM draft, —FRAGO 07–189—on the subject of command relationship, and provided a proposed response for review by MG Blackman, our chief of staff. I was pleased to report to LTG McKiernan that all of the proposed changes we suggested when this FRAGO was first released had been incorporated and it was a good product from the CENTCOM J3. The only further change we recommended had to do with who would be in command of campaign in the extremely unlikely event both GEN Franks and LTG Abizaid were unable to continue in command. We suggested that LTG McKiernan temporarily assume command until LTG DeLong arrived in theater from Tampa.

As close as we were to execution, I reported that we had reviewed a draft CFC FRAGO, unnumbered, for updated guidance on CFC Phases II and III. The CFLCC C35, future operations section, was coordinating the CFLCC response.

The good news I reported was my C5 senior NCO, Sergeant First Class Penor, would return from attending the Advanced Non-Commissioned Officers' Course at Fort Benning on 20 March.

I made time on 16 March to attend the V Corps Baghdad operations after-action review. I spent the afternoon at the theater on Camp Doha listening to the presentation on how V Corps would approach fighting in Baghdad. LTG Wallace directed that the senior commanders and staff of the 1st Armored Division do research and develop a concept of operations on how V Corps would conduct this fight. Based on the outcomes of exercises and wargames, V Corps believed it could launch one mounted brigade-sized raid into Baghdad every 48 hours. There was a very interesting presentation on brigade raid tactics, techniques, and procedures, TTPs. Wallace, as well as all other senior commanders, did not want to let a fight in Baghdad devolve into street-by-street fighting akin to Hue City in Vietnam, or in Berlin, or in Manila in 1945.

LTG Wallace approved the concept presented by the 1st Armored Division commanders. In essence, V Corps planned on establishing operating areas on the outskirts of the city. The focus of psychological operations would be on convincing the people to flee the city and move to less urban areas where aid agencies, civil-military affairs units, and other non-governmental organizations would take care of them. The intent was to remove as many civilians as possible from the city before conducting mounted raids; these raids would be informed by intelligence collected and developed by special operating forces and "other government agencies"—our euphemism for the CIA. This remained the basis of intended V Corps operations in Baghdad until US forces actually closed on the city.

This was, for me, an excellent afternoon. I got to see many of my friends who were serving in key roles in V Corps and I MEF: Steve Boltz, the Corps G2; John Coleman, chief of staff, I MEF; Bill Weber, ADC of the 3rd Infantry Division; Jack Sterling, chief of staff of 3ID; Ben Freakley and "E.J." Sinclair, ADCs of the 101st Air Assault Division; and Mark Hildenbrand, who was commanding an engineer group in support of the 3ID. I was struck by the potential, however small, that I might not see some of these men again. It was some kind of afternoon, exciting and sobering.

I also learned of a concern among the 11th Attack Helicopter Regiment which involved the AH-64D (Apache Longbow) jammer which countered the J-Band radar used by SA-8, ZSU-23/4, ROLAND, and 2S6. Longbow countermeasures involved overpowering the J-Band radar frequency, so that the aircraft itself became a J-Band emitter. The root of the problem was the HARM anti-radiation missiles launched from F-16CJ and EA-6B would lock onto the more powerful emitter. V Corps requested a test with an EA-6B on a mission to see if it could discern the AH-64D. COL Heidi Brown, the Patriot brigade commander supporting V Corps, and COL Marc Workman, USMC, of the CFLCC fires cell, were also present when I learned of this concern and took note.

Refinement of Cobra II continued as well. We sent the CENTCOM J5 the Phase IV products which our Washington team presented to the Army staff in order to help them prepare for Elaborate Crossbow/Prominent Hammer, Joint Staff-level wargames. CENTCOM J5 sent a planner to Washington during the upcoming week to brief the key sections of the Joint Staff on the overall campaign plan, 1003V. Finally, the C5 non-commissioned officers briefed the CFLCC CSM Sparks on Cobra II. I wanted to ensure 1) the CSM was fully informed of the totality of the planning effort, and 2) I wanted to highlight the work my superb NCOs had done in support of that planning effort.

At this point in my story, I feel I must note we began talking of Phase IV as a sequel to Cobra II on 1 March. We also named the plan which would succeed Cobra II—Eclipse II —on 4 March, yet when I spoke with LTG McKiernan on the evening of 17 March he was surprised that 1) we were writing a sequel, and 2) Cobra II would only get us to Baghdad.

In my daily report I mentioned another report from the team we sent to Qatar to work on what we were calling the Iraqi Army "after next." This team had formed the opinion that we were farther along in our thinking about the reform of the Iraqi Army than CENTCOM J5. Our interest in this was to clearly articulate that this very large task was not one that could be done in Phase IVA—the portion of Phase IV assigned to CFLCC in campaign plan 1003V. I wanted our team to make clear that CFLCC could begin an assessment process, but the actual restructuring would have to be carried out on a much longer timescale, if in fact CENTCOM ought to do it at all. The Iraqi Army as it was at the time was a national institution which pre-dated Saddam. The J5 team, in Qatar and supported by the section in Kuwait, also engaged with CENTCOM J5 on some of the campaign "assumptions" for CENTCOM's Phase IV. In terms of reforming Iraqi military forces, CENTCOM intended to change as little as possible, preferring to leave the issue for the government which emerged to address in detail. CENTCOM planners did agree with the CFLCC proposed planning directive and its concept, Eclipse II, such as it was at the time. CENTCOM planning was in line with our CFLCC vision for the new Iraqi military's size, structure, and effort of reformation.

Other assumptions made by CENTCOM planners at the time were:

- The assumption that a CFLCC/CJTF-4 transition would occur during November or December 2003. (This did not come to pass; the handover, of a sort, was accelerated.)

- The assumption that I MEF would redeploy before the end of Phase IVA.
- The assumption that CFLCC would establish a stable environment during Phase IVA.

CENTCOM was also pondering how to "operationalize" LTG Garner and ORHA at the strategic and operational level.

I reported that the CFLCC plans section Phase IVA team continued to refine the draft plan (Eclipse II) with V Corps, I MEF, and 377th TSC. We also sent updates to the air, Marine, naval, and special operations components, and to CENTCOM J5. The team coordinated with the JTF-4 planners writing the Phase IVB/C plan, "Aurora." This plan was intended to fit into the CENTCOM J5 campaign plan for the recovery portion of the overall campaign.

My team also continued work on the redeployment portion of Eclipse II. The team coordinated the effort with C4 and 377th on the more detailed portions of the plan, which included phasing the recovery of APS equipment and stores, and the sequencing-out of units.

We also learned that Secretary Rumsfeld had decided to postpone taking the decision briefing on the continuing force flow until at least 19 March. I acknowledged LTG McKiernan's requirement to prepare a short presentation that would serve to keep the senior Army staff informed, for McKiernan's review and approval.

On 16 March, the CENTCOM J3, MG Renuart, wrote to MG Webster, our DCG (Operations), asking if CFLCC could seize the southern Iraqi oil fields on four hours' notice. I wrote a proposed note in response for MG Webster to review. It was very clear that MG Renuart was the leading staff officer on the CENTCOM staff, and that GEN Franks relied on him. I outlined the depth required behind this task and emphasized that it required coordination across the components that would carry it out. This was yet another example of the traffic received via electronic mail by MG Webster and LTG McKiernan. The date, 16 March, was also significant, as the question and its timing indicated D-Day was getting very close. I also inferred that MG Webster himself did not yet know that D-Day was at hand.

The next day, 17 March, was a frantic day beyond even the level of the earlier "frantic days." We answered email queries from V Corps, I MEF, and CENTCOM. In my journal I noted we had been informed—by a confirmed report—that the Baghdad Republican Guard division had chemical rounds for its artillery. The UN force which had been monitoring the demilitarized zone between Iraq and Kuwait would be gone from its posts, effective 17 March, 1100hrs. We were told that D-Day had been set as 19 March for "planning only." There were no decisions, diplomatic or otherwise, as of yet. The secretary of defense did not want to commit the nation to war until 30 minutes prior to H-Hour. This framed the atmosphere in which our continued wargaming on Phase IV was taking place.

Meeting with LTG McKiernan, 17 March 2003

On the evening of 17 March, I was able to schedule a meeting with LTG McKiernan. I did not realize it at the time, but aside from some casual meetings, this would be the last time I would be able to talk at length with LTG McKiernan until mid-April, when he was getting ready to go to Baghdad.

I went to see him about our Phase IV wargaming efforts. I told him the wargaming we were doing on Phase IV was the most complex I'd ever done, and that I felt that this phase was be more akin to a sequel plan than a continuation of Cobra II. As such, I told him we needed to develop an entirely new plan for Phase IV, and that I would need to have some of his time if we were to wrestle with the challenges of completing regime removal and reestablishing the level of security in Iraq that CENTCOM had envisioned in the campaign plan, conditions that had to be met before we could hand over operations to the follow-on headquarters.

LTG McKiernan looked at me with a somewhat fierce expression. He said, "Kevin, I cannot think about Phase IV until we get through Phase III." He paused and then said, "Men are going to die in Phase III." I was stunned. Clearly I had not communicated well enough about what I felt Phase IV would entail. I said, "Sir, men are going to die in Phase IV and I cannot even tell you how long that phase might last." He put his hand up, palm toward my face, and repeated that he had to get through Phase III first, and that I was to work with MG Whitley on plans involving Phase IV activities. I said "WILCO," and left his office.

When I got back to my desk, I reflected on what had just happened. In the past, LTG McKiernan had continually admonished me to think operationally, but in that moment he was going to focus his energies on the tactics of Phase III. My instincts told me that he must know we were going to war, and soon.

March 18, 2003 was another busy day. CFLCC told V Corps and I MEF to move into attack positions on order. We expected D-Day to be 19 March, thus 18 March was D-1. Our C2 analysis indicated lots of enemy movement of forces in response to the President's speech on 15 March. The Republican Guard was moving out of garrison to dispersal areas, and a regular army brigade was moving from the north to An Nasiriyah. There was both tension and expectation in the air in our headquarters.

On D-Day, 19 March, the C5 Phase IVA team continued to refine the draft plan with V Corps, I MEF, and 377th TSC. We sent updates to the components and CENTCOM planners. We began daily meetings with MG Whitley, in accordance with LTG McKiernan's directive. The C5 Phase IV team briefed the Garner group on the status of our Phase IV planning effort, as a part of the Garner group, inbriefs given by the staff.

We were on the verge of starting the war, and work continued on the redeployment portion of our Phase IV plan, Eclipse II. My C5 team worked on developing redeployment preparation task lists—specifically, the framework and system CFLCC would use to redeploy forces. We worked to obtain APS disposition from the Army staff to include prioritization of the reconstitution effort (APS-3 vs. APS-5K/Q), location (Camps Arifjan and/or Doha in Kuwait, Qatar), and turn-in criteria. We drafted a message requesting CENTCOM J5 assistance in getting access to Saudi Arabian ports.

We continued work on a presentation ultimately for the secretary of defense. We had no definitive word on when Secretary Rumsfeld might take the presentation generated by his snowflake on the humanitarian efforts involved in the campaign, and the corresponding requirement to publicize these efforts.

The team completed the Army staff presentation LTG McKiernan had directed us to develop and, on his approval, sent the presentation to a trusted agent on the Army staff. The last mundane task I did on D-Day was to complete a review of the state of C5 personnel in the coming months. We would lose a number of key officers to new assignments, and at this point only a few replacements had been identified and assigned projected arrival dates.

Commanders' Huddle, 18 March 2003, and the D-Day Announcement

LTG McKiernan held a final commanders' huddle on 18 March 2003, at 1530hrs. In it, he told us this was a historic day. D-Day would be 19 March 2003, and H-Hour would be 1800hrs. The execution order would be by verbal order of the commander (VOCO). We would cross the line of departure as a full-scale rather than a limited attack.

The enemy was moving forces in response to the President's speech. Saddam was moving six battalions of artillery to the south, and we were within range of it. In response, the corps and MEF would focus on the close fight, while CFLCC would focus on the Republican Guard in and around Baghdad. McKiernan reiterated there had been some intelligence indicating the Baghdad Republican Guard division had received chemical rounds for its artillery, and that if the enemy used WMDs, retaliation would be a national decision.

McKiernan also let us know he had informed the Kuwaitis that if they completed cutting their defensive berms, we would provide force protection, counter-reconnaissance, and counter-fire. LTGs Wallace and Conway agreed. They also agreed that they would move into the border area on the morning of 19 March.

LTG Conway said he had ordered the 1st Marine Division to the 23 northing, and that the 3rd Marine Air Wing would be the first of the Marines to engage the enemy. He would send his force reconnaissance units north of the border just after H-Hour.

LTG Wallace told us he had ordered the 3rd Infantry Division to attack on order, in zone, to Jalibah if the MEF ended up being ordered to attack early. McKiernan told LTGs Conway and Wallace that if we were ordered to seize the oilfields, "we all go."

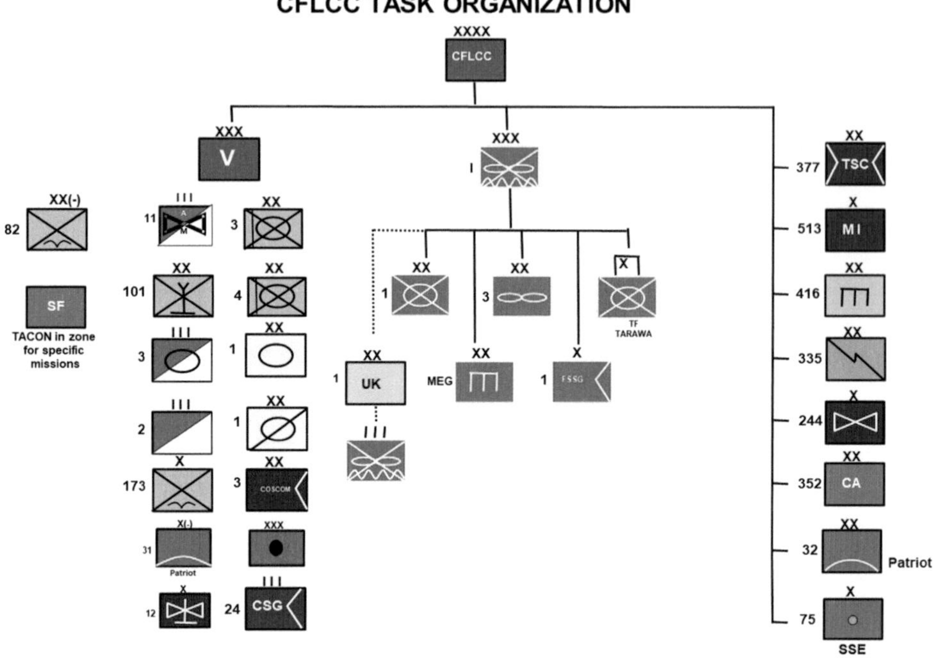

Chart 4. This chart highlights the major units apportioned to CFLCC for operation COBRA II and how these units were task organized under the major subordinate headquarters of CFLCC. (From the author's personal files, and prepared in 2003 by officers working for the author.)

McKiernan wrapped up by telling us Washington had ordered that we weren't to have any US or UK flags flying from our tanks or other vehicles when we crossed the line of departure. He told LTG Wallace that CFLCC would try to get the 101st Air Assault through its staging areas as soon as possible, to join the fight. We learned there were one thousand six hundred registered media and they had not stopped coming to theater. The strategic deep battle included taking advantage of the media presence to have our Soldiers and Marines represent us to the American people.

McKiernan concluded with the old joke about plans. He said, "This is a pretty good plan … it might just work."

The final comment I wrote in my journal on 18 March was, "the fight is Phase III, the campaign is Phase IV."

CHAPTER FOUR

Planning While Fighting, March 2003

The next chapters will cover the planning activities that took place from D-Day in March 2003 until the handover of command of Iraq operations in June 2003. There were trials and triumphs during this period. Once again, I must address the myth which held no one in the Army did any planning for Phase IV. This myth is now widely held conventional wisdom and a symbol of the "foolish" Army which wanted to fight the "last war," thus refusing to see how conditions of warfare were changing. This is truly a myth; we did plan for what to do after we completed the decisive maneuver which delivered two corps formations to Baghdad and isolated Saddam Hussein's regime from the country.

In this chapter, I will relate how my officers developed an entire new plan for dealing with the transition from combat to post-hostilities, and how we would address reestablishing conditions which would lead to a handover from military to civil control, and then ultimately to handing the country back to the new Iraqi government. Planning was undertaken and completed, but convincing senior leaders in Washington of what needed to be done was another effort entirely.

The start of this war was the most challenging experience of my professional life. I brought together my team of planners, and balanced getting them to focus on the respective tasks at hand while attempting to keep a longer-term perspective in mind, so we could think through the length of the campaign.

I was coming to grips with the key difference between an academic approach to campaign planning—Clausewitz on paper—and the reality of planning in the modern age—Clausewitz in action. In this age of the 24-hour news cycle, social media, and the perceived instant effect of tactical actions on the strategic realm, I realized the requirement for considered speed in planning. We had to produce, promulgate, and refine a plan swiftly while operating under the unblinking eye of CNN/FOX and other media. That is an amazingly high standard to have to meet, but it was becoming almost an absolute requirement for planning in this age.

Professor Roger J. Spiller, one of the best minds I have ever encountered and a professor at the Command and General Staff College, wrote to me and reminded me that what can be controlled in Washington will be controlled in Washington.[1] I realized this as a truism—21st-century communications technology permits the illusion of the ability to take "immediate" decisions that will be executed instantly. Thus, as Spiller highlighted, people in Washington, D.C., both in the White House and in the Pentagon, will want to "control" the ongoing events in the field. I came to believe they also labored under the feeling that they could delay taking decisions until they felt it was necessary to take a decision. I was—and remain—unsure that we fully understand the limits of this span of control, and I feel certain it will continue to be overplayed until we all learn the limit of control from afar.

The education I received at SAMS gave me the wherewithal to envision the totality of a campaign. I started asking about what we would do when we got to Baghdad even before I arrived at Third Army. Backward planning, a time-honored Army technique, drove me to think about the transition conditions at Phase IVA when—according to the CENTCOM campaign plan—CFLCC would hand over the responsibility of controlling Iraq to another Joint Task Force. This was the start point for envisioning how the Third Army/CFLCC plan would unfold, because we had to think of how we would arrive at those transition conditions at the same time as we planned for the arrival of forces, how our forces would fight the Iraqis, and how we would sequence and sustain the battles of our major operation.

The Central Command campaign plan 1003V, Operation *Iraqi Freedom*, envisioned Phase IV in three stages: A, B, and C. The Third Army/CFLCC part of the campaign concluded at the end of Phase IVA, or at least this was how the initial campaign plan was written. Events occurring in May 2003 would end up leading us in other directions, but the focus of our planning efforts from July 2002 to April 2003 was directed toward the handover conditions that would be required of CFLCC and our assigned forces.

CENTCOM portrayed the campaign in the phrase "5-11-16-125," a reference to the number of days for which the initial phases, 0–III, of the campaign would last, although we never really war-gamed those phases with any rigor. Even I just accepted this timescale as it had been set out, although I was not sure about the 125 days associated with Phase III, Decisive Maneuver. My team of officers war-gamed the actions in Phase III, refining them as we presented the plans to LTGs Mikolashek and then McKiernan.

Three events accentuated the focus on Phase IV before D-Day: the announcement that ORHA, led by Lieutenant General Jay Garner (Ret.), would come to theater; the decision of General Richard Myers, chairman of the Joint Chiefs of Staff, to establish JTF-IV, led by BG Hawkins; and our own internal wargaming. My team

1 Professor Spiller, one of America's foremost military historians and theorists, died Sunday, 13 August 2017, at his home in Leavenworth, Kansas, after a long struggle with cancer. He was 72. I had the honor of being his student.

of officers war-gamed the actions in Phases III and IV, refining them as we presented the evolving plans to LTG McKiernan. The results of our wargaming of Phase IV led me to conclude we were facing a sequel to the initial operation-Cobra II- and thus had to develop an entirely new plan for post-hostilities operations. Events on the battlefield and in Washington dictated the direction of our planning.[2]

D-Day was 19 March 2003. Our headquarters remained just outside of Kuwait City, and our subordinate forces were near the Iraq–Kuwait border. Our headquarters staff remained focused on the continued arrival of our forces. I told LTG McKiernan in my report for this day, as "close as we are to execution we are at the point where we have what we have and we recommend letting the force flow as is for a few days until we see where METT-TC [mission, enemy, terrain, troops available, time, and civil considerations] conditions take us." LTG McKiernan agreed with this recommendation.

We continued refining our operations plans. I began my daily Phase IV meetings with MG Whitley on 19 March, and we focused on the mutual work of the C5 and JTF-4 Phase IV teams. MG Whitley repeatedly made the point that our Phase IV work needed to be closely coordinated, and I agreed with him. At the same time that we were hard at work crafting our Phase IV plans we were also—in conjunction with the C4 logisticians—working on the overall development of the turn in apportioning redeployment. My folks were also charged with writing a personal message from LTG McKiernan to GEN Franks asking for the latter's assistance in coordinating for the use of Saudi Arabian ports for redeployment. This was an extension of the "tug" of war we were dealing with, which involved competing requirements.

My section also received a draft message from the CENTCOM J5 concerning handling of the interagency "blacklist." No individual Iraqis were explicitly named in the message itself, but this was the start point for the deck of 52 cards later produced. The pertinent sections of the message were:

- Among enemy combatants are people of special interest who appear on the interagency blacklist.
- US Central Command should initiate planning to identify, apprehend and take these individuals under US control.
- The first 55 individuals on the list are designated for active pursuit and apprehension by US/Coalition forces.
- These individuals are prioritized by degree of criminal culpability, degree of influence, and by the ability to pose a serious threat to the stability of a post-conflict Iraq.
- All others on the list are to be apprehended as US/Coalition forces encounter them.

---

2 See Chart 1 on page 2.

- When captured, these individuals should be identified, detained (in theater) and isolated from other blacklist individuals and other prisoners.
- Individuals apprehended should be processed in accordance with applicable directives and regulations to determine their status (e.g. EPW, detainee, internee), and held under US control until otherwise directed.
- No public announcements of actions associated with blacklist individuals should be made without further guidance.

Finally, I reported that I'd focused LTC Reilly, my senior planner, and his crew on some planning "what ifs," as opposed to the constant overwatch of the force flow. I wanted to take advantage of the force flow on automatic pilot to think through potential branches beyond the horizon of C35, future operations section.

D+1, 20 March 2003, I spent with the Garner group (what we were calling ORHA) working Phase IV issues. MG Whitley and I had some wide-ranging discussions with LTG Garner. The first major point I made was to tell the Garner group that a stable environment in Phase IVA did not mean CFLCC would provide guards to every contractor working on reconstruction projects. MG Whitley told the group that CFLCC would have fewer troops in theater than California had police officers, just to put security into perspective.[3]

We learned the Garner group reconstruction effort had a potential $2 billion for use in Phase IV, but only $110 million on hand; the rest depended upon a supplemental bill which was pending in Congress. Emergency repair of vital infrastructure was a CFLCC task designed to establish handover conditions to JTF-4 and LTG Garner's ORHA, so we were concerned about this money and how it would be administered.

LTG Garner told MG Whitley and me that the US Government's position was to not have a Special Representative of the Secretary General until much later on in the Phase IV effort. He told us the UN High Commission on Human Rights, chaired at the time by Libya, intended to bring a charge against the US for violating Iraqi human rights. This was interesting, but not really an area of concern for me. LTG Garner also relayed that there was a plan of sorts (whose exactly he did not say) to provide monies to pay Iraqi bureaucrats and police in Phase IV; $100 million would be on hand for this, delivered by USAF planes on pallets. CFLCC would have to guard these money pallets. Finally, LTG Garner told us Vice President Cheney's daughter, Liz, would serve as the head of a group charged with rewriting the Iraqi Constitution. He was not sure whether Ms. Cheney would come to the Iraq Theater or accomplish this task in Washington.

I spoke with both LTGs (Ret.) Garner and Ron Adams about the daily secretary of defense VTC. The latter was acting as the Deputy Director of ORHA and

---

3 Majors Grieme, Sparling, and Innocenti came up with this comparison. We found this really assisted in visualizing land mass, population, and security forces.

chief of staff for Garner. It was Garner who told me that Secretary Rumsfeld had ordered him to report daily, so he would. Adams told me that Garner did not want to spend three hours coming to Doha for VTCs, and that Secretary Rumsfeld was sending Garner a portable secure VTC package. Adams further told me that if ORHA could not get the VTC package to work, he had no doubt that OSD would order CENTCOM to provide communications. I made sure LTG McKiernan knew this, as it was important to our planning effort to know how Garner saw the situation.

While I was at this meeting with ORHA, CFLCC endured its first missile attack, I remember the meeting very clearly. I thought to myself, *this is surreal*—I was wearing civilian clothes, in a hotel on the beach, a Filipino waiter had just offered me a soft drink, and my cell phone went off. Sergeant Teltoe, a wonderful Soldier and my administrative NCO, was screaming at me that the headquarters were being evacuated because there were missiles inbound. I thought to myself ... *Am I really at war?* It was very, very surreal.

So, on 20 March I spent time at ORHA with British Colonel Colin Boag and MG Whitley. The meeting was solely Phase IV focused.

I also briefed the CFLCC operational plans group, OPG, on the ever-changing Eclipse II concept of operations. We forecasted the delay of the arrival of 4ID and the uncertainty of where it would enter the fray, and receiving more definitive detail on the integration of the joint special operating areas in the north and the west of Iraq into the CFLCC zone of operations. The final note of the day concerned V Corps and the force it would establish in Baghdad during Phase IV. V Corps planners proposed—and I assumed LTG Wallace concurred with them—using 3ID, reinforced with a brigade of the 82nd Airborne Division, as the major force of TF Baghdad. V Corps wanted to retain the 101st AASLT for covering the rest of the proposed V Corps zone. (See Chart 5.)

The C5 Plans Update for 21 March 2003, was focused primarily on developments in Washington and the Pentagon. It was D+2, and we were already getting inquiries on the flow of forces to theater.

My planners sent out a new set of force flow charts based on the latest information from TRANSCOM. We noted there was no change to TRANSCOM 4ID's assumption that there would be no movement of the division until a decision from the Turkish government. I reported to LTG McKiernan that the CENTCOM J3, MG Renuart, had gone to GEN Franks recommending that 4ID move south to Kuwait immediately, as the Turks were not going to approve a northern attack through their country, at least not in the foreseeable future. I anticipated GEN Franks taking a decision on the evening of 21 March, and confirmed this with COL Fitzgerald of the CENTCOM J5. I also received a note regarding a briefing which was being prepared for Secretary Rumsfeld on the continuing force flow.

The focus of the briefing was on the 1st Armored Division. From the note:

Chart 5. This chart was developed during the wargaming effort to for Phase IV of COBRA II. The purpose was to identify the initial operating areas for V Corps and I MEF. (From the author's personal files, and prepared in 2003 by officers working for the author.)

> Tomorrow's session with SECDEF will focus on the First Armored Division. Our recommended outcome, at this point, is that he not make any decision on the First Armored—continue to let it flow, and gain additional clarity that will come in the next couple of weeks. J5 will put a front end on this, and then we'll take it forward. We're tasked to brief OPSDEPS [the operations deputies for all the services] at 0930, and SECDEF at 1730 EST. We have the following from the briefing. "-- SecDef stated he wanted to 'engage' with GEN Franks mid next week on forces needed for Phase IV." SecDef told us to let the CENTCOM staff know about this. -- In order to prep the SecDef for that discussion with GEN Franks he gave this tasker [*sic*] to J5 / 4: a. Develop 3 scenario to develop speed of success … Rapid Success [1 Week], Medium Success [2–3 Weeks], Slow Success [Month or Months] b. Based on those 3 scenarios … and the assumptions for each … determine which units [combat, combat support and combat service support] we would want to flow for each scenario … and the timing of that flow. --SECDEF asked us to get back to him NLT Tuesday [25 March].

This exchange was indicative of a challenge we would face for the remainder of the time we were in theater: obstacles introduced by senior people viewing the ongoing operations through television and the lens of drones and satellites who believed they could understand the flow of battle and determine what precisely would be needed, as if the deployment of forces was a faucet they could easily turn on and off. These people did not think to raise questions regarding the social and historical factors which would affect the conditions in Iraq, or on what it would take to establish secure conditions for a new government.

I engaged with COL Fitzgerald in the development of a supporting product for this effort. This was the first indication of intense interest in the flow of forces, and a harbinger of future thoughts about limiting forces. I sent a note to Rear Admiral (Lower Half), RDML, Clingan, the deputy CENTCOM J5, in which I outlined our priorities in the upcoming days. I was pleased by the note I received in response from MG Blackman, our chief of staff. He wrote, "WELL SAID."

We continued refining the Phase IV major operations plan, Eclipse II. A part of this effort was figuring out how to depart the region. In support of this effort, we developed a personal message to send to GEN Franks. I sent the message requesting the use of Saudi Arabian ports to MGs Webster, Stratman, and Blackman for review and approval.

My C5 planner representative had been left out of the concluding session with the Garner group. Nonetheless, we picked up interesting information regarding the development of LTG Garner's plans for his organization in Iraq. LTG Adams traveled to Qatar. He took a small group and met with CENTCOM planners all day. An interagency group in Washington was working on a "mega-resolution" for submission to the United Nations Security Council. This group would brief Secretary Rumsfeld on the resolution. We did not have the specific details, but learned the intent was to make post-hostilities work easier for CENTCOM. LTG Garner reiterated that we would have to wait for details, and this would take a while given the feelings within the secretary of defense's office toward UN participation in post-hostilities Iraq.

We continued our engagement with the CENTCOM J5 team on the synchronization matrix for Phase IV. This was a total team effort. My team wrote and updated the tasks included in the effort to develop this matrix, ensuring the development effort was linked up with the tasks from the CENTCOM J5 Campaign Plan 1003V, Phase IV, tasks to CFLCC, and our own Eclipse II plan, as well as working with JTF-4 planners. JTF-4 was developing tasks within CONPLAN Aurora, the JTF-4 plan which refined Phases IVB and IVC of the CENTCOM campaign plan. Our Phase IV team was working with the CFLCC operational plans group on supporting annexes for Eclipse II.

A new member of the C5—C5 Space—was working with CFACC, who was tasked with coordination of Space operations for CENTCOM. The problem of the moment was the designation of V Corps and I MEF Army tactical missile system (ATACMS) fires as hostile tactical ballistic missile (TBM) launches. ATACMS was the primary counter headquarters weapon used by V Corps and I MEF. The counter TBM detection system generated alerts every time one of our ATACMSs was launched. Resolving this issue was an important effort.

My plans team was also looking at the "what if" question related to a potential Turkish operation. We were attempting to outline possible ramifications of the Turks execution of Operation *Rain* immediately after A-Day, and what would happen if it this crossed the Kurds' "red line." *Rain* involved expansion of a buffer zone between the Turkish border and Kurd operating bases, all inside Iraq. Our conclusion at this point was that we did not have many options if the trigger for *Rain* was A-Day. We reported this back to LTG McKiernan and CENTCOM.

Finally, there was some good news for my section. My senior non-commissioned officer, SFC Penor, had returned from his course at Fort Benning. As I mentioned previously, I had tried to get his attendance delayed given the impending D-Day, but since I could not share this classified information with the infantry school I had to send my senior NCO to school just months before the war began. The school was vital to SFC Penor's record and promotion to master sergeant. Ultimately it was the correct call, but I was sweating his return once the war began.

The C5 Plans Update for 22 March, D+3, reported on a continued focus on getting forces into theater and refining our sequel plan for Phase IV. The force package work continued as we sent out a new set of force flow charts based on the latest information from TRANSCOM. The EAD/LAD window of 4ID, based on TRANSCOM data, was shown as 3–7 April. This TRANSCOM estimate did not quite match the way we saw the arrival of 4ID. We engaged with TRANSCOM to better understand its appreciation of the situation. On the topic of the 4ID, I sat in on a phone-only conference with FORSCOM, USAREUR, III Corps, and 4ID on 22 March. The passenger and ship flow of the division was discussed. LTG Cody, the Army G3, also briefly dropped in to the VTC portion. The discussion covered a range of topics.

MG Speers, US Army Europe G3, stated that USAREUR was reluctant to reload the USNS *Capella* and her cargo until there was more clarity on whether or not another heavy force might transit Turkey for entry into the Iraq theater. *Capella* was one of the ships which had carried Army prepositioned afloat stores, and since she had been unloaded, TRANSCOM intended to use her to continue moving forces into the Iraq theater.

An officer from the Army staff, whose name I did not catch at the time, reported that "rhetoric" from the Office of the Secretary of Defense was leading folks to conclude Rumsfeld was too impatient to wait for the Turkish process to play out, and thus would not support another heavy force waiting for clearance into Turkey. This was news to us.

MG Ray Odierno, commanding general of 4ID, stated he had some concerns about the force moving to the south. He said he had some forty people from his signal company on the ground in Turkey, and he wanted to ensure these folks would be linked up with the division. USAREUR would handle this transport problem. Odierno wanted the 44th Signal Company, which was essential to his division's digital communications system and the digital backbone of the division. The 4ID was the "digital" division of the Army.

From the USNS *Cape Horn*, he wanted to ensure cargo-handling cranes were re-embarked for cargo transfer use in Kuwait. This was a lengthy conference but a necessary one, as the 4ID was finally moving toward Kuwait for the fight in the main effort.

The scheduling of passenger and cargo flow was discussed. I felt I needed to make the points that our movement planners were completely involved in the process, and scheduling would be handled by validating the arrival of passengers tied to the unloading of ships as they arrived in port. We learned the 4ID advanced party of 516 troopers and a port support activity of 200 with some pallets would depart Fort Hood on or around 25 March. BG Speakes, a 4ID assistant division commander, would coordinate with the V Corps rear headquarters for space in one of the desert camps. The Forces Command G4 coordinated with our C4, MG Christianson, on the coordination of the arrival of the 4ID and the continued flow of force packages 186 and 187, elements needed to complete the 101st Airborne Division and V Corps support units. I assured all involved in the conference that we could accept the arrival of both sets of forces.

We also continued work on the redeployment portion of our Phase IV plan, Eclipse II. As ironic as it felt at times, this was an important portion of Phase IV, as we had to coordinate the entry of forces into theater along with the departure of others. We also coordinated with the Defense Threat Reduction Agency (DTRA) over the process of disabling expected Iraqi WMDs, primarily chemical weapons.

On the subject of WMDs, I spoke with a US Navy Captain, Captain Weyrick of DTRA on the task of disabling WMDs. Captain Weyrick would work in the JTF-4 area but participate in sensitive site exploitation (SSE) work to keep situational awareness over the anticipated WMD sites. He would also write portions of the JTF-4 Aurora Phase IV concept plan.

On 24 March, I told LTG McKiernan that the redeployment operational plans team would meet to finalize our list of redeployment preparatory tasks (mostly construction related), and also perform a walk-through of the redeployment system we wanted to put in place. We would plan for US forces redeployment through current Kuwait air- and seaports.

British forces would use the Iraqi port of Umm Qasr. We planned to designate a set of existing "temporary" camps to support redeploying forces, and another set of camps to serve deploying follow-on or rotation forces. Camps Doha and Arifjan were the two primary sites used for washing vehicles, containers, and helicopters. Our goal was to have the capacity to move a brigade combat team-sized unit through both camps simultaneously. We would wargame both the outcome of using Kuwaiti air- and seaports alone, and outcome of using both Kuwaiti and Saudi Arabian ports to achieve this.

I finished by reporting that I was reviewing the "what if" product on what would happen if the Turks executed Operation Rain and this execution crossed a Kurdish "red line." Lastly, I met Michael Gordon, the embedded reporter from the *New York Times*. He wanted to talk with me about the planning effort for the book he was going to write about the beginning of the war in Iraq.

On 23 March, D+4, the planners continued to focus on force package work concerning the decision to move 4ID to the south, and on entry into the Iraq theater through Kuwait. The coordination effort began with planners sending out a new set of force flow charts based on the latest information from TRANSCOM. We were still working on getting the division into Kuwait earlier than the TRANSCOM projected dates of 3–7 April. We coordinated with Joint Movement Center at CENTCOM and we both pressed TRANSCOM to realistically program in the personnel flow of 4ID. I kept the CENTCOM J5 planners informed about this effort as well.

CFLCC operations, C3, requested we check on the flow of Mortuary Affairs, Military Police units, and asked my planners to check on the mobilization and possible flow of remaining Reserve Component light infantry units in light of a possible increased rear area threat. The Army would be charged with coordinating mortuary affairs for the joint force, and we needed to ensure this important task was carried out swiftly and honorably. The 54th Quartermaster Company (Mortuary Affairs) closed on 22 March, so the theater mortuary affairs unit was set. All of us in plans, future and current operations, were concerned about a rear area threat as V Corps and I MEF advanced on Baghdad. As the Corps and MEF rear boundaries moved forward, Third Army/CFLCC was responsible for the protection of the rear area. We programmed three reserve component light infantry companies to arrive in theater in early April.

Given the decision to move the 4ID to the south, we supported a request from the commanding general of US Army Europe to relieve 1ID headquarters of the mission to serve as the Army Forces headquarters, Turkey. USAREUR tasked the 1ID headquarters to run the staging areas and supply centers for 4ID if it moved into the theater of operations from the north. USAREUR wanted to bring the advanced parties of 1ID back to Germany and then back to the US

Our OPLAN refinement continued apace as we pressed for use of Saudi Arabian ports to use when moving units out of Iraq. I spoke with CCJ5 on the evening of the 23rd on integrating Phase IV planning efforts between my planners, CENTCOM J5, JTF-4, and ORHA. LTG Adams, during his visit to Qatar, suggested a mutual planning session in the near future. COL Fitzgerald agreed to let me know when LTG Adams provided some dates. In the meantime, I continued our ongoing efforts with JTF-4 and ORHA. I kept our greater plans team updated as well.

I presented a revised format to the OPG for our daily update. The primary focus for the OPG remained on Phase IV, including daily updates on Eclipse II, Aurora, and redeployment planning efforts. Intelligence updates focused on implications for the Phase IV environment. The OPG also worked on providing input to the Task Force Baghdad decision briefing.

The essence of the decision briefing was centered on three proposals: the V Corps proposal for TF Baghdad; our initial proposal; and a third course of action. V Corps intended to use two brigades of the 3ID, plus a brigade from the 82nd Airborne under command of the 3ID headquarters, as the initial TF Baghdad. The CFLCC proposal for TF Baghdad was to use the 101st Airborne Division. The third proposal was the use of the 4ID as TF Baghdad. I wanted to ensure the decision briefing was coordinated with all the proposed units and get it to LTG McKiernan for decision quickly. We were closing on Baghdad.

I informed LTG McKiernan that we had sent out coordinating draft 14 of the Eclipse II OPLAN. The Phase IV team had worked with CENTCOM and all components on this task. This latest revision reflected the decision for 4ID to come into Iraq from the south. Finally, I reported the next Garner–Rumsfeld VTC was scheduled to take place on the evening of 24 March, and I would attend it and report back to him on the outcome.

I informed LTG McKiernan that my planners had finished the "what if" product on projected outcomes of the Turks executing Operation *Rain* which might cross a Kurdish "red line." My planners and I were also preparing another "what if" concept plan regarding an increased rear area threat which disrupted our lines of communication while CFLCC fought the enemy's conventional forces. By McKiernan's direction I was working this effort through MG Webster, the DCG (O).

Communicating with LTG McKiernan

On 24 March, Terry Moran informed me that I should stop sending my updates to the CG. Evidently, reading into Moran's note, I was distracting McKiernan from the ongoing tactical challenges faced by V Corps and I MEF with my focus on what to do after we arrived at Baghdad. I did not protest; rather, I continued to write the notes to the chief of staff and deputy commanding generals. COL Mark Eshelmann, McKiernan's executive officer, told me he would incorporate my notes into his own so that McKiernan would continue to see some of our planning efforts. I made an error here by accepting the note of a contractor—Moran—on limiting my ability to interact with my commanding general. I trusted COL Eshelmann to put critical information in front of McKiernan, but at this point I was never really sure if what I was doing actually made it to my commanding general.

Starting with my update of 24 March, D+5, I sent my notes to MGs Webster, Stratman, Blackman, Whitley, and COL Eshelmann. The 24th was a significant day, at least I thought so given what occurred at the daily secure VTC. This was an important note to the command group as it contained the first indication that our previous expectation that we would be able to recall the Iraqi regular army and bureaucracy might not become fact. My planners continued the daily battle to get forces into theater by developing force packages to go through the process to reach the Office of the Secretary of Defense for approval. Based upon the growing threat to the V Corps and I MEF lines of communication, we were directed by LTG McKiernan to accelerate the deployment of the 2nd Cavalry Regiment.

I acknowledged the mission of determining the requirements of moving elements of the 2nd Cavalry by air. The 2nd Cavalry would address the combat requirements of defeating the Saddam Fedayeen and Ba'ath militia from the Kuwait border to the Euphrates River, and possibly beyond, as the forward line of troops advanced. We were working with CFLCC, C4 Joint Movements Center, US Army Forces Command, CENTCOM, and Transportation Command. I assured our command group that my planners would have the necessary data for movement validation on 25 March. I am certain that this development in the close fight consumed the focus and energies of the command group.

Our work on OPLAN refinement continued. I reported on the daily VTC, our Phase IV plan work, and our work on redeploying the force when directed. I attended the Garner–Rumsfeld VTC. Deputy Secretary of Defense Wolfowitz chaired the VTC for a short period, although he was replaced by Mr. Douglas Feith when Wolfowitz had to go to another meeting.

The VTC covered a range of topics, most of which were echelons above our CFLCC concern until ORHA really stood up in Iraq. I learned planners at the Department of Defense were working on a memorandum of agreement with the Department of State which would place all Disaster Assistance Response teams under LTG Garner's control. This seemed a bit late in the effort to me, but for Garner it was better now than never.

Learning about De-Ba'athification

LTG Abizaid delivered a short talk on how Iraq would rid itself of Ba'ath Party members. He said that the smart party members with money would flee the country, the smart ones without money would turn themselves over to US forces, and the stupid ones would likely be killed by other Iraqis. After this talk by LTG Abizaid about dealing with the Ba'ath Party, Mr. Feith pounded on the table in the Pentagon conference room to punctuate his point, sternly stating "de-Ba'athification is the policy of the United States Government." Then he went on to qualify that mere party membership would not automatically disqualify someone from working in the new Iraqi Government. In February 2003 I'd told LTG Casey, the Army G3, that we were planning on recalling the Iraqi regular army and the Iraqi bureaucracy to assist in securing post-Saddam Iraq. Feith's forceful statement and then his qualification was confusing. When Feith stopped talking, I stated we were planning on the recall of the army and bureaucracy, and I really needed clarification on this point. Abizaid cut me off and said "Kevin, I've got this."

I trusted Abizaid, and so deferred to his judgment and had faith that he would be able to find clarification on the point of "de-Ba'athification." I also sent a note to my former regimental commander, LTG Sharp, who was now the director of the Joint Staff. Neither of these men ever got back to me with any clarification on the status of the policy. Given the press of events, I also never followed up on the issue. I did not know then, and do not know now, if this indication of trouble ever reached LTG McKiernan. I only know I was never able to talk to him about it.

I told our command group I would seek clarification from CENTCOM J5 and officers I knew on the Joint Staff. This policy statement was counter to our understanding of the guidance which LTG Abizaid had given earlier, during Phase IV planning, and what he reiterated during the VTC. All of our planning to date had been based on a recall of the Iraqi bureaucracy, but when I queried the possibility of this shift in the plan causing an issue, I never heard back from anyone within our command group. I also never received any clarification on this policy statement from CENTCOM or from people in the Pentagon. This was unsettling on many levels as we continued to refine Eclipse II.

I reported that CENTCOM J5, my planners, JTF-4, and ORHA would hold a Phase IV meeting on 26–27 March with the purpose to coordinate a common framework for the campaign Phase IV. The team also: met with DTRA representatives to clarify roles and responsibilities for SSE and WMD disablement/elimination requirements in Phase IV; completed course of action development for WMD disablement tasks; refined course of action analysis and presentation for TF Baghdad; arranged a 25 March meeting with LTC Polk, lead planner for ORHA, to discuss joint planning between ORHA and CFLCC; and finally, Phase IV planners were working with future operations in developing CFLCC options to set conditions for the Baghdad fight.

I ended the report with a detailed overview of the latest redeployment plans team meeting. The team had been doing solid work on establishing a system which would sustain both return of forces to home station and the reception of relieving forces entering theater. We outlined camps in Kuwait for Marine and Army use, the steps needed to reestablish the Army and Marine Corps afloat prepositioned sets of equipment, and the refurbishment of the land-based Army stocks of equipment in the Gulf. I was rather proud of the range of tasks my planners were taking on.

The enemy situation on 25 March was interesting. I had written in my journal that the enemy was having a good day. Given the advancing units of I MEF and V Corps, a salient was developing along Iraqi Highway 6 which I felt the enemy was using as a reentrant in the classic sense (but not for ground forces). Missiles fired from the Basrah area could now range south to Kuwait, but also back to the north and northwest, essentially firing into the rear of V Corps and I MEF. Patriot units were in a 360-degree defense, and radar coverage was overlapping. The CENTCOM J2 reported the enemy was still in tight control of his military and the civil population.

CFACC was also having a good war, as I also recorded in my journal. CENTCOM had not yet declared air supremacy, but in essence nothing flew which CFACC did not know about, and nothing was really interdicting our advance. Ordnance and fuel were coming into theater at a sustained rate, and the sortie rate remained high. CENTCOM, CFLCC, and CFACC intelligence was tracking the Iraqi Republican Guard divisions and concentrating fire on these formations. CFACC was having a good war indeed.

The major news I reported from this day was the firm arrival date of the advanced headquarters of the 2nd Cavalry, accompanied by one ground cavalry squadron and an air cavalry troop of OH-58D helicopters. This initial element moved by strategic airlift. The remainder of the regiment would follow via a combination of air and sea lift.

The first increment would arrive between 31 March and 5 April. The other good news was this accelerated movement of elements of the 2nd Cavalry would not disrupt the flow of other forces into theater. We also continued our work on refining our Phase IV plan, Eclipse II, and coordinating planning with ORHA, JTF-4, and CENTCOM. MG Whitley really pressed for a coordinated Phase IV effort with all headquarters. It took him using his rank to make this happen, along with his personality. It was good to have a general officer involved in Phase IV planning.

There was no secure VTC with the Pentagon this night. At the end of my 25 March journal entry, I recorded that GEN Franks had told us he could not be more pleased with the operation thus far.

I quietly celebrated my 48th birthday that evening, in my chemical suit listening to alert sirens and Patriot launch reports.

Under Fire in MOPP 4

It was a long night during which I got little sleep. I decided to go into the office, and discovered the hallway outside my room was filled with troops who just arrived in theater. The lights were out, and all were in MOPP 4—chemical protective suits and masks. There was only red light in the corridor. I could smell fear through my mask. The incoming missile siren was going off, and we heard the double boom of a Patriot launch. I said, for my own morale as well as theirs, the improved Patriot hasn't missed yet so we were in good shape. I heard a voice come from the dark, muffled by the protective mask, which said "What if it DOES miss?" I replied, "Well if it does, I am going to be pissed off. I own stock in TRW and I will damn sure write the president of the company." There was a pause, then a short laugh, followed by another, then even more laughter. It was the best I could come up with. I said goodnight, wished all Godspeed, and headed into the plans office.

My update on D+7, 26 March, was very short. I rendered a report on the status of the arrival of the 2nd Cavalry Regiment and on our continuing work honing Eclipse II. This work continued our refinement of a broader understanding of the conditions which could be extant in Phase IV of the campaign.

The accelerated movement of the 2nd Cavalry was going well. The system for moving forces into a theater of war was working exceptionally well. Forces Command and Transportation Command validated the movement of regimental personnel and equipment. MG Burns, the Forces Command G3, operations officer, reported air loading of the regimental units would begin from England Air Park on 30 March. This news meant the programmed early and late arrival date would be met.

TRANSCOM dedicated six to eight C5s for the force flow of the initial elements of the regiment. The remainder of the regiment would arrive in accord with the established flow of DEPORD 190. This was but one of the instances in which the solid work LTC Reilly and my planners had done to develop the TPFDL paid off. We were able to reach into the force flow, select a critical unit, and accelerate its arrival based on the commander's needs and battlefield conditions.

Some people were advocating a static defense of the southern oil fields, but I recommended that 2nd Cavalry not be considered for a static defense use. The regiment was a mobile force; I recommended making use of the tactical agility afforded by the regiment in the destruction of irregular forces along our lines of communication. This was in fact how LTG McKiernan ended up using the regiment. We remained engaged with the CENTCOM J3 and J5 on continuing to flow the remainder of the force in accordance with established priorities.

JTF-4 proposed placing planners with the Garner group, which was a good idea. Our thinking on the relationship between CENTCOM, CJTF-Iraq, and ORHA was changing. Based on our ever more complex wargaming, we believed our Phase IV transition/battle handover might be to both CJTF-Iraq and ORHA in the form of an interim civil authority, although we were not sure what the latter's exact title would be.

CENTCOM planners coming forward for a visit were weathered in, thus our Phase IV conference only lasted one day. I told the chief of staff that on 27 March I would spend all day with the Garner group. The purpose of the conference was to agree to a structure for the civil–military mission plan for the campaign after 1003V was concluded.

Regarding other tasks, I let the chief of staff know I had replied to a note from RADM Robb, CENTCOM J5, concerning our use of Arab forces, if the use were offered. RADM Robb's CENTCOM J5 planners were beginning work on the political decisions to gain the use of the Peninsula Shield Force of the Gulf Cooperation Council, less the Saudi force. There was no Rumsfeld VTC on 26 March, but I would attend the next VTC on 27 March and would continue to report on further VTCs.

Finally, I reported I had my whole section thinking on how to reduce the salient from Al Amarah to Basrah.

The C5 Plans Update for 27 March, D+8, focused on three major points, one of which was an indicator of things to come—though we missed the significance of it at the time. I reported that my planners were engaged with the CENTCOM J3 and J5 on continuing to flow the remainder of the force in accordance with established priorities. We were continuing to track the closure of the 4ID into Kuwait. I also learned Secretary Rumsfeld had agreed to continue the force flow up to the 1st Cavalry Division, and then review the follow-on requirements with GEN Franks. I reported this meant Third Army/CFLCC would receive the 1st Armored Division and the remainder of 2nd Cavalry. At the time, this was very good news, as we were depending upon the 1st Armored and the remainder of the 2nd Cavalry to extend our control of the CFLCC zone of operations. While the 1st Cavalry Division was equally important to the overall operations plan, I felt this was an indicator of yet another effort to refine a request for forces. Later on, I would see this was a much larger decision.

My planners were also back in the fight, so to speak, as MG Webster, DCG for Operations, directed us to develop charts for the VTC with GEN Franks on continued offensive operations beyond Baghdad. This included looking into how we would link up with the Joint Special Operations Task Force in the north of Iraq, as well as operations in the west of Iraq to the Syrian and Jordanian borders. We were also thinking on how to expand our work on expanded offensive operations into a plan to coordinate Corps/MEF counter-reconnaissance and counter-irregular forces operations.

The Iraq Survey Group

The Rumsfeld VTC of 27 March was chaired by Dr. Stephen Cambone, the under secretary of defense for intelligence. The topic of the VTC was the Iraq Survey Group. We learned the mission of the group, its specified tasks, and its make-up (including key units). The mission, which I copied from a chart shown during the VTC, was:

> The Iraq Survey Group (ISG) will provide the expertise and capabilities to identify terrorist operations; identify, examine, and support elimination of WMD; identify and exploit key Iraq individuals; determine and resolve fate of people detained by Iraq; and identify and control evidence of war crimes and crimes against humanity.

The group's expected capabilities, requirements, and make-up included:

- Forward presence with reach back to CONUS-based expertise;
- Access to select Phase III CFLCC assets;
- Integrated in Phase IV command and control structure;
- Full British and Australian integration;

- CJTF-Iraq provides necessary support (security, counterintelligence, tactical communications, transportation, billeting and messing, contracting, etc.);
- Operates against prioritized interagency requirements;
- At a minimum, be prepared to support the following requirements:
    - Identify and disrupt terrorist operations;
    - Identify, examine and eliminate WMD;
    - Identify, seize, secure, and exploit key Iraqi individuals;
    - Determine and resolve fate of people detained by Iraq (e.g. CAPT Speicher);
    - Identify and control evidence of war crimes and crimes against humanity/ environment;
    - Prepare a post-Saddam operating environment for US intelligence.

The group faced a pretty exhaustive list of tasks. I realized this was important; the point of the operation was to find WMDs, component parts for making chemical weapons among other things. I spoke up when Dr. Cambone mentioned that "key elements" of the 513th Military Intelligence Brigade would be retained as a part of this effort. I told the audience key elements of the 513th had been deployed for close to two years, and many were reservists on their second call-up. By law, since the brigade was activated under Presidential Selected Reserve Call-Up, we had to send them home starting in June 2003. Judging from the expression on Cambone's face, this interruption did not make me very popular.

28 March was an auspicious day, although we did not realize it until some days later. Our work on monitoring the force flow was falling into a routine. We monitored the loading and potential arrival of major units from the remainder of the 2nd Cavalry Regiment to the 4ID. I reported that the first ship bearing elements of the division would close on Kuwait on 30 March. The refinement of our major operations plan continued apace.

The conference with the CENTCOM J5, JTF-4, and Garner group concluded on 28 March. I reported there had been some small progress made, and that there was a growing realization on the part of the Garner group of the enormity of its task. Our Phase IV planners gave an Eclipse II presentation to the group. We came to a rough overall agreement that the ending conditions for Eclipse II would become the starting conditional assumptions for JTF-IV and the Garner group. This was no small agreement, as we'd argued a great deal over what CFLCC would do in-country and under what conditions the operation would be handed over to the JTF, and further to Garner. The CENTCOM J5 left a team of planners with the Garner group planners to assist in writing its mission plan.

I was happy to report, as tasked by MG Webster, that the bulk of my planners spent most of the day developing concepts, along with support briefing materials, in support of an 1830hrs VTC with GEN Franks on upcoming offensive operations.

These operations would conclude Phase III, and included a series of link-up operations with the Joint Special Operations Task Forces in the north and west of the country. We continued to look at what I described as the changing nature of the enemy and how to fight him. I was glad to be back "in the fight," even though, as I knew, Phase IV won the campaign.

I ensured the deputy commanders and chief of staff knew the planners would conduct a mission analysis of the Cambone concept for an Iraq Survey Group (ISG) for discovery, exploitation, and interrogation activities in Iraq during Phase IV. We knew this was extremely important to Washington, and gave it a major effort. We would provide the results of our work to the CENTCOM J5. The campaign was not over, but we also continued the hard work of planning how our major forces would depart the region.

A section of the overall plans group continued to refine our work on redeployment and the potential use of Saudi Arabian ports. At this point in planning, I reported that unless we received massive help from the CENTCOM J5 and CENTCOM headquarters—meaning GEN Franks—the use of these ports would be more than merely problematic, especially in the area of Saudi customs. The biggest potential advantage of redeployment using Saudi ports would be achieving more throughput of forces returning home and reducing the impact of ongoing Army Prepositioned Sets of equipment, APS, recovery, and reconstitution activities at Camps Arifjan and Doha. The disadvantages the team identified included increased costs of contracts (movement, food services and life support, etc.), achieving few economies, redundant troop/unit requirements needed to operate ports in Kuwait and Saudi Arabia, and the prohibitive Saudi border restrictions currently in place. We had Army Materiel Command representatives in our group. There were over eleven thousand pieces of rolling stock (HMMWVs, all manner of trucks, etc.) from APS out in the field at the time. This complicated our reconstitution effort for the APS stores.

"The enemy we're fighting is different than the one we war-gamed against!"

The event causing a great deal of angst in Washington, Tampa, and Qatar was a story published in the *New York Times*.

Jim Dwyer of the *Times* and Rick Atkinson of the *Washington Post* had been embedded within V Corps headquarters. These men were traveling with LTG Wallace. A few days previously, LTG Wallace had spoken with the two reporters. At the time, we were coming to grips with the changes in the conditions of the fight toward Baghdad and along our lines of communication from Kuwait forward. Both men published articles in their respective papers on 28 March 2003. Dwyer reported, "'The removal of the Iraqi government is likely to take longer than originally thought,'

Lt. Gen. William Wallace, the commander of the Army forces in the Persian Gulf, said today. 'The enemy we're fighting is a bit different than the one we war-gamed against, because of these paramilitary forces,' General Wallace said. 'We knew they were here, but we did not know how they would fight.'"[4]

LTG McKiernan went forward into Iraq to meet with LTGs Conway and Wallace on 28 March. The weather was turning bad on us, with sandstorms closing on our formations. LTGs McKiernan and Wallace discussed how best to make use of this weather to close the remainder of the 101st Airborne and conduct a series of attacks along the line of communication, while the 3ID would attack to the north toward Baghdad.

It appeared the Iraqi main effort was concentrated on attempting to use irregular forces to disrupt our line of communications to the north. A dual attack within the V Corps zone to the north and along the line of communication would crush the irregular forces and cause remaining Iraqi Army and Republican Guard formations to mass in an attempt to stop the 3ID. I MEF would continue to attack to the north to split the attention of the Iraqis, while also turning to the south to complete the defeat of Iraqi forces in zone between the I MEF and British forces near Basrah.

This was a tremendously difficult tactical maneuver within the two corps-sized zones of operation. LTG McKiernan approved the schemes of maneuver and supported the efforts of LTGs Wallace and Conway with fire and resupply efforts. LTGs Wallace and Conway demonstrated extraordinary tactical command abilities in the conduct of these operations.

LTG McKiernan and our entire staff only learned about the article and Rumsfeld's subsequent displeasure late on 28 March. The challenge faced by LTG McKiernan was in responding to GEN Franks, who in turn was responding to Rumsfeld. When the articles were published, Rumsfeld was pressed by the media on how the plan was unfolding. LTG Wallace, in talking to Dwyer and Atkinson, had told the truth of the situation as he saw it. The enemy gets a vote. I knew the truth of LTG Wallace's statement, as I had led the wargames. We'd never considered an extended irregular threat to the lines of communication in the magnitude we were facing at the time. From the desert and LTG Wallace's command post, this was obvious. From Washington, D.C., this appeared as the first chink in an unbroken chain of success. The end result was that GEN Franks inquired of LTG McKiernan, at the behest of Rumsfeld: was LTG Wallace fit for command? LTG McKiernan had to fly to Qatar and CENTCOM headquarters to allay concern. In the end, LTG Wallace retained command of V Corps, but it certainly was a strange event.

The plans update for D+10, 29 March 2003 mostly concerned the action officer-level work that underpins planning during war. My section was addressing

4 The *New York Times*, p. 1, 28 March 2003.

a multitude of issues concerning force flow, Phase III/IV planning, and trying to link our actions into the expected handover of operations when CFLCC reached its end state conditions for CENTCOM Campaign Plan Phase IVA.

The flow of forces into theater continued. Colonel Terry Wolff and the command group of the 2nd Cavalry would arrive on 1 April. His arrival was a key event, as V Corps would use the regiment to keep its lines of communication open. Also of note, I reported the first ship containing elements of the 4ID had arrived in Kuwait.

As directed, the section was working with C35, the future operations section, in developing products and thought pieces on how to counter the irregular/Saddam Fedayeen threat.[5] This in response to a directive from GEN Franks and the first use of suicide car bombs. On this date, 29 March, four Soldiers were killed by a bomb in a taxi. The irregular threat was a growing concern.

LTG McKiernan's assessment of the situation, as of this date, was that V Corps and I MEF were doing good work on the Saddam Fedayeen. Daily attacks were going down, and the question all were addressing was: Are the Fedayeen repositioning to a different defensive belt farther north or remaining on place to continue attempting to delay our forces? At this time, we were sure Saddam Hussein and his general staff had realized the only ground threat to Baghdad was coming from the south. McKiernan pressed us to think of maneuver options to take advantage of either use of the Fedayeen.

LTG McKiernan covered this with GEN Franks during the daily VTC. He said that were continuing to refine our maneuver options, and were working closely with the CENTCOM J5. Franks asked McKiernan how we were covering the supply columns moving north, and what would happen to our convoys if a dam on the Euphrates was blown. At this point in the VTC, Franks was speaking rhetorically. He was pressing McKiernan to remain on the offensive and search for opportunities to advance to Baghdad.

Due to the VTC with GEN Franks and the preparation it required, we had no meetings with the Garner group. Our next scheduled meeting with them would be 31 March. The other good news, for me at least, was that there were no VTCs with the secretary of defense and staff over the weekend. This did not mean there would be no work on Pentagon-directed projects: work continued on the Cambone proposal for an Iraq Survey Group to execute WMD destruction, terror network disruption, and war criminal apprehension. I sent a draft presentation to MG Blackman, the chief of staff, for review. I noted I would work with CENTCOM J5 on the effort. I was also working on a proposal for LTG McKiernan on how to control Baghdad.

We named Baghdad as the Iraqi center of gravity in Cobra II. The Phase IV team and I were working on how to remain in control of the city once we completed

5 The "Saddam Fedayeen" was the title our intelligence section used for the range of irregular forces which our units were fighting in the town, along our lines of communication.

regime removal. We called the proposal TF Baghdad. At this time, 29 March, I was telling MG Blackman that we were close enough on our proposal to run it by him before asking to see LTG McKiernan.

There was a great deal of action officer-level work on the changing conduct of operations by Saddam: the irregular forces roaming up and down the lines of communications, indications of weapons caches in mosques and schools, etc. We were reviewing several presentations made by the CENTCOM J5 on the changing nature of the conflict. Additionally, we were assisting the CFSOCC by reviewing presentation on Phase IV and on countering the irregular threat in our rear area.

In an incident indicative of how heavily I was sleeping, when I got any sleep, occurred in the early morning hours of 29 March. My team and I averaged working 16 to 18 hours a day, and all this time we were in our chemical protection suits.

Iraqi forces near Basrah launched a Silkworm anti-ship missile at Camp Doha. The missile flew over, or at least near, Camp Doha, but landed in Kuwait City and on a posh shopping mall. My officers reported that the noise of the missile had been deafening, and the impact had shaken the buildings. I slept through the incident, learning about it in the morning as we watched reports on CNN. My folks were incredulous. They told me the noise was thunderous and the building shook. I believed them, but I honestly slept through the event.

"Think outside the damned box, Benson"

Our C5 Plans Update for 30 March, D+11, indicated that our focus continued to be on getting forces into theater, refining our sequel plan for Phase IV, and, for the first time, factored in the arrival of new equipment to deal with anticipated enemy countermoves. My planners coordinated with our operations section on a response to headquarters, US Army Europe, regarding the requested arrival dates of the 1st Armored Division. We were attempting to manage the flow of forces through the necessary reception, staging, onward movement, and integration process to ensure units arrived in the Iraq theater of operations in good form.

We informed US Army Europe and the Department of the Army that our desired EAD/LAD for the division was the window of 16–27 May 2003. We were balancing the closure of 4th Infantry Division, 3rd Armored Cavalry Regiment, the remainder of the 101st Air Assault Division, and in general the ability of the seaport of debarkation to handle the equipment of the 1st Armored Division until that time. This meant the division needed to begin moving to the directed European port of embarkation near the middle of April based on both European Command and US Army Europe's best judgment on rail movement to the port. The pressure was on to move the 1st Armored Division to Iraq. Any delay in movement could reinforce Secretary Rumsfeld's preference to stop the force flow.

I understood this array of factors very well. I also kept on telling people—especially when well-meaning people told me to "think outside the box"—that my particular "box" remained bounded by Newtonian physics, wherein it took time to move mass over distance. We continued to work on refining our Phase IV plan as well as dealing with the growing array of efforts in support of Phase IV, from building the alliance to finding evidence of WMDs.

MG Blackman, our chief of staff, tasked us to provide a response on the use of Czech troops with Kuwaiti humanitarian assistance convoys and distribution. We were also figuring out how to incorporate the use of a Czech hospital unit. I would coordinate drafting the response with MG Whitley in a note back to the US ambassador to Kuwait. As shown below, I highlighted to the chief of staff how we were coordinating all Phase IV work with MG Whitley.

Officers on the staff of the secretary of defense remained engaged in thinking about post-hostilities Iraq. We were tasked to review a draft Department of Defense message providing guidance on vetting of Iraqis for post-hostility positions in the post Saddam Iraqi government. Given the earlier stated de-Ba'athification "policy," we were somewhat confused regarding the intent of the message, but we chose to consider this a shift in the absence of other information. The Phase IV team reviewed the message and suggested changes with MG Whitley. The latter provided a recommended response to the chief of staff for transmission to the CENTCOM J5.

MG Whitley and I attended a meeting with ORHA on 31 March. The announced subject of the ORHA meeting was a proposed "Model Iraqi Village." I stressed to the command group that this really was the topic, and that I wasn't making it up; there was no further information at the time.

I continued to serve as the CFLCC representative at the daily secretary of defense VTCs. I remained a notetaker, but also informed the command group of the intended topics for the 31 March VTC in case they had any thoughts or input. The topics were: the Iraqi interim authority, vetting Iraqis for potential ministerial and military positions, and the "White List."[6] The Phase IV planners completed work on the Cambone proposal for an Iraq support group to execute WMD destruction, terror network disruption, and war criminal apprehension, on 30 March. I was to review the response with MG Whitley, and would coordinate the official response with the chief of staff. I informed the command group that we had received and forwarded to them a memorandum signed by the deputy secretary of defense naming the secretary of the army as the executive agent for war crimes prosecution.

Finally, I reported that MAJ Whitlock of the C5 had met with COL Bruce Jette, who worked for the vice chief of staff, Army. COL Jette suggested we might

6 The so-called "White List" was a group of expatriate Iraqis and Iraqis who were still in Iraq who had been screened by intelligence agencies and were free of any link to the Ba'ath Party.

want to request the Shortstop, an electronic protection system designed to detonate incoming enemy artillery well above lethal range, as a reinforcement device for the 173rd Airborne Brigade. Shortstop also functioned as a local jammer which could interrupt radio-detonated explosive devices of the kind the 173rd might encounter in the Kirkuk oil fields. We were preparing a message requesting this device. It was the first of many "suggestions" we would receive from the Army staff.

Strategic Exposure

I started the C5 Plans Update for 31 March, D+12, in a different manner than was usual, though I did still report on my planners' efforts towards getting forces into theater and refining our sequel plan for Phase IV. I opened with a note on our thinking about the changing conduct of the fight and on future fights:

> Been thinking about strategic exposure, and also talking to C2 Plans. Think we are at a point where we are offering regional Arabs a chance at jihad against us. I know we are killing lots of irregulars, but buses are still crossing the Syrian–Iraqi border with Iraqis filled with nationalist zeal. Arab TV is showing that Americans can be killed and there is a way to defeat high technology. We must think of ways to counter this or we can face a longer-term regional problem, irrespective of the outcome of the war. Arabs will see we can be hurt, and take the chance to strike us acting in an asymmetric way, ala the USS *Cole* and Khobar Towers. We must counter the move to jihad in active ways; from IO that stresses what was said this morning, "The enemy is shooting and we are killing." We must also press CENTCOM to declare the borders closed and that we cannot guarantee the safety of traffic moving on the roads toward Baghdad. We could do this in non-lethal ways, use of police nail strips to puncture the tires of the buses, for example. Intend to put this to the OPG [operational plans group] for a brain storming session. My instincts tell me we have the immediate enemy, the Iraqi regime, and we have a potentially vast long-term enemy, a motivated pan Arab element in the region both of which must be considered. This has large implications for PH IV as well.

I never got any general officer feedback on these thoughts.

There was a great deal of message traffic and some work on Phase IV, and our associated plan, Eclipse II. Most noteworthy; we received notice that Deputy Secretary of Defense Wolfowitz had approved the concept of a CENTOM sponsored initial interim Iraqi authority meeting in Umm Qasr, possibly to take place the week of 7–11 April 2003. The CENTCOM J5 was working on a warning order which we saw during the week. We also learned CFLCC would be directed to accept some seven hundred Iraqi "fighters" coming in from Kurdish areas. The Iraqi "fighters" had been exiled during the '90s, had some rudimentary military training, and prior to exile had all lived in southern Iraq. The CENTCOM deputy commander's guidance was "get them into the fight." CENTCOM fragmentary orders on both topics were being written at the time.

We were not linked into the secretary of defense's VTC on 31 March. I reported we provided a proposed response to MG Whitley on a draft Department of Defense message providing guidance on vetting of Iraqis for post-hostility positions in the Iraqi Government after next. We also completed work on the Cambone proposal. CENTCOM J5 planners, DTRA, ORHA, JTF-4, and our Phase IV team would meet on 1 April to discuss this proposal for an Iraqi support group. I hastened to point out the mission of this group would greatly expand the WMD mission. I expected a good session, as we also had the CFSOCC planners with us at Camp Doha. I sent our proposed response to MG Whitley for review, and then to the chief of staff.

I actually got out of Camp Doha on this date and went across the border into Iraq. When I had been a junior officer, I'd dreamed of crossing the line of departure at the head of my tank or cavalry unit. On this day, I crossed into recently captured enemy ground in a rented car: a Lancer, driven by a British officer. I consoled myself that at least the car was named something military. We went to just short of Umm Qasr to observe the media event of the official turning on of the US Army engineer-surveyed, Royal engineer-built, and Kuwaiti-funded water pipe into Iraq. There were 25 water trucks waiting to be filled, which would then move out to distribution points. Lieutenant General Ali (Ret.), a former Kuwaiti chief of defense staff, was present and gave several interviews to Western and Arab media. MG Whitley had really worked hard to get this water pipe project off the ground. The nickname of the project was "General Albert's pipe"— the joke being that MG Whitley was a pipe smoker.

As March 2003 ended, we were working non-stop on the Phase IV plan, Eclipse II, while monitoring the flow of forces into theater. We worked hard to protect the force flow, arguing when needed to continue the flow of the entire apportioned force. April would prove a momentous month in terms of the fight and our planning efforts.

CHAPTER FIVE

April in Iraq

April 2003 was a remarkable month for the planners at CFLCC. My small group of planners acted as a fire brigade for critical tasks; we continued to monitor the ongoing actions in Cobra II and our development of the plan for Phase IV, Eclipse II. Under the pressure of war and a shared drive to ensure our operations were successful, the personalities of the key staff officers influenced their relationships with each other. This included LTG McKiernan's "alter ego," Terry Moran.

Around D-Day, 19 March, Terry Moran moved from doing J5 plans work to being LTG McKiernan's lead effort in the J35, future operations. He had a very unique relationship with McKiernan; it was almost as if the latter used Moran to prod others into thinking in creative ways, or ways McKiernan felt he was not getting out of us ordinarily. For example, below is a note written after McKiernan took Moran on a visit to the front, something I never got to do during the march up. It is indicative of their relationship, and how Moran operated outside our more formal channels of information to accomplish the tasks McKiernan gave him. On 7 April, Moran wrote to LTG McKiernan and "cc'd" in the other senior staff and key colonels—the folks who had to get the work done.

> Subject: Coordinating Baghdad Effects and Efforts
>
> Sir,
>
> Per discussion on the helo yesterday afternoon. Spoke with MG Blackman this morning and the C2 guys and OGA on trying to pull together a coordinated attack into Baghdad with TF20, CFSOCC, V Corps and the MEF. Intent would be for CENTCOM to lay down a marker to the Regime Leadership (telephone, loudspeaker, news conference, whatever) that the Coalition expects a regime leader to give us the keys to the city 1800 Local, Thursday on the front steps of Saddam's Palace in Zone 2. Failing that, Coalition operations will increase in scope and intensity putting the Iraqi people at risk (some smart guy can figure out precisely what the message is). Prior to this warning (ultimatum), <u>CENTCOM</u> attacks into Baghdad Wednesday night with TF20, CFSOCC, OGA and the two Corps all stepping off at roughly the same time to seize limited but high visibility objectives in the city. Operations would include (if viable), a prison break out, a couple of snatch actions and some very serious (noisy) CFACC delivered air strikes that completely decimate a Regime node or military base. Need to prep (saturate) the city with

> leaflet and radio as part of the run up. If you OK, will ask the 35 guys and the 2 guys to work with the Corps for targets and objectives for this attack and will also begin working this at my level with the CENTCOM bubbas.
>
> T

CENTCOM, GEN Franks, and CFLCC, LTG McKiernan, were under great pressure from Washington to conclude the operation swiftly. This note from Moran to McKiernan, written after a visit to V Corps and I MEF, arose from a sincere desire to respond to this pressure and conclude the operation. Coordinating the details of an action involving five organizations would be massive and, to my knowledge, this operation was never executed. The colonels in the future operations section and MG Thurman, the J3, did not have a role in this planning effort. As the pressure on the headquarters built during the march up, we were all trying to figure out how to win this fight. This note and the corresponding action it started was also indicative of the fact that while my J5 team was working hard on what to do after got to Baghdad, aside from MG Whitley, no one else in our command group appeared to be very interested in what we were finding.

At first we thought to use an Arabic name for our Phase IV plan to communicate to the Iraqis that we were in the effort for their good. We were coming to grips with the effects of information delivered through the media and other means; leaflets, etc. Since we really had no Arabists in the plans section, we quickly realized this was beyond our area of expertise. As we did with Cobra II, we looked into the history of Third US Army to find a name for our plan. The name of the plan written for the reconstruction of Germany was Eclipse. We settled on Eclipse II as the name of our new plan. The first major effort in the development of the plan was to describe the range of enemies we thought we would face.

Eclipse II/Phase IV Efforts

In my 3 April 2003 daily report, I wrote I'd been thinking about the nature of the threat to Phase IV operations:

> Believe we should explore asking the TRADOC Threat Directorate to review ECLIPSE II and red team the plan based on how the Saddam Fedayeen fought in PH III. Given de-Ba'athification is US policy we must think through the potential problem this could cause us as an asymmetric threat. We could face an insurgency problem or at least a terror problem in PH IV.

This was the beginning of a long conversation between J5 and the planners in J2 on how to describe the threats we would face in Phase IV.

Our Eclipse II plan described the threat situation as boiling down to a range of groups that would fight us depending upon their interests. The group we felt most likely to pose challenges in a post-regime environment was the Sunni minority group, primarily represented by the remnants of the regime-sponsored paramilitary

(Fedayeen Saddam, and Ba'ath Party militia). The post-regime environment would also be destabilized by ethnic conflicts by and between the Kurds (PUK, KDP) and Shia Arabs against other ethnic groups, especially the Sunnis.[1] We did not think either the Kurds or the Shias would directly oppose the Coalition-sponsored interim regime, unless they perceived their long-term political interests would not be furthered through cooperation with the Coalition. The Kurds in particular might actively oppose the interim regime if they perceived the interim regime structure was set in a way they found unacceptable in terms of Kurd autonomy.

The greatest risks for sudden and violent outbursts existed against the Sunni minority, where Kurd and Arab areas meet in northern Iraq, and in Shia population centers in southern Iraq and Baghdad, where long-repressed Shia citizens might lash out against governmental, Ba'ath Party, and security officials. North to south, the most significant urban flashpoints would be Mosul and Kirkuk (Kurd territorial claims and oil infrastructure); Baghdad (especially the Shia neighborhood, Saddam City); Karbala and An Najaf (Shia holy cities which had experienced violence in the past decade); and Al Basrah.

The Kurds and Shias would look to the Coalition to protect their interests, and Sunni populations might require Coalition protection against Shia or Kurd retribution. External interference by Iran and Syria might also pose problems, as these countries might attempt to influence the post-regime government. Volunteer Arab fighters from throughout the Middle East might enter Iraq through numerous border crossings, particularly along the Syrian border, to fight Coalition forces. Before the collapse of Saddam's control, upwards of three hundred to six hundred fighters per day were estimated to have entered Iraq, to a total of five thousand to six thousand fighters. After regime collapse, additional fighters were expected to infiltrate in lesser numbers across unsecured border sites, especially from Syria. Among these volunteer fighters were members of Hezbollah, at the time the only known terrorist group to infiltrating and operating in Iraq post D-Day.

Upon regime collapse, we expected the Iraqi armed forces to be in one of three statuses: defeated/capitulated, resisting, or of unknown intentions. Determining the status of those unknown units, along with defeating resisting units, would be paramount to success during stability operations.

Elements of the regime's security organizations could take a variety of actions. Some could go to ground and seek to blend in with the civilian populace in an attempt to disappear and distance themselves from the regime. Others could continue to resist as individual and small groups attacking soft targets—both civilian and Coalition. Those who had a part in hiding and securing WMDs might see an opportunity to use them to their advantage. They might seek to sell information or devices to

1 The Patriotic Union of Kurdistan (PUK) and the Kurdish Democratic Party (KDP) are major factions within the Kurdish area of Iraq.

Coalition forces or, more significantly, they might work to sell WMD devices to hostile states, criminal elements, or terrorist groups for personal gain.

We felt much of the populace was unsatisfied with Saddam's reign and desired a more representative government. Once citizens were assured the Coalition was here to remove the regime for good, we expected the people would be emboldened to take matters into their own hands and rid themselves of the yoke of oppression put upon them by the regime and its paramilitary forces. However, we stated this would not mean the people would be happy with the Coalition presence. We felt that most of the people would take a "wait and see" attitude, expecting conditions to improve without their action. If basic needs were not met, or if infrastructure was slow in being restored, popular dissatisfaction would grow and present problems for Coalition forces.

We recognized the importance of the Sunni tribes. Tribes played an important role in maintaining stability in Iraq. We knew tribal leaders and relationships were as important to the stable functioning of a region as the formal governmental structures. In some cases, Saddam had given a tribe's leaders official powers (e.g. to act as the judiciary in a region, or even collect taxes). Saddam had routinely used relationships with tribes to strengthen his power. He bought the loyalty of some and coerced the loyalty of others, while some tribes remained in, or fell into, opposition to his regime. As a result, understanding tribal dynamics would be essential to identifying and responding to inter-factional competition or fighting.

We highlighted the role we felt groups using terrorism would play. Paramilitary and terrorist groups would play a role in post-Saddam Iraq. Groups like the Mujahedin-e-Khalq (MeK), Supreme Council for the Islamic Revolution (SCIRI), and Ansar al-Islam, which were operating in Iraq, might pose a threat to Coalition forces. Other groups, such as volunteer fighters (from Syria and other Arab countries) and well-established terrorist organizations like Hezbollah, would seek to infiltrate Iraq to recruit members, exploit targets of opportunity, or attempt to gain control of WMDs.

Based on our appreciation of the situation, we felt the most likely situation would be that the Coalition would face opposition from a range of forces in a post-Saddam Iraq. The regime-sponsored paramilitary groups would continue to try to retain a stranglehold on the civilian population as a whole. Once the regime fell, we expected a certain number of these paramilitaries to hold out and continue operations on a smaller scale, attacking soft targets—particularly reconstruction entities. We also expected an emboldened civilian population who would take matters into their own hands. A rash of internal factional territorial claims and score settling could lead to local rioting and violence in major urban centers.

In Baghdad we felt competition for leadership in the post-regime government and control of city between Shia and Sunnis could lead to factional violence. In southern Iraq we felt the flow of displaced people and repatriation of Shia throughout

Iraq into Basrah could cause factional violence internal to the Shia community as well as against the Sunni minority. Islamic clerics in Karbala and An Najaf could attempt to establish these cities as centers of influence to influence Shia roles in the post-regime government. Finally, in northern Iraq we felt Kurdish territorial claims for the Kirkuk oil fields and a reversal of Saddam's Arabization resettlement in Kirkuk and Mosul could lead to inter-factional violence.

De-Ba'athification, Again

In drafting Eclipse II, we had to make certain assumptions. One of these—to our later chagrin—was that the Iraqi civil authorities would continue to run essential local and regional services. Since I'd not received any more information regarding Mr. Feith's declaration—made during a VTC on 25 March—about de-Ba'athification, I did not think these people being Ba'ath Party members would make a difference. The people we were interested in for running services were not among the deck of the 52 key members of Saddam's regime. We also stated that one of our principal tasks was to reintegrate designated Iraqi military units. Given I'd briefed the JCS J3, and then LTG Casey, that we intended to recall Iraqi regular army units, we felt this task was on solid ground. We were mistaken, because we did not anticipate changes in policy made by leaders in the Pentagon. As we were working on the post-hostilities plan, events continued apace.

On 1 April, D+13, I wrote to MGs Webster, Stratman, and Blackman. In my report, one I'd highlighted as a "first report," in accordance with an old Army adage that the first report is always wrong, I'd just learned that LTG Garner's ORHA, specifically Brigadier General Buck Walters (Ret.), was moving into Umm Qasr, possibly as early as the next week. I did not think this was wise at all; at this stage of Phase III, ORHA could best support CFLCC by coordinating relief supplies with the humanitarian operations center (HOC). As much as ORHA was in my thoughts, I also wrote about the nature of the threat that I felt we would face.

I was continuing to think about the nature of the enemy and strategic exposure. We—the J5 Plans section, along with the J2 planners—would conduct an operational plans group brainstorming session on 2 April. The J5 night crew would put together a short opening presentation based on my note of 31 March. We were really thinking hard about the conditions we needed to have set for the fight for Baghdad. The night crew would think through these, along with some other thoughts for more refined work on 2 April by the day crew. I concluded with my continuing theme: "If we assume the allure of a wider jihad we will face a longer and tougher fight for Baghdad. Again, implications for Phase IV."

Establishing some form of control along the Iraq–Syria border was a hot topic. I learned that my friends in the CENTCOM J3 were considering the forces needed to close the border between Iraq and Syria, or at least control the flow of people and goods. This was another example of responding to symptoms and the concern of the moment in Washington, to my mind. I had to pay attention, though, as good ideas quickly became directives, and given our limited forces I was sure they were thinking about diverting 2nd Cavalry, at least, and the regiment we were planning on using to guard our lines of communication had not completely closed on theater.

We continued to work and re-work the force package requests. This included assisting the MEF. I received a note from I MEF G5 on 1 April. He requested assistance in getting the 4th Light Armored Reconnaissance Battalion (LAR) flown over instead of coming by ship. The "fighting load" of the 4th LAR was 17 C5 loads. We checked with the Joint Movement Committee on the potential disruption to the established force flow. This was a longer-term project. I reported that based on our meetings with ORHA, CENTCOM J5, and JTF-4, on the expanding WMD sensitive site exploitation mission, as well as the arrival of more special equipment teams to support this mission, we needed to develop a special request for forces for equipment to support the increase in the number of teams.

We continued to receive "help" from Washington for the refinement of our Phase IV operations plan. I reported we would receive a CENTCOM J5 FRAGO sometime late on the night of 1 April on the use of the free Iraqi forces, FIF, coming from the north of Iraq. The development of FIF was raised earlier but we'd not heard any more about them since. We knew there was an effort to recruit and train these forces, but we didn't have any information on the number of troops, their training, or when they might arrive. Now we learned that people in Washington had directed that these Iraqis would be used in the ongoing fight.

The FRAGO outlined our CFLCC responsibilities, and those of CFSOCC. I informed our future operations section and told the chief of staff that my planners would assist C35 as needed on the effort to develop the tasks to incorporate the arrival of free Iraqi forces into the MEF and V Corps. I also reported that the Umm Qasr conference on the interim Iraqi authority had now been put "on hold" by Washington, per the CENTCOM J5.

I was learning that the information age demanded control of information, and if this was not possible then any media report somewhat contradictory to the preferred message should receive a response. Thus, I acknowledge receipt of a chief of staff task to review the V Corps force flow in response to James Kitfield's article in *National Journal*, in which he wrote:

> This "pause" was the result of a critical prewar decision made by Defense Secretary Donald Rumsfeld to cut the planned size of Army forces essentially in half and focus on agility and high technology rather than on more conventional force packages.[2]

2 James Kitfield, "The Plan Unfolds," in *National Journal*, 5 April, 2003, pp 1044–51, 1047.

I provided a response to the chief of staff. Kitfield, embedded with V Corps headquarters, wrote about the effect of the decision to rely on requests for forces as opposed to the flow of an entire deployment list and an emphasis on bringing attack helicopters into the fight. The 11th Attack Helicopter Regiment's defeat during its first operation led to a change in thinking about the employment of these aircraft. When the sandstorms prevented these aircraft from flying, V Corps needed to rely more heavily on the precision guided fires provided by USAF and USN aircraft. In essence, everything in our proposed reply was firmly based in fact. The answer would not be very popular with the staff in the Pentagon. I never found out if our CFLCC response was ever sent forward by CENTCOM.

We were working hard to finalize just what the security conditions for handover of the Phase IV task from CFLCC to a follow-on headquarters would be, thus I acknowledged receipt of a chief of staff task to review and provide an official response to a policy memo on weapons in post-Saddam Iraq. We were reviewing documents from post-WWII to more recent policies from Haiti, Bosnia, and Somalia.

The folks at ORHA were, from my journal notes, "getting froggy." It appeared someone within ORHA was writing RFFs in CFLCC's name and sending them directly to the Joint Chiefs of Staff for action. I let the CFLCC command group know I would raise this with MG Whitley and then directly to ORHA's chief of staff. I understood, somewhat, the need on their part to get into the fight. ORHA also wanted to investigate when the Iraqis could begin oil production from the Rumaillah oil fields. Again, there appeared to be hints that people in Washington might direct the production of oil sooner than we, CFLCC, might want to invest effort in such a task, although there was no definitive timeline as yet. The talk during the OSD VTC indicated a desire to get the recovery started and have the Iraqis start to pay for it with oil revenue.

My team had completed work on the Cambone proposal on 31 March. We had a good meeting with ORHA, CENTCOM J5, JTF-4, 75th Field Artillery Brigade, and the Phase IV team on 1 April. The topic was the now-completed proposal and our response, as well as how to handle the longer-term effort of WMD SSE. The session assisted in refining the work on our response to RADM Robb, the CENTCOM J5. CENTCOM J5 scheduled a VTC between CFLCC, CCJ5, and the OSD (Policy) lead for this effort sometime later that week. I received a decision from MG Whitley and the chief of staff in the form of further guidance on refining the answer. We continued work based on received guidance and provided a response to CENTCOM J5 through MG Blackman.

Regarding our work on the Phase IV plan, I reported I was awaiting thoughts on the proposal for TF Baghdad from MG Whitley. I reported that the Phase IV team meetings with CFSOCC Phase IV planners had been superb; we now had a better understanding of the scope of tasks ahead for CFSOCC, and CFSOCC had what we required of SOF during Phase IVA. The meetings helped us refine Eclipse II.

I went to Kuwait City International Airport on the evening of 1 April to greet the arriving officers and troopers of the 2nd Cavalry. The regimental commander's plane broke down at England Air Park in Louisiana. COL Wolff would arrive early on the morning of 2 April.

On the evening of 1 April, TF 20 conducted a raid into An Nasiriyah and rescued Private Jessica Lynch of the 705th Maintenance. It was well conducted and Lynch was rescued.

The C5 Plans Update for 2 April, D+14, covered a number of topics. The planners were answering a range of questions, from getting forces into theater to refining our sequel plan for Phase IV. I offered the caveat that my note could be another "first report," but I learned that ORHA's MG Bruce Moore (Ret.) was moving into Irbil on 4 April. I told the command group and MG Whitley that I had not changed my opinion about the wisdom of these moves at this stage of the campaign, but recognized there was nothing we could do to stop it.

Refining our plan for Phase IV had to move to the back burner given incoming tasks from CENTCOM and the Office of the Secretary of Defense. CENTCOM J5 continued work on writing a FRAGO on the use of the Free Iraqi Forces coming from the north. OSD directed these folks will be used in the fight. I had planners ready to assist C35, future operations, as needed on the effort to develop the tasks to incorporate the arrival of Free Iraqi Forces from the north. In addition to the FIF tasks, we also received guidance from Washington on a proposed meeting of Free Iraqi People. This would be a meeting of key Iraqi leaders inside Iraq and from the expatriate community. CFLCC would support such a meeting. ORHA would act as the host.

The deputy CENTCOM Commander, LTG Abizaid, conducted a VTC the night of 2 April with Secretary Rumsfeld and Mr. Tennant, the Director of Central Intelligence, regarding the proposed Umm Qasr conference on the interim Iraqi authority. I was not invited to link in to this VTC. I learned from COL Fitzgerald that the conference would take place. CENTCOM J5 would prepare a paper on the agenda for the conference, and how it would run for Secretary Rumsfeld to take to the President by 3 April. Secretary Rumsfeld did tell LTG Abizaid that CENTCOM could make the call on when and where the conference would be held. Firm guidance was given regarding the location of the conference. It would be in a city under Coalition control. CENTCOM J5 requested CFLCC make a proposal on the date and place by the morning of 3 April.

I learned the FRAGO would task CFLCC to provide a concept of support for the conference. I let the chief of staff know I would discuss our response with MG Whitley on the morning of 3 April and propose a date and place for the conference. I did attend the regular SECDEF VTC. Secretary Rumsfeld, LTG Sharp, Mr. Feith, and others were present. The topics covered were the DoD "vetting" policy message and the ORHA proposal to move to Umm Qasr to establish a "model city" as tangible proof of the benefits of liberation. The essence of the vetting policy was that, before we could appoint any Iraqi to a position of responsibility, we must check with the Office of the Secretary of Defense. The Department of Defense was building a database to allow a 24-hour turnaround on the name of any proposed Iraqi office-holder. Feith suggested that the term "model city" not be used. Rumsfeld and Garner agreed.

I reported on a range of tasks my planners had received, such as that from the chief of staff to query CENTCOM J5 on guidance regarding the destruction of captured weapons, given the fact we must arm Free Iraqi Forces. The request was received and acknowledged by CENTCOM J3 Plans and CENTCOM J5. The answer we received was: "Wait, Out." The chief also tasked my planners to coordinate the response on the development of a weapons-carrying policy in post-Saddam Iraq. I acknowledged receipt of a task to review and propose a response to another DoD/JCS policy message on Iraqi police and security. I reported I'd settled the ORHA RFF issue reported earlier. I had rather forcefully told the folks at ORHA to knock that shit off as I was tasked to speak for CFLCC on requests for forces.

Finally, I reported that our Phase IV planners had met with I MEF C5 rear planners to provide a Phase IV update and coordinate actions with CFSOCC planners for the southern transition in Phase IVA. The concerns we covered included vetting Iraqis, ORHA integration, definition of security, and law enforcement. Phase IV planners also visited Camp Virginia with CFSOCC planners to conduct coordination on the northern and western transitions with V Corps planners. We continued our work on finding evidence of WMDs and follow-on analysis. Planners, along with officers from DTRA and the 75th Field Artillery/Exploitation Task Force, met to wargame equipment and personnel requirements for the TF headquarters, in accordance with the proposed answer to the Cambone proposal. My planners developed operational needs statements and the follow-on request for forces. I told the command group we would continue our work based on guidance and provide a response to CENTCOM through MGs Whitley and Blackman.

The final thing I noted in my journal that day was all about Baghdad. I wrote, "We are closing on Baghdad. 3ID had no fight of significance and 1 MarDiv is across the Tigris. SIGINT has directions to Ba'ath to not fight and Baghdad division fleeing Al Kut. Why is he [Saddam] sacrificing pawns? Have to think."

In the C5 Plans Update for 3 April, D+15, I again raised a point about the nature of the fight we would face after closing on Baghdad:

> Thought about the nature of the threat to PH IV. Believe we should explore asking the TRADOC Threat Directorate to review ECLIPSE II and red team the plan based on how the Saddam Fedayeen fought in PH III. Given de-Ba'athification is US policy we must think through the potential problem this could cause us as an asymmetric threat. We could face an insurgency problem or at least a terror problem in PH IV.

Again, I was trying to start a conversation, and again, I never got a response to this note. I had to assume the generals were talking among themselves.

I reported that we continued to focus on CFLCC priorities, getting forces into theater, and refining our sequel plan for Phase IV. The force package work covered two main points. First I informed the G5, I MEF that movement of 4th Light Armored Reconnaissance Battalion by air alone was not feasible. The MEF accepted this news and we continued to plan for the arrival of this unit by sea and air. I also reported I'd answered a FORSCOM request for clarification on the 1st Cavalry Division deployment for our C3. I reiterated that we wanted the 1st Cavalry Division to flow in accord with our priority. This meant the division would begin movement to the port of Beaumont, Texas, the week of 7–11 April 2003. Our response went to the Forces Command G3, and was acknowledged by the same. This was the first question about the movement of the cavalry division. Later on, when the division's deployment was cancelled, we realized we should have seen this coming and planned accordingly.

We continued refining our Phase IV plan. The Phase IV team refined the battle handover briefing for Eclipse II. I reported we would coordinate/refine the briefing with MG Whitley until it was required for presentation to McKiernan. Along with plan refinement, I reported that we had sent the CFLCC proposal for a date and place for the interim Iraqi authority conference to the CENTCOM J5. Our proposed date was 14 April and the place was An Nasiriyah/Tallil Air Base. The CENTCOM J5 would send a draft FRAGO for our review on 5/6 April. Since the proposed site was in the I MEF zone, I let the command group know I'd sent a heads-up note to I MEF G5 on the task. My planners would write a draft warning order for our C35, future operations section consideration.

I informed our command group of the range of other tasks my planners had been having to juggle: we were waiting for a FRAGO on Southern European Task Force (SETAF); unit employments into the Kurdish autonomous zone (KAZ)/northern Iraq; and that the last information we'd had from CENTCOM J3 Plans was that the Joint Staff J3 had not yet released the FRAGO. CENTCOM J5 acknowledged receipt of our request for guidance regarding the destruction of captured Iraqi weapons and took our point that these weapons could be used to arm the post Saddam Iraqi Army.

We coordinated with the CFSOCC Phase IV planner on a response regarding the introduction of ORHA into the north. CFSOCC was less than enthusiastic about the idea. We answered the task to review and propose a response to another DoD/JCS policy message on Iraqi police and security. Our planners, along with DTRA, and 75th XTF, met to continue the wargame regarding equipment and personnel requirements for XTF headquarters, in accordance with the proposed answer to the Cambone proposal. We would refine the operational needs statements and request for forces.

Missile Attack

Finally, I reported on the next tasks for C5 upon Phase IV plan handover to C35. We would review another pending regional operations plan, the refinement of redeployment, and theater engagement strategy. We were already working on redeployment, and would receive a briefing from the Army Materiel Command representatives on the recovery options for Army pre-positioned equipment sets 3/5. Our theater engagement strategy would require some brainstorming. I said we would build on the articulated vision of a brigade combat team in Kuwait with a division tactical command post. Last, I reported I had spoken with BG Bromberg the night of 3 April on his view of regional Patriot presence after the war. We continued to do what the C5 Plans was supposed to do: look at the next phase and continue planning for what happens next; handover of our Eclipse II plan, redeployment, and post-Saddam theater engagement strategy.

It was during my talk with BG Bromberg that we endured another missile attack on Camp Doha. The alert siren started to go off and was quickly followed by the double boom of two Patriots launching at an incoming missile. Almost instantaneously after the launch boom came the intercept explosion, and the clatter of missile pieces on our roof. Then the devices BG Bromberg had on his field gear went off, as he was connected to all manner of early warning systems. He ran from my office; I decided it was not worth putting on my protective mask and returned to work. *Thank God*, I thought, *for the PAC-II Patriot.*

The concluding note from my journal:

> Confused fight, enemy merging units and directing his units to hold off on engagements with US Really amazing, fight could really be ugly, or enemy could be falling apart… Must think about the threat in PH IV. Will we face an insurgency and terror threat?

Our work on 4 April 2003, D+16, revolved around messages to and from the secretary of defense. I received a proposed briefing for Secretary Rumsfeld from the CENTCOM J5. This Joint Chiefs of Staff J5 presentation for the secretary was on whether or not to flow the 1st Cavalry Division and 1st Armored Division into theater. The question posed was, "is this the right mix of forces for Phase IV?" Based on all the information we'd been sending to Washington through CENTCOM, Forces Command, and the Army staff, I was frankly surprised by this proposed briefing. I reported to the command group I would get on this immediately. There was no suspense for review and comment, but I knew this was something we could not wait on. I would coordinate our responses through MG Blackman for delivery to the CENTCOM J5. At the time I did not get any response from the command group, but I felt, perhaps, this was a vote of confidence. There was also movement on the meeting of the Free Iraqi People.

I reported I'd received a call from the CENTCOM J5 on the conference. The ORHA—Iraqi Opposition Group—OSD conference would be on 12 April at

Tallil. We would receive a warning order from the CENTCOM J5 sometime on the night of 4 April.

The Secretary Rumsfeld VTC was interesting that night. Its major focus was on the establishment of the police force in a post-regime Iraq and how the Defense Department was coordinating the effort at getting civil police and gendarmes from other nations to enter the fray. As far as the effort went, I reported, "Not much joy right now in all candor." Mr. Feith asked the CENTCOM J5 if it was true most Iraqi police were tied to the regime, and thus unsuited for duties post-Saddam. RADM Robb answered that it was too early to tell.

The direct impact on CFLCC operations regarding police functions was really limited, in my estimate. Nothing said this night negated our assumption CFLCC forces would have to provide the law & order force for some time in Phase IVA, aided by such Iraqi police as we could find and use. Of note, LTG Garner told Secretary Rumsfeld he was sending BG Walters into Umm Qasr 8 April 2003. Rumsfeld said, "Good."

Other details came in regarding the northern operations of US forces in the Kurdish area. I passed the orders on to C35, future operations, along with notes on several calls and emails from the SETAF J3. I directed his calls to C35 as well. Work on redeployment continued as I met with COL Newton of Army Materiel Command. We discussed the procedures of turn-in and how we would accomplish this portion of redeployment, as well as how it fit into the reconstitution of the APS equipment and stores.

Finally, I reported on a VTC with CENTCOM J5. Our links to the Pentagon failed, thus we did not accomplish the purpose of talking about the Cambone proposal for an Iraq Support Group. I did take the opportunity to talk about Phase IV tasks with the J5. I learned the CENTCOM J5 would prepare a presentation by 30 April on the long-term theater engagement and presence strategy for the Chairman of the Joint Chiefs of Staff and Secretary Rumsfeld. I assured our command group that I would get engaged in the effort. We had not yet closed on Baghdad and my planners were engaged in refining our Phase IV plan, working on redeployment of our forces and what the post-Saddam theater would look like from the Army perspective.

The final note from my journal entry of this day was about the SecDef VTC:

> Another astounding VTC w/SecDef. We talked about the Iraqi police and ways ahead. Another plan drawn up in DC w/o input from the field. Am wondering if we should drop off these though as they are a window into our own US decision making process that I am not sure our British cousins should see. I am sure this goes right to Whitehall and No. 10 Downing St.

The 5 April, D+15 report reflected the range of work my planners and I were doing at the time. We were engaged in the previously reported Rumsfeld presentation refinement on flowing the 1st Cavalry Division and 1st Armored Division into theater. Primarily, at least on this day, the main effort continued to be focused on planning refinement and preparation for handing over Eclipse II to our future operations section. Planning refinement covered many aspects of Phase IV.

The first note was on a call I received from the CENTCOM J5 regarding a meeting of the Iraqi peoples. The ORHA, Iraqi Opposition Group, OSD conference would be held on 12 April at Tallil Air Base. The J5 sent out a draft planning order for our review. Tallil Air Base was run by the 377th Theater Support Command, although it was in the V Corps zone. I let the command group know my planners would work closely with C35, future operations, on the requirements for running the conference. This effort would grow in complexity as we drew closer to execution. MG Whitley informed us there would be no military involvement inside the building or tent.

I reported I learned a brigade from the United Arab Emirates would join our forces. The UAE agreed to guard the Rumaillah oil fields. This proved to be a classic "first report"—no Arab troops ever joined our Coalition.

People in the Office of the Secretary of Defense were growing concerned over the status of the police in Iraq. I received a request from CENTCOM J5 to find out about the police situation in Umm Qasr and whether the situation in Umm Qasr might be a representative sample of the state of the police across the country. My instinct was that the situation in Umm Qasr would not be representative, but our civil affairs staff section, C9, would check its sources to answer the specific question on Umm Qasr police. The C9, my good friend COL Marty Stanton, provided a very straightforward answer—the Umm Qasr police had bugged out, and 42 Commando was providing security in the town of Umm Qasr. This was a clear indicator, for us, that we would have to reconstruct the Iraqi police. Work on Eclipse II and specifically coordinating it with CENTCOM, ORHA and JTF-IV continued as well.

We had an excellent session with the CENTCOM J5 Phase IV planners on 5 April. On 6 April we planned an all-day meeting with CENTCOM J5 and ORHA planners at the ORHA location; their hotel on the beach, south of Kuwait. In my report I stated there was no daylight between our Eclipse plan and CENTCOM J5. At the time this reflected our understanding CFLCC's participation in the campaign concluded on accomplishing the handover security conditions which marked the end of CENTCOM campaign plan Phase IVA. Our next step was to focus on the Aurora effort underway by JTF-4. As I mentioned earlier, Aurora was the name of the plan for Phase IVB. Additionally, my planners were working with CENTCOM J5 on the post-Saddam theater engagement strategy briefing for the Joint Staff.

On 30 April, CENTCOM would present its thoughts on the long-term theater engagement and presence strategy to the chairman of the Joint Chiefs of Staff and Secretary Rumsfeld. I reported that we were basing our portion of the presentation on six force size and positioning assumptions. These were that there would be:

- A division tactical command post with a rotating brigade-sized force in Kuwait;
- "Warm" (minimum manning on a rotational basis) operational-level headquarters in Kuwait (Camp Doha, then Arifjan);
- APS5 on the ground in Kuwait, with some in Qatar, leaving room in Qatar for CENTCOM forward headquarters;
- A "Green ramp" kind of projection capability staged/built out of Kuwait City International Airport (to support the launch of US Kuwait presence forces rapidly throughout the area of operations);
- Pre-positioned equipment (more C4ISR/CSS than combat) forward in the "Stans" region[3], with a remote command post linked to our "warm" headquarters in Kuwait;
- US Patriot units moved out of Saudi Arabia with batteries stored in Kuwait, Qatar, and Bahrain, along with a battalion headquarters in Kuwait.

We recognized the assumptions above required review by the CENTCOM J5 and the Army G3. I asked Army G3 for the latest thoughts on the future of APS and equipment.

I sent the following note in response to a request from COL Fitzgerald for input as to a developing briefing to Rumsfeld. COL Fitzgerald sent it on to the Joint Staff. My note, and COL Fitzgerald's reinforcing note, follow:

> Subject: FW: secdef brief
>
> In addition to the excellent comments below. We need to consider the following [*sic*]
>
> - The presence mentioned below immediately following hostilities is essential. It will require a significant force (depicted in previous 7–8 Div sector layout). There will be a requirement for a relief in place prior to prep to redeploy. If you need 7 Divs doing ops and want to redeploy two, you will need 9 on the ground for ~60 days (time to do a RIP and significant activity required by forces to redeploy)
> - Those that will argue the 7–8 Div requirement don't understand the dynamic Kevin has listed below. We will need a period of time with enough presence to regain control, assess the situation and then make the decision to redeploy. Until then we need to make sure we maintain a strong presence until a full assessment can be made and force requirements determined
> - Additionally, the assumptions we made going into this included use of capitulated units and police to rapidly reestablish internal and external security. This is a bad assumption. We care [*sic*] killing lots of Iraqi soldiers and the remaining units won't be useful. The police in the south are part of the regime and will not be useful and I suspect we will see the same in the central part. All of this translates to a higher troop to task requirement to maintain stability long enough for the new government to take hold.
>
> Hope this helps. Please pass comments you think are worthy to LTG Sharp. He asked us to provide [*sic*]

3 The "Stans" referred to Uzbekistan, Kazakhstan, Turkmenistan, Kyrgyzstan, all countries being considered for inclusion in the CENTCOM area of responsibility.

Subject: RE: secdef brief

Mike,

Here are some thoughts on why the force flow should continue. It is more than just a troop to task calculation that makes the continued flow important—it is an issue of psychological impact that will shape dramatically the post-hostilities environment we will face. Bottom line—for the best Phase IV stability environment we need an initial post hostilities perception of growing/ consolidating US power—not growing vulnerability.

Consider:

- Right now the Iraqis are crumbling in part because we continue to surprise them with how quickly we get to places. It is likely that they have a perception of our strength and numbers that exceeds the reality of it.
- As things sort out and we disperse our forces to more and more missions—north, west, etc— we will not only be lighter in many places but more significantly will also look smaller/less present than we are now. There will be a gradual realization that there aren't as many of us as they thought. This perception will lead to an idea of growing vulnerability in two respects: 1) of US forces to terrorist attack and 2) among the populace—that there are not enough of us to guarantee their safety against resurgence/vengeance of former regime enforcers.
- Additional force flow can counter this perception before it takes hold—seeing new troops continue to flow in will reassure the populace, feed understanding of our strength as growing not diminishing, and lessen enthusiasm for terrorist action. The psychology of it is perhaps more important than the troop-to-task requirements as the reason we should continue the flow. This is **not** to say that we will need large numbers remaining on the ground for the long term—it is to say that there is a critical period post hostilities where both the population and potential adversaries will be trying to make sense of what just happened and understand the new environment—during that period we want them cowed by a perception of growing US presence/strength.

Kevin

Finally, I reported my planners had held the first in a series of presentations to future operations, C35, designed to inform them of the depth and detail of Phase IV and the Eclipse OPLAN. I did not believe we would have the opportunity for a formal handover of Eclipse, like we had done for COBRA. I reported I would discuss this with the C3, MG Thurman. I felt we would have a "blurred" transition. I proposed conducting a key C5/C35 planner handover with MG Whitley on or around 12 April. Then I would have the entire Phase IV team work with future operations, C35, until the forward headquarters deployed to Baghdad. Then three C5 planners (two US, one UK) would remain with C35, and the original C5 planners (one US, one AUS) would return to C5. This was my plan to keep a core of planners in my section while still supporting ongoing operations.

Once we completed plan handover, the upcoming C5 efforts would be focused on: the redeployment stage of Eclipse, completing the force closure of Cobra II, developing a classified planning effort, and assisting the CENTCOM J5 in developing the theater engagement strategy presentation. Work never stopped, and we were closing in on Baghdad.

In my journal entry of this day, I noted that during the CENTCOM VTC, MG Renuart, the CENTCOM J3 had referred to the "Thunder Run" by 2nd Brigade, 3ID as a "Saturday drive." General Franks directed CFLCC to continue the armored raids into Baghdad while also continuing efforts to isolate the city from the remainder of the country. The raids were "1. Killing bad guys, and 2. Great IO."

The C5 Plans Update for 6 April, D+18, again reflected the range and complexity of the work my planners were doing from getting forces into theater to refining our sequel plan for Phase IV.

Secretary Rumsfeld received the Joint Staff presentation on the status of the CENTCOM campaign to date on 5 April. I did not get to connect to the secure network to see the presentation. In the aftermath of the briefing, I received multiple queries from the CENTCOM J5 related to force flow. I kept firm on the line that the force winning the battles of Phase III was smaller than the force needed to win the war in Phase IV. I also reiterated we required the 1st Cavalry Division in theater. My response to the CENTCOM J5 was acknowledged, but I never heard about OSD reaction to this line of reasoning.

We were seven days away from holding the first conference of Free Iraqi People. I reported that my planners and folks from the future operations section were working together on the requirements. This conference was growing in difficulty, but we all did realize how important it was for the future of Iraq.

I attended a VTC on the Iraq Survey Group. An action officer from the Joint Staff presented the concept. It was just that, a concept. It was not a completely thought-out plan for action. The CENTCOM J2 proposed that some senior decision-making planners come over to theater to organize the effort and gain an understanding of the situation on the ground. I was really glad CENTCOM took this position.

I reported on Coalition-building efforts. I also sat in on meetings and lunch with the Spanish force representatives on 6 April. The day's good news was that it appeared the Spanish would be somewhat flexible on the placement of their hospital in the Umm Qasr area. At the time, the Spanish Prime Minister was under pressure to show Spanish troops doing good works for the Iraqi people. Force security was very important to the Spanish, a point which would come back to the fore later when we were building the Coalition force for Phase IV.

The Phase IV team went to ORHA with the CENTCOM J5 planners. On 6 April we received the CENTCOM order placing ORHA under OPCON of CFLCC. This was a big deal and I wanted to ensure our command group had as much detail as possible on this event. ORHA would receive a more comprehensive communications suite from Raytheon which served to solve our problem of information sharing via the classified system of computer servers. Given the new OPCON status, I recommended and offered to draft a short order which recognized ORHA as major subordinate command. We formalized some procedures, granted direct liaison authority for planning with I MEF and V Corps, and requested an ORHA liaison officer at CFLCC.

Our team also went over another CENTCOM FRAGO regarding ORHA and CFLCC. CFLCC now had the requirement to declare an area "permissive," which was the trigger to allow ORHA entry into the area. This declaration also cued in contractors working for ORHA and other non-governmental organizations. ORHA remained engaged and busy.

ORHA Team South would deploy into Umm Qasr over 7/8 April 2003. The ORHA team coordinated with I MEF, 1 UK Division, and the UK Port & Maritime Regiment running the port at Umm Qasr. ORHA had two contracts which went into effect upon arrival: a long-term port management contract designed to phase in Iraqis and allow the British to phase out; and a dredging contract with a Kuwaiti company to keep the shipping channel open.

Secretary Rumsfeld's public affairs office cleared LTG Garner to speak to the media. He held his first press conference on 7 April 2003. Garner really pressed for this clearance as he felt it was necessary to get news of reconstruction out to both the US media, and also to the people in the Gulf region through Arab media.

The Phase IV team continued talks with ORHA on the new Iraqi Army. Getting the Iraqi Army back in operation was a key requirement in Eclipse II for the transition from CFLCC to JTF-IV. We received a presentation on 6 April from a company called RONCO. This company held the contract to disarm, demobilize, and reintegrate the Iraqi military. On 7 April the team heard the Military Professional Resources, Inc. (MPRI) contractor's portion of the operation. I promised a more detailed report after hearing all the presentations and the conclusion of our meetings with ORHA. At the time, we were continuing to operate based on the "fact" that we could recall the regular Iraqi Army.

Finally, in this report, I acknowledged the guidance to proceed on refining the theater engagement strategy in accord with notes from 5 April. I would coordinate with Mark Eshelmann, McKiernan's executive officer, on keeping the latter informed of progress. I also acknowledged guidance that my section would retain responsibility for Phase IV for some time. MG Thurman felt his section was too busy for handover at present. I would continue to keep future operations informed of Phase IV tasks and concepts.

The final note in my journal of this day was, "The effort to keep forces flowing is remarkable. I am afraid the valor of 3ID and 1 MarDiv will convince the SecDef he was right to reduce the size of the force."

The C5 Plans Update for 7 April, D+19, reflected the pressing questions we continued to receive as a result of the Joint Staff presentation to Secretary Rumsfeld on 6 April. We continued receiving multiple queries relating to force flow from the CENTCOM J5. Once again I stood firm—the force winning the battles of Phase III was smaller than the force needed to win the war in Phase IV. I also reiterated we wanted the 1st Cavalry Division to flow into theater. I was certain I was angering folks in higher headquarters, but I knew I was in accordance with LTG McKiernan's desires. Our planning efforts continued as well.

My section had the lead on the interim Iraqi authority meeting coordination. My planners wrote a warning order on this meeting, and our OPG would meet on 8 April to refine a FRAGO. I highlighted to our command group that the effort included the C8, comptroller, Public Affairs Office, and the Secretary of the General Staff, as well as Protocol. Before the warning order went out, we sent a "heads up" note to the 377th Theater Support Command as the owner of Tallil. We continued coordinating with CENTCOM J5. The J5 told us to expect one hundred Iraqis and at least that many media, OSD, and State Department people. The VTCs with the Secretary and senior staff continued as well.

The topic of the daily VTC was building the military Coalition. Secretary Rumsfeld, Mr. Feith, Dr. Dov Zakheim, Under Secretary of Defense (Comptroller), GEN Myers, GEN Pace, and LTG Sharp were in attendance; there were others too who I did not know by sight. RADM Robb represented CENTCOM. LTG Garner was on the VTC as well. Secretary Rumsfeld directed the JCS and CENTCOM to develop lists prioritizing the nations we would approach for: divisional-sized units, brigade-sized units, money, police/constabulary forces, and WMD elimination-type units. When I was asked for comment, I told all in attendance that we would proceed with our current assumption that the ground Coalition forces would establish the stable environment in early Phase IV, and further Coalition nations would join later. There was no comment.

We continued coordinating with ORHA on Phase IV efforts. The CFLCC Phase IV security team went back to ORHA on 7 April to meet the MPRI representatives selected to play a contractual role in the rebuilding of the next Iraqi Army. ORHA Team South remained on line to complete deployment by 8 April. The deployment of Team North was on hold, pending determination of a secure environment in the KAZ. The Secretary cleared Garner to speak to the media, but his press conference was delayed until after the Belfast meeting between President Bush and Prime Minister Blair.

The final point on Phase IV concerned acknowledging receipt of guidance on redeployment. I was scheduled to meet with MG Stratman, the DCG (Support), on 8 April. I had a team working on redeployment, as a portion of Phase IV, for two plus weeks. We also continued to work with the CENTCOM J5 planners on longer range post-hostilities efforts.

My planners and I continued our work on developing input to the CENTCOM J5 effort on a theater engagement strategy. I exchanged information with officers within the Army G3 to keep them informed. I sent our points and noted the only difference was—based on information available to it—that people on the Army staff were proceeding with the position that Third Army/ARCENT would be

ALO 1 (the highest readiness rating) and a stand-alone major command. This was good news for our outfit. My concluding thought for the day? "PH IV is hard, redeployment is harder."

The C5 Plans Update for 8 April, D+20, covered refinement efforts on our Phase IV plan, as well as events related to ORHA moving north into Iraq. Top on my task list was the meeting with the interim Iraqi authority, a meeting which was now scheduled for 15 April (vice 12 April). I reported that ORHA no longer had any tasks associated with the effort. A representative from the White House, Ambassador Crocker of DoS, and an OSD representative were now in charge of the agenda inside the tent; the White House and OSD representatives had not yet been named.

People in Washington were aware that Iraqi National Congress founder Ahmed Chalabi was at Tallil, but there was no real plan to prevent him from attending a meeting intended to be an "action officer" meeting. We would continue to hear from Mr. Chalibi as we pressed in on Baghdad. My Phase IV team remained hard at work.

The Phase IV team wrote a FRAGO on the command relationship between ORHA and CFLCC, and the ORHA regional teams and V Corps/I MEF. We placed the ORHA regional teams under the TACON of the Corps/MEF until battle handover of CFLCC to CJTF-Iraq. The efforts to establish control of the ORHA teams moving into the respective corps and MEF zone were problematic as the teams never really reported to either headquarters. The retired generals in charge of the teams preferred to continue to report to ORHA and LTG Garner, though this was not a real problem as the commanding generals of V Corps and I MEF were more concerned with fighting Iraqis and accomplishing the tasks of Phase III.

I reported that ORHA Team South arrived in Umm Qasr on 8 April, reportedly to throngs of cheering Iraqis, many of whom kissed the senior ORHA member, BG Walters. The deployment of Team North remained on hold pending a determination of a secure environment in the KAZ. ORHA was working hard to enter the fray and conduct its mission. More disturbing were the reports on the effort to rebuild the Iraqi Army at the conclusion of hostilities.

According to the Phase IV security team, the MPRI presentation on the future of the Iraqi Army was sub-par. The MPRI guys would have another product in a few days. This was an important note I passed on to the CFLCC Command Group. I never got a question back on this report.

Even though MG Stratman knew this already, I reported it to MGs Webster and Blackman that I had a very productive meeting with MG Stratman on the afternoon of 8 April on the subject of redeployment. The full OPG Team was there, as well as representatives from the MEF, Corps, and 377th. Based on LTG McKiernan's guidance, and refinement by MG Stratman, we would continue to develop a mission analysis presentation for McKiernan to update him on our work thus far. We also incorporated Stratman's feedback into our review of the CENTCOM J5 draft redeployment guidance.

I reported I'd completed the task to inform GEN Franks of how long it would take for 4ID lead elements, a brigade combat team, a division tactical command post, plus artillery and logistics to reach Kirkuk. We calculated elements of 4ID could reach Kirkuk by 26 April. I let the command group know that MG Thurman had the chart we made.

I also reported I'd reviewed the regime capitulation presentation developed by the future operations section and based on earlier work done by my planners. My comment was, "What do we do if the regime accepts?" Judging from looks I received from MG Thurman, I shook some people up with this question.

My final journal comment of 8 April concerned the CENTCOM VTCs. I wrote:

> These things are so boring. We miss the point of these things, should be an assessment of the fight and a synch of forces…Need to be able to personally red team the situation. What can the enemy do to hurt us and likely more important how can we hurt him. This must include information ops from STO [special technical operations] and open source. Always ask why should we bomb, what else would be effective.

Stopping the Force Flow

The C5 Plans Update for 9 April, D+21, contained the first official indication that the Joint Staff in the Pentagon, likely at the direction of the secretary of defense, was thinking about not flowing the 1st Cavalry Division into the theater of operations. My planners continued to work on the range of tasks we were given, but this one indicator made us all pause.

I reported I received a call from COL Fitzgerald saying the J5 needed help in answering Joint Staff J5 RFIs on the need for 1st Armored Division in our force flow. The implication in the series of RFIs was that 1st Cavalry Division was not going to come to Iraq. I continued working on this overnight with my planner team and sent a first draft to MG Webster, the DCG (O).

I also acknowledged receipt of LTG McKiernan's guidance to prepare courses of action which had been developed given a force of the 3rd Infantry Division, I Marine Expeditionary Force, 101st Airborne Division, 2nd Cavalry Regiment, 3rd Armored Cavalry Regiment, and the 4th Infantry Division, with a recommended position back to CENTCOM. I wrote I would look deep, and would not discount the 1st Armored and 1st Cavalry Divisions if course-of-action analysis led us to conclude we needed them. I knew the I MEF would remain in theater for a while. I informed the command group we would outline what units in remainder of force flow we could turn off immediately.

I would also work in logistics and in our lines of communication as part of each course of action. LTG McKiernan directed we complete our first cut about midday on 10 April. I wrote that I would try to incorporate V Corps/MEF planning input, but would not wait on it. I also pointed out we would try to factor in the 377th Theater

Support Command recognizing that this would be particularly tough due to reserve component mobilization timelines. I reminded the command group that I also had to factor in the time required to reconfigure the Army ship- and land-based prepositioned sets of equipment, and the Marine Corps maritime prepositioned squadrons' sets of equipment. This was an item of concern at the Pentagon.

Given all of this, I reported our redeployment team was on track to finish a mid-course in-progress review on redeployment for LTG McKiernan the week of 14–18 April, as directed. The team met 9 April and would meet again 10 April. The 377th TSC and C4 were major players in the effort. The CG update would cover some of the details of retrograde, equipment turn-in, recommended retrograde priority, and requests for information which were due out. The bulk of these information requests were to the CENTCOM J5 and the Army staff. The requests regarded Army Prepositioned Stocks and the developing theater engagement strategy. I reported that we had received the first word of a redeployment conference to be held in Qatar, on a date to be set later.

In my report, I mentioned I'd attended the first meeting of the effects board focused on the information operations, humanitarian assistance, and public affairs effects we wished to generate during Phase IV. The "killers" of the effects board—our field artillery and USAF members—declined to attend, as the only effects they cared about were lethal effects. This meant the first meeting was, in a hoary Army descriptor, a ***clusterfuck***. Finally, I acknowledged the requirement to brief LTG Garner on Eclipse II on 10 April and a possible requirement to meet with Mr. De Rita, special assistant to the secretary of defense, on 13 April.

In my journal, I noted that LTG McKiernan said as that day, 9 April, the campaign was in Phase IV. I also wrote:

> Amazing day. Watched a statue of Saddam topple and an American flag be put on his face. I watched this as I was in a mtg on the new direction of effects and was called out to talk about 1) the meeting of free Iraqis at Tallil and 2) the SecDef desire to stop the force flow and reduce the number of RC units awaiting deployment. Celebrations in the streets of Baghdad, Basrah, and Irbil.

It was D+21 and American forces were in Baghdad.

In the C5 Plans Update for 10 April, D+22, I continued showing the command group indicators that I was receiving concerning intentions on refining the force flow in Washington. In this report, I also wrote of the annual US Army exercise in Egypt: Bright Star. We were engaged in fighting a war, but the mundane efforts of theater engagement had to continue as well.

I acknowledged the command group guidance on refining the rotation and redeployment briefing input to the CENTCOM J5. My planners and I would continue to refine our input with an eye toward more detail from the CFLCC C4, our logisticians, and the 377th Theater Support Command on combat service support forces required for sustainment and redeployment. In this manner we were attempting to look longer term for Phase IV efforts. For the Army we also planned on the early return of the 2nd Squadron, 6th Cavalry, an AH-64 Apache attack helicopter battalion, as it was scheduled for Longbow transition.

The Iraqi peoples' meeting at Tallil moved closer. I reported I would attend a late-night, our time, VTC with Joint Staff, representatives from the Office of the Secretary of Defense, and the CENTCOM J5, on the meeting in Tallil on the Iraqi interim authority. I recorded a note taken during this VTC on simultaneous translation during the meeting. I rather forcefully reminded all that; 1) we were still engaged in combat and 2) I had nowhere near the high-level translators required for "UN-like" simultaneous translation. We were meeting in a tent in the desert, not New York City. (My language was actually more "colorful.") Our deputy chief of staff, COL John Dellajocano, led a VTC with the 377th Theater Support Command on the Tallil meeting. The meeting served to focus the effort and get staff tasks identified. We continued to hold these conferences daily until we executed the operation.

As I reported for the previous day, I once more briefed LTGs Garner and Bates on the state of CFLCC Phase IV planning, and on integration of ORHA into our view of Phase IVA. It was an interesting session, and received well enough by LTGs Garner and Bates, though I still felt that execution would be a challenge for both of our organizations.

My planners continued the work on the scope of our redeployment effort. We were preparing to brief LTG McKiernan on our progress thus far before he took the command group to Baghdad to link up with the CFLCC early entry command post.

The point I really stressed was my concern regarding refinements on a force flow presentation for Secretary Rumsfeld. I was growing more and more concerned about whether or not we would receive the entire apportioned force: the number of units we needed to complete the mission. I reported we were engaged with the CENTCOM J5 planners on refining assumptions for the Rumsfeld briefing on force flow. All of this effort was linked with a session held in Washington this day, 10 April, on the 1st Armored and 1st Cavalry Divisions' deployment and continued force flow. The preparation also involved the assumptions for planning Phase IV overall.

At that time, all of the proposed assumptions were in line with the assumptions CENTCOM made for continued Phase IV planning. The rub, as I saw it, came in with the assumptions about "not a normal rhythm of redeployment" and "not a standard six-month rotation." I believed the drive would be to keep the same units overseas to complete the stability and transition missions from military to policy lead (ORHA) before redeploying any units, save those required to reconstitute the MEU/ARG rotations, APS/MPS, and the 82nd Airborne Division's ready brigades. This meant the Marines and paratroopers would depart Iraq to reconstitute the nation's ready forces while our conventional forces—3rd, 4th Infantry Divisions,

1st Armored Division and so on—would remain in Iraq to conduct stability and support operations through handover.

We were in effect trying to think through a successful end of the war. My unease was that we were doing this well before we'd reached any of the proposed end of Phase III conditions for transition, and before even attempting to define our war termination criteria. I informed the command group that I would stay engaged on this effort.

The Bright Star update was just that, an update. This was an important annual exercise conducted with Egyptian forces. The initial planning conference was held in Tampa from 31 March to 4 April. The main concept for the exercise was a field maneuver exercise in late September to early October, followed by an after-action review, after which there would be a senior leader seminar and command post exercise conducted by Joint Forces Command in Suffolk, Virginia. CENTCOM would handle the details, including sending a senior general officer to Egypt to brief the Egyptian general staff. I mentioned this in my journal, as it struck me we were attempting to return to "normality" a bit too soon.

My planners' growing workload also included a requirement to develop an Army prepositioned equipment set strategy for review and a requirement to capture ideas for the "future Army," a first attempt incorporating observations on current operations into doctrine and training requirements. We were also asked about a replacement for JOPES as well as input on force structure and the post-Saddam theater engagement strategy.

On the evening of 11 April, LTG McKiernan went to Baghdad. The night before, LTC Reilly and I had been summoned to see LTG McKiernan. Neither of us had seen McKiernan—other than casually in the hallway of the headquarters or during a morning briefing—since the start of the ground operations. Now, he was going north to enter a conquered city.

I expected he would want to take a briefing on the overall details of Phase IV. I brought this information and directed Tom Reilly to bring along updated information on the status of the request for forces packages we were waiting on for secretary of defense approval. We went into his office just outside the war room and above the enormous operations center hall. COL Eshelmann told us the CG was on the phone with GEN Shinseki. LTG McKiernan beckoned us to enter his office. He was in a very expansive mood. I told him we were prepared to brief him on the status of Phase IV and our flow of forces into theater, but he waved away those topics.

He looked at LTC Reilly and said, "Don't get too comfortable up there at Carlisle." Tom Reilly was set to head to the Army War College as a student once he returned to the United States. McKiernan then looked at me and told me he knew where I was headed—I was selected to be the Director of the School of Advanced Military Studies—but I was where he could reach me. He told us we were doing a good job and dismissed us. We walked out of his office and back down to the plans area. We were both puzzled.

LTC Reilly suggested the call from the chief of staff was likely to tell LTG McKiernan where he was headed after he returned home from Iraq. We both thought that perhaps McKiernan was headed back to Washington to be the next vice chief of staff, Army. When he left the next day, it meant that I did not get to brief him on how we'd war-gamed the unfolding of Phase IV until later on in the month.

My final note of the day served to remind me that the fighting was still ongoing, and could be brutal. I wrote "Hell of a Baghdad fight today. Marines had 1 KIA, 23 WIA, 2 M1A1 & 1 AAV mobility kills. Looking for Uday I think." Ominously, a cleric sent into Karbala by a government agency was killed that same day by people loyal to Moqtada al-Sadr, an indicator that al-Sadr was consolidating power and would not tolerate rivals. I may have been doing what planners should do—looking ahead—but there still remained tough fighting to do.

War is an Extension of Policy through Other Means, Really

My update for 11 April, D+23, was proof—if such is truly needed—that war is an extension of policy, and policy is guided at times by local politics. We continued to focus on CFLCC priorities: getting forces into theater, and refining our sequel plan for Phase IV and redeployment.

The movement of force packages, in particular the 1st Armored Division from Europe, was delayed due to a city government election in Rotterdam. The Dutch government requested US troops did not transit the town until after the election. I confirmed this news with a source in Washington. The 1st Armored Division was still flowing toward the Iraq theater of operations. Our planner work went on amid a background of continuing, albeit diminishing, combat.

We were learning of competing, as yet unidentified Islamic factions in Al Amarah, the I MEF zone of operations. We had our first suicide bomber in Baghdad, and I asked if this was a harbinger of things to come. MG Marks and his J2 folks were working extremely hard on this and learning of the range of enemy forces we might face as we moved into Phase IV. This work tied in with the refinement of Eclipse II which we carried out in between VTCs and work on building the Coalition.

I reported candidly on the previous day's Washington-led VTC on the Tallil meeting—the session with the Joint Staff, and representatives from the Office of the Secretary of Defense and the CENTCOM J5, was not well focused. People in Washington, in my view, were more concerned about the media event, which I granted was important given embedded reporters and other media were flocking to the theater since we were now in Baghdad. The message we were giving them was important. However, we were looking for real answers on the monies needed to pay for what we needed to support the effort. I said my section would remain engaged.

During the 11 April VTC, attended by Secretary Rumsfeld, Mr. Feith, Dr. Zakheim, GEN Myers, and LTG Sharp some good news was shared. The chairman delivered some reasonably good news on our developing Coalition—Poland, Ukraine, Romania, and the Baltic States had all indicated they would be willing to entertain talks on contributing division-sized forces for Phase IV. The plan on the approach was discussed during the VTC. Joint Staff representatives would begin talks with these countries on 12 April. Secretary Rumsfeld was convinced that these Coalition contributions should relieve US forces by mid- to late summer 2003.

I also reported that I had taken the opportunity to talk to LTG Sharp about the need for the 1st Armored Division. I delivered the message that the 1st Armored needed to deploy with its equipment based on the need to reconstitute and refit the APS fleets. LTG Sharp acknowledged my message.

I also acknowledged that I was the lead on Coalition integration into Phase IV with our civil affairs section, the C9 in direct support. My planners would write the major portions of FRAGOs and then hand over the product to our future operations section, C35, for finishing touches. Along those lines, I also acknowledged a task from MG Webster to engage with the Republic of Korea (ROK) Army engineers on their mission to Iraq. The ROKs had been charged by their government to do visible reconstruction efforts which would help the Iraqis. I worked with a Colonel Jeong, the senior officer and representative of the ROK Army, on 12 April.

My C5 planners would conduct another presentation on Eclipse II to the C35 operational plans team on 12 April. This was in accord with directives from LTG McKiernan to perform the handover very deliberately. I reported we were also working with JTF-4 planners on a schedule for the writing of OPLAN Aurora. The expected completion date for this plan was 1 June.

I once again acknowledged the task to meet with and brief Mr. De Rita, Special Assistant to Rumsfeld, on Sunday, 13 April. I suggested that the De Rita meeting would be a good opportunity for us to inform the man who had Secretary Rumsfeld's ear on redeployment and force flow. The command group thought there was some merit to this suggestion, but we did not take a decision that day. My final journal entry was:

> What an amazing day. This VTC w/SecDef is remarkable, we talked around topics. Thankfully tonight's was interesting and potentially of some real use in getting coalition divisions into Iraq to relieve US divisions. The task of coalition support will really become a drain on us. I can sense this with the Koreans.

The C5 Plans Update for 12 April, D+24, contained one line which, at the time, really resonated above the others. Before he left for Baghdad, LTG McKiernan had tasked me to develop a schematic breakdown of our Phase IV stance and to assume the 1st Cavalry Division was not coming. Later that day (12 April), I learned from McKiernan's XO, COL Eshelmann, that the 1st Armored Division would move to theater but we should not plan on the arrival of the 1st Cavalry. I did not know with certainty to whom McKiernan had been talking, but I assumed it was with GEN Franks. I knew McKiernan was determined to bring both divisions into theater, but he had given the task to me without showing his emotion; he gave orders in his own name, and I trusted he fought the good fight to the last. Washington directives, as they ought to have done, directed our strategy. The remainder of my day was spent with Coalition affairs.

I worked issues on the employment of the Korean engineer group and medical unit. The Koreans were satisfied they would do independent operations under I MEF control. COL Chris Guenther, I MEF G5, really helped out in this effort. The Koreans had to show Seoul the engineers and medical unit were accomplishing important tasks assisting the Iraqi recovery. They also had to operate in a secure area due to their government-directed restrictive rules of engagement. After a lot of telephonic coordination, COL Guenther and I worked to get the Koreans on an airplane to coordinate directly with I MEF planners.

I passed on notes I received from COL Fitzgerald from the SecDef meeting on bringing the 1st Armored Division to theater. From my journal:

> SD [Rumsfeld] approved flowing the 1st AD DEPORD [people and equipment] minus the EAD [echelon above division] FA Bde. He would like you all to look at whether the 1AD should use their own equipment or whether they should fall in on 3ID APS equipment and put 1AD equipment immediately into APS stock. Think real answer is some combination of both. Working hard on POW vetting policy, amnesty for IZ scientists, and Phase IV coalition force contributions (military, Carabinieri/gendarmerie, NATO, and police monitors).

I appreciated working with COL Fitzgerald, as he understood the value of cross talk among planners. He kept me informed and I did the same for him.

I acknowledged we had been informed that a Jordanian hospital would move to Baghdad in the near future. The Jordanians—based on their own intelligence, I reckoned—had given us four proposed locations for this military hospital. I told the command group that I would direct our plans group to develop information on the four suggested locations. I suggested that the Jordanians were determined to offer their hospital to support the Iraqis and we would also need to try to anticipate the longer-term support needs, which would range from securing Jordanian convoys coming from Amman to coordinating site security.

I reported the C5 held another update briefing to C35 on Eclipse II. I told the command group that we were beyond the PowerPoint stage in the development of the plan. The OPLAN, Eclipse II, had been written and vetted through MG Whitley. We sent it out to V Corps and I MEF electronically, and posted it to the internal secure CFLCC website. I wrote we would begin the process of burning disks and sending out formal copies to components and the CENTCOM J3 and J5. I was indicating I intended to formally hand over the oversight of this plan, as we were in execution mode and clearly my planners had a great many other tasks to do for the commander.

Brigadier Bradshaw, the first senior British liaison officer assigned to CFLCC. (UK MoD)

Chairman of the Joint Chiefs of Staff during OIF, GEN Myers, USAF. (US DoD Public Affairs)

Under Secretary of Defense for Policy, Mr. Douglas Feith, so-called architect of the Iraq War. (US DoD Public Affairs)

Under Secretary of Defense (Comptroller) Dov Zakheim. (US DoD Public Affairs)

Vice Chairman of the Joint Chiefs of Staff GEN Pace, USMC. (US DoD Public Affairs)

Secretary of Defense Rumsfeld, President Bush, Chairman of the Joint Chiefs of Staff General Myers, and Vice Chairman of the Joint Chiefs of Staff Pace, watch troops pass in review at Fort Myer, Virginia, on October 15 2001. (US DoD Public Affairs)

Commanding General of US Central Command, GEN Franks, touring the ruins of one of Saddam Hussein's palaces in April 2003. (US Navy)

The US Army's M1A1 Abrams tank, "the best tank in the world." (US DoD Public Affairs)

Command Sergeant Major Sparks (left), Major General Marks, CFLCC senior intelligence officer (center), and McKiernan (right) somewhere in Iraq. (US DoD Public Affairs)

Patriot missile launch. It was this kind of missile which saved the author's life. (US DoD Public Affairs)

Ambassador Bremer, leader of the Coalition Provisional Authority. (US DoD Public Affairs)

Dr. Cambone, the first Under Secretary of Defense for Intelligence, briefing reporters in May 2003. (US DoD Public affairs)

Major General Whitley (center), Senior British Liaison Officer to CFLCC, in Baghdad. (Personal files of MG Whitley, used with his permission)

Deputy Secretary of Defense Wolfowitz. "We have a brigade on the ground. Why can't we go now?" (US DoD Public Affairs)

Lieutenant General McKiernan explaining his commander's intent for execution of Cobra II, 14 February 2003. (Personal files of the author)

Lieutenant General Wallace describing the V Corps scheme of maneuver in Cobra II, 14 February 2003. (Personal files of the author)

LTG Conway describing the scheme of maneuver of I MEF in Cobra II, 14 February 2003. (Personal files of the author)

The author on the Iraqi Army parade field in Baghdad in May 2003. He is carrying the sidearm worn by his grandfather in World War I. (Personal files of the author)

Regarding the Free Iraqi People meeting in Tallil, I reported the C5 team and the entire headquarters team had worked details of the 15 APR Iraqi people's representatives meeting. I wanted to ensure the command group knew about all the moving parts in support of this operation. The 377th Theater Support Command was totally engaged, as were all staff sections. CENTCOM J5 sent a representative who was on the ground with us and making things happen. The air component, CFACC, was supporting the operation with C-130s. Major movement to Tallil Air Base began on 13 April. I wrote in my journal, "Thankfully Willie Davis & Winston Gaines are on top of the Free Iraqi meeting on 15 April. MAN!"

In addition to the Phase IV refinement, 1st Armored Division movement, handing over Eclipse II, and the Tallil meeting, my planners continued to work redeployment and force flow options. Our OPG was on an accelerated timeline to scrub deployment orders to identify units we assumed would not need in Phase IV. We also worked on the logical sequencing of medical units with the surgeon. This was very important for a number of reasons, one being a potential problem with mobilization times for individual physician augmentation. We deployed active component Army medical units augmented with the professional filler system (PROFIS), doctors, and staff, and were at the point of considering demobilizing reserve component medical units. We had to consider a replacement flow for medical units which sustained our force in theater without emptying the troop medical clinics and hospitals back at home stations.[4] Finally, to my great relief given all our other tasks, I acknowledged that the meeting supposed to be held the next day with Mr. De Rita, Special Assistant to Rumsfeld, had been cancelled.

We remained busy with short-range targets in spite of efforts to look longer range. As I reported on 13 April, D+25, we continued to focus on CFLCC priorities, getting forces into theater, and refining our sequel plan for Phase IV and redeployment.

I let the command group know we were into Phase IV operations: completion of regime removal. As I'd been portraying for the last days given the range of tasks my planners had at hand—planning for Phase IVB/C (Aurora OPLAN), Coalition integration, redeployment planning, a classified operations plan, the 15 April meeting of Iraqi opposition groups, and the review of the headquarters functions—I recommended that the oversight of Eclipse execution pass to C35, future operations. I had coordinated this recommendation with the C35 directors: Colonels Barry Fowler, Plaudy Meadows, and "Brownie" Brown, USMC. I also reported that it had been confirmed the 1st Armored Division would move to theater, but we should not plan on the use of the 1st Cavalry Division.

4 The PROFIS, or professional filler system, is used by the Army to fill critical, unfilled positions in medical units. Most often during peacetime, battalion- and brigade-level medical teams do not have a medical doctor assigned. The PROFIS doctors fill this vital need for doctors at battalion-level aid stations during war.

CHAPTER SIX

Off-ramps and Phase IV

On 13 April my planners and I continued work on the employment of the Korean engineer group and medical unit. My planners wrote a FRAGO placing the Koreans under the operational control of I MEF, with administrative control (for logistics) being given to the 377th TSC.

The initial focus of the effort by the Koreans in support of I MEF operations would be humanitarian assistance and reconstruction in the An Nasiriyah area. As I'd arranged, the senior Korean representative in our headquarters would attend the CFLCC battle update briefings, starting 14 April. This took some work, as the senior representative of the Korea group was a colonel, and the "war room" was reserved for flag officers only. I worked hard to convince the Chief of Staff, MG Blackman, it was important to include the Koreans. He agreed and made room available.

We continued oversight of the Tallil meeting. The first airplane of equipment left for Tallil on 13 April in support of the conference on 15 April. I was sending input for GEN Franks's briefing on the meeting to our J5 liaison officer, LTC Stan Stewart, who kept CENTCOM action officers informed of our supporting efforts. I reported aircraft for 14 April and delegate movement was coordinated with CENTCOM and CFACC. My C5 team would depart for Tallil Air Base on 14 April and stay there for the duration of the conference. Further, the C5 advanced team left for logistics support area Adder in support of the 15 April Iraqi people's representatives meeting. My people moved with the 377th TSC main body ground convoy. The final element of the group moved to Tallil by C-130 on 15 April. We also continued work on the details of redeployment. This was getting tougher all the time.

My C5 planners continued to work redeployment and force flow options. We developed a draft presentation and proposed message for review by MGs Webster and Stratman. I stressed for information only, not action. We were cross talking with our fellow planners at Marine Forces Central Command, MARCENT. I wanted to make sure our command group knew we were certain the MARCENT proposal would be for all Marine forces to be gone from theater by the time we reached "stable" conditions. The Marines were really pressing to depart from Iraq as soon as possible, reminding everyone that there was a Joint Staff requirement to reconstitute the Marine Expeditionary Units and Amphibious Ready Groups for the regional combatant commands. This pressure would grow along with the intensity of combat in Iraq. I wanted to let my command group know this was ongoing and we planners continued to cross talk and work together with no rancor. The rancor would come later.

I also acknowledged a task from MG Whitley to review the headquarters functions of CFLCC-Iraq with a view toward crafting the follow-on role of CJTF-Iraq. I would look at maximum reach back to Kuwait in order to minimize the forward presence of CFLCC-Iraq, focused on the essential functions of the forward headquarters in support of stability and humanitarian assistance operations. I believed this crafting of the headquarters would allow CFLCC the ability to incorporate Coalition staff and attain a steady state of personnel rotation of Third Army/ARCENT personnel. It would also, I felt, reduce security force requirements as we would keep our forward presence at an effective minimum. I wrote we would have the analysis/recommendation done prior to the deployment of the forward headquarters to Baghdad.

I had the Army Space element working for me, and these folks did terrific work. The space element continued to work with the C9 section to support private volunteer and non-governmental organizations' communications needs, and to ensure there was no frequency interference. C5 Space also continued to shift toward providing more commercial imagery products, as we got more involved with Phase IV activities.

From my journal:

> CINC concerned about looting. His staff sending clarification/instructions that prevention of looting is authorized by ROE. Use all force necessary to prevent any further action counter to our efforts in Najaf done by "punk" cleric who killed OGA sponsored cleric two days ago.

The press was focusing its cameras on people looting Ba'ath Party buildings, which made it look like we were not in control of Iraq. These were indicators of trouble with the range of opposition we'd cited in Eclipse II; regime diehards, Sunni–Shia violence, "jihadis" who wanted to kill Americans, al-Qaeda, and criminal elements trying to exploit confusion for profit.

My C5 Plans Update for 14 April, D+26, focused primarily on refinement of our Phase IV operations plan and redeployment. I also reported on the Rumsfeld VTC. Again the effort to look longer range was hindered by the real need to take care of short-fused projects. We were well into our Phase IV.

My first note to the command group concerned the daily SecDef VTC. Directly from my report:

- Plans on track for 15 April meeting.
- Message should be that this meeting is a discussion about the future of Iraq—the process rather than the personalities. This is the first time for Iraqis to talk about the concept of the IIA [Interim Iraqi Authority].

- Planned output is the press availability after the meeting.
- Play down the expectations—not necessarily leading to a specific national-level conference.
- Have developed proposed scripted statements for host, Jay Garner, and other US, UK, and Polish representatives.
- Debate on using the term "democracy" because of possible perception of imposing a specific governmental process on Iraq.
- "Big tent" and "interim" are good terms to associate with this meeting.

During the VTC, Secretary Rumsfeld mentioned he had spoken with GEN Franks concerning his desire that the payment to Iraqis working for CFLCC and ORHA be kept at reasonable and consistent levels. The conversation was based on media reports that the Marines in Baghdad were paying Baghdad police $10/day. A CFLCC directive on pay scales established $10/month for unskilled workers, $15/month for skilled, and $20/month for managers, although this referred to oil workers only. I could not confirm the media reports at the time, and had asked the public affairs office for help. We were concerned about the details. I followed up on Secretary Rumsfeld's comments on payment amounts in Iraq. I called the CENTCOM J5 and let them know I MEF was paying $10/month vice per day. I reported, "Message received."

The CFLCC main body supporting the execution of the meeting would depart for logistical support base Adder early on the morning of 15 April. We'd been tracking bad weather but MG Renuart made a weather decision to go with the operation. There would be a weather update on the morning of 15 April as well. I noted reports from Tallil were about standard—lots going well and small hiccoughs being worked through. One major point was that US government representatives allowed some delegates to bring armed bodyguards. We were engaged with the on-ground CENTCOM J5 representative on this report.

CENTCOM was taking an interest in our Phase IV planning effort. I reported I'd received a message directing CFLCC, and other components, to brief GEN Franks on Phase IV plans on 20 April by VTC. The presentation was due to MG Renuart on 18 April. I let the command group know my Phase IV team was on it, and would be done well prior to suspense for LTG McKiernan's review.

I acknowledged the task from MG Whitley to brief LTG McKiernan on a proposal for the CFLCC-Iraq headquarters. I would present the proposal at a meeting on 15 April at 1400hrs. I reported I was also prepared to brief our revised redeployment and our updated Phase IV presentation. Whitley was extremely interested in an assessment of the worthiness of the Iraqi railroad from Umm Qasr to Baghdad. I reported the assessment of the Umm Qasr to Baghdad rail line should begin 20 April, but I would remain engaged with the engineers on this effort.

Two notes from my journal:

> Received a note from CCJ5 containing the following questions from SecDef. Will develop answers as input to CCJ5 response. 1. Why 3ID around Baghdad, why not 4 ID who is fresh and will have continuity [1 year rotation]? 2. Relief in place, why 45–60 days? Seems like it would be less. 3. Do we have 1AD fall in on 3ID equipment and use 1AD equipment for APS

> reconstitution? Or do we have 1AD use its own equipment? Or is it a combination? CCJ3 [MG Renuart] indicated that #3 has been resolved. CCJ3 wrote though that the other questions deserve thought. CCJ3 indicated that the CINC has an opinion on #1, but did not elaborate.

I also noted a concern on growing Iranian influence or attempts at influencing events in Iraq:

> Iranian influence: no structure in Basrah but intel indicates attempts, Al Qurnah = infighting among Iranian backed factions, Al Kut = structure seen in terms of Iranian influence.

We were seeing signs of what was to come in the theater while we were trying to retain the forces we felt we needed to keep some form of control as events sorted themselves out.

The C5 Plans Update for 15 April, D+27, focused on CFLCC priorities, getting forces into theater, and refining our sequel plan for PH IV and redeployment. I reported that while I would talk to the CENTCOM J5, I thought we must convene a force rotation board in order to begin the process of redeployment. If we were to meet requirements then we had to provide orders to TRANSCOM so the staff could anticipate the need for shipping and aircraft. I was trying to establish the process of planning for either our departure or the movement of forces into and out of the theater to sustain operations.

Phase IV Meeting with LTG McKiernan

On 15 April, MG Whitley and I had a Phase IV meeting with LTG McKiernan. I was able to give him a thorough briefing on where we were regarding Eclipse II, and get his thoughts on the plan. McKiernan expected a "rush to get out of Dodge," and he was insistent that we control the pace of battle handover. He wanted these events tied to conditions on the ground and forces arriving in theater. He laid out his thoughts on which units should leave as early as possible; 2–6 Cavalry, an AH-64 squadron slated for conversion to Apache Longbow, the headquarters of the 82nd Airborne Division, 173rd Airborne Brigade, the elements that made up the Marine Expeditionary Units, theater missile defense units (Patriot), MLRS battalions, medium bridge companies, and the equipment sets associated with Army and Marine Corps afloat equipment sets.

LTG McKiernan wanted us to outline where we were on handover conditions, something we could easily explain to GEN Franks and others in Washington. He directed "no seams in the headquarters … the coordinator for Phase IV and civil-military operations is MG Whitley." He empowered Whitley with the authority to give subordinate units directions and to task the staff. Finally, McKiernan directed Task Force Baghdad would remain under the command of V Corps and the battle space for the 1st UK division was set as the four Iraqi governates around Basrah.

My planners and I continued to work on the refinement of our operations plan. We coordinated with the Korean contingent. The Koreans were working on their plans for employment based on their visit to I MEF. We refined the draft order on Coalition force integration and contributed to the CENTCOM RFF with information on the type and suggested source for US forces to support the range of Coalition forces we expected in theater.

Our Coalition integration planner worked all day on updating the movement plan of the Jordanian hospital—it was going to set up in Baghdad—as well as the refinement of the Korean engineer order. I assured the command group that we would continue to lead on this effort, but needed help. I let them know I was coordinating with the civil affairs section, C9, for more access to the officers in Coalition Liaison Center and reminded them that this effort would become increasingly difficult as we, hopefully, started receiving Coalition divisions. Regarding the movement of the Jordanians I reported I'd received word a Jordanian hospital reconnaissance team and medical supply convoy would depart for Baghdad on 16 April. I communicated to the CENTCOM J3 that V Corps was not in a position to make a link up and escort the column into the city. I also passed the report on to MG Thurman. Rather grimly I wrote, "Do not know what will happen." Thankfully the movement was without incident. We worked to close out the report from the Free Iraqi People conference as well.

I reported that LTC Gaines rendered the final report on the conference. He was forward at Tallil AB. The planes carrying delegates got out just before there was a thunderstorm. Our trail party of six people and one pallet would return on a C-130 flight 16 April, and "Mission accomplished." We'd heard on CNN, not from CENTCOM, the next meeting would be within ten days, not unusual in the electronic age.

In a rather tongue in cheek way, I told the command group I called the CENTCOM J5 and nominated the Special Operations Command element for the lead on the next conference with a location in the Kurdish autonomous zone. My CFSOCC counterpart did not think this was too funny. We were also working on questions and tasks from the Office of the Secretary of Defense.

I reported we were working on answers to the Secretary's questions posed yesterday: use of divisions in theater, reconstitution of the stocks of equipment and so on. I had the night crew work through a rough draft of these answers and said I would bring a final version to MG Webster the morning of 16 April.

Even though we were already into Phase IV operations and I was pressing to handover the plan to the operations section, we did not have a commander's intent for the plan. I was not able to get a decision on the intent during the meeting with LTG McKiernan. I delivered a copy of the Phase IV intent to COL Eshelmann and reported I was standing by for guidance. My proposed intent was:

> CFLCC Commander's Intent for Phase IV Operations.
> Purpose. To create a secure and stable environment for transition to follow-on-forces and the full engagement of civil agencies to accelerate/enable recovery.
> Key Tasks. Lead lies with CFLCC: Build Iraqi, regional and international support through positively influencing the Iraqi populace, coalition, regional and world perception; Establish a secure and stable environment within IRAQ to permit CFLCC transition to CJTF-Iraq; Maintain civil order by exercising control through published proclamations and the existing legal system where possible; Begin infrastructure recovery by enabling restoration of critical civil infrastructure; Mitigate human suffering by enabling civilian engagement in Emergency Humanitarian Assistance (HA); Provide governance and civil administration through the exercise of military authority; Continue to locate and secure WMD and initiate disposal process; Reintegration of designated Iraqi military units and Capture of designated high value targets, HVTs.
> Endstate. CFLCC has established a secure and stable environment in which CFLCC has conducted battle handover to CJTF-Iraq, recovered forces and completed redeployment.

I wrote regarding the requirement to brief GEN Franks on Phase IV plans on 20 April by VTC. We completed a rough draft of the presentation we would refine and staff through MG Whitley before sending it to Baghdad. I would incorporate all relevant notes from the Phase IV session and continue to work through the night. I also acknowledged receipt from Terry Moran of the task to provide some Phase IV slides on zone expansion. I sent him charts in response, including a slide depicting ORHA zones. We were making some progress, even though we did not know what headquarters would take over from us at the end of Phase IVB. LTC Hendricks, my deputy, had a betting pool going and the odds-on favorite was CFLCC.

The C5 Plans Update for 16 April, D+28, reflected our continuing focus on CFLCC priorities while also responding to questions, notes, and snowflakes from Washington. The thrust of force package work involved pressing the CENTCOM J5 on convening a force rotation board in order to refine the processes of redeployment and establishing priorities. As LTG McKiernan had anticipated, everybody was getting anxious to get the "hell out of Dodge."

I reported on our efforts to balance the workload of refining our Phase IV planning with responding to Washington and Pentagon priorities. War, the use of force, integrating Coalition forces, and the conclusion of wars was certainly an extension of policy. My C5 Coalition integration planner coordinated with the C9 Coalition Liaison Center, CLC, on the process of Coalition integration. I would meet with a CLC representative and COL Fowler once a week to review the status of incoming Coalition units. CLC would receive information from CENTCOM and coordinate the arrival of the units, while my C5 planner would integrate Coalition units in accord with their capabilities and write the "80 percent" solution FRAGO. Then COL Fowler and his C35 would refine the FRAGO for release. We made this process work.

I learned from COL Fitzgerald of the CENTCOM J5 there'd been another VTC with Deputy Secretary Wolfowitz the evening of 16 April. He'd directed CENTCOM to send a recommended location for the next meeting of the Iraqi people's representatives within 24 hours. COL Fitzgerald told me that LTG Abizaid favored a palace located near Baghdad International Airport for ease of transportation, security, and to remove the "mystique" of Baghdad from the process. I expected to receive some message from the J5, either later on in the evening or early on 17 April, with more guidance. This event would land in our laps.

I attended the daily SECDEF VTC. Deputy Secretary Wolfowitz chaired the meeting, GEN Pace, the vice chairman of the Joint Chiefs of Staff, LTG Sharp the J5, Mr. Feith and Dr. Zakheim were in the Pentagon in Washington. LTG (ret) Garner and Mr. De Rita were linked from ORHA. The focus of the VTC was on the continuing humanitarian assessment. People in Washington were concerned by the difference between what the media was portraying as an impending humanitarian disaster and the on-the-ground reality, which was not as bad as shown on TV. LTG Garner led the people in the Pentagon through the linkages between water, power, fuel, and security, and emphasized that security was the most important condition which must be set. This was indirect, but welcome, support for flowing the entire apportioned force.

I acknowledged receipt of guidance on the development and refinement of the Phase IV presentation to GEN Franks. My planners and I would rework the first draft presentation, as needed, and continue refinement on 17 April. I wrote I would send a revised draft for review on 17 April. I told the command group I was receiving information from Terry Moran, who was in Baghdad with LTG McKiernan.

I let MG Blackman know I had submitted answers to the Rumsfeld questions through MGs Thurman and Webster, and that the former had approved the answers which we had then submitted to CENTCOM for inclusion into notes back to the JCS J5. I was keeping all the major generals informed, since they were all interested in this effort. I had to balance "guidance" from all of them, as well as from LTG McKiernan. Of course, McKiernan's "guidance" carried the most weight. Other work went on concerning redeployment.

My C5 redeployment planner spent the day at Arifjan with 377th TSC planners working on the tactical-level details of redeployment. I also received word from V Corps on units that could redeploy within sixty days, and those that should be stopped in the deployment process. I needed to cross-check the V Corps work with the work done by our plans group. I let MG Blackman know I would write a message to FORSCOM on units we feel we could stop deploying, subject, of course, to approval.

I informed MGs Blackman, Webster, and Stratman that I was reviewing two slides from the Army G3 on 1st Armored Division (1AD) and 3rd Infantry Division (3ID) for the C3. The Army G3 wanted to know if it was feasible for the 1AD to deploy without its equipment and fall in on the equipment in use by 3ID. MG Thurman asked for my help, and of course I gave it; I would have a response to him in on 17 April.

Lastly, I acknowledged the requirement to host Ambassador Barbara Bodine's visit and her desire to talk with Phase IV planners on 18 April. Ambassador Bodine was ORHA's coordinator for Baghdad. From my journal:

> Call from Mike Fitzgerald. Seems CINC intent is to accelerate the redeployment as a prod to get more coalition spt. Not sure that will work but will support to get the troops home. Seems too ambitious and really infeasible, we are trying to leave while troops arrive.
>
> Bde Cmd list came out today and altho [*sic*] I knew I wouldn't be on the list there is that feeling of disappointment. Not even on the alternate list. Ah well. Sean MacFarland was picked as was H. R. McMaster. Am still satisfied that I'll be the director of SAMS.

The C5 Plans Update for 17 April, D+29, reflected the true nature of war at the cusp of the operational and strategic level. While my planners remained engaged with refining our Phase IV plan, a great number of us engaged in answering a question from the secretary of defense, one he posed to the vice chief of staff of the Army, GEN Keane. We continued our focus on CFLCC priorities, getting forces into theater, coordinating the integration of Coalition forces, and refining our sequel plan for Phase IV and redeployment.

I reported I'd met with MG Stratman on redeployment. We received notes on the crisis at the numbered continental US armies. The stop and start of the request for forces process was having a dramatic effect on the Army reserve and National Guard. There was only a finite number of days during which a unit could be mobilized short of general mobilization. The President had not declared general mobilization, thus the starting and stopping of the deployment clock on units was heading toward limiting the length of time a reserve or National Guard unit could remain on active duty. This materially affected the type and number of forces we could rely upon to come to theater and relieve units on the ground. We received the V Corps redeployment unit list. We received a proposed MARCENT redeployment list. In my report I wrote,

> I am going to need some time to do a thorough analysis of this paper, as well as a review of all of our force flow. We are still in the process of flowing the V Corps CSS troops. I will need **five days** starting tomorrow [18 April] to do the thorough analysis with the OPG of the units we have in the flow, those we do not need and are here, those we do not need and have not yet moved out, and those we need based on our stance in theater over time. We will include the work done by V Corps in this analysis. From this work we will have, a list of units that can redeploy within 60 days, a list of units we can "turn off" in the flow, and a list of units we will need who are either here now or flowing that will allow us to sustain the force over the expected/assumed length of the mission. **Two days** after the completion of the analysis we will have messages for release that will state officially what our positions are regarding the deploying force flow and the redeploying force flow.

The point I was trying to make—as forcefully as I could—was that we were rapidly approaching the point of being overwhelmed, what with units wanting to go home, finding units to relieve these units, and still maintaining the forces in theater necessary to maintaining security. We still had not even begun to try to find Saddam and his sons, let alone the other high-ranking members of the Ba'ath Party.

The big effort regarded a task per direction of MG Webster in response to a question from GEN Keane. The question from GEN Keane had itself been generated from a rhetorical question posed by Secretary Rumsfeld. The multi-day effort towards answering it began when Rumsfeld asked why it took 150,000 Army troops to deliver the 3rd Infantry Division to Baghdad, but only 50,000 Marines to deliver the 1st Marine Division to Baghdad. My planners screwed themselves into the ceiling to produce an analysis of combat support and combat service support units in theater across the entirety of the CFLCC force, focusing on general logistical, theater ballistic missile defense, air base guard forces, Special Operations Force base support, and Army Title X requirements. In essence, we developed picture of how Army units supported the theater effort of the campaign. I could not help but wonder why we were answering GEN Keane's note. I felt surely there were folks on the Army staff who could assemble the necessary information and send it to us to verify and update. I also wondered about the WHY behind Secretary Rumsfeld asking such a question, and just what was going on in Washington.

We were also working on a Phase IV presentation for GEN Franks. The updated draft of the presentation was due no later than 20 April. I would deliver it to CENTCOM headquarters in Qatar and would personally stand by for further guidance on the development/refinement of the presentation. I acknowledged that either LTG Garner or Bates would accompany my plans group to Qatar. I would coordinate with ORHA to ensure the generals and their staffs received all information on the presentation. We were working on the handover criteria of CENTCOM Phase IVA to Phase IVB, as this marked the exchange of authority from military to civil lead in the reconstruction effort. It was a rather important milestone in the overall campaign.

I also informed the command group of our response to a CENTCOM J5 request for a recommendation on the location for the next Free Iraqi People meeting. CFLCC units would again provide all the support and security required for this event. I recommended Baghdad International Airport as the general location, with a specific location to be determined in conjunction with V Corps planners "in the next few days." I was stalling for time here as I asked the command group to reinforce the requirement for a CENTCOM representative to come forward in Baghdad to accelerate the planning to MG Renuart, CENTCOM J3, and RADM Robb, CENTCOM J5.

My redeployment planner spent a good day at Arifjan with 377th TSC planners working on the tactical-level details of redeployment. I reported we had a good handle on the detailed effort which must occur to make turn-in of Kuwait- and Qatar-based US Army equipment and stores. Additionally, I provided MG Thurman with a proposed rewrite of two slides from Army G3 on the 1st Armored and 3rd Infantry Divisions. I believed this effort would finally kill the notion of 1st Armored falling in on 3rd Infantry equipment.

In my daily update for 18 April, D+30, I reported we were continuing work on answering the vice chief of staff's question along with our other tasks. There were well over 15,000 Soldiers in support of I MEF. They ranged from truck companies to Military Police, Patriot units to a rocket artillery battalion (MLRS). The Army had Patriot units all over the Gulf, Israel, and Turkey, along with corresponding support units. The scope of tasks given to the Army led to the "150,000" number which Secretary Rumsfeld questioned. We'd completed the development of our first draft charts and were awaiting approval by LTG McKiernan. He was in Baghdad.

My planners and I completed an updated draft of the Phase IV presentation for 20 April. I reported that my understanding was it would be delivered via VTC on 21 April. I acknowledged a requirement to see MG Blackman on 20 April at 0900hrs for further guidance on the development of the presentation.

I let the command group know I would continue to work with our deputy chief of staff, "DJ" Dellajocano, on the development of CFLCC participation in the next Free Iraqi People meeting. We recommended the airport as a suitable location to CENTCOM. We also recommended that LTG Garner and ORHA be in charge of this and other meetings. CFLCC simply could not devote the attention required for this meeting, especially on a schedule of one meeting every ten days.

We were also done with a good 80 percent solution on the redeployment review of forces to redeploy in the next 60 days, and those in the force flow we could stop. My Phase IV team delivered a presentation to MGs Marks, Thurman, and Whitley on the way ahead for the ISG. The team continued to refine the proposals for ISG integration and receive the senior-level DIA planner in the coming week, as well as continuing to write and refine the Aurora OPLAN for the continuation of Phase IV. We were very busy.

Finally, I informed the command group that I had received a draft order from US Special Operations Command for review. The CENTCOM J5 had sent it to us, and MG Thurman said he had no time to review and comment on it. The subject was the prosecution of the global war on terror. It was a remarkable document.

Notes from my journal of this day:

> The tenor of intelligence analysis changes from war/combat to peace support operations. A sheikh declared himself administrator of Basrah today. C2 learning about him. Iranians really trying to take advantage of the power vacuum. Power struggle among ayatollahs in Iraqi Shia groups. Syrians developing insurgent effort in north of Iraq (first report).

Finally, "CG and Garner will see Chalabi. Low key… no media … Zubadi—self-proclaimed mayor of B-dad. Chalabi says not true and does not support this guy."

And from a letter sent to my wife, Kate, on 18 April 2003:

> I am taking advantage of a break in between another in a series of briefings to write you. We are now in the process of bringing our C2 (senior intelligence officer—a major general), C3 (senior operations officer—major general), and Deputy Commanding General for Post Hostilities (a British major general) up to speed on how we will integrate the Iraq Survey Group—of which you might have heard of in the open press—into our operations.
>
> In my personal opinion this is a good idea that is six months late thus once the group is established the fleeting opportunity to exploit intelligence that is literally lying about the offices in Baghdad will long gone.[*sic*]
>
> Nonetheless this is a good idea that emanated from OSD thus is far superior to anything that we lesser mortals could possibly conceive. What can be controlled from Washington will be controlled from Washington. I am sure you can hear the sarcasm in this.
>
> The fight in the city of Baghdad that never happened, to a large degree. Well, after An Nasiriyah, Samawah, An Najaf and Al Hillah we all felt that if we entered Baghdad it would be house-to-house fighting, à la WWII. I wish I could tell you we had an epiphany and the complete situation and solution came crystal clear but that is not correct. As we demonstrated our overwhelming superiority in close combat and faced the enemy in literal hand-to-hand combat AND BEAT HIM the enemy realized at the lower soldier level he was losing. Marshall De Saxe, a late 18th-century French soldier, said courage had to be reborn every day and in this instance the enemy could not find his courage.
>
> I really think the irrefutable fact that we did not flinch from close combat and could kill efficiently and remorselessly will serve us well for the foreseeable future. The people over here do not respect restraint nor do they see restraint as strength. Restraint to the Arabs is weakness.
>
> To return to why no city fight in Baghdad [*sic*]. The enemy had organized himself to fight along the roads to Baghdad. Since we went out into the desert and the enemy stayed put we turned his flank. He abandoned his positions and weapons, and fled at night. The fierce but limited resistance in Baghdad came from Saddam's forces that could not flee the country. The soldiers, those who did not flee, died. The TV story of 2,000 Iraqi KIA on the first reconnaissance in force is true. A Brigade of the 3rd Infantry Division fought its way into the city, fought all day in the heart of the city and then fought its way out. This broke the enemy resistance. The one tank lost was worn out and broke down and could not be recovered. It was destroyed by the ground force and further by a precision guided bomb, so-called JDAM. It did give the enemy a momentary TV moment.
>
> After that first recon the resistance reduced every day. The V Corps guys reported that they captured a colonel from the Special Republican Guard as he walked around the city amazed that we were there. He was trying to organize resistance above platoon level. He failed. We remained on plan, in general, (my favorite quotation of a dead German, Moltke the Elder, is; *No operation plan extends with any certainty beyond the first encounter with the main body of the enemy. It is* ***only the layman*** (my emphasis) *who, as a campaign develops, thinks he sees the original plan being systematically fulfilled in every detail to its preconceived conclusion*) that being to isolate the city by establishing an outer cordon and raiding into parts of the city. The decision to go in and stay was a key decision because the Iraqis believe what they see.
>
> As long as we bombed the people believed they were winning because the planes left. The city had experienced bombing before. Tanks in the streets had not happened since 1941. The people saw us, believed we were there to stay, and started pulling down statues.
>
> Tanks and mechanized infantry worked well in the city. The battle, I think, was already won because the enemy lost heart. That is why I was happy to see the American flag on the face of the statue [the statue of Saddam]; the people watching Al Jazeera needed to see Americans and

> Iraqis pulling down the statue and the American flag on it. The Arab street needed to know we beat them soldier-to-soldier. This will pay dividends for some time.
>
> Now we are engaged in the remarkably difficult planning and execution of post-hostility operations. We are fighting and turning on electricity. We are collecting weapons, looking for WMD and delivering humanitarian assistance. We are also responding to DC pressure to stay the course as long as needed so long as we have only one division in Iraq by 1DEC. This will be amazing.

I used this letter to vent some of my frustrations to my wife. These were thoughts I felt I could not express to my subordinate officers and to my commander.

The War is Over, but the Campaign is Not

On 19 April, D+31, Soldiers from the 3rd Infantry Division found 600 million dollars while searching one of Uday's palaces. I saw pictures of the bales of money. We made some "Kelly's Heroes" jokes and wondered what to do with the money. I proposed we immediately put the money to use in the rebuilding effort.[1]

That day, LTG McKiernan spoke with some passion in our daily morning update. He told us that if we were thinking that we ought to be doing something, we were right. All our energy must be put into winning the campaign now, and the campaign is Phase IV. He said our units were de facto sheriffs and "the law," and that "No one else but us will make things happen in Iraq." My concluding thought from this meeting: *War is over in the US/UK, but the campaign is not over.*

My planners and I continued to focus on CFLCC priorities, getting forces into theater, coordinating the integration of Coalition forces, and refining our sequel plan for Phase IV and redeployment. We also had a number of other tasks to accomplish.

On 19 April, LTG Abizaid arrived in Kuwait for a meeting with LTG McKiernan. Larry DeRita of Secretary Rumsfeld's office also attended the meeting. LTG Abizaid told us CENTCOM owed us a policy on armed groups. We were dealing with the Kurdish Peshmerga in the north, armed groups of bodyguards around emerging Iraqi leaders like Chalabi, along with increasing indicators of various armed Shia groups aligned with the Hakim brothers and Moqtada al-Sadr.

LTG Abizaid made the point that the Shia do not want us here for a long time. He said we should consider Phase IV a sprint with a goal of no US divisions in Iraq by March 2004. Continuing the track metaphor, he described our task ahead as a 440-yard relay; completion of Phase III was a military task and the first leg, Phase IVA, was the military/ORHA leg, IVB the ORHA/military leg, and the final leg, Phase IVC, was the Iraqi civil government/the US country team leg. We were to focus on the transition between CFLCC and ORHA at the end of Phase IVA. Based on Abizaid's thoughts, I refined the 21 April Phase IV presentation for GEN Franks.

1 I never found out what happened to the money.

LTG Abizaid also established 26 April as the date for the next Free Iraqi People meeting. It would take place at the Baghdad International Airport complex, as we had recommended. My C5 planners would continue to work with D/CofS, COL Dellajocano, on the development of CFLCC participation in the next Free Iraqi People meeting.

I told MGs Webster, Stratman, and Blackman I was prepared for the meeting with LTG McKiernan on 20 April, 0900hrs, regarding the priority of redeploying forces, and forces we could return to the force pool and not deploy. I would also go through the VCSA presentation on Army forces in theater.

My planners and I were earning our pay. LTG McKiernan presented me with a Bronze Star on this day. He also presented LTC Reilly with a Legion of Merit. I appreciated this, as LTG McKiernan had to go out on a limb to get this medal for LTC Reilly as it was out of the ordinary for a lieutenant colonel to receive it.

20 April, D+32, was an interesting day. While we continued to focus on CFLCC priorities, we were also working very hard on tasks associated with the coordination of our Phase IV efforts, namely getting forces into and out of theater and coordinating the integration of Coalition forces. We continued to work on messages regarding the return of forces. We were receiving input from V Corps and 377th Theater Support Command, and would continue to coordinate our total efforts.

The plans group also continued to review all products with the view of continuing to refine the force list of those units that could retrograde earlier into Kuwait to begin the force regeneration process. We focused on field artillery, attack aviation, a deeper look at combat service support units with the view to determine the requirements of sustaining the force over time, and the dual task of returning forces to home station and deploying them into theater. This was hard, detail-oriented work; we were trying to sort out how to sustain a longer in-theater effort while looking at what units to bring over vis-à-vis the tasks we assigned ourselves for Phase IVA. This was living the dictum of Moltke the Elder, as related by Jim Schneider at SAMS: an error in the initial placement of forces cannot be corrected over the duration of a campaign.

I sent the final drafts of the GEN Franks's Phase IV briefing and the response to the vice chief of staff's project to LTG McKiernan for review. I was able to spend some time with him this day (20 April) going over both of these efforts, and he was satisfied with the level of detail in both. I had the impression that LTG McKiernan was sending his own notes back to Washington regarding the response to GEN Keane, and ultimately Secretary Rumsfeld. This was important for the Army, as we were also anticipating what I was calling the post-war "Battle on Capitol Hill," the inevitable budget battles and force reductions that always follow a war. Secretary Rumsfeld had talked about reducing the Army by a few divisions before the wars in Afghanistan and Iraq started. I figured this would come up again, hence my focus on getting this response correct, or as correct as possible.

My C5 planners continued to work with our deputy chief of staff on the development of CFLCC participation in the next Free Iraqi People meeting. Their impression was officers on the CENTCOM staff were not too keen on using the Baghdad International Airport, BIAP, as the location of the meeting. It was a good thing LTG Abizaid told us to develop the plan using the airport.

Another group led by my planners was working on integrating the ISG to float the proposal that the headquarters of the ISG should be based in Qatar with CENTCOM's forward headquarters. I endorsed this idea and directed more research. I felt the idea would cut down on the footprint required in Baghdad and importantly the communications requirement that we needed to establish the ISG forward. The investigators could operate from Baghdad while the analysts could do their work in Qatar. A smaller footprint forward also reduced the amount of security CFLCC would need to supply to the ISG.

I mentioned to MG Blackman I spoke with Colonel Jeremy Robbins of the Senior British Liaison Activity. COL Robbins offered an additional staff officer for work in the Coalition liaison cell, and I accepted on behalf of the C9. We also spoke about the force generation conference which the British would host in London on 8/9 May; COL Robbins told me both CENTCOM and CFLCC would be invited to attend. I also learned that the British were in talks with the Danes, Spanish, Norwegians, and Dutch regarding the provision of peacekeeping forces. The Spanish, Danes, and Dutch would likely provide battalion-task-force-sized units. The Norwegians would have a somewhat smaller force. The countries would operate under the OPCON of the UK division. I believed this meant we could probably expand the British zone and allow MEF forces to either better cover high-priority cities or retrograde forces to begin the force regeneration process.

Along this line of thought, I told MG Blackman that we had received a note from the CENTCOM J5 concerning questions on the quick reduction of forces in the Corps and MEF zone, and asking how we would integrate the expected Coalition division(s) which might come into assist in establishing and maintaining the desired secure and stable environment in post-hostilities Iraq. I told our chief of staff that we would brainstorm on how to redraw zones for Phases IVB/C. We would operate under the assumption of a more rapid progression from IVA to IVB, an assumption which certainly did not become fact. Finally, I reported that my C5 Coalition integration work continued. My planners had written another FRAGO providing details of upcoming arriving Coalition forces for the operations section.

I also recorded these events in my journal. The International Committee of the Red Cross was reporting an outbreak of "Black Fever" in southern Iraq. We were hearing about Iranian imams worrying that Qom, in Iran, would cease being the center of Shia Islam as Shia could now travel to Karbala. We were watching Chalabi as he was attempting to build alliances with the Kurds and thus building a broad-based political coalition.

The C5 Plans Update for 21 April, D+33, covered our continuing focus on our CFLCC priorities (the mundane work of being a planner at the time). The Phase IV briefing for GEN Franks was completed and approved. We also learned the presentation to Franks was postponed. I informed MG Blackman that we were prepared for the proposed new date and time, which was 22 April at 1830hrs. This was an important presentation as through it we would get GEN Franks's thoughts on the conduct of Phase IV, which we had not yet heard from him. I also sent the completed VCSA project to LTG McKiernan, who was forward in Baghdad.

My planners continued to work on the development of CFLCC participation in the next Free Iraqi People meeting. We received a fragmentary order from the CENTCOM J5 informing us of the arrival of ten to twelve CENTCOM J5 officers at the Baghdad International Airport on 22 April. These people would coordinate the CENTCOM-level effort in support of the meeting. The order also directed that this meeting would not take place at the airport. This was different to normal, and we were working on this with the J5 folks. It was also annoying since LTG Abizaid had told us to find a location on airport grounds.

The C5 Coalition integration work continued. We were working on finding office space for a British officer in the Coalition Liaison Center. The best news was that there were indications the Poles would commit a division headquarters and a brigade to Phase IV operations. I mentioned this to MG Blackman because it would take more than four officers to integrate a division into Phase IV operations. We were trying to balance looking well into future with how to integrate Coalition divisions into the battle space, as well as actually getting the units into the theater.

Senate Staff Visit, 21 April 2003

The most important event this week, at least in my estimate, was a meeting with two Senate Foreign Relations Committee staffers. General Franks lifted the ban on congressional delegations visiting theater, and this was the first of many such visits. The two staffers were Dr. Andrew Parasiliti, who worked for Senator Chuck Hagel, and Mr. Puneet Talwar, who worked for Senator (at the time) Joe Biden. Dr. Parasiliti and Mr. Talwar were escorted by Mr. Gene Delbianco (from the embassy). These men asked many questions on Phase IV and operations leading up to the capture of Baghdad. They asked about the MeK, urban operations, and integration of the various groups of "Free Iraqi Forces" into our operations and how we were working with ORHA. What was disturbing was how apparent the disdain for these two staffers was on the part of briefing officers from our C9.

Brigadier General Kern was the commander of the 352nd Civil Affairs Command at the time. When I learned about the visit, I did some research on who these men were, where they were educated, and anything they'd written, etc., to prepare for the meeting. I offered this information to BG Kern. Clearly it was ignored.

About 15 minutes into the presentation, and after seeing the raised eyebrows of Mr. Delbianco, I suggested a break for coffee. I let BG Kern know the meeting was not going our way, and asked whether he realized just who these men were. Kern and his staff dismissed my concern; he and his people continued to talk down to these staffers.

I went to MG Blackman when the meeting was done to let him know of the potential bad news. Perhaps I was overreacting, since I hadn't been able to discern any immediate effect or results from the meeting. I was convinced we'd reinforced in the minds of these two men that the military held lots of people in contempt.

While the meeting was alleged to be "off the record," I did not believe it for a second. This meeting reinforced in my mind that professional Soldiers needed the ability to speak to policy makers and staffers in language they'd understand without being condescending. We needed to be able to render politically aware military advice.

The C5 Plans Update for 22 April, D+34, reflected the nature of the war we planners were fighting since we had seized Baghdad and moved to control the entire country. While we tried to focus on CFLCC priorities, we were also working on a range of other actions ranging from the profound to the mundane. We worked with our C4, supply and logistics section, planners on the CCJ4/CCJ3 conference on theater sustainment and basing, which was set for 24/25 April.

The conference would be held at Camp As Saliyah, Qatar, and co-hosted by the CENTCOM J3 and J4. The CENTCOM J3 and J4 asked that it be attended by two to three planner-level component representatives who had prepared to present our CFLCC commander's intent, and state detailed requirements for theater-wide sustainment and basing for the long-term Operation *Iraqi Freedom* Phase IV, Operation *Enduring Freedom*, and the Global War on Terror.

The CENTCOM C4 was looking ahead to try to coordinate the disparate requirements of sustaining two theaters of war with completely different ranges of requirements. Our planners had to be prepared to present/formalize a range of movement, sustainment, reception, staging, onward movement and integration of forces requirement, along with the complete range of issues with sustaining a long campaign. I was happy someone was taking the long view, and taking it seriously.

We also kept on working on the range of presentations and papers dealing with Phase IV issues and requests from the Pentagon. I sent the completed GEN Keane project answering the secretary of defense's questions to LTG McKiernan for his final review. We were finally putting the last touches on this action. We all realized it was very important for the Army to ensure the secretary of defense really understood what the Army was doing throughout this theater of war, not to mention supporting and fighting in the Afghan theater as well.

We completed the Phase IV briefing for GEN Franks. I sent it to Baghdad and our early entry command post. Terry Moran confirmed that he received it. My planners and I stood ready to give the briefing from Kuwait if needed. We learned the Phase IV VTC was scheduled for 23 April. My planners continued to work on the development of CFLCC participation in the next Free Iraqi People meeting. C5 officers went into downtown Kuwait City for a coordination meeting on this event. It was also an opportunity for some of my folks to get off Camp Doha, a place we fondly referred to as a medium-security prison.

CENTCOM had other work for us as well. I reported I'd spoken with COL Fitzgerald about another Rumsfeld query. Secretary Rumsfeld had supposedly asked the chairman of the Joint Chiefs of Staff, GEN Myers, to think about adding Syria, Israel, Lebanon, India, Georgia, Armenia, and Azerbaijan to the CENTCOM area of responsibility. Fitzgerald asked me for my thoughts, and told me he was working on a reply for GEN Franks's signature, but he did not think it was a serious request for information but rather another snowflake. Dealing with snowflakes was getting old hat for us, as by this time we'd endured a small blizzard of these notes.

We also received a copy of a CENTCOM task from Secretary Rumsfeld concerning reserving the holding facility in Guantanamo Bay for illegal combatants of special intelligence value, and directing CENTCOM to develop a holding facility for illegal combatants of no special intelligence value but who were dangerous nonetheless. CENTCOM was directed to develop a plan—working with the "developing civil authority" in Iraq—to deal with various types of detainees, Iraqi and non-Iraqi. Fitzgerald told me he had to produce a first draft of this plan for Secretary Rumsfeld by 30 April. This was not going to be an easy task.

A plans team brainstormed some options for the integration of Coalition divisions into the Iraq theater of war battle space. I told our chief of staff we would further develop the options into true courses of action for final review. At the time we were certain that the British and the Poles would send a division headquarters and associated units, but there were no other firm offers of troops for Phase IV.

Finally, I reported that I understood Major General Dayton, commanding general of the ISG, would have an office call with LTG McKiernan on 28 April. I was ready to give the latter a presentation on the options for the integration of the ISG into the CJTF-Iraq structure. I said I did not believe the previously mentioned suggestion that MG Dayton remain in Qatar would stand up, based on input from officers in the CENTCOM J5.

While these tasks and others were my focus of main effort, in the background Iraq was simmering. We were learning of Shia clerics in the south inciting violence against the Coalition. The security situation in Mosul had been improving with the arrival of the 101st Airborne Division, but there was at least one prominent Sunni sheikh, al-Jubari, spreading hate against us in the north.

We were dealing with balancing a range of requirements in administering this country. Water needed to be released from a reservoir in order to run generators at a dam on the Tigris that provided power to Mosul. The release of water would cause the river to rise, flooding fields in the south. Saddam's birthday was 28 April, and we were preparing for "events" celebrating this date. He was still out there somewhere. In my journal, my final comment of the day was on the CENTCOM video teleconferences. I wrote, "CINC had no words of wisdom today. We just don't make good use of the SVTCs." Also, directly from my journal: "Another day of balancing looking long term from the operational level of war and meeting the day to day mundane, yet important, tasks of a headquarters at war."

To convey a sense of the tasks set for small group of planners, this is my report of 25 April 2003:

> MG Webster, MG Stratman, MG Blackman,
>
> The C5 Plans Update for 23APR03, D+35. We continue to focus on CFLCC priorities, getting forces into theater, coordinating the integration of coalition forces and refining our sequel plan for PH IV and redeployment.
>
> Force Package Work:
>
> - Force flow charts went out based on latest TRANSCOM data.
> - We have a planner going with the C4 to the CCJ4/CCJ3 conference, 24/25APR, on theater sustainment and basing conference.
> - We continue the work on refining the requirements to sustain the force as it rotates in and out of theater. Will meet with C3 on establishing a system of control for the process of early redeployments to ensure we have proper movement orders for TRANSCOM, FORSCOM, DA, and JFCOM.
> - Received a request from the Army G3 asking that they be included in redeployment information distribution groups for CCJ5 messages and email. Do not think this is a problem.
> - We received an official message announcing that there will be a lieutenant colonel/colonel-level conference in Qatar on redeployment 27/28APR but there will not be a formal TFPDL conference for the overall redeployment. Coordinating with V Corps and I MEF to send a planner along with C5 to Qatar this weekend for the CCJ5 planner-level conference on redeployment. I MEF responded in the affirmative, anticipating that V Corps will do likewise. Will coordinate for billets and transportation.
>
> OPLAN Refinement:
>
> - Acknowledge the CofS decision to make soon to be LTC Frank Jones senior LNO to ORHA in Baghdad, not real thrilled with this but WILCO.
> - C5 continues to work with D/CofS on the development of CFLCC participation in the next Free Iraqi People meeting. C5 officers went downtown again today for a coordination meeting on this event. It appears that we will be able to convoy supplies up to Baghdad for this event. All acknowledge the slip of two days to 28APR.
> - C5 team went on a recce of the port of Umm Qasr today. Excellent trip. Port appears to be very good and could be made ready as another SPOE. The port needs dredging and soon. The team talked to the UK Port and Maritime Regimental commander while there. Every three days enough silt builds up to require a day of dredging. ORHA let a contract, we think, but the company has a 30-day mobilization period to get organized for the effort. Will dig deep, no pun intended, into this effort with ORHA. Also potential trouble regarding dockworker pay. Have seen something about this in other notes but in essence the $10/month minimum wage is far less than the pay with allowances and bonuses dock workers made pre-war which was $48/month average according to reports.

- C5 team will translate brainstormed options for the integration of coalition divisions into the Iraq theater battle space into presentation charts for review tomorrow.
- Acknowledge the guidance given during the PH IV/Redeployment VTC today. Will continue to coordinate with CCJ5 and Corps/MEF on a tight retrograde/redeployment schedule.
- SecDef VTC with LTG (Ret.) Garner tomorrow, topic as yet unknown.

Will meet tomorrow with C35, CofS, C2, C3, on HQ refinement for CJTF-IZ, etc.

I pressed MG Blackman to "frock" MAJ Frank Jones to lieutenant colonel in the hopes this would allow him a better reception among the people in ORHA.[2] Jones did a superb job as our liaison officer with this organization and later on with the CPA under Ambassador Bremer.

Given my report above, the daily background was full of alarms and intelligence reports on fears of growing Iranian interference with Iraqi affairs. We were told by his agents that Grand Ayatollah Sistani was worried about the infiltration of Iranians crossing into Iraq; Sistani wanted the Coalition to control the borders. Al-Sadr was now in Baghdad and making noise about receiving a post in the next Iraqi government. He was using his bully pulpit to build a power base.

Marines of the I MEF were patrolling the streets of Al Kut. The 101st Airborne Division, reinforced by a tank battalion, conducted patrols in Mosul. The people of Tikrit were putting up Saddam pictures in advance of his birthday on 28 April. There was an amazing statement from the CENTCOM Public Affairs Office. The public affairs officer reported to the entire command that there were fewer than two hundred embedded reporters remaining in theater. He said, "The war is over." I was not so sure.

On 24 April, D+36, I mentioned Mr. Walt Slocombe and the reorganization of the Iraqi Army for the first time. I did not know if the general officers in the command group had heard of Slocombe before, but they might have as they all worked in the Pentagon at some time. I reported I was sending two officers to Qatar on 25 April for a conference on the reactivation of the Iraqi Army. As we did not know much about Mr. Slocombe at the time, my officers would render a report and their impressions upon their return. Additionally, I sent in my first report on the development of courses of action for the integration of Coalition divisions into our Phase IV battle space.

Force package development work continued apace as well. We kept our higher and subordinate headquarters informed of projected incoming and outgoing units based on data we received from TRANSCOM. I reported the arrangements were

---

2 Major Frank Jones was selected for promotion to lieutenant colonel but had not yet been officially promoted. Frocking him to LTC allowed him to officially wear the rank insignia of an LTC before his official promotion.

settled for the trip to the lieutenant colonel/colonel-level conference in Qatar on redeployment scheduled for 27/28 April. We were taking a V Corps and I MEF planner along with us to Qatar. We completed a review of the I MEF concept for redeployment and sent it on to the chief of staff. My planners worked on scheduling a date for a thorough review of units and redeployment based on the morning's intelligence update VTC.

My C5 team refined the potential courses of action for integrating Coalition divisions into the Phase IV battle area. We developed three courses of action: 1) establish division zones along exiting governate lines, 2) establish non-contiguous division zones focused on population centers, and 3) establish non-contiguous division zones task focused on border control and ORHA support. I would forward the draft charts for review upon completion. We knew the Poles and the British were sending divisional headquarters to support our campaign. We did not assume other nations would send division-level headquarters, but we were prepared to continue our refinement of the battle space if this occurred.

There was great emphasis on reorganizing the headquarters to conduct both our Iraq theater of operations mission as well as serving as the Army component for Central Command, wherein we were responsible for the sustainment of Army forces in the wider CENTCOM area of operations. I met with representatives from the chief of staff's office, C2, C3, C35, and others, on reorganizing the headquarters. I stressed that time was not on our side. We could not reorganize and retrain, therefore we had to adapt and apply what we were familiar with (our established procedures) to the unfamiliar of stability and support operations, SASO.[3]

The C5 team continued to work on a range of tasks, all with particular milestones and attention from higher headquarters. We worked with the overall CFLCC group moving supplies and people to Baghdad in support of the next Free Iraqi People meeting. I reviewed the proposed agenda for the CFLCC commanders' meeting on 1 May. LTC Mike Hendricks and I refined the presentations suggested, and prepared them for review in the coming week. We reviewed a Phase IV briefing we received via the CENTCOM J5 which originated in the Joint Staff. I reported I would send it on to Baghdad and work with COL Fitzgerald of the CENTCOM J5 to stop the nonsense. I recorded in my journal this was another example of our officer corps' predilection with the tactical level of war.

The final notes from my report concerned arrangements for MAJ Jones's promotion to LTC and his travel for duties in Baghdad. The daily SecDef VTC with LTG

3 SASO was the Army and joint doctrinal term which covered all post-hostilities efforts. We were operating in unfamiliar areas as our preparatory training, indeed all Army training focused on winning force-on-force battles. None of us, save time spent on peace-keeping operations in Bosnia and Haiti, spent much time thinking about how to restore a country while replacing a government.

Garner was cancelled and the C5 team forwarded some explanatory charts on the ISG as a means of preparing LTG McKiernan for his meeting with MG Dayton.

Our daily operations and intelligence meeting kept me informed on what was happening while I was focused on planning. In the MEF zone, Al Kut seethed. The Iranians worked to establish influence there. In the V Corps zone the situation in Mosul improved as the 101st Airborne became established. Reports from Tikrit led us to anticipate an "event" of some sort on 28 April, Saddam's birthday. We also asked CENTCOM for guidance on how to deal with the MeK. A brigade of the 4th Infantry Division was tasked to establish contact and keep the group under control.

My final note of the day in my journal concerned our daily CENTCOM operations and intelligence VTC. I wrote, "Amazing. These CC VTCs are horrid wastes of time. When CC ought to be issuing operational guidance we get tactical focus. When we need theater intelligence we get snipers at patrols. Terrible. I only hope more gets done one-on-one btw CGs & CINC."

The C5 Plans Update for 25 April, D+37, reflected the hectic nature of the work the section was doing at this time. We continued to focus on CFLCC priorities, getting forces into theater, coordinating the integration of Coalition forces, and refining our sequel plan for Phase IV and redeployment. We also dealt with a range of related tasks.

Small things can take up a great deal of time. MG Thurman had a prodigious appetite for work, and he wanted to be aware of everything. He had to personally approve every order and message leaving our headquarters. I asked to take a "rock out of his rucksack" by asking he get out of the business of approving the deletion of companies from the existing force flow. Since my section continued to be responsible for the force flow in and out of the theater, I requested permission to approve/disapprove individual unit deletions and speak for CFLCC on these matters. My caveat was that, of course, I would continue to get appropriate senior staff concurrence/input.

I tried to make this request as politely as I could because the bottleneck of MG Thurman's inbox really was slowing down the force flow process. Additionally, I was working to get MG Thurman, as the C3, out of the action officer business on turning off unit movements. It was very interesting, working with MG Thurman. He felt he needed to have a hand in the fine details of deployment and redeployment to have a feel for the totality of the operation.

We were also continuing work on refining our Phase IV plans. The two C5 officers in Qatar for the conference on the reactivation of the Iraqi Army sent a short update. They had the presentations from the conference and would carry them back from Qatar. They reported that Mr. Slocombe from the Pentagon had stated the goal was establishing an Iraqi Corps of the new Iraqi Army as quickly as possible. The conference report was much in line with LTG Abizaid's thoughts on getting the process moving very swiftly.

I acknowledged LTG McKiernan's approval of three courses of action for integrating Coalition divisions into the Phase IV battle area. Based on his approval, I reported the C5 would continue on a fast course for continued refinement and decision on the way ahead. Additionally, in talks with Colonel Robbins we learned the UK military preference was for the UK divisional zone to mirror an ORHA zone, specifically the one in the south with Basrah. This preference, according to Robbins, was based on lessons learned from similar operations (Northern Ireland) and, in Robbins's words, ensured a "seamless effort" in the zone. We worked toward adapting the selected course of action with this UK national preference in mind.

I acknowledged receipt of a task to refine the command and control relationship of the Spanish contingent and I MEF/1UK Division. Rear Admiral Moreno, Spanish Joint Task Force commander, was adamant about only working for the British. The Spanish were also basing most of their logistics on board a ship moored near Umm Qasr to reduce exposure to potential threats.

My planners were also tasked to prepare a presentation on the Umm Qasr area regarding future tasks and the security situation for the next six months. MG Blackman would take the presentation. We were also continuing our work on redeployment of forces currently in theater.

My C5 redeployment team held another session on the overall sequence of redeployment tasks and integration of movement to Kuwait and within Kuwait. In the short term, there was one key chokepoint—wash racks for heavy cleaning requirements. CFLCC had to closely monitor the flow of units through the vehicle cleaning area in Kuwait. All US equipment, especially equipment returning to the continental US, HAD to meet US Department of Agriculture (USDA) standards, and be inspected by USDA personnel. We pointed out that if the Saudi port of Al Jubayl was not available for use by Marine forces, then redeployment through Kuwait would need to be sequential, and thus would be longer in duration. The Saudis would never allow us to use their ports to depart the theater, but we did not learn this until much later on.

I received a proposed briefing on CENTCOM's Phase IV from LTC Agoglia of the CENTCOM J5. GEN Franks would receive the presentation on 26 April, and pending his approval it would go to Secretary Rumsfeld on 28 April. There was nothing surprising about the presentation itself, as my planners put a great deal of effort into refining the presentation, and LTG McKiernan approved what we proposed. I was headed to Qatar on April 26 for a redeployment conference, and I reported I'd try to get into GEN Franks's briefing.

There were other actors in play. The enemy continued to exercise his vote on our operations. Our J2 reported Tikrit was the most contentious city in Iraq. The city was a safe haven for forces attempting to disrupt Coalition stability operations. Near al-Kut, various Shia factions were contending for power. I MEF had its hands full in the area. Finally, al Qaim was still a hot spot and we were trying to find troops to send there.

CJTF-Iraq

I traveled to CENTCOM forward headquarters on 26 April, D+37. This was one of "those" days, as it revealed how decisions are really taken when people are under pressure and seeking some release therefrom. I wrote my daily report from Qatar.

The ostensible purpose of the trip was to attend a redeployment conference. The team which accompanied me spent time coordinating for our presentations at the redeployment conference. I continued to stress the need for CENTCOM action on Saudi Arabian ports as an absolutely necessary part of any thought of a rapid retrograde from theater. My point was that without a Saudi port we would be in a sequential retrograde situation given the known chokepoints of wash racks at Arifjan, Camp Doha, and the Kuwait Naval Base. While I met with COL Fitzgerald, I learned that GEN Franks was holding a meeting on what headquarters would serve as CJTF-Iraq. He would also go over the final draft presentation to Secretary Rumsfeld on the CENTCOM view of Phase IV. I knew I had to attend.

I went to see the CENTCOM J3, MG Renuart. I told him I learned of the meeting, the topics for discussion and I was here to represent LTG McKiernan. Renuart said he was not sure GEN Franks would allow me to attend. I suggested we go to see GEN Franks and ask. Renuart demurred. He then told me I could attend the meeting but not to speak at it.

It was a very interesting meeting, an understatement to be sure. GEN Franks sat at the head of the table, his long legs resting on top. He was smoking a cigarette and very much at ease. LTG Abizaid, MG Renuart, RADM Robb, MG Whitcomb, the CENTCOM chief of staff, COL Halverson, and COL Fitzgerald all sat around the long conference table. I sat along the wall of the room.

The first topic of the meeting was the final draft COMCENT presentation to Secretary Rumsfeld on Phase IV. The discussion on the briefing revolved around chartology vice what would be spoken. Franks wanted to convey a concept in the charts, a concept of stability operations and retrograde over time; he also directed no unit symbols be used on the charts as "map symbols have no meaning for this guy." Franks wanted color-coded unit areas along Iraqi governate lines. The areas covered by colors associated with units would show the pace of retrograde and increasing span of control of a decreasing number of units, US and Coalition. The chart in the final draft presentation showing the decreasing units over time would be modified to show the components' retrograde of forces, again reinforcing the pace of retrograde. I reported I would send the latest briefing as soon as I could get a copy. I assured my generals I would remain engaged in the development process.

RADM Robb remarked that Rumsfeld would likely want to discuss the long-term theater posture. LTG Abizaid agreed this topic would come up. Franks talked at length, saying his words were not guidance but thoughts. I wrote as fast as I could. Franks directed his CCJ5 to prepare a map of the region to include the countries currently under consideration for addition to the CENTCOM AOR: India, Georgia, Armenia, Azerbaijan, Israel, and Lebanon. He wanted the following placed on the map: CENTCOM FWD in Qatar with a three-star flag, CENTAF FWD in Qatar with a two-star flag, NAVCENT in Bahrain with a three-star flag, SOCCENT in Qatar with a crisis response element and a one-star flag, ARCENT FWD in Kuwait with a two-star flag, along with the land- and sea-based forward-positioned stocks of equipment, Special Forces companies in Djibouti, Afghanistan, and Uzbekistan.

Franks said since we did not have assigned forces in the region, we could not have the principal headquarters in the region, but we could put forward headquarters. The presence of forward headquarters would give the regional combatant commander the capability to stand up various air-, sea-, or land-centric joint task forces. Franks said he wanted a squadron of USAF fighter aircraft based at Al Udeid Air Base; this squadron could train with Gulf Cooperation Council air forces. Franks demonstrated a real depth of understanding of both the direction he felt Washington would go in, and what Secretary Rumsfeld would support. It was a bravura performance by a man who really understood his region. Then he turned to Iraq.

Franks directed JTF-Iraq be a numbered Joint Task Force (JTF-7). The story of how CFLCC became CJTF-7 was much more interesting. LTG Abizaid spoke of the need for a seasoned headquarters to establish the conditions required for attaining policy objectives. Franks agreed and said, "CFLCC." There was a pause, then LTG Abizaid asked what number the JTF headquarters should receive. There was another pause. Whitcomb chuckled and said, "I recommend JTF-69." The men around the table laughed. Mike Fitzgerald looked at me as I scribbled in my notebook. Franks took a deep drag on his cigarette and said, "Nah, call 'em JTF-1369 cause they're gonna be some unlucky cocksuckers." There was another eruption of laughter.

Mike Fitzgerald poked MG Renuart, who looked at me and quickly said, "I recommend JTF-7." General Franks said, "Approved." Then LTG Abizaid saw me taking notes and said he did not know I had been there since the start of the meeting. He directed I come to see him immediately afterward. Franks laughed again, looked at me, and asked if I'd gotten the gist of the discussion down. I assured him I did, to more laughter. This was how the decision was made to put CFLCC in charge in Iraq, and how the number of the task force was decided upon. The CENTCOM map board reflected JTF-180 in Afghanistan and JTF-7 in Iraq.

As far as post-hostilities Army training in the region, GEN Franks said he thought the right presence level was two battalion rotations/year based on prepositioned equipment in Kuwait and two battalion rotations/year based on prepositioned equipment in Qatar, to exercise the equipment. Franks also wanted to base an Army tri-hulled high-speed transport in Qatar to move the Qatar rotation units around the region to extend training opportunities with Oman and Pakistan. He also suggested an ARCENT-"Stans" for consideration, as Secretary Rumsfeld was considering adding the "Stans" region of former Soviet republics to the CENTCOM area.

Africa was also mentioned; GEN Franks directed the map used to brief Secretary Rumsfeld also show all of Africa as hash marked, and stated he would suggest Africa be designated a four-star sub-unified command under the commander CENTCOM.

This was a breath-taking meeting. We had not yet met any of the conditions for attaining the policy objective, but we received sweeping guidance on the proposed future development of the CENTCOM area of operations, where headquarters would be, and the scope of Army training opportunities in a post-war theater.

Thankfully, some C5 officers I had brought with me, MAJs Huelfer and Innocenti, attended the meeting on the new Iraqi Army. They de-briefed me, and I directed they write an executive summary report attached to the briefing presented by officers from the Department of Defense. I reported I believed we would receive a FRAGO directing many un-resourced tasks associated with the stand-up of the new Iraqi Army, and that I would remain engaged in the development of these Rumsfeld briefings. I also stated our C5 liaison officers in Qatar, LTCs Stewart and Sutherland, were doing a great job representing CFLCC.

The final note I recorded at the end of the day had to do with my thoughts on SAMS. I wrote, "Must have Army officers and GOs in all CINC-doms, esp. TRANSCOM. SAMS thought: remember 507th Maint… everyone must know how to fight."

I wrote the C5 Plans Update for 27 April, D+38, from Qatar. I attended the redeployment conference, as well as running down answers to questions which popped up during the meetings on 26 April concerning CFLCC being named CJTF-7. I earned my pay this day.

Retrograde, CJTF-7, and Who Follows Whom?

I reported on the first day of the conference. It began with a VTC with officers from TRANSCOM. A TRANSCOM colonel articulated a series of assumptions TRANSCOM was making regarding planning for the redeployment of forces. While there was nothing too radical in the presentation, we made it a point to acquire a copy of his paper before we left Qatar.

The CENTCOM J5 representative proposed all components have periodic planner-level VTCs/meetings to review redeployment priorities and flow. There was no opposition to this proposal, as we all understood the retrograde from Iraq was conditions-based, and a change in conditions might affect the flow of forces. This concerned TRANSCOM in its legitimate quest for effective use of ships and planes. This conference reinforced LTG McKiernan's intuition that everyone would be itching to get the hell of out Dodge. There were other extant assumptions at play in this conference.

The folks in the CENTCOM J5 worked under the assumption V Corps would follow CFLCC as CJTF-7. Since GEN Franks took the decision naming CFLCC

CJTF-7 on 26 April, I did not know where this assumption came from and no one in the CENTCOM J5 could explain it either. It made some sense to think along this line, however. The further assumption was that the ARRC would follow V Corps as CJTF-7. There was absolutely nothing to really substantiate this assumption. I rather thought it represented wishful thinking.

I repeated LTG McKiernan's presentation from the component commanders VTC on our view of Phase IV and redeployment. I added to the presentation the two charts of anticipated priority Army forces and Marine forces for retrograde. There were some inconsistencies in our priorities and the charts from the CENTCOM presentation to Secretary Rumsfeld, primarily in the timing of the retrograde of divisions. This was not a problem, as we were consistent in stating that the retrograde is conditions based. MARCENT planners believed there would not be a problem in simultaneous retrograde of Army and Marine units.

MARCENT intended to retrograde the regiments based on the amphibious task forces first. These regiments had less heavy equipment than the MPS based regiments, the 5th and 7th Marines. MARCENT believed the wash racks being built at Kuwait Naval Base could handle the washing and loading requirements of the amphibious task force, ATF. The challenge of MPS based regiments remained on the horizon, but in the short term this meant we could or should be able to retrograde both elements of the 1st Marine Division and the 3rd Infantry Division.

CFSOCC intended to send a message releasing all conventional units back to CFLCC for retrograde. The British did not intend to use Umm Qasr for retrograde, which would mean returning to England based on the shallow channel to the port. The British intended to use Shuaybah port and Kuwait City International Airport.

The Australians stated they needed to return to Kuwait and needed to use two of our Doha wash racks for about forty-five days to meet the really stringent Australian Ministry of the Interior requirements for cleanliness. We had to work with the Aussies. We suggested they investigate the use of Qatar and ARCENT-Q wash racks. The retrograde of forces, our own and Coalition, was going to be difficult (another huge understatement).

The ongoing effort to continually refine and update our operational plans was going reasonably well. While I was in Qatar, I assisted in refining the charts for the Rumsfeld Phase IV presentation and sent a copy back to the command group. I learned that LTG Abizaid would give the presentation, although I did not know when the briefing would take place, but reported I felt certain I would not be able to get into the room. I also talked to RADM Robb, who requested CFLCC help in getting information out to NGOs and PVOs regarding military points of contact in various cities within Iraq. NGOs/PVOs needed to know what the on-ground situation was in the familiar terms of permissive, semi-permissive, and hostile. RADM Robb requested this information be made unclassified and accessible via the Internet. I knew COL Stanton was already working on this with our computer technicians.

I learned there would be a third in the series of Interim Iraqi Authority meetings. The third meeting would be held in the north, likely in either Kirkuk or Irbil. This meeting would be held within ten to fourteen days, possibly sooner. The final meeting would be held in Baghdad, and was scheduled for the end of May.

Finally, I spoke with MAJ Kevin Marcus, V Corps planner, regarding the battle handover of CJTF-7 from CFLCC to V Corps. I reminded MAJ Marcus that LTG McKiernan had not yet weighed in on this proposal, especially given, as far as I knew, he just learned CFLCC had the mission much less having time to consider a handover to V Corps. I told MAJ Marcus CFLCC C5 would continue our work on courses of action for the incorporation of Coalition forces, and the general conditions for the end state of Phase IVB, as we saw it. I told MAJ Marcus we would continue to refine this and other planning tasks, and handover to him as complete a product as we could in order to assist in the V Corps planning and execution effort, pending LTG McKiernan's guidance. Marcus requested that CFLCC issue a formal warning order and planning directive as soon as possible. We did not know it yet, but we were anticipating another headquarters transition.

The C5 Plans Update for 28 April, D+39, reflected our continued focus on redeployment. There were other signs indicating directions of thought from Washington which were interesting but at the time did not seem to be overly important given our tasks at hand. I was in Qatar for another day of the redeployment conference and thus did not have a picture of what was going on in Iraq.

It was day two of the CENTCOM sponsored redeployment conference. We learned CFSOCC could not retrograde the 10th Special Forces Group through Turkey, therefore we had to expect to execute the retrograde through Kuwait. This added more units through the few vehicle wash points available there. I stressed to the CENTCOM J5 that GEN Franks needed to articulate a priority among components in order to reduce the potential for friction. Colonel Fitzgerald asked me for an estimate on the number of USDA certified inspectors we would need to sustain throughout through the wash racks. All our equipment had to meet USDA standards, especially equipment headed back to the US Our logistics planners estimated we needed three times the number of wash racks in use in order to sustain 24hr operations at the wash points. Going home was going to be difficult.

During the buildup of forces, we built an elevated causeway from floating pier assets embarked on our MPS ships. The NAVCENT planners raised the point of the elevated causeway and asked for an estimate on how long we would need to retain it in theater, as NAVCENT needed to reembark the causeway system onto MPS shipping. The causeway reduced friction with the Kuwaitis, as we were taking up berth space for our resupply ships in the Kuwaitis only port.

RADM Robb concluded the conference by announcing that his planners would be sending out a draft redeployment message for review. The message would contain a request for details on redeployment TPFDD development in force modules in order to assist TRANSCOM in the running of feasibility models for shipping and airplanes. The anticipated suspense for the effort was 21 May. Robb recognized the CFLCC piece was the largest of this effort, and said he would understand requests for an extension if it became necessary.

OPLAN refinement such as it was focused on Phase IV and redeploying forces. I also sent an update on the initiative to rebuild the Iraqi Army, along with an executive summary of the effort to COL Eshelmann.

I acknowledged a task set by LTG McKiernan to lead a plans team to write and release a redeployment order by 4 May. The team included V Corps, I MEF, 377th TSC, ARCENT-K, MLC, and others from the CFLCC Staff.

I sent out an updated version of GEN Franks's presentation to Secretary Rumsfeld on Phase IV and redeployment to McKiernan. I learned Phase IV would not be named as such, but I could not find out the "why" behind this. My friends on the CENTCOM staff, COLs Mike Fitzgerald and Dave Halverson, told me the expectation was that President Bush would announce a cessation of hostilities on or about 1 May. The three of us could not see the sense in this, given we had not captured or killed Saddam and his sons. The best we could discern was that such a declaration would meet requirements for other nations to join the Coalition stabilizing Iraq. We also talked about the post-hostilities version of the theater engagement strategy.

Colonels Fitzgerald and Halverson speculated that the developing theater engagement strategy, which had been outlined in a slide shown in the Rumsfeld presentation, would be based in part on CONPLAN 1025 or, and this was a big difference, OPLAN 1020. These operations plans were focused on Iran. Our discussion was limited on this topic, as it was mostly COL Fitzgerald's speculation. I observed that given his standing with GEN Franks, he was usually a good source.

I was returning to Camp Doha and acknowledged a meeting with LTG McKiernan on redeployment and Phase IV. I also reported that I had sent a proposed Phase IV mission and commander's intent to COL Eshelman and MG Blackman, as directed.

My plans update for 29 April, D+40, continued in the current vein of work on redeployment and update work on post-hostilities plans. I also reported on a SecDef VTC. These were my priorities for CFLCC. Planners were looking ahead.

In my journal entry of this day, I noted a great session with the 377th TSC on redeployment. Once again, I acknowledged the requirement to have our redeployment order done by 4 May. The first session with the redeployment plans team was scheduled for 30 April. Our guidance: write an order, not a telephone book-sized campaign plan. CFLCC would focus on the larger operational level, referring to the more detailed 377th order for back up.

I acknowledged a task to write a "personal for" note, P4, to GEN Franks requesting policy guidance on Turkish forces in northern Iraq. As we moved forces into northern Iraq, we increasingly encountered Turkish forces operating there to conduct counter-guerilla operations against Kurdish irregulars.

I sent the latest version of my proposed Phase IV mission and intent back to COL Eshelmann and the chief of staff. This version was based on feedback from LTG McKiernan. I reported I would stand by for further edits as required. McKiernan, recalling his time during the First Gulf War, stressed that our units would be akin to "horses smelling the barn." In writing this order and working with our subordinate units, I was to stress the importance of attention to detail and teamwork. McKiernan told us going home would be twice as hard as getting to the war. He was "more interested in getting people home than equipment," but clearly recognized the importance of getting our Army and Marine Corps reset for the next fight.

I attended a SECDEF VTC on 29 April. Deputy Secretary of Defense Wolfowitz, Mr. Feith, Dr. Zakheim, GEN Myers, GEN Pace, and LTG Sharp were present. Deputy Secretary of Defense Wolfowitz and LTG Garner did most of the talking during this session. The latter described the Baghdad "town hall" meeting he and MG Webster held on 29 April. Garner described how a series of citizen committees focused on security were the outcome of this meeting. Garner appointed MG Strock, based on an Iraqi request for an American, as the de facto "city manager" for Baghdad for the next thirty or so days. Mr. De Rita, Rumsfeld's on the ground representative, also gave a short but positive description of the interim Iraqi authority, IIA, meeting; in so doing, he was very positive about the CFLCC contribution. Mr. De Rita announced the next meeting would be in about thirty days and would be held in the north. I recommended CENTCOM J5 and ORHA select the site.

I reported my planners remained engaged with the redevelopment of the Iraqi Army effort. There was no new information on this effort to pass on. Finally, I reported my planners also remained engaged on the development of theater engagement strategy and CONPLAN 1025.

Our plans work went on while our intelligence folks were reporting on the activities of SCIRI in Iraq. SCIRI, we learned, was quietly supporting Coalition efforts in Iraq. Our assessment of this SCIRI effort: SCIRI was angling for a larger role in the post-war Iraqi government, and in society. The CENTCOM J2, from my notes, was covering tactical-level detail and passing on the development of credible intelligence indicating al Qaeda was planning attacks on the US from within Saudi Arabia.

The C5 Plans Update for 30 April, D+41, reflected the mundane work of being a planner. My officers were hard at work crafting the order to redeploy the forces which started this fight while coordinating the arrival of relieving US and Coalition forces. I highlighted key officers loaned to us from other organizations who were leaving, and the range of other tasks my team was completing. 30 April was also the day Secretary Rumsfeld visited Baghdad.

Redeployment planning work was going full bore. I led a session with our full OPG to inform all these great folks of the redeployment effort. I then held a follow-on session with the smaller redeployment plans team. My planners and I put out the timeline required to meet a 4 May deadline. My planners collected all staff planning efforts done at the time and would meet the deadline. We found a copy of the 1991 retrograde and redeployment plan. It was 35 pages in length and was our standard. Our liaison officer from the Center for Army Analysis, Captain Max Moore, departed 30 April. He had developed superb force tracking tools which materially assisted our efforts in monitoring the flow of forces into theater. As we anticipated, there was growing competition for the use of space on the vehicle wash racks.

We were beginning to see the extent of the demand for the limited wash points as unanticipated units from other components arrived asking/demanding time on the wash racks. Coordinating wash rack use demanded careful and hard-nosed management. I mention this as the 377th TSC needed LTG McKiernan's top cover, given that units' demands would quickly escalate to general officer level. We were also seeing more units arrive at Camp Doha looking for hardstand and billets. A potential friction point was the impending demise of Marine Corps led Joint Task Force-Consequence Management, JTF-CM, and the retrograde of the Coalition chemical defense units, all of whom, in the short term, had to go through wash procedures of varying degrees and redeploy through the Kuwaiti port. My planners worked with the 377th to incorporate these Coalition units into the overall flow.

We were not really refining operations plans at this moment but responding to a range of tasks from LTG McKiernan and our command group. I completed the final draft of LTG McKiernan's "personal for" message to GEN Franks requesting policy guidancc on Turkish forces in northern Iraq and was standing by for final approval.[4] I acknowledged approval of the proposed stability operations mission and intent. My planners coordinated with CENTCOM J3 and J5 on a proposed meeting in Qatar to write a plan of action for ORHA. We completed a draft of the C5 presentation for the CFLCC commanders' conference and sent copies to COL Eshelmann, Terry Moran, and MGs Webster, Stratman, and Blackman for review.

My planners remained on standby to answer ORHA questions regarding the redevelopment of the Iraqi Army. ORHA coordinated the release of requests for proposals to a range of companies interested in bidding on this important work.

4 A "personal for" or sometimes "P4" message is a special communication between commanders. The personal for message is delivered directly to the addressee and no one else. This type of communication is only used to raise important issues.

We also continued to refine courses of action on incorporating Coalition forces into ongoing stability operations, since we were now responsible for all of CENTCOM Phase IV. I reported we were sharing this work with V Corps under the assumption V Corps would follow CFLCC as CJTF-Iraq. LTG McKiernan was not pleased with this, but pending GEN Franks's decision there was nothing we could do.

In the background of my planners' efforts, we were dealing with issues ranging from reorganizing an Iraqi police force, giving permission for these people to carry sidearms, and working with returning finance ministry workers to re-establish Iraqi currency. The Saddam dinar was a favorite souvenir, but Iraqi merchants would only accept US dollars, which was not good for long-term economic growth. Suddenly, officers with MBAs and undergraduate economics degrees were in demand. We were monitoring Chalabi's efforts across Iraq to build a power base.

April 2003 was a momentous month for me and my planners. We watched Cobra II unfold as we scrambled to develop and write Eclipse II. At the month's end we were anticipating another headquarters transition, and I was worried about how we would establish the necessary minimum security conditions for success as we looked to the ultimate end of, as LTGs Abizaid and McKiernan constantly said, "put[ting] an Iraqi face on the government."

Below is a message GEN Franks sent to the chairman of the Joint Chiefs indicating his intent to establish a three-star-level command headquarters for post-hostilities. I do not know when it was actually sent.

> DELIVER DURING NORMAL DUTY HOURS//
>
> PERSONAL FOR CJCS, GEN MYERS; INFO SECDEF, SECRETARY RUMSFELD; DEPSECDEF, DEPUTY SECRETARY WOLFOWITZ: VCJCS, GEN PACE; CSA, GEN SHINSEKI; CNO, ADM CLARK; CMC, GEN JONES; CSAF, GEN JUMPER; CUSAC, LTG MCKIERNAN; CUSNC, VADM KEATING; CUSMC, LTGEN HAILSTON; CUSCA, LT GEN MOSELEY; CSC, BG HARRELL; CJTF180, LTG MCNEILL FROM GENERAL FRANKS//
>
> MSGID/GENADMIN/CCJ3-PP//
>
> SUBJ: ESTABLISHMENT OF COMBINED JOINT TASK FORCE IRAQ (CJTF-4)
>
> RMKS/ 1. CHAIRMAN, AS PREVIOUSLY DISCUSSED, IN ORDER TO ENHANCE UNITY OF COMMAND FOR POST-HOSTILITY OPERATIONS IN IRAQ, I INTEND TO ESTABLISH COMBINED JOINT TASK FORCE IRAQ (CJTF-4).
>
> 2. THE MISSION OF CJTF-4 WILL BE TO CONDUCT SECURITY, STABILITY AND CIVIL-MILITARY OPERATIONS AS APPROPRIATE IN ORDER TO ENHANCE REGIONAL SECURITY.
>
> 3. BASED ON CAREFUL ANALYSIS, A 3 STAR CORPS EQUIVALENT COMMANDER, ESTABLISHED DURING PHASE III OF THE CAMPAIGN, WILL ALLOW ME TO

> OVERSEE AND EXECUTE PHASE IV OPERATIONS WITHIN IRAQ. MY DESIRE IS TO EXECUTE THE TRANSFER OF AUTHORITY, O/O, DURING PHASE III OPERATIONS. WE WILL CONTINUE TO EVALUATE OPPORTUNITIES TO EMPLOY COALITION FORCES TO COMPLEMENT OUR EFFORTS.
>
> 4. ONCE AGAIN CHAIRMAN, I WANT TO EXPRESS MY THANKS FOR YOUR CONTINUED SUPPORT. WE STAND READY TO EXECUTE BASED ON YOUR EXORD. RESPECTFULLY, TOM.//

At the beginning of a briefing I was giving to MG Webster, and prior to him leaving for Baghdad in late April 2003, MG Webster asked me, "Kevin, how long is Phase IV going to last?" I replied "Sir, I think it will last three to five years." To which MG Webster replied, "Oh, bullshit."

I was incorrect. We were in Iraq much longer.

CHAPTER SEVEN

Building the Coalition, May 2003

The month I cover in this chapter was truly significant. Decisions taken during this month set the stage for what came to pass during a very long campaign. Our attempts at thinking through key decision points were for naught, as we were unable to communicate effectively with senior leaders in Washington. We could not convey what we understood to be the facts on the ground and the ever-changing nature of the situation in Iraq.

I did not render a report on 1 May 2003, as I traveled to Baghdad for a CFLCC commanders' conference. I had been looking forward to this event, as it would allow me a chance to talk to the division commanders and receive their feedback on how the plan was received and how it fared during execution.

The CENTCOM J2 reported that ISG investigators had found an underground facility the size of a football field. Investigators found reports dated back to 1990. The document exploitation folks were very excited. The J2 also reported on Badr Corps activity in southern Iraq based on the British intercepting a courier. We had the Badr Corps plan on how it would extend influence in the south. J2 also developed credible intelligence on impending al Qaeda operations in Saudi Arabia.

We learned from CENTCOM that the President had authorized us to use seized funds. This approval took only two weeks, which was remarkably fast. Finally, on 1 May CFLCC officially became CJTF-7. I hoped we would not be as unlucky as GEN Franks had joked.

The highlight event of 2 May, D+44, was the commanders' conference held in the ballroom of Al Faw Palace. At the time, we faced isolated incidents conducted by remnants of regime forces across Iraq. The conference focus was on training, what we had learned from the initial fighting to Baghdad, ongoing stability operations, and redeployment. LTG McKiernan proposed thinking about training and readiness akin to the Navy's carrier battle group approach. He suggested our Army forces would spend three to four months on alert or deployed, three to four months getting ready for alert status or deployment, and three to four months in a cadre status, during which time individuals would move, go to school, and so on.

He also stated he believed in the standing joint force headquarters' approach to command and control of forces. These standing headquarters would organize around land, sea, and air specific missions. McKiernan also told the assembled senior commanders and staffs that the Third Army was the correct land centric basis for a standing joint force headquarters. In my journal entry of this day, I wrote that this approach "means breaking lots of rice bowls."

I noted that CFLCC needed to remain sensitive to the Coalition chemical units which were a part of CJTF-Consequence Management. The CENTCOM J5 sent some notes indicating our State Department wanted us to find out whether or not these chemical units could be used as a form of site reconnaissance teams for sensitive site exploitation. Using Coalition chemical units in support of these missions would enhance the willingness of the Coalition to take steps to find and destroy these weapons.

My section continued work on the draft redeployment FRAGO. LTG McKiernan indicated he wanted us to fly a copy of the order to Baghdad on 4 May for his personal review and mark up. I intended to send copies to planners from V Corps, I MEF, and the 377th TSC so those commanders would not be surprised. My planners were working with 377th TSC on the detailed agenda for the daily redeployment VTCs scheduled to begin 6 May. The commanders at the table in the ballroom were interested to hear about the details of these conferences. My other planner work continued unabated.

I was still receiving notes on a possible meeting with the CENTCOM J3 and J5 to "write a plan" for ORHA. I did not think this was necessary, but informed the MG Blackman that I would find out why there was a perceived need for the meeting. My C5 planners remained on standby to answer ORHA questions regarding the redevelopment of the Iraqi Army. Finally, my planners continued to refine courses of action on incorporating Coalition forces, as well as other work that would have been a part of Aurora, the base plan of the now defunct JTF-4. I indicated we were sharing this work with V Corps under the assumption that V Corps follows CFLCC as CJTF-Iraq.

I took advantage of the presence of the fighting commanders to ask their views on SAMS graduates and what I would need to stress in my role as the incoming director of the school. MG Chuck Swannack, commanding general of the 82nd Airborne, told me SAMS educated planners needed to know the decision-making process so well that they could accelerate it. He found that during operations, he relied on a running estimate and the products from this running estimate. He said he did not have time for the process of decision making; rather, he needed clear options and executable decisions.

MG Dave Petraeus, commanding general of the 101st Air Assault, told me to balance theory with tools for the fight. He said the commander's intent was so important that he gave writing this short paragraph his full attention and trusted his planners to 1) understand his intent, 2) derive tasks and the purpose of those tasks for his brigade commanders, and 3) most importantly, to determine resources for the brigades in accord with determining the main and supporting efforts.

MG "Buff" Blount, commanding general of the 3rd Infantry Division, told me he relied on his planners to assist him in developing his personal running estimate during the fight. He suggested instructing SAMS educated officers on how to balance process and product before the fight began.

MGs Swannack, Petraeus, Blount, and Kratzer of the 377th all told me they would come to SAMS and speak to officers in class. LTGs Wallace and Conway also committed to come to Fort Leavenworth to speak. This was a historic day. I gathered my thoughts on the flight back to Kuwait. I was trying to balance my excitement for my impending upcoming new job with the feeling we were not yet done with Iraq.

I returned to my routine of sending a planning note to the chief of staff and two deputy commanders on 3 May, D+45. In this note I made certain these three knew about a proposed speaking role for CFLCC at the Polish force generation conference in Warsaw. My planners continued to work on refining our force packages. We received word that the Czech chemical unit in CJTF-CM would redeploy to the Czech Republic and would not be available for use in sensitive site exploitation in Iraq. Czech national policy precluded this use. My planners monitored the redeployment, as it might have affected our own movement of forces. We completed a draft redeployment FRAGO on 3 May.

I reviewed the draft redeployment. It was very good, and cross-walked with MEF, Corps, and 377th orders and planners. I wrote that I would transmit the order on 4 May. We were still trying to arrange a flight up to Baghdad for two planners to talk through the order with LTG McKiernan. I also reported we sent a draft agenda and slides to 377th TSC on the daily redeployment VTCs. I recommended we should stick with starting the VTCs on 6 May, pending the release of the redeployment order and sending out the proposed slides for the VTC.

My planners also continued work on OPLAN refinement. I reported that there were two conferences on force generation coming up. The first was on 8 May in London hosted by the British Permanent Joint Headquarters, PJHQ. There was no speaking role for CFLCC/CJTF-7, but we would participate in the conference. The second was on or around 15 May in Warsaw. This conference required a speaking role for CFLCC/CJTF-7, at the request of the Polish Land Forces Command. European Command hosted this conference. We were asked to speak on the role that we expected a Polish led division to assume in post hostility operations. At the time, I wrote that I did not expect I would be the one to attend both of these conferences, thinking one of our general officers would represent the command.

As usual, my section was dealing with a range of tasks from the Pentagon and CENTCOM. I received a tasking from CENTCOM to review a series of questions from one of the many deputy assistant secretaries of defense on the CENTCOM response to Secretary Rumsfeld's regional strategy questions. CENTCOM developed its product based on the input we gave to the CENTCOM J5. I sent the CENTCOM J5 briefing and the list of questions to Baghdad and the command group. I assured the command group my planners and I were working on this effort and would meet the suspense of 6 May for review. C5 planners also worked on a review of a draft CENTCOM J3 FRAGO on the initial operations associated with the establishment of the new Iraqi Army. We non-concurred with a number of tasks the CENTCOM J3 proposed CFLCC take on in the development of this force.

Finally, I reported my planners wrote a proposed email for MG Thurman to send to the CENTCOM J3 on Coalition force integration. We were trying to set conditions for a better integration process of forces as we faced the potential (and hoped for) integration of Coalition divisions. Bearing in mind "hope was not a method" we remained hopeful our Coalition partners would send complete divisions for operations, much as the British had from the start. As we learned later, only the Poles volunteered to do this, and even they sent no more than a brigade's worth of troops along with a division headquarters.

Of course, our operations in Iraq continued. On this date, I noted in my journal that al Sadr was telling his followers to cooperate with the Coalition, which was outwardly good news. The SCIRI leader Hakim was coming to Baghdad to talk. Around Iraq it appeared the Shia communities were coming together in a political sense. They were not, as yet, opposing the Coalition, but I asked myself what this might mean for Iraq.

Ahmed Chalabi and his representatives were posting police in Tikrit. These police carried a vetting letter to US forces from the Iraqi National Congress. The Kurdish Democratic Party began displacing people from homes in the north, Kirkuk, ostensibly to counter Saddam's Arabization policies. The people being displaced were Turkomen, a Turkish "red line." The center of Iraq was outwardly calm. In Baghdad, there was a growing shortage of liquid propane gas. This raised the potential for demonstrations, as the people were dependent upon the government supplying this cooking fuel. There was a reminder of the second theater of war in CENTCOM's area. We were directed to move CH-47 Chinook helicopter units to Afghanistan. CJTF-7/CFLCC would receive National Guard C-23 Sherpa units, a fixed-wing aircraft, as a backfill for inter-theater transport missions.

The report of 4 May, D+46, reflected shifts in the political landscape of Iraq, as well as in our view of the situation. It also provided further evidence that the use of force is an extension of policy. I reported I was continuing work on the London force generation conference. Our role in this one was observer as all of the invited nations; Spain, Denmark, Holland, and Norway, expressed a desire to work for the UK division and in the UK zone. More specifically, we were to answer questions on likely tasks that would come up in Phase IV, and others that might arise. The Warsaw conference was now scheduled for 22/23 May. The Poles, we learned on

4 May, did not want to be assigned to the northern sector between the Kurds and the Turks. I expected there would be more to follow on this situation. It appeared there were no other nations willing to send a division headquarters. This looming fact meant more mission analysis by my planners once the force generation conferences had concluded.

From my journal notes, I wrote that two groups had emerged on the Iraqi political landscape, the National Front for the Salvation of Iraq, and the High Commission for Iraqi Liberation. The National Front was attempting to expand across the country and form a legitimate political base. Our intelligence assessment concluded this was a potential obstructionist group. Our intelligence section focused on refining our knowledge base of this group and its leaders. The second group, the High Commission, based its operations in Baghdad. Its first task was to arrange a march of a hundred thousand men in the city. We had no conclusion as yet on this group.

Our Washington, D.C., based Department of the Army staff was becoming aware of the potentially long-term nature of this campaign. We were working with them on a replacement headquarters for the 377th TSC. I wrote, "We will be here for a long time. DA needs to look at the fix as the Arifjan mission will be continuing for at least another eight more months." Clearly I was in an optimistic mood on this day.

My 5 May daily report was rather thin, although there was a great deal going on in theater. In my journal I recorded notes from our operations and intelligence update from the southern, northern, and central regions of Iraq. In terms of the south, I noted the British were "working on a pair of bad guys in the city government of Basrah. The people don't like the two either." I did not write down the names of the two bad guys.

In the north, V Corps was also dealing with the difficulties of governance and the local peoples' response to government officials. I noted a key factor the growing difficulties was the lack of fuel for cooking. We were in a country which was producing crude oil but finding it difficult to sustain a supply of liquid propane for cooking. I wrote, "Maslow's hierarchy in play again."

The central region of the country, primarily in terms of action in Baghdad, revolved around rumors of who would be the future prime minister. The favorite, based on intelligence gathered 5 May, was a former pre-Saddam minister named Pachee, although I was not sure of the exact spelling of his name. There were also reports of a planned assassination attempt on LTG Garner. We increased Garner's security detachment and continued to follow up on this information thread. The final report was on the development of political party related media. The Kurdish PUK had a newspaper and radio station in Baghdad. The Iraqi National Congress and SCIRI both had newspapers, radio, and TV stations. The Iraqi Communist Party also published a newspaper.

We conducted our standard secure VTC with Central Command as well. Of note from it were comments from GEN Franks on the news; he wanted us to consider having our Public Affairs Office give periodic tactical event news updates in conjunction with scheduled ORHA press conferences. GEN Franks told us we had "dropped off the scope as far as news since Wilkinson [the White House press office representative] left."

Our chief of staff, MG Blackman, asked if our staff was properly organized for Phase IV, and also said that he had some misgivings, although when I asked him he could not cite any specific examples. He asked me to consider where the Coalition was going, not where we wanted it to go. Of major significance, we learned that LTG McKiernan was starting talks with former Iraqi general officers about the future of the Iraqi Army. This was good news, as my planners and I did not assume we could recall the Iraqi regular army, we accepted this as a fact, since the army was one of the two institutions in Iraq which pre-dated the Ba'ath Party and Saddam. The other was the Iraqi bureaucracy. Later on, we learned to our dismay that both of these presumed "facts" were in error. I also followed up on the upcoming force generation conferences.

I reported I spoke with COL Fitzgerald on the London and Warsaw conferences on the evening of 5 May. I learned it seemed the Poles did want to go into the north, which is not what I had initially thought. It turned out it was CENTCOM J5 and our Joint Chiefs of Staff that suggested the Poles take the central division sector. The reason was we, CJTF-7/CFLCC, had to supply them and the array of forces making up the Polish-led division. I also learned the Polish "division" would consist of some 4500 soldiers (essentially a division headquarters and one brigade). The remainder of the division's troop units would come from other nations. I offered we might be forced to assume either a population focused or task focused course of action for the employment of Coalition divisions in the latter stages of this portion of the campaign. I wrote I believed we could only count on three divisions—UK, Polish, and US—for the continuation of Phase IV. I assured MG Blackman I would remain engaged in this process and keep all informed.

The C5 Plans Update for 6 May, D+48, reflected our continuing work refining our operational plans and preparing our forces for redeployment. My planners and I were also monitoring CENTCOM J3 and J5 actions on the new Iraqi Corps and ORHA.

We held the first redeployment VTC this day, and as we expected it was well attended. This was the preliminary session, thus we went through proposed slides to monitor the flow of forces through the process of redeployment. Based on feedback, my planners held an after-action review within C5/35/4 and with the 377th TSC planners after the VTC to further refine the slides. We established the sequencing of the conferences, and given the pressure from Washington to up the pace of bringing troops home, we determined there would be five working sessions per week. General officers attended the VTC once a week for a wrap-up of the effort and for potential problem resolution. Majors Whitlock and Davis of C5, and Colonel Dougherty of

377th TSC, acted as the lead planners for the redeployment effort. We posted the redeployment operations order on the CFLCC/CJTF-7 website.

At LTG McKiernan's request, my planners and I briefed him on command-and-control relationships we had and did not have with Coalition forces in the Iraq theater of operations, ITO. McKiernan directed that we establish a relationship with the Saudi, UAE, and Jordanian hospitals through the HOC in Baghdad. We also covered the upcoming force generation conferences and the current state of potential Coalition contributions.

As I departed Kuwait for the UK force generation conference on 7 May, I reviewed a range of subjects for the command group in this report. My planners reviewed RFF 203 for the Iraq Survey Group, and would brief MG Thurman on it 7 May. We greatly reduced the scope of the RFF based on talks with the ISG second in command and reports from our own recon team in Baghdad. I outlined the construct for our approach to developing redeployment force modules and how we intended to integrate them into an overall redeployment flow for use by TRANSCOM. MG Renuart required us to submit a picture of our first 90 days of redeployment to the CENTCOM deployment/redeployment planners by 21 May. I assured the command group that this effort would enjoy my plans group's full attention.

I reported we continued our engagement on the new Iraqi Corps through staff-to-staff talks. My planners wrote a message containing our views, and were awaiting approval of our proposed message. I believed we must respond officially to the task of building this Iraqi Army unit.

There was a great deal of activity for and against our efforts throughout Iraq. I recorded notes in my journal by sector, from the south, north, and the Baghdad zones. The south was stabilizing, although we were not sure who held greater influence in local politics: Iraqi Shia or Iranian backed Shia groups. I wrote, "We can't overstay our welcome in this country."

In the north, we knew Turkish special operating forces were in all the northern cities, reporting back to the Turkish General Staff. I could not really find fault in this move, as the Turks lived in the region and a stable Iraq was in their best interests. The MeK continued small unit engagements against the Badr Corps. The 4th Infantry Division received the mission to compel the surrender of the MeK. Our question was, "What does the Badr Corps do after the MeK is eliminated as an opposing force?"

In Baghdad we learned Adnan Pachachi, a 78-year-old former minister, was definitely returning to Iraq. Apparently, he intended to challenge Chalabi for the presidency of Iraq. Baghdad was stable, but as I have mentioned, there was a growing shortage of liquid propane. ORHA was working feverishly to get the Iraqi Civil Service back on the job and to get the economy going, and the people back to work. We were working on how to establish the conditions required for our policy to succeed in Iraq.

Force Generation Conferences

I never anticipated that I'd be going to war and then attending conferences as the senior American representative from CFLCC. I did not think to bring a dress uniform, or more appropriate civilian clothes, with me. I went to a force generation conference for Phase IV forces in London, actually at the UK's PJHQ in Northwood, and one in Warsaw at the Polish Armed Forces Land Forces headquarters. From my journal:

> London: met with then LTG John Reith, UK, commander of the UK's permanent joint headquarters. Arrived by train from London in Levi Dockers and a polo shirt and went directly into a high-powered negotiation as I was the senior American representative from CFLCC. The British object was to convince the Spanish as a "first tier" NATO nation it was Spain's duty to join with the Polish led multi-national division and not the UK division. I really believe the British had the exact force they wanted in exactly the Iraqi governates they wanted so the addition of the Spanish brigade would entail an expansion of the UK led multinational division zone of operations. The Spanish were represented by a vice-admiral whose name I've forgotten. I left the NATO politics to LTG Reith and concentrated on convincing the Spanish vice-admiral the Quahdasiyah governate was within the medical evacuation helicopter range of the port of Umm Qasr where the Spanish would dock their class one medical facility, aboard a Spanish warship. The Spanish agreed with the caveat that they would command multinational division center-south, the division the Poles would command. Reith successfully deferred this discussion to the next conference in Warsaw. Our British cousins retain a smooth operating ability and focus on what their interests are, to my disadvantage because neither the OSD nor JCS reps had any guidance to offer about these conferences.

I reported to LTG McKiernan on the UK-sponsored force generation conference. LTG Reith had sent his regards, as did MG Fry. The former said he expected to be back in the region sometime soon, and would pay his respects in person. I shared my impression about the UK conference with LTG McKiernan, which was that the British were focused on their interests; precisely, on the kind of forces and nations they wanted in their zone. The British had done well in organizing the arrangement of forces in the proposed expanded UK zone of four governates, almost an embarrassment of forces actually.

I reported there were representatives from OSD and the JCS there, which I found interesting. The OSD and JCS representatives did not say anything, instead deferring to RADM Jaskot, the deputy J5 of EUCOM. Knowing I would not get to see LTG McKiernan face to face and render a report, I spent time in the written report covering the wheeling and dealing around the Spanish contribution of forces and the Spanish "red line" to not work for the Poles. I stressed that LTG Reith was hard at work on this, and would likely want LTG McKiernan's support in moving the Spanish to serve under the Polish led multinational division in the center-south area. I shared my impressions of the Poles as well.

The Poles were very professional about this brouhaha. They were well aware of the Spanish position, but did not openly say anything. I reported to LTG McKiernan the Poles were willing to go to the north or south central, wherever we determined the Polish division could make the best contribution to the Coalition effort. I made sure McKiernan knew I had stressed to the Polish division commander that if the Polish division went north or south central, they really ought to bring at least one, but better two, regiments with organic combat support and combat service support (vice one regiment of two battalions). I informed MG Blackman that the Poles wanted to come for site reconnaissance during the week of 18 May, or sometime prior to their force generation conference. The reconnaissance party would be rank heavy, with the CG, chief of staff, G2/3/4/6, and medical officer in attendance. The Poles would coordinate through the EUCOM Staff and US military attaché in Poland for arrangements.

The JCS representative did mention the Department of State and Joint Staff continued to work on getting an Indian division into the Coalition mix. He could not say when we could expend to know whether or not the Indians would accept. He also mentioned the possibility of the Koreans providing some force in battalion strength, a combat arms formation rather than the engineers who were currently arriving, which would serve in the north with whatever Coalition division went there.

I traveled to London on 7 May. I was booked into the famous Grosvenor Hotel in London. I knew Eisenhower and Patton stayed in this hotel during World War II. I do not recall much about my stay. This was the first night since March I did not sleep in my chemical protective gear, and I slept well.

D+50, 8 May, was a long day. I took a train from London to Northwood and the UK Permanent Joint Headquarters. A British major met me at the train and took me to the opening reception. Officers from Denmark, Italy, Portugal, Spain, Poland, the Czech Republic, Norway, Romania, and the Netherlands attended this British-sponsored conference. This conference really tested my abilities as a military diplomat.

I met LTG Reith at the door of the conference building. He immediately introduced me to a Spanish vice admiral, the senior Spanish Ministry of Defense representative. LTG Reith very clearly wanted my support in convincing the Spanish they should agree to serve in the multi-national division center area with the Poles. The Spanish admiral was equally clear that the Spanish would not consider that the Spanish area of operations should be anywhere but in the south, and within a one hour round trip flight from the Spanish hospital ship off shore from Umm Qasr. I told LTG Reith we would not make headway with this decision at the conference, as it was clearly going to be a political decision on the part of the Spanish.

The Spanish admiral would not consider serving under the command of the Poles. His nation was a "first tier" NATO nation, and thus deserved to serve with the British. The Poles were very professional about this development and the rather curt pronouncements made by the admiral. As no one from either our Defense Department or European Command stepped up to engage with the admiral, I let this lie, as it reinforced my thought this was a political decision.

LTG Reith started off by introducing the chief of staff of the 1st UK Armoured Division, now operating in Basrah and in the south of Iraq. He said we must be prepared to "think through to the finish" regarding operations in Iraq. He also said the pace of recovery in the south was remarkable, and that the Iraqi people would prefer to have a new dinar as opposed to continued use of US dollars.

Reith then proposed that countries coming to serve with the UK division in the south should arrive self-sufficient in terms of logistical units in the short term. The long-term solution was shared logistics and maximum use of contractors. He proposed a multinational logistics brigade. Basrah would serve as the divisional airport of debarkation, and Umm Qasr as the seaport.

Reith also proposed the Spanish base their operations in Al Qadisiyah under UK or Polish command. I noted that if this area was under UK control, ORHA must change its operating boundaries of south and center. It was very clear the Spanish did not want to go to the Al Qadisiyah area. I noted that LTG Reith would press this point. The British felt they were at the limit of their ability to exercise command and control, and that adding the Spanish would stretch them too far. Reith informed the conference the 3rd UK Division would complete a change of command with the 1st UK Armoured Division by 12 July 2003. The British would form a multinational division headquarters and integrate officers from Coalition countries into the staff. The agenda shifted to national updates.

The Dutch reported they were awaiting political approval of participation in operations in Iraq. The decision depended upon where Dutch force might go in country. The Dutch reported they were considering sending their forces to either Al Muthanna province or Basrah, both under UK command. The Dutch stated they required assistance in the form of support helicopters for at least the first six months of their deployment. The Portuguese reported they expected their parliament to approve the deployment of a company of military police this day, 8 May. The Portuguese agreed to serve with the Italian force and stated they would need logistical support.

The Spanish stated they intended to deploy helicopters as a part of their force; the Spanish government had already approved the deployment. The Spanish government also decided Spanish forces would operate in Dhi Qar Province. I noted that the British had entered into talks with the Italians to operate in Dhi Qar. The British had to deal with this friction point. The Spanish reported their force consisted of a brigade headquarters, three battalions of infantry (which was later reduced to one battalion), helicopters, logistical units, and riverine craft. The Spanish force expected to be tethered to a Spanish logistical force in Umm Qasr.

The Spanish people were very sensitive to the conditions of the deployment, as Spanish politicians had told their people that the deployment was tied to the conduct of humanitarian tasks. The Spanish could not stress stability and security tasks. This would come back to bite the Spanish government when conditions changed. Once again, the Spanish stressed they would only go to Dhi Qar, as this area is within the one hour flight window from Umm Qasr and the Spanish hospital there. The Spanish government took this decision, and it was final: the Spanish force must be in the south and under British command.

At this point in the morning's session, MG Fry rose to re-state the UK's position on the composition of the UK-led multinational division. He made his points precisely, and politely. It was again clear that Soldiers were not going to resolve this point of friction. These exchanges took us up to lunchtime, and a series of continuing informal discussions. Much as I wanted to support the British, my guidance was CFLCC/CJTF-7 wanted as many division headquarters as possible to assist in the conduct of stability and support operations. The composition of the Coalition forces within the multinational divisions was up to the nation providing the division headquarters. CFLCC/CJTF-7 would assist in providing sustainment, ensure intelligence and common operating positions were shared, and that all contributing nations received tasks within national rules of engagement. I attended the logisticians working group in the afternoon.

The operational level of war is all about logistics and sequencing and sustaining battles. This is also true in regards to stability and support operations. The discourse of the logisticians working group covered the expected size of deploying forces, who might need various types of support, and when CFLCC might expect various national elements to come to theater and conduct site reconnaissance.

The Czech Republic committed a hospital for service in the south. The Czechs said the hospital would be self-sufficient, and its purpose was humanitarian assistance only. The Czechs would operate under British command. The Danes would send a battalion of Soldiers, along with an engineer detachment. The engineers would build the Danish operating base and then return to Denmark. The battalion would be 450 Soldiers strong. The Danes expected to be a part of a British unit and operate under British command.

The Italian government approved the deployment of a mixed Carabinieri and Army troops up to three thousand strong. The Italian brigade headquarters would have under its command some Poles and Romanians. The Italians wanted to conduct two recons of the operating area, 13–24 May and 17–29 May. The Portuguese company and Romanian battalion deployment timeline was advance party arrival on 1 June 2003, with an expected declaration of full operational capability of 15 July 2003 (with the caveat this was all dependent upon politics).

The Dutch planned on contributing a brigade of one thousand Soldiers, and would be relatively self-sufficient, though they did ask for short term assistance with medical evacuation helicopters until theirs arrived, and no time was given. I took a note on this and the possibility of these helicopters operating at Tallil Air Base.

The Norwegian contribution was an engineer company of 120 troops. The company was scheduled to arrive in June 2003 and to be fully operationally capable by 1 July. The Norwegians requested permission to conduct reconnaissance the week of 12–16 May 2003.

Our CFLCC/CJTF-7 headquarters would be busy coordinating the arrival not only of US and UK troops, but the troops of up to twelve different countries in the upcoming weeks. The British intended to structure their logistics to support Coalition partners and little to no reliance on US assistance.

Our British cousins ran a very effective conference. Aside from the issue with the Spanish, which would not be settled until the Polish-led conference in a few weeks' time, there were no other issues, large or small, which were not settled at this conference.

This was my very first experience in working at the international level. I did my best to represent LTG McKiernan's interests, and our national interests insofar as I understood them. The other US representatives from the Pentagon and European Command were remarkably silent, but I suspected their work was done before the conference began. I departed for Kuwait early on the morning on 9 May 2003.

I used the C5 Plans Update for 9 May, D+51, to report on the UK force generation conference. It was unsettling being out of touch with the intelligence situation in Iraq, but I knew I could catch up on my personal situational understanding. The officers in the C5 continued to focus on CFLCC priorities, coordinating the integration of Coalition forces, refining our order for redeployment and monitoring CCJ3 and 5 actions on the new Iraqi Corps and ORHA. To return to Kuwait, I had to travel for most of the day.

I shared my report and the questions I took down at this conference, as well as ones I thought of myself, with the staff principals. Coalition integration was my task, supported by the civil affairs section. MG Thurman was not really interested in the development of the Coalition divisions. His concern was of the moment, and what was happening in theater right now. He would make time to see the Poles when they arrived. MG Marks spent time thinking about how to incorporate the range of multinational forces into the intelligence network. I spent the most time with MG Christianson, the C4, as we played a great role in at minimum overwatch of Coalition resupply and sustainment efforts.

I used the C5 Plans Update for 10 May, D+52, to report on the series of tasks which had stacked up for the section over the three days I was gone. LTG McKiernan had been in Baghdad, but returned for the first in a series of farewell dinners for key members of the staff. The section continued work on what we called force packages, but what was mainly work on redeployment. I reported that the C5 held another in our continuing series of redeployment VTCs. Slowly but surely, we resolved issues and answered unit questions. The general officer redeployment VTC was set for 15 May 2003. The remaining five VTCs aimed at working sessions for action officers.

We continued our work as the utility infielder of the staff, as I reported on another in a series of strange tasks which the SAMS graduates in my section received. We were tasked to coordinate the answers to a series of questions from the Government Accounting Office concerning our stewardship of the monies we spent on the preparation for the war. I acknowledged receipt of the task to refine a history of the operation from January 2002 to the present, this clearly because MAJ Huelfer held a Ph.D. in history.

My great deputy, LTC Mike Hendricks, completed the refinement of the Operation *Enduring Freedom* (OEF) message on the fourth series of unit rotations into Afghanistan. Third Army retained the task as the Army Service Component for the CENTCOM area of operations. Mike Hendricks did the painstaking work of reviewing the units slated to go to Afghanistan. He coordinated this work with the C3. I also acknowledged receipt of the task to develop a task organization for our forward headquarters, CFLCC-FWD, to include statements of functions for the forward and functions for the main command post. This task required the review of our entire operational plans group.

Finally, I reported I would meet with the Korean senior liaison officer, Colonel Jeong, on 11 May. He wanted to discuss his concerns about the potential transfer of the An Nasiriyah area from US to UK and ultimately Italian control. The Korean Government directed that its forces would only work for the US and not another nation. This remained a big deal for the Koreans.

While my section and I dealt with the expected general staff-level tasks, in the background was the situation of continuing threat in Iraq. In the south of Iraq, Hakim of SCIRI/Badr Corps was making a grand tour of the region. We learned the British had approached the Iranians with a message about this tour and were demanding the size of the group traveling with Hakim be limited to 25, and only 5 of these armed. We remained concerned over reports of growing direct and indirect Iranian influence in the south.

In the north we learned of an impending Turkish operation against KADEK, the Kurdish terrorist group which was using northern Iraq as a safe haven for its operations in Turkey. The Turks intended to use seven battalions and over twenty SOF teams. This was a first report, but we had to pay attention to these operations. GEN Franks was concerned about the Turkish operation but there were no other indications of troop movement. From past experience, we knew the Turks always named their operations, and as this one did not yet have a name we were not overly concerned for the time being. There was other activity in the north.

In the early morning of 10 May a mine exploded near Mosul. We lost an M577 headquarters vehicle and trailer in the attack. There were no reports of personnel losses. There was also a shooting incident between an ORHA convoy and an alleged "civilian." We learned of two media teams on the scene, so our public affairs section was checking on the reports. CID was directed to investigate the incident.

In the central part of the country, the MeK was conducting reconnaissance of its area and the Badr Corps, and Iranians were monitoring this MeK activity. These two groups were well aware of our efforts to disarm the MeK. LTG Abizaid passed on comments from the President and Secretary Rumsfeld concerning the MeK. Abizaid stressed the MeK was a terrorist organization. The MeK surrenders, and we dominate the group. Washington did not want to be seen as quavering on this point. Abizaid passed on that the President stressed we must impose our will and get security set as we want it. People in D.C. believed there was too much "fractious behavior." We were to do what we needed to do, "a JDAM or two is okay."

LTG Abizaid reported that Ambassador Bremer was on the way, and that he would act as the "500lb gorilla" we needed. Bremer was coming to be our boss. The number one security issue was security in Baghdad. Events were underway, and the concern in Washington on Iraq was growing.

Finally, this night our C5 section said farewell to LTC Reilly. I have already mentioned this, but it is worth saying again. I recommended Tom receive the Legion of Merit for his superb work on the range of OIF plans, especially his work on the development of the TPFDL and subsequent pain of devising requests for forces in accord with Rumsfeld's directives. LTG McKiernan endorsed my recommendation and pinned this great medal on LTC Reilly in April. Tom Reilly left after two very hard years of planning. He headed for the Army War College. I would miss him.

Sunday, 11 May, D+53, was a busy day. We focused on CFLCC priorities. We also spent time dealing with the Koreans and actions on the New Iraqi Corps and ORHA. I reported I'd met with COL Jeong in the morning, and that COL Jeong intended to report to his government that the zone in which the Korean forces would operate, vicinity Tallil AB under TACON of the MEF, would transition into an expanded UK zone within thirty–forty-five days. This was a true statement based on my sojourn to London the previous week. Colonel Jeong shared three major points he had to consider when speaking to his MoD and government, and requested my help in formulating an answer. The points were:

1) Military. The RFF which brought the Koreans over here specifically stated that the Koreans would work with the US only. The current Korean zone of operation was now in a UK division zone, in a governate commanded by the Italians, and with a battalion of Romanians.
2) Political. The Koreans had taken the decision to come over here when the situation was very tense. The Korean Government also withstood some rather large civilian protests, as well as opposition party resistance in the Korean National Assembly. A shift in zone or shift in relations with the US could spark renewed questioning of the mission, and about whether the Koreans were being "tools" (COL Jeong's words) of the Americans.
3) Finally, there were national economic interests. The Iraqis owed Hyundai Corporation about $1.1 billion. The Korean Government hoped that by operating in its own autonomous zone they could foster some good will, be in a position to enter the new Iraqi market, and thus recoup some of their losses to the ex-regime.

Colonel Jeong told me he saw only three possible courses of action for the Korean government: stay in the same location and deal with the British and Italians; move to a new zone in a US sector; or withdraw its forces. I did not think we could afford to have the Koreans leave the Coalition before the completion of the closure of their forces. I suggested to LTG McKiernan that we needed some higher headquarters policy help in this instance, possibly from the Joint Staff. It would not be an easy operation for the Koreans to move from one zone to another. The Koreans (in my impression) appeared to be somewhat deliberate in their approach to planning and execution. I had never worked with them before. Colonel Jeong said he was surprised the Koreans had not been consulted about this change in zone, or even informed of this potential change when they first entered into negotiations with CENTCOM for commitment of their force. The remainder of the Koreans were set to arrive on 14 May. They were temporarily at Camp Commando, but must move forward into zone to ease some crowding at the MEF base camp. This was not the only Coalition issue I worked on this day.

I spoke with COL Fitzgerald on the placement of the Polish division into a zone in Iraq. I specifically asked if the CENTCOM J3 or J5 had any guidance on this from the Joint Staff or OSD. I was not surprised to learn there was none, indeed I learned, again not surprising, that CENTCOM looked to CFLCC for a decision on the placement of the Polish division. I reminded LTG McKiernan that I'd written earlier the Poles would go wherever we asked them to go. I stated I'd work on some pros and cons of the placement of Polish forces in the north- and south central-zones and make a recommendation on the placement of the Polish division. This work was of some urgency as the Poles wanted to make a reconnaissance of their area before the Warsaw force generation conference. I told our command group I intended to take a V Corps planner with me to Warsaw to keep V Corps more fully informed on Coalition forces.

We worked on a range of Coalition moves, from a Polish chemical company under tactical control of CFSOCC to a Singapore medical team, and from Romanian and Ukrainian units from JTF-Consequence Management to a Macedonian infantry platoon and medical team inbound at the end of the May. We understood the Polish senior representative wanted the chemical company to stay in country and link up with the Polish division once it entered country. There was no CENTCOM FRAGO or indeed guidance on any Coalition units. I told the chief of staff I intended to pose questions on the range of Coalition forces and tell CENTCOM what I thought the answers should be, and would keep him informed.

I informed our command group I received a Joint Staff presentation on the command-and-control relationships between US forces, ORHA, and Ambassador Bremer. I learned that ORHA retained responsibility for recruiting, training, and equipping the Iraqi defense forces. CJTF-7 would exercise command and control over Iraqi forces until completion of the reestablishment of the Iraqi military and

Ministry of Defense. At the time, I believed we could influence the development of the new Iraqi Corps (NIC) through this relationship. I was seriously incorrect, but this was not apparent at the time. I rendered an NIC update. Directly from my journal:

> My C5 team had a conversation on 11 May with Darrell Crawford, MPRI rep, who just came from a meeting with ORHA (COL Hughes), CENTCOM Chief of Staff, MPRI and RONCO. Mr. Crawford stated MPRI signed a contract with ORHA to plan the stand-up with the NIC. We learned there would be no CMATT. (After our meeting we called MAJ Scott at CENTCOM and learned that CENTCOM was still generating a PLANORD asking for a CMATT-and asked for our input on what the CMATT should look like. Scott said CENTCOM is assuming a large amount of CMATT work will be contracted to MPRI but that the CMATT would still have to have a military face.) Mr. Crawford further stated at the ORHA meeting it was decided the first training at the Recruitment Centers would be done at Al Hillah and there would be a recon to determine what needed to be contracted at Al Hillah on or about 1 June. More recruiting centers would follow as additional MPRI teams become available. He stated the NIC basic training cycle would be 6–8 weeks in order to prepare recruits for coalition support missions. The training would be divided into blocks of instruction for recruit enlisted, junior officers and senior officers. Additionally he stated RONCO would be establishing three "DDR" (disarm, demobilize, rehabilitate) centers which would train civilian skills to "angry young men" to make them employable (this being a throw back to the concept RONCO was selling before the war for reintegrating the hordes of EPWs we planned on capturing). MAJ Scott was not totally unaware of these big changes coming from ORHA, but had not gotten any instructions from COL Fitzgerald on how to proceed yet. He did say the DRAFT FRAGO would change quite a bit and would not be out for the next couple of days. He did say the underlying tasks for CJTF-7 probably would not change. Learned there will be a VTC on this subject coming up on Tuesday, the 13th between CENTCOM, TRADOC and FORSCOM. Will plan on attending.

The work we were doing was paying off. The Hakim road trip in the south generated only positive public statements about the US and the Coalition. We had no indicators or warnings of the Turkish operation against KADEK, and best of all the UN Security Coordinator for Iraq declared Baghdad a "permissive" security environment. He passed on this recommendation to the UN in New York. This was a big deal for us as we could now expect the UN to arrive in some force and pick up work in theater.

In the C5 Plans Update for 12 May, D+54, I highlighted a suggestion made by MG Christianson regarding the Korean engineers, which was that we place the Koreans at Tallil Air Base. The Korean engineers would live on Tallil Air Base, which remained under CJTF-7 control, and would thus take work directions from the 416th Engineer Command. The presence of the Koreans would add to the security of Tallil, remain under US control and contribute to reconstruction work in zone. I passed this suggestion on to COL Jeong as another COA for the employment of the Korean forces. I covered other Coalition topics as well.

The V Corps G3 asked to go along for the Warsaw Force Generation conference. I offered that at first glance this was a good time to include the G3, but I needed to coordinate more fully with him to ensure we sang off the same sheet of music. I still intended to bring along a V Corps planner on the trip.

We also continued to hear that we might get an Indian division as a member of the Coalition. I continued to engage with the CENTCOM J5 on this topic. I offered that I personally had doubts on this as the Indians, at the last read of message traffic, wanted the cover of a UN mandate as well as the monetary guarantees a UN mandate brings before considering committing their forces to Iraq. The Indians never did commit forces.

I reported to the chief of staff that I was sending COL Roland Tiso to Baghdad on 14 May to represent C5 in the effort that was standing up the Iraqi Defense Force and the new Iraqi Corps. I told the chief this was the best use of COL Tiso's talents and contacts, as he had known Mr. Slocombe from his time as executive officer to the previous CENTCOM Commander, General Peay. The chief also asked me to review our headquarters structure for a future battle handover of the CJTF-7 role. At the time we projected a battle handover in August. We did not know it yet, but we were off by several months in this estimate.

MG Blackman directed me to look 30 days into the future, and specifically at what we, Third Army, would be doing by then. I wrote Third Army would revert to its role as the theater-wide Army Service Component Command, as the role of CFLCC ended when the last MEF Marine reembarked. Third Army would then be responsible for: sustaining the force in Iraq, redeploying forces in Iraq, reconstituting the Army Prepositioned Sets of equipment, managing the Kuwait battlespace, conducting operational protection throughout the CENTCOM region, and maintaining regional situational awareness. Third Army would sustain the fight but would no longer serve as a war fighting headquarters. This assessment did not make me very popular.

General Franks directed us, as CJTF-7, to prepare a briefing on how to improve the security situation in Iraq. The presentation was due at the end of the week. We also learned Ambassador Bremer intended to locate his headquarters near CJTF-7 and V Corps.

In another form of Coalition efforts, I had dinner at the Korean ambassador's residence on the evening of 12 May. In my journal I wrote, "Very nice time." Never having served in Korea before, I was truly unprepared for how much the Koreans drank. My good friend COL Jeong met me inside the ambassador's residence and informed me we were now in Korea where General Order #1 did not apply, before handing me a water glass dark with whiskey. He toasted me and drank his down. I did the same. It was my first drop of liquor in months. Colonel Jeong kept my glass full all night. I poured a great deal of good whiskey, Johnny Walker Blue, into the potted plants in the ambassador's residence. Colonel Jeong thought I was a strong drinker and this would come back to haunt me some weeks later.

Of course, Iraq continued to simmer as we approached the summer months. Most interesting was the movement along military and political lines by the Turks and KADEK, the Kurdish independence/terror group. KADEK recruited from among a "pagan" tribe in the northern mountains in an effort to build combat power.[1] The group was also planning on a move into Syria and away from the reach of the Turks. The Turks announced an amnesty plan aimed at lowering troop levels among KADEK, then isolating and attacking the group. The Turks were also rebuilding a presence in Iraq as they re-opened their embassy in Baghdad.

The C5 Plans Update for 13 May, D+55, reflected yet another busy day for me and my planners. We continued to focus on CFLCC priorities, coordinating the integration of Coalition forces, refining our order for redeployment, and the order of redeployment. We also monitored CENTCOM actions on the new Iraqi Corps and ORHA. The work on redeployment was time consuming and the frustration felt waiting for the word to go home was exacerbated by the time it took to bring in Coalition forces.

We conducted another redeployment VTC on 13 May. I told all of the delay in sending the message requesting release of the 3rd Infantry Division and associated units. I knew the Soldiers in the 3ID were anxious to go home, but given the pace of the arrival of Coalition forces we could not afford to lose the 3ID. The 377th TSC prepared to conduct an Arifjan flag officer "terrain walk" of the Arifjan site redeployment and APS turn in procedure area vice holding a redeployment VTC on 15 May. This was a large part of ensuring the process of redeployment went as smoothly as possible. We also continued to work on Coalition force generation issues.

I continued coordination for the 22/23 May trip to Warsaw to attend the force generation conference. I submitted information to the attaché for country clearances. I told our chief of staff that the CFLCC team consisted of three officers, two from C5 Plans and one C4 Plans. I planned on linking up in Warsaw with our CENTCOM liaison officer and the CENTCOM team. As previously reported, I planned on V Corps planners attending the conference as well.

I acknowledged LTG McKiernan's decision on a proposed zone for the Polish division. I sent the zone decision to CENTCOM J5 for review and action. I needed to coordinate the execution through the CENTCOM J5 and the Polish, British, and Spanish, given the proposed shift in governates for the Spanish brigade. We were still trying to persuade the Spanish to operate under command of the Poles in the center-south division area. The sticking point remained that the Spanish preferred to operate under the British. To that end, I reported my conversation with the chief of staff of the senior British liaison element.

To accommodate the Spanish, the proposed Polish zone included the expansion of the UK zone into five governates, one of which being Wasit. The British chief of staff relayed in a VTC with the UK PJHQ that this proposal would not be accepted by the UK. Unbeknownst to me, we apparently bumped into a British "red line"

1 The tribe the Iraqis called "pagan" was the Yazidi sect. Shia and Sunni sects of Islam believed the Yazidi people were heretics. This group was later persecuted by ISIS in 2014.

in this proposal. The UK government only offered to take five governates if the Spanish would accept Al Qadisiyah governate and operate under UK command. I learned that the Spanish government's answer was Spanish forces would operate in either Dhi Qar or Al Basrah governates, as these were within the range of their organic medical evacuation helicopters and their own military hospital. The issue was bigger than one Army colonel, and I needed help.

I told MG Blackman I attended a VTC with Joint Staff, CENTCOM Tampa, CENTCOM forward, and European Command on the upcoming Polish force generation conference. COL (P) Kevin Bergner of the Joint Staff ran the conference from Washington. RADM Robb, CENTCOM J5, MG Kohler, EUCOM J5, and BG Trautman, CENTCOM J5, attended. I told all about the Spanish message and the British position. I suggested the real issue was to address where the Spanish fit into the scheme of maneuver. We spent most of the VTC talking about how to set the Poles up for success. I reported that this was not a fruitful VTC but at least JCS had what we believed was the current information on distribution of Iraqi governates in operating areas for Coalition forces. The work on operational plan refinement continued as well.

I acknowledged that the draft FRAGO on CJTF transfer of authority, TOA, had been reviewed and approved by LTG McKiernan. I wrote I would continue to monitor the CENTCOM J5 response and keep the CG and V Corps informed. Based on this, my planners began work on our own order. I also reported on my talk with the senior Korean LNO about the C4's suggestion on how to deal with the placement of Korean engineers and the Korean requirement to work only for the US Colonel Jeong had been receptive to developing the idea of placing the Korean engineer group under operational control of the 416th Engineer Command. This was good news, and I began the process of refining the proposal into an order, working with our staff engineer and the planners at the 416th. This was a small victory but significant. We had demonstrated to the Koreans we listened to their concerns and acted to address them.

Lastly, I reported on a Department of the Army-level VTC I attended with MG Thurman, subject: the new Iraqi Corps. The Army G3 himself, LTG Cody, led the VTC. The essence of the VTC was that the Army G3 wanted to ensure a contractor largely executed this effort, which was in accord with LTG McKiernan's intent as well.

MG Thurman and I relayed to LTG Cody our understanding of the tasks we, CFLCC/CJFT-7, performed in support of establishing the NIC. We would designate sites for reorganization of the Iraqi units, assemble arms and ammunition, and then turn this over to a contracted company for training. LTG McKiernan stated he wanted the Iraqis to wear national uniforms, not US desert camouflage uniforms. We acknowledged our understanding of Mr. Slocombe's responsibilities: re-establish the Iraqi Ministry of Defense, review and approve all former Iraqi military officers wishing to serve in the NIC, and get the contractor up and running in country as soon as possible. V Corps and I MEF were in direct support of this effort, as it was one of the key tasks that had to be completed before we could begin to redeploy.

Iraq continued to simmer as the backdrop to all of my activities. In the southern part of the country, we watched Hakim of SCIRI continue his sojourn. He continued to be well received. He openly stated rejection of an "occupation force." He was clearly setting conditions for his brother's entry in the political realm. I wrote in my journal, "Wonder if this is a harbinger of inter Shia struggles." In the north there were still no indicators of overt Turkish moves against KADEK. Turkish special forces were conducting reconnaissance operations, as the Turks were concerned about the Kurdish Peshmerga re-equipping with Iraqi military arms and vehicles, especially armored vehicles. In Baghdad, we observed the actions of the Iraqi senior leadership council. Council membership expanded to accommodate new parties whose platforms countered Shia fundamentalists. We were on alert for demonstrations on 14 May, the birthday of the Prophet. Of note, on this day there were multiple terrorist suicide attacks across Saudi Arabia. Our reports indicated a number of westerners were killed in the attacks. The leaders of the attacks knew what they were doing. We saw all the hallmarks of al Qaeda operations. This was another danger to think about.

The C5 Plans Update for 14 May, D+56, again reflected the mundane nature of planning. We continued our focus on CFLCC priorities. My report touched on actions concerning the redeployment of a rocket artillery battalion to a report on changes to the Polish force generation conference. The Poles also intended to conduct a theater reconnaissance in May, possibly starting as early as 16 May. As was to become the usual pattern of activity we were seeing, Iraq continued to simmer.

In the south, we observed the emergence of two competing Shia groups; SCIRI and what we thought was Hezbollah. We later identified this group as supporting Moqtada al Sadr. We noted both groups received support from Iran. SCIRI had an armed faction, the Badr Corps. The other faction had no organized militia, as yet.

In the north, we watched the Turks and KADEK. The good news continued to be that there was no indication of any movement on either side. We assessed that action by KADEK was not in the interests of either the PUK or the KDP, the main Kurdish parties, thus these groups were pressuring KADEK. V Corps was monitoring these groups. V Corps was also mounting raids against Ba'ath Party remnants in Mosul.

In the center of the country, we observed the Badr Corps continuing to watch US forces and the MeK. There were also incidents of small arms fire near Baghdad International Airport. Mr. Pachachi continued to move around Baghdad talking politics. He expressed the desire for elections, as he wanted to be put into office by the Iraqi people.

My planners and I continued our work in refining our unfolding operation in Phase IV.

Baghdad, the Center of Gravity

I sent the C5 Plans Update for 15 May, D+57, to MGs Blackman, Webster, and Stratman as usual. Against the backdrop of a simmering Iraq, my planners and I remained focused on CFLCC priorities, coordinating the integration of Coalition forces, refining our order for redeployment, and the sequence of unit redeployments. The main thrust of our activity, though, centered on information operations. This was one of the rather busy days.

LTG McKiernan told us he had two main concerns: the message being sent via Western media on the situation in Iraq, and the distribution of liquid propane gas, gasoline, and diesel in Baghdad. By this stage of Operation *Iraqi Freedom*, many of the embedded reporters had returned home. McKiernan told us he wanted to "go on the offensive in IO," information operations. He said his impression was the Western media currently in theater was the "B team." The news' focus was exclusively on Baghdad. The hotels in Baghdad were operating, and since the media did not want to embed, they relied on "suspect" sources. The stories being presented were all sensational, and were making Baghdad look like *Tombstone*.

LTG McKiernan directed our current operations section, supported by the intelligence section, to prepare a daily summary of activities. He tasked the public affairs section to arrange battle space visits for the media in Baghdad to get them out of the city to see American units in action around the country. The essence of what McKiernan was looking for was the correct mix of information to portray a balanced view of what was happening in the entire Iraq theater of operations.

Baghdad remained the center of gravity of the operation, as it was the center of media focus. Given this reality, McKiernan directed maximum effort towards using the Iraqi fuel distribution system to address the perceived gas shortage in Baghdad. He directed our Army Corps of Engineers Task Force RIO (Restore Iraqi Oil), our own C4 logistics section, and ORHA to make this issue their top priority. Sufficient stocks existed in Iraq, but the distribution system was fragile and, we suspected, rather corrupt. McKiernan directed a "brute force" approach to addressing and solving this distribution challenge.

The political and military situation in Iraq continued to simmer as well. In the south, we were seeing efforts by Chalabi to counter the Hakim brothers' moves towards establishing a political power base. Chalabi was working very hard to establish a power base in Basrah and the south. He pointed out a Hakim weakness: the fact that he got his financial support from Iran while decrying "foreign" influence. The Ayatollah Hakim had also lived outside Iraq for 23 years. In the north, V Corps was reporting indications of Hezbollah activity. V Corps also assessed a downturn in cooperation among the main Kurdish parties, the KDP and PUK. Both groups were vying for power in the Kurdish autonomous zone. We continued to monitor Turkish operations but saw no indicators of preparations for conventional operations.

Turkish special forces were still conducting reconnaissance in Iraq. V Corps also reported the 4ID conducted two raids, but when I recorded this we had no definitive information on their results. Our C2 continued to develop intelligence and track a range of "bad actors" in Baghdad and across Iraq.

CENTCOM also directed all of the 1st Armored Division close on Baghdad by 28 May. An armored division operating in a city made no sense to me, but I anticipated this was the move designed to get the 3ID back home. Finally, CENTCOM informed us to expect the arrival of several congressional delegations coming for visits. More information would follow. The mundane routine of conducting combat and stability operations in an active theater of war.

Our force package work ranged from reviewing a spreadsheet from Forces Command which outlined units at mobilization stations to refining the battle space for our Phase IV operations. Forces Command wanted our input on what forces could be released from call up and which should continue to come to theater. I projected our plans group would finish our review by 16 May and recommend units for release from active duty. We engaged in this review as we were starting to realize we were in this campaign for the long haul, and we needed to focus on sustaining the force. The battle space refinement effort was growing equally complex.

I informed our command group we had no word on the force generation conference in Warsaw. I continued planning based on the assumption the conference would run 22/23 May. The Poles were coming to theater for a reconnaissance. I informed our command group of the details of the visit and who was in charge of sponsoring the Polish command group. I worked with LTG McKiernan's executive officer to arrange an office call for the Polish division commander. There was other news on the coalition-building effort.

I also received word from the US liaison officer to the Ukrainian Army, Captain Schaefer, Special Forces, that the Ukrainian President and Ministry of Defense had decided to send a brigade of infantry to reinforce the Polish division. More information followed. I stressed to CPT Schaefer and the Ukrainian major on the phone with him that the brigade needed to be as self-sufficient as possible, especially in terms of logistics and sustainment. We also heard from the British.

We met with the G3 planners from 1Div (UK) on 15 May and discussed Coalition integration, command and control transition and the future of senior British liaison activity. The primary issue which arose was the command-and-control transition of 1Div (UK) from I MEF to CJTF-7. The British believed on 1 June, 1Div (UK) would come under the operational control, OPCON, of CJTF-7 (CFLCC). Their concern was that on 1 June they would lose their US communications support from the MEF and would have no communication with CFLCC. This communications support ran the gamut from VTCs, telephone, CENTRIX (the technical means through which US developed intelligence was passed to Coalition members), other G2 links, etc. The British were very concerned about this problem and asked that this issue be raised with CFLCC immediately. The interest extended to the following transition of CJTF-7 from CFLCC to V Corps on 15 June, and the implication for them regarding links with their higher headquarters. CENTCOM and our own Army staff sent messages as well.

CENTCOM J5 intended to issue the TOA order during this week. This would settle the date for the handover between V Corps and CFLCC regarding CJTF-7. I learned this day sometime in the coming week an Army G3 party was coming to theater to discuss the future of the APS. This was all I had, but I expected to get more information on this visit soon. The CENTCOM J3 sent a request for information asking us to provide details of our plan to move major combat units out of Iraq from the end of April through 30 June. This request was in addition to a requirement to provide our first 90 days of redeployment flow by 21 May. We were well and truly engaged in a theater of war, but exercise planning was also on the burner.

I received notice this day of GEN Franks's approval for a re-scoped Bright Star, our annual exercise with the Egyptian Army. The field training exercise portion would continue with the tentative participation of the 49th Armored Division, Texas National Guard, as controlling headquarters and the 278th Armored Cavalry Regiment, also a National Guard unit, as the maneuver unit. There would be no larger scale command-post exercise with Bright Star. CENTCOM directed the final event be a senior leaders seminar in Egypt, with discussions on consequence management, rear area operations, and joint targeting. A message would be out soon announcing these changes. I reported we received a read-ahead copy of the message for review and comment. Finally, I reported COL Fitzgerald that ORHA representatives and contractors would meet at Camp Doha on 18 May to discuss the NIC.

De-Ba'athification

This day, 16 May 2003, was unsettling. Ambassador Bremer issued CPA Order 1. This order removed all government employees associated with the Ba'ath Party from current and future employment with the Iraqi Government. The C5 Plans Update for 16 May, D+58, covered our ongoing focus on CFLCC/CJTF-7 priorities, which was hard to do given the CPA order. This news did not go over well on the "Arab/Iraqi Street."

My report focused on the Poles' upcoming visit and our planning for the handover of the CJTF-7 role to V Corps. LTG McKiernan understood all of this, and demonstrated a real understanding of the situation in theater. Amidst all of our planning efforts and current operations activities, he told us his issue of the day was "Iraq-wide fuel distribution." He stated this was the "number one quality of life issue, gas for cooking and transportation." This issue was not in my purview, but all my planners remained aware of it. It truly had implications for future planning and establishing the security conditions necessary for transitions during Phase IV of the campaign. Coalition building showed solid progress.

I reported that the Polish-directed force generation conference was set for 22/23 May in Warsaw. I would represent CJTF-7 and bring along two planners, a logistician from our C4 and one of my C5 planners. We completed the final coordination for the Polish reconnaissance party. On 17 May we planned briefings for the Poles on theater-wide issues. The Poles would then spend the remainder of their time in theater with I MEF.

We learned more about the Ukrainian contribution to the Polish division. The brigade included a logistics organization, akin to a US forward support battalion. The force was built from a Ukrainian airborne/air assault brigade; according to Janes (our standard open-source reference book) the airborne force was one of the Ukrainians' best outfits. I would gather more information at the Warsaw conference.

Our plan refinement work centered on continuing our mission analysis and order production based on the CENTCOM TOA order. I reviewed the presentation for the JMD meeting with V Corps. The JMD outlined the other service support required to build a joint headquarters based on the V Corps Staff. This document listed the skills required of incoming Navy, Air Force, and Marine Corps staff officers and NCOs by the specific staff sections, from personnel administration to future plans. I reported our staff was on a glide path to review the JMD with the V Corps Staff and establish a timeline for CJTF-7 task handover to the V Corps Staff. I provided more details as we refined them.

I reviewed a presentation on our headquarters functions for the main and forward command post structure. This was a good product intended to focus on a CG decision. The presentation laid out staff and command and control functions per each headquarters element, in Atlanta, and at the forward headquarters in Kuwait. MAJ Huelfer, the lead planner, continued on a path to present this decision briefing to LTG McKiernan in the coming week, 19–23 May.

I reported I completed an answer to the CENTCOM J3 request for information regarding the CFLCC plan for redeployment of major combat formations through the end of June. From my journal, here is a synopsis of the answer:

- CFLCC published a redeployment order on 5 May 03. The redeployment order is linked to our CFLCC home page. The order, along with CFLCC operations order ECLIPSE II (published 19APR03), also found at the home page, articulates the stability and security conditions required for redeployment.
- In accord with CFC Redeployment guidance CFLCC will plan to redeploy the following Army and Marine forces through June. All redeployments, in accord with CFLCC and CFC operations orders, are conditions dependent. As of 16MAY, all redeployments of major combat units are on hold.
- Army Forces
- During MAY 03: Patriot and select attack helicopter units, selected elements of 82nd Abn, and 173rd Abn.

- During JUN 03: 3ID and associated forces. 75th Field Artillery BDE after SSE transition is complete.
- Marine Forces
- During May 03: Amphibious Task Force, ATF, East forces and ATF West forces on amphibious shipping, logistics and aviation forces no longer required, stop loss personnel and other personnel required to attend joint duty and formal schools, forces required to deploy to Okinawa.
- During JUN 03 to DEC 03: Plan to redeploy and/or rotate forces while maintaining a minimum 1.0 ARG/MEU presence in the northern Arabian Gulf, NAG.
- CFLCC published a redeployment order on 5 May 03. The redeployment order is linked to our CFLCC home page. The order, along with CFLCC operations order ECLIPSE II (published 19APR03), also found at the home page, articulates the stability and security conditions required for redeployment.
- In accord with CFC Redeployment guidance CFLCC will plan to redeploy the following Army and Marine forces through June. All redeployments, in accord with CFLCC and CFC operations orders, are conditions dependent. As of 16MAY, all redeployments of major combat units are on hold.
- Army Forces
- During MAY 03: Patriot and select attack helicopter units, selected elements of 82nd Abn, and 173rd Abn.
- During JUN 03: 3ID and associated forces. 75th Field Artillery BDE after SSE transition is complete.
- Marine Forces
- During May 03: Amphibious Task Force, ATF, East forces and ATF West forces on amphibious shipping, Logistics and Aviation forces no longer required, Stop loss personnel and other personnel required to attend joint duty and formal schools, Forces required to deploy to Okinawa.
- During JUN 03 to DEC 03: Plan to redeploy and/or rotate forces while maintaining a minimum 1.0 ARG/MEU presence in the northern Arabian Gulf, NAG.

My planners and I focused on this work but remained aware of the ongoing daily situation reports coming in from around the theater. We were still in a combat zone, as the reports indicated. In the south, we learned that Bakir Hakim had met with senior Shia cleric Grand Ayatollah al Sistani on 15 May. We did not know the specifics of their discussion, but there were indications that in it they reviewed a nationalist agenda for the Shia. British reports indicated a militia forming in al Amarah. The militia intended to work with the British and the leader, Hatim, fought alongside UK forces during Phase III.

We were reminded, by a Department of State message, that KADEK was a terrorist organization, as if we had forgotten. The Turks showed no signs of a major operation against KADEK. The 4ID headquarters received mortar fire over the night of 15/16 May. There were no reported casualties. The 3rd Armored Cavalry Regiment in Ar Ramadi and Hit were on alert for hostile acts. Reports indicated that these were to occur in the upcoming 48–72 hours.

In Baghdad, criminal activity was on the rise, which not surprising given the lack of cooking oil and gasoline, as well as the lack of an Iraqi police force. Our SOFs believed high value targets remained in Iraq. They were working on establishing safe houses and operating bases for future operations. Detecting and killing these people was a focus for our SOF as well as our intelligence section. Convoys coming to and from Kuwait were receiving small arms fire on a more regular basis. Based on our intelligence updates and the recent attacks across Saudi Arabia, LTG McKiernan directed all units to review force protection measures. We needed no reminder that we were still in an active combat zone.

I sent MGs Webster, Stratman, and Blackman the C5 Plans Update for 17 May, D+59. While overall, my planners remained focused on CFLCC priorities, the main elements of the report were on a request from the air component, the Poles' visit, and the work on building the NIC. The request from the CFACC was in the nature of a "first report." From my journal:

> Received a fascinating note from CFACC. Seems they've been tasked to increase the air defense of the embassy in Nairobi against a potential air threat. My counterpart at CFACC wanted to know if we had any SHORAD [short range air defense] we could contribute. I suggested to him that the closest SHORAD might be embarked with the MEU. Am pursuing the request and asked for more information.

We had no intelligence to immediately back up this request, but our intelligence planners promised to look into the traffic.

I reported that I had sent an updated presentation to the US military attaché in Warsaw for use at the preliminary planning sessions with the Polish General Staff. I gave MG Tysczkiewicz (pronounced "Tis-kay-vitch") a personal hard copy for his immediate use. We spent a good day with the Polish reconnaissance party. During the afternoon, our plans team gave a major presentation to the entire party which covered intelligence, planning, communications, and medical areas. At the start of the presentations, I stopped our briefers for a moment and asked for a short recess. While I did preview the presentations to cut down on acronyms, I did not rehearse the speakers. I reminded my people that English was likely a third language for our Polish visitors. The speakers needed to speak clearly and avoid American slang, which was untranslatable. I knew our Polish guests picked up on this and were grateful for the change. Upon completion of the presentation, we broke into small group discussions. MG Tysczkiewicz then met with MG Blackman.

I sat in on the meeting between MG Blackman and MG Tysczkiewicz. MG Tysczkiewicz made a "joking" request for US forces to round out the Polish division. This request was based on a statement of requirements which the Polish had gotten from somewhere. I learned later it was a paper (not staffed through us) written by our British cousins which proposed that US/UK reconnaissance; engineer, aviation, and civil affairs battalions be assigned to the Polish division. This was a big deal, and caught MG Blackman—and me—by surprise. I knew I needed to do some expectation management/control during the force generation conference.

MG Tysczkiewicz asked MG Blackman if we would reinforce his division with a US brigade as he had assessed that he might need a US brigade and perhaps a battalion as a framework for Coalition forces to form around. Tysczkiewicz also mentioned a conversation between the Polish deputy minister of defense and Dr. Zakheim about Poland "leasing" some four hundred US HMMWVs for the Polish division. It was the first we'd heard of this proposal as well. The Poles had left Washington believing they'd be supported by the US logistics system. I said I would check on this with CENTCOM. I learned later on that COL Fitzgerald, CENTCOM J5, knew nothing of this support arrangement or HMMWV leasing either. Mike Fitzgerald said he would check with Tampa for more information.

MG Tysczkiewicz had many other questions, all of which we could defer to I MEF as they had to do with billeting for troops and local intelligence. He and his party would spend 18 May with I MEF on an in-zone reconnaissance. The final bit of news on Coalition building was that JTF-Consequence Management was ready to handover the Romanian and Ukrainian chemical units to CFLCC. The Ukrainian chemical unit ultimately joined the Ukrainian brigade in the Polish division. The Romanians were awaiting parliamentary approval to remain in theater.

My impression of MG Tysczkiewicz and his staff was very positive; the former impressed me as extremely talented and capable; a tough leader. His staff gave the impression of calmness and confidence. These were Soldiers you would want on your team. I looked forward to working with them.

Work on developing the NIC continued apace. COL Fitzgerald arrived on the evening of 17 May in advance of a conference on the Iraqi Corps. We held talks with ORHA and contractors on 18 May on the NIC and future Iraqi Armed Forces development. I learned from COL Fitzgerald that Mr. Slocombe might come down to Camp Doha from Baghdad on 19 May for a briefing on the status of the NIC based on the 18 May talks. This was also news to us, and I made sure LTG McKiernan knew of it immediately.

I reported I had completed a review of a proposed de-Ba'athification letter for MG Blackman. He received a proposal from CENTCOM about how to carry out a program of de-Ba'athification based on Bremer's CPA order. I had warned our command group about this notion back in March and it never went away. My suggestion was we limit this notion to the highest-ranking members of Saddam's regime, and this was as far as it should go, to no avail given the order. I returned the letter to MG Blackman. We never heard anything from CENTCOM on this again. In the coming months, the notion would truly come back to haunt us.

We learned from LTC Jones, our liaison officer to Ambassador Bremer's organization, that the ambassador had missed a chance to get out to see some V Corps activity. LTC Jones strongly recommended that Ambassador Bremer be scheduled to attend a V Corps operation. Such an event was in keeping with LTG McKiernan's concept of an information operations offensive, plus it was good press for Ambassador Bremer and the Coalition effort. I seconded LTC Jones's suggestion.

I sent the C5 Plans Update for 18 May, D+60, to LTG McKiernan. I did this even after having been told to not bother him with my notes because I felt I was getting more and more out of synch with his thinking. I had a conversation with Terry Moran on this day about our input to the CENTCOM theater engagement strategy for the post-Saddam times. My understanding of LTG McKiernan's views were at odds with Moran's, so I decided I needed to see LTG McKiernan. Once I did this, I decided to communicate directly with the commanding general. I reported we were still chasing down information on the request from CFACC for air defense support to the US Embassy in Kenya.

The only note we could find on the CFACC request for SHORAD read as follows:

> Just received a heads-up call from COL Phalen (Chief, SOD). He advises that State Department is sending a request for DOD assistance in countering a possible aerial terrorist attack on the American Embassy in Nairobi, Kenya. According to COL Phalen, the request has not yet made it to SecDef, that we may not see it until Monday or Tuesday (19–20 May) and that the proposed suspense for a plan is 23 May. I have passed this to CJTF-HOA via phone. Recommend we pass to all components soonest. BG Fruchtnicht requests, in addition to CJTF-HOA, particular attention by CFACC and CFMCC.

This note originated in the CENTCOM J3 Joint Operations Center. There was nothing further on either the request or intelligence which led to the request. We never sent air defense units to Kenya.

Our force package work focused on the Poles, although other nations were speaking with the Department of Defense. 18 May was a good day for the Polish reconnaissance party. I MEF showed the Poles a large portion of the proposed south-central zone. There was no further word on the status of a "lease" of HMMWVs for the Poles, nor any other of the CSS-related issues raised by the Poles. I continued to press on the logistical support issue at the force generation conference. I wrote a complete report on the Polish reconnaissance team visit once the Poles left. I included observations from I MEF. The Coalition integration continued as we refined the request for forces transportation support for the Mongolian and Philippine contributions, a company and battalion respectively.

Operations plan refinement focused on a review of the NIC structure and presentation coordinated with Ambassador Bremer's CPA Staff, and CENTCOM J5. I reported to LTG McKiernan that Mr. Slocombe would be at Camp Doha on 19 May to receive the presentation.

CHAPTER EIGHT

A Bad Feeling

I exchanged notes with LTG McKiernan about the presentation review and his stating the two "principles" or caveats of which I needed to be aware. I sent him what I called a "90 percent solution" for the presentation. He replied with a note saying that when I spoke with Mr. Slocombe, I needed to bear in mind that he was coming from D.C.—D.C. had determined that no Iraqi above the rank of lieutenant colonel would be allowed into the new Iraqi Corps. He wanted us to be ready to address the effect this would have on recruitment, any additional "anti-Coalition" effects this would produce, and where would we find leadership for the NIC. The second "principle" from D.C. was there would be no re-establishment of a ministry of defense type organization, at least in the short term. LTG McKiernan told us Mr. Slocombe would await his input on Iraqi former general officers and whether they could be "advisors" in the process. He told me Terry Moran had details. Of note, Moran never gave me any details on what Mr. Slocombe was bringing with him in terms of dealing with the NIC. Evidently, this was why McKiernan was not as surprised as I was when Mr. Slocombe just said, "Thanks for the briefing" after I stressed during the 19 May presentation we needed to know if we were still acting in accord with policy regarding the recall of the Iraqi Army.

Slocombe and the Iraqi Army

19 May 2003. Mr. Slocombe arrived late, as his flight had been held up for some reason. He brought a UK general officer along, a Major General Richards. I sat in on the discussions with Mr. Slocombe, LTG McKiernan, MG Blackman, and MG Thurman concerning the NIC. Mr. Slocombe redirected the effort to a force that would focus on external security vice the direction the ORHA and CENTCOM group had been going in, which was more constabulary in nature.

During the meeting, I told Mr. Slocombe that we were operating under the assumption we could recall elements of the regular Iraqi Army to form this "new" corps. I told him we had teams of officers on the ground identifying barracks and staging areas which the Iraqis could rebuild, and that we were assembling arms and equipment for this reorganized force. I asked if we were still acting in accord with policy. Mr. Slocombe looked at me and said, "Got it, thanks for the briefing Colonel." I was taken aback, to say the least. I reiterated what we were doing and again asked Slocombe if we were acting in accord with policy, and again he said, "Thanks for the briefing." I looked at MG Blackman and he shrugged his shoulders. Mr. Slocombe left the room with LTG McKiernan. I learned later on that Slocombe intended to return to Camp Doha on 23 May to take one more presentation, and that he would then take this final work to Washington for presentation to the chairman of the Joint Chiefs, GEN Myers.

I was stunned at this response. I had the feeling we were in for a surprise regarding the recall of the Iraqi Army. I shared my feelings with MGs Blackman and Thurman, and found out that they too did not quite understand what was coming. As mentioned previously, we had not just assumed we could recall the regular Iraqi Army, but we had taken it as a fact given the theme of the messages we were sending to the Iraqis in our psychological operations messages and leaflets. When I told all of this to my team of planners, the group asked, "What do we do now, boss?" I replied, "It beats the shit out of me."

The Coalition Provisional Authority issued CPA Order 2 on 23 May. This order dissolved the Iraqi Army and its associated elements.

The C5 Plans Update for 19 May, D+61, covered my final meeting with the Polish reconnaissance party. I held final talks with them on 19 May. The group had to remain overnight at Tallil the night of 18 May due to dust conditions and visibility. The Poles got a real feel for the zone. I reported I would render a separate report on issues raised by MG Tysczkiewicz and his staff. The Polish division would begin deploying into theater on or about 15 July, and expected to be mission capable between 1 and 30 September.

I told LTG McKiernan that we were prepared for the Warsaw conference, and I needed some guidance on what we were allowed talk about to the Poles. I reported I believed the Poles might formally request US forces under their command in order to effectively control the south-center zone. At a minimum, I felt they would ask for US MPs, aviation (lift and medevac), and logistics support teams to remain in zone. I also opined the Poles might ask for a US brigade headquarters (and at least one combat battalion) for command and control within the Polish zone. At this time, no other countries (save the Poles themselves and the Ukrainians) were offering brigade-level headquarters. I took down a number of questions ranging from how the Poles would receive air support to what the sequence of the relief in place with the Marines would be. I promised MG Tysczkiewicz I would have the answers when I arrived in Warsaw for the force generation conference.

All the while, Iraq was still simmering in the background of our planning efforts. In the south, we saw multiple religious groups vying for power and asserting leadership over the Shia. One consistent actor on this stage was the Grand Ayatollah Sistani, who was acting as a peacemaker. He was the leading Shia cleric and was not moving into politics. What we observed was his canny use of his bully pulpit to defuse tension. In the central region of Iraq, we observed what we perceived as the waning influence of the Ba'ath Party. We also observed the rising influence of Wahabi-influenced extremists acting as a counterbalance to the rise of Shia activism. In Baghdad, a Wahabi-oriented imam had called for attacks on all who supported the Coalition. There was no evidence of any impending attacks, but this contributed to an atmosphere of tension in the city.

My report to LTG McKiernan on 20 May, D+62, covered all the loose ends I had tried to tie together before departing for Warsaw. These loose ends ranged from a recommendation on redeployment to the impending arrival of a team from the Army G3, led by MG David Huntoon. Regarding redeployment I recommended we ask CENTCOM now for permission to redeploy the 3ID and its associated echelon above division support force modules so when conditions were met for their redeployment we already have approval in hand and are ready to act (issue the C35 FRAGO directing movement back to Kuwait). Otherwise, I offered it would take a week to gain CENTCOM approval, thus slowing down the process to order ships and planes to support the redeployment. McKiernan took this under advisement.

I reported I put the Polish reconnaissance party on the plane to Poland that morning. The Poles were extremely satisfied with the visit and were eager to maintain contact for continuing planning. I wrote MG Tysczkiewicz would send a liaison team to link up with the I MEF staff by the end of the month. MG Tysczkiewicz and his staff would lead the execution of the Force Generation conference. The senior American representative would be RADM Jaskot, the deputy J3 of European Command. I concluded with a note the C5 team would leave for Warsaw early on 20 May.

My planners incorporated the results of the staff to staff talks with the V Corps staff into the effort to complete the writing of our transition order. The plans team remained on track to complete a first draft of the FRAGO by Thursday, 22 May.

I reported my C5 planners continued to work with ORHA and CENTCOM J5 on the new Iraqi Corps effort for Mr. Slocombe. Mr. Slocombe planned on remaining on his schedule of returning to Camp Doha on Friday, 23 May for one more review of the presentation. He then planned to take it back to Washington with him. I reviewed the product and sent it on to the command group for one more round of review and comment. Our presentation retained our planned recall of elements of the regular Iraqi Army.

Lastly, I reported an Army G3 team, led by MG Huntoon, would visit from 27–31 May. They were sending an updated list of discussion topics for our review. My executive officer would send this list to the command group upon receipt. I also told LTG McKiernan that I had sent out a synopsis of our short talk on our

ARCENT input to the theater engagement strategy to senior staff today. We would use this as our constant input to CENTCOM J5's development of the CENTCOM theater engagement strategy. It was a catch-all report, but I wanted my boss to know that the section would keep all the plates spinning while I was in Warsaw.

Polish Land Forces Force Generation Conference

21 May 2003 was a travel day. I took MAJ Bill Innocenti, one of my SAMS-educated planner reinforcements, with me to Warsaw. This was the first time in my career that I realized another army had a dossier on me. When I flew into Warsaw, I was greeted by a Polish Army captain who had a sign with my name on it. He spoke superb English. On the drive to our hotel in Warsaw, he talked with me about my career and what I thought about my next posting as the director of the School of Advanced Military Studies. Not even my officers knew about the possibility of my upcoming assignment to SAMS. We were billeted in the Marriott Hotel in downtown Warsaw.

Chart 6. This chart was developed during the wargaming effort to develop operations plan Eclipse II. The purpose was to display how the entire Iraq theater would be divided into operating areas for the two multinational divisions and US forces. (From the author's personal files, and prepared in 2003 by officers working for the author.)

22 May 2003, and the first day of the conference. I linked up with RADM Jaskot, who told me that the US would "pony up forces if the Poles can't fill out their division." He attributed this to Secretary Rumsfeld. RADM Jaskot then went on to tell me that no American at the conference held the authority to commit to this. We would "let the dust settle" but "must be prepared for this eventuality, as "the US will not let the Poles fail." He also told me that his goal was to fill out the Polish division without US troops. I was rather happy about this, since what he told me was news to me as well as COLs Fitzgerald and Halverson. The morning session of the conference was dedicated to opening remarks and presentations.

Ambassador Kobieracki opened the conference. He said the North Atlantic Council had tasked NATO to develop options to support Poland in the successful accomplishment of this mission. He went on to say the UN Security Council would soon pass a "Phase IV"-type resolution. Based on these occurrences, Poland intended to reopen its embassy in Baghdad. He concluded by calling for "deeds, not theoretical discussion" from the conference participants. I learned from MG Tysczkiewicz that the ambassador was being considered for a post as the Assistant Secretary General of the UN.

The next speaker was Ambassador Krystosik. I did not record his position within the Polish government. He stated the Polish mission was to secure and guarantee appropriate conditions for the development of a stable political process in Iraq. The ambassador said Polish Soldiers "are not occupiers … Iraq belongs to the Iraqis. The territorial integrity of Iraq will not be put in danger." I watched MG Tysczkiewicz as the ambassador said all this, and saw a true poker face. I suspected this was news to the general.

The next speaker was RADM Martinez, the senior Spanish representative, who said he could commit liaison and staff officers now. He had no authority to commit forces at present, but he felt that this authority would come after the Spanish elections which were slated for 25 May.

A Polish officer whose name I could not catch, but who was from the land forces intelligence staff, followed RADM Martinez. I recorded in my journal I felt he was a bit off base in his assessment of threats and potential Shia-on-Sunni violence. This potential, in his assessment, was the major threat to the security of the Polish zone and to the troops of the division.

MG Tysczkiewicz's presentation followed the intelligence briefing, and this presentation was first rate. He focused his remarks on the contributing nations' representatives. He outlined his scheme of maneuver which revolved around where he intended to place his division and brigade headquarters. He stressed that, for the scheme of maneuver to work, he needed three brigade headquarters and right now he only had two. In order to ensure smooth development and transmission of orders, he stated he wanted to have a staff that was 50 percent Polish, with the other 50 percent made up of staff officers from contributing nations. His chief medical officer gave an overview of the medical plan, which was first rate. The signal officer followed with a lay down of the signal backbone within the division zone, and how the brigades and division would link into the JTF command-and-control system. This was another superb presentation. MG Tysczkiewicz concluded the morning session by announcing the Poles would host another conference in June.

During lunch I was cornered by South Korean BG Choi. He said the South Koreans would send an engineer colonel to serve on the CPA Staff. All Ambassador Bremer had to do was ask the South Korean ambassador to do it. I told BG Choi I would carry this message back to theater. Then BG Choi told me my good friend COL Jeong had told him I was "strong with drink." After the conference, BG Choi said we would go out into Warsaw and "drink much whiskey." At the time, I wondered how I could escape this proposal with dignity. I also learned I had a speaking role at the start of the afternoon session.

Immediately following lunch, I found myself standing in front of a collection of officers from Poland, Hungary, Romania, the Czech Republic, and Slovakia. I confessed to them that even in my wildest dreams as a young officer, I'd never imagined standing before a group of officers whose armies I'd studied as potential adversaries, and be briefing them on combined operations in Iraq. The group laughed.

I was speaking through five translators, although most of these officers spoke English. I assured these officers the joint task force would ensure we shared a common operating picture of the range of threats in Iraq. We were all professional Soldiers, and we would not let them down; any challenge which came up we would work through, because Soldiers take care of Soldiers, especially those sharing the dangers of battle together. I gave them my assessment of the operation thus far. I concluded my short talk by encouraging the potential contributing countries to send complete combined arms teams to theater. My feeling was the talk was well received.

The remainder of the afternoon was taken up with short proposals and statements from the potential contributing countries. The common caveat was that just about every nation was awaiting parliamentary approval of a commitment of Soldiers to the Coalition. The western European NATO countries, Denmark, the Netherlands, and Norway, had all committed troops to the British Coalition division in the south, thus could not commit further troops to the Poles. The Danes and the Dutch, pending parliamentary approval, might send staff officers. The Lithuanian representative said his army was also considering sending staff officers to support to the British.

The Spanish said they would only be observers, however they were willing to send staff officers to augment the multinational division staff. This was the official position, pending further talks. The Canadians would not commit troops as they were fully committed to Afghanistan and ISAF. The representative said his government offered full political support and airlift support.

The Bulgarians offered to commit a mechanized infantry battalion. There was consensus among the political factions in Bulgaria, and parliamentary approval was expected soon. The caveats were that the battalion would need financial aid for transportation and logistical support for the duration of the operation.

The Parliament of the Czech Republic approved the dispatch of a hospital and a company of military police for security. The Czech NBC company would remain in Kuwait. There was no support for any further troop deployments, but the Czech representative indicated his general staff and parliament were willing to listen.

Estonia and Latvia offered an infantry platoon each. The Hungarians offered 300 Soldiers, either a transportation battalion or two infantry companies and a water purification unit. Staff-to-staff talks would refine the offer based on need. The Slovakians offered an engineer company for mine clearing, with the caveat the company would need logistical and medical support, as well as assistance in getting to Iraq. The Ukrainians repeated their offer of a brigade of 2,000 Soldiers, with the caveat that the brigade would require strategic lift to get to Iraq and logistical support to sustain operations.

The Dominican Republic offered a commando battalion of 250 Soldiers. The El Salvadoran representative reported he was awaiting policy guidance from his government, and could not make a public offer of support, yet. The Honduran representative offered a mixed battalion of infantry, special operations, and engineers, pending government approval.

The Fijian representative offered a light infantry battalion of 700 Soldiers. The Filipino representative had four proposals, ranging from a 500-man mixed battalion of Army and police to a much smaller military police mix, all dependent upon the budget appropriated for the operation by the Philippine government. The South Korean representative said the South Korean engineer group and hospital in zone would stay, and would provide general support. The ROK government would not send any more units to Iraq. The Thai representative reported he could not make an official offer, as his government had not yet taken a decision to send troops.

The remainder of the afternoon was taken up by a series of talks about national caveats, the need for communications, logistical and transportation support, and so on. A lawyer on the Polish General Staff cornered me to press for a framework agreement between our Department of Defense and the Polish Ministry of Defense covering precisely who was going to pay for what, how supplies would be delivered, liabilities and limitations, and so forth. I pointed the lawyer to RADM Jaskot as the senior American officer present, as I did not have the authority to discuss this kind of topic. All in all, it was a fruitful first day. The Poles then hosted a social for all the officers and officials attending the conference. As we left the conference site, I noticed a small demonstration outside the gates of the headquarters. They were protesting against Polish troops going to Iraq.

Whereas MG Tysczkiewicz was tall and lean, the Polish lieutenant general who commanded the Polish Land Forces was a big, barrel-chested man. He looked as hard as woodpecker lips. I learned from him that there were factions within the

Polish officer corps; one favored going to Iraq, and the other was opposed to NATO "out-of-area" operations. This was not, he told me, reducible to younger, Western-educated versus older Soviet-educated officers, as the factions contained both young and old, Western- and Soviet-trained officers. He told he personally was very much in favor of standing with the Americans. While he was explaining these difficulties to me, he called over his aide-de-camp. He presented me with a Polish Land Forces coin, and I gave him a CFLCC coin, in the name of LTG McKiernan. The general laughed and then said we must drink vodka together.

The aide-de-camp brought over some dark bread, a spread with some substance I was sure I did not want to know what exactly was, a pickle, and a glass of vodka. The general told me his heart surgeon did not want him to eat any more of this "good Polish peasant food," but the vodka made it all right. He explained to me that the order was to take a bite of pickle, a bite of bread and the spread, and then chase it all with vodka. The Polish general led the way and looked on approvingly, as I did likewise. We had two more vodkas and then the aide-de-camp said the general had another appointment. As he left, I turned to look at the officers from CFLCC who came with me to Warsaw and I said, "Never tell me what I just ate." I think they hurt themselves by holding in their laughter. I still do not know what it was I ate. The adventures in military diplomacy did not end there. During lunch I met Debra Cagan, whom I had seen during some preliminary video teleconferences. Debra Cagan was the Office Director of the State Department's Bureau of European and Eurasian Affairs. Debra Cagan certainly acted with power and first named all the senior American officials and flag officers at the conference. Debra was "a player."

As I joined a circle of officers to talk about day one, Debra walked over to us, put her arm through mine, and said, "Well, boys, who's taking me to dinner? … Kevin." How could I refuse? Off we went. This invitation also allowed me to skip going out to drink with BG Choi. As we walked to the restaurant, she raised the issue of getting medical evacuation helicopters from the Norwegians for the Poles.

Her main purpose at the conference was to appeal to the Norwegians as NATO members and humanitarians. She knew of the political dissension in Norway over the invasion of Iraq, thus she resolved to stress the humanitarian nature of our Phase IV operations and how medical evacuation helicopters and a hospital could support both the Iraqi people and the Poles. Debra repeatedly asked me if I thought this was a great approach. I assured her that from my perspective she was on the correct track and was, again as far as I could see, making real progress in convincing the Norwegians to assist the mission. I was somewhat uncomfortable with this, as most of the topics in the conference were classified at some level, yet Debra continued to talk about this as we walked, and when we were seated in the rather charming restaurant near our hotel. Debra announced that she was so pleased I thought she was making progress that she was going to "call Condi."

I was not sure I'd heard her correctly, but she reached into her purse, pulled out a cellphone, punched in a number, and the next thing I heard was, "White House operator, how may I direct your call?" "Condoleeza Rice, please," Debra said. Her next statement was, "Condi, Darling how are you? Where am I? I am in a funky restaurant in Warsaw with Kevin Benson … He's CFLCC, you know." Debra went on to describe her ploy to convince the Norwegians to provide medical evacuation helicopters and medical support, that I fully supported this proposal, and how well the conference was going. I was hoping that she would not hand me the phone to talk to the National Security Advisor, and thankfully, she did not. This was certainly a different sort of experience for me.

23 May 2003. The second day of the conference was the most revealing. The Spanish came back to the conference and did indeed offer a brigade headquarters—of course, pending governmental approval—and one infantry battalion. The Spanish also demanded command of the division as they would send a major general, but did not offer a headquarters and staff. I really thought this was "Rather cheeky," as our British cousins were whispering. The Poles were very gracious in dealing with the Spanish demand to immediately command the division. The Poles explained that command of the division was a national priority given the Polish Army was split on the mission, as was the greater population of Poland. It was very important politically for the Poles to have a western European unit within the multi-national division. The Poles proposed the Spanish command the multi-national division during the second year of the mission, pending the Spanish government's decision on whether to send a division headquarters. The can was kicked down the road. The successful end result: the Poles potentially gained the third brigade headquarters they needed for their scheme of maneuver. The actual commitment of the Spanish brigade took some time to nail down. Who would serve under whose command was not limited to the Spanish.

The Bulgarians wanted to serve directly under the command of the Poles. The Ukrainians wanted to have the Bulgarian battalion under the command it its brigade headquarters. All national formations needed helicopters for troop transport and medical evacuation, and helicopters were expensive to operate and maintain in the desert. The Polish Land Forces Command's commanding general made a point of telling me that if the Poles were going to send a helicopter squadron to Iraq, they must be reimbursed for the use of their helicopters, and would look to the US for this monetary support. The Ukrainians were not going to bring level two medical support, and the entire division was short level three medical units. Other challenges remained in organizing this headquarters.

Chief among the challenges of the Polish division was the lack of a common language. Orders written initially in Polish and translated to English went to the Spanish, who translated it into Castilian Spanish, but had to further translate it into other Spanish dialects as the Hondurans and Dominicans were brigaded with the

Spanish. The common language between the Poles, Hungarians, Czechs, Slovaks, and Romanians was Russian, as many of their officers were graduates of a variety of Soviet era staff colleges.

I was very impressed with the bearing of MG Tysczkiewicz. He gained a real appreciation for the task he faced. He took swift decisions where he could during the conference and passed those which he could not take to his higher headquarters, Land Forces Command. I learned more about the split in the Polish Armed Forces over NATO out-of-area missions. The factions were defined by background. The faction favoring out-of-area engagement was mostly composed of air assault officers, and those who opposed it were mostly mechanized force officers. The air assault faction dominated the Land Force Headquarters, with the mechanized faction in the General Headquarters. The "old-school" officers, those with limited exposure to NATO, were looking east at the Russians, and felt out-of-area operations were exotic but did nothing to contribute to the defense of Poland. The "new-school" officers had more NATO experience, and felt the contribution to the defense of Poland was in shared experiences with other nations while on an active campaign. Major General Tysczkiewicz was "new school," and determined to accomplish the mission in Iraq.

I compiled notes on "what ifs" for my planners. The biggest uncertainty regarding the commitment of forces by the potential troop-contributing nations was government approval and sustained support. I asked "What if": the Spanish did not send a brigade headquarters; the Ukrainians left early; the Norwegians did not send medical evacuation helicopters and a hospital; and so on. What mattered was getting two operationally capable division-level headquarters to cover down on the MEF zone, thereby allowing the Marines to redeploy and reconstitute the MEUs which all the regional combatant commanders wanted. Any shortfalls in the Polish multinational division would fall back on the US to fill. I also noted the transportation planners needed to cross walk the arrivals and departures during the upcoming months, as all flowed in and out through Kuwaiti ports.

Return to Kuwait

I spent 24 May traveling back to Kuwait. The day was a blur of airports and cramped airline seats. In my C5 report to LTG McKiernan on 25 May, D+67, I plunged back into the mix of planning efforts and trying to refine conditions for security handover associated with the handover of our CJTF-7 mission to V Corps. As I wrote in my journal, this day was "Lost in a blur." I also apologized for sending a lengthy report. Upon my return from Warsaw, I learned my daily reports from the embassy had not reached Kuwait. I had to get back up to speed on what was happening in theater, and quickly. The first effort was getting back into the flow of our force package refinement efforts. We were engaged with CENTCOM and FORSCOM in trying to establish a common picture of what I was coming to think was going to be a rather longer campaign than had been initially expected in Washington.

The urgency of our force package work revolved around a review of Army reserve units and how long they'd been in theater. We provided a complete review on 21 May, as requested by CENTCOM. CENTCOM believed we were at the 80 percent solution. We also did a review of reserve and National Guard units to finalize our 16 force modules. We intended to provide specific available-to-load dates when a unit rotation policy was decided upon, or conditions existed to redeploy units, whichever happened first. US TRANSCOM did not like blank movement dates because the programmers needed dates to do joint flow and analysis system for transportation studies. These studies determined the requirement for the full range of transportation assets needed to move units from the US to theater. We worked with FORSCOM to identify reserve units in the ITO as we were approaching one year since mobilization. These units needed to be evaluated so they may be extended past one year of mobilization, redeployed, or rotated. It was tough, detailed, but necessary, work.

In my daily report I wrote:

> Realize there is a perception of worsening conditions in Iraq in general and Baghdad in particular; however continue to recommend that we ask CENTCOM for permission to redeploy 3ID and 3ID EAD Force Modules. Once we have managed the perceptions and established such conditions as required for redeployment we will already have that approval in hand and be ready to act.

I reported that I would render a complete report on the Warsaw force generation conference in a separate note, but included the following points: I highlighted the excellent work done by MAJs Bill Innocenti, Mack Hagin, and Sim Ripley during the conference.[1] I mentioned that the Poles had ended the conference with a request for another one 2–6 June. The purpose of this second conference would not be force generation but rather the integration of known forces into the Polish plan for the Polish zone. I urged LTG McKiernan to support this request, and further recommended we send representatives from C2, intelligence, C4, logistics, and C6, signals.

During the conference, MG Tysczkiewicz announced he would stick with the timeline proposed during his reconnaissance, which was for his liaison and advanced party to arrive at the end of June and integrate with I MEF. MG Tysczkiewicz and his headquarters staff intended to arrive on or about 1 July. The Polish element

1 Majors Innocenti, Hagin, and Ripley all retired as lieutenant colonels. All three served multiple tours of duty in both Afghanistan and Iraq. Major Innocenti, military intelligence, contributed greatly to our Phase IV plan, Eclipse II. Major Hagin, a superb logistician, assisted in the development of both Cobra II and Eclipse II. Major Ripley, a signaler, also assisted in the development of both major operations plans. These three officers were among the handful of "go to" guys I depended upon to get tough jobs done.

main body was to arrive on or around 15 July. MG Tysczkiewicz requested all other nations' troops be in theater by 15 August so the Polish multi-national division could complete the relief in place of the Marine Expeditionary Brigade by 1 September. I also reported I learned our Joint Chiefs of Staff intended to send a team to New Delhi after Memorial Day 2003, to open talks with the Indian General Staff on the role for an Indian division in Iraq. I was not sure anything would come of this, given the history of Hindu–Muslim tension and the British Indian Army's history in Iraq.

Our operations plan refinement, such as it was, focused on two major efforts; the upcoming handover of the CJTF-7 task to V Corps, and the development of the new Iraqi Corps. While I was in Warsaw, LTC Hendricks had incorporated the results of the staff-to-staff talks with the V Corps Staff into our final draft of the TOA FRAGO. I planned to review the FRAGO on 26 May (I was having trouble overcoming jet lag) and then send it on for command group approval. The TOA operations order, in final draft, was submitted to MG Thurman for review. Once Thurman reviewed and approved the order, LTG McKiernan would receive it for final approval within 24 hours.

LTC Hendricks also completed our headquarters restructure assessment (which was a part of the transfer of authority) and presented it to the Council of Colonels, and then to MGs Stratman, Thurman, and Blackman while I was in Warsaw. I recorded that we presented the restructure and transfer of authority plan to LTG McKiernan on 25 May. The highlights of the plan are below:

- Army Service Component Command ASCC/CJTF-7 Division of Responsibilities Brief. Third Army reverted to the theater ASCC role when V Corps assumed the mantle of CJTF-7. The Third Army Staff developed information papers and by section checklists for the TOA to coordinate with their V Corps counterparts.
- TOA timeline: action officers meeting in Baghdad 26 May (28 CFLCC officers went to the headquarters to coordinate with V Corps). Staff Principals TOA synchronization conference at Camp Doha (3–5 June). Commanders VTC for TOA—9 June. Right-Seat-Ride (12–18 June) TOA to take effect 15 June.

  o ASCC / CJTF-7 TOA Division of Responsibilities Brief: portions presented to CG today. The staff is working on Information Papers and by section checklists for the TOA to coordinate with their V Corps counterparts.
  o TOA timeline: Action Officers Meeting in Baghdad tomorrow (28 CFLCC officers going to EECP to coordinate with V Corps). Staff Principals TOA Synch Conference here at Camp Doha (3–5 June). Commanders VTC for TOA - 9 June. Right-Seat-Ride (12–18 June) TOA takes effect 15 June.

New Iraqi Corps

While I was in Warsaw, the C5 hosted a week of planning meetings and briefings on the NIC. CENTCOM and ORHA/CPA planners attended these meetings. The primary goal of the planning sessions was developing the briefing Mr. Slocombe would give to Secretary Rumsfeld on 29 May. CJTF-7, CENTCOM, and the CPA reached final agreement on many issues which would be carried forward as recommendations to Rumsfeld. These issues included NIC structure, recruiting and vetting, the required training plan, and the number of battalions to be trained, and the size of the NIC for the next year.

The necessity for a Coalition Military Assistance Training Team (CMATT), the requirement to contract for logistic support, and the requirement to contract for trainers were also key parts of the briefing. Mr. Slocombe, MG Blackman, MG Thurman, RADM Robb, and staff made good progress on the NIC this week. The CPA, CENTCOM, CJTF-7 also agreed on site selection criteria, priorities, and methodology. C3 drafted an order to conduct site selection recons for NIC recruiting center, training center and garrison sites. Recons were completed by 6 June. The Corps of Engineers expected to do building refurbishments.

Other logistics support and training contracts were solicited by open bid in Washington. Mr. Slocombe requested that C5, with assistance from CENTCOM, develop cost estimates for the first year of the NIC so he could ask for that amount of money from Rumsfeld while he was in D.C. He also asked C5 to develop a draft statement of work he could give to the Defense Security Assistance Agency for final development so bids could be solicited for contractors to start training the NIC. The product deadline was 27 May. This was ambitious work.

Finally, I reported we continued our preparation for the visit of the Army G3 team. I coordinated with Terry Moran on the agenda for the visit and scope of activities. I acknowledged we intended to focus on a few items as opposed to the entire list proposed by the Army G3. The day truly did pass in a blur, and I knew I was fortunate to have LTC Mike Hendricks and the other great folks in the C5 to pick up the slack while I got my head back into the war.

My report to LTG McKiernan on 26 May, D+68, in large part covered the final details of the impending arrival of the Polish multi-national division and our refinement work on the transfer of authority of JTF-7 to V Corps. McKiernan was in Baghdad preparing for GEN Franks's visit to the city on 27 May. Iraq still continued to simmer in the background.

I reported on my meeting with the Ambassador to Poland, Chris Hill, while in Warsaw. Ambassador Hill asked me to pass on to LTG McKiernan that the Poles wished to reoccupy their embassy in Baghdad. He believed the Polish President might mention this to President Bush in the next week, sometime during Bush's visit to Poland.

The Poles wanted to have an escort from the Jordan–Iraq border to Baghdad. They had arranged security for the embassy. I did not commit anything to Ambassador Hill, save that I would pass on this information. I also ensured that LTG McKiernan knew, at the time, that the CENTCOM policy allowed movement, but not the provision of US security escorts. I acknowledged McKiernan's guidance to inform the Poles that the relief in place of the MEB would be conditions based, and a decision would be taken on the ground by CG, Polish MND, CG, MEB, and CG, CJTF-7. I sent this information to Poland via the Defense Attaché in Poland. I let McKiernan know I had begun coordination for sending a plans team back to Poland for another conference 2–6 June, and that I had suggested to CENTCOM J5 that this June conference be held in Qatar, though as yet there was no word on if the suggestion had been accepted.

Our staff action officers were in Baghdad on 26 May for TOA talks with the V Corps Staff. I let LTG McKiernan know the team had continued to refine the TOA order, and the complete TOA operations order was in its final draft and had been submitted to MG Thurman for review. McKiernan directed V Corps to co-locate its headquarters with Ambassador Bremer's CPA. There were other items to report.

I acknowledged guidance on holding fast on developing requests for redeployment instructions for the 3rd Infantry Division and associated units. McKiernan wanted to wait on this effort, pending the results of his 27 May talks with GEN Franks. I updated the statement of requirements for a northern division at the request of CENTCOM J5. The Joint Chiefs of Staff team would carry this statement as a basis of discussion in staff talks with the Indian General Staff. I stated the basic requirement as a division of motorized infantry of three brigades, with organic combat support units (engineers, and military police) and logistics units. Finally, I let LTG McKiernan know I was coordinating with the deputy chief of staff and secretary of the general staff on arrangements for the Department of the Army, DA, visiting team. The DA team's scheduled arrival was 27 May. I received all of the DA presentations and, along with Terry Moran, refined the CFLCC opening presentations, especially the proposed theater posture.

Opposition activity continued across Iraq. In the south, the Da'wa Party moved to consolidate its position. Leaders of the party worried about Ba'ath Party's activities and requested Coalition patrols to contain the Ba'athists. In the north, we also received reports of Ba'ath activity, although Mosul was relatively quiet. The Ba'athists we discovered were now calling themselves the Return Party.

The 173rd Airborne Brigade reported finding 999 bars of gold. In the center of the country the 3rd Armored Cavalry Regiment reported finding 1,176 bars of gold near al Qaim. The 3rd Cavalry also reported that one of its convoys was attacked, and reported the losses of one Trooper killed and one wounded. The 4th Infantry Division reported a grenade attack, thrown by a woman. No losses were reported. The 4ID felt the attack was conducted on orders of the Badr Corps. Badr continued reporting to the Iranians on Coalition operations. Finally, in Baghdad, Chalabi criticized the lifting of UN sanctions on Iraq as "legitimizing the occupation." This was an interesting shift in Chalabi's position, and one we continued to follow.

Risk Going Out

The most amazing event of all that took place on 27 May, D+69, occurred during a phone call with Terry Moran, who had called me from Baghdad. Moran began the conversation with, "Kevin, are you sitting down?" He then said, "The CINC [GEN Franks] just told the old man to take as much risk going out as we did coming in, and he wants the 3rd ID home by the end of June." I paused before answering. I told Moran I knew he was serious, and then asked how LTG McKiernan had responded to GEN Franks. Moran told me he thought LTG McKiernan handled it well, telling GEN Franks, "We'll get right on it," and not bringing it up during the remainder of the day. Ambassador Bremer had banned Ba'athists from returning to the government and disbanded the Army, and now GEN Franks wanted us to get the 3ID out of theater by the end of June. It was an amazing start to the day.

I received a response from the military attaché in Warsaw regarding the conditions-based relief in place between the Polish division and the Marines. The attaché acknowledged receipt of our message. He then spoke with MG Tysczkiewicz and reported that the latter intended to stick to his timeline, mainly as a forcing function for the Polish General Staff and other troop contributing nations. Again, MG Tysczkiewicz impressed all of us as a tough, decisive leader. We continued coordination for sending the team back to Poland for 2–6 June. The attaché informed us the conference would be larger in scope, as we would assist in developing/refining the Polish initial operations plan. V Corps, I MEF, and C5 would all send teams to assist. I continued to engage with Coalition sustaining efforts.

I told LTG McKiernan that the South Korean senior LNO had requested a warning order and formal order on the change of operational control from I MEF to the 416th Engineer Command upon expansion of the UK national zone. My team began drafting a warning order for release through the C3, once approved by MG Thurman. Our plans section's activities ranged from refining the transfer of authority order to developing the retrograde of forces from theater. I reported that due to the arrival of GEN Franks in Baghdad, the scheduled USAF C-130 flight left behind my lead writer of the transfer of authority order in Baghdad. Refinement work carried on via email and secure phones to incorporate changes requested by V Corps.

I reported I'd acknowledge receipt of a CENTCOM J5 tasking, suspense for the product 29 May, for a detailed month-by-month retrograde plan to a steady state presence in Kuwait. Due to the arrival of the DA G3 team on 27 May for three days of talks, I intended to ask for an extension. The intent in the CENTCOM planning order was to develop a product for a GEN Franks's presentation to Rumsfeld. I intended to use the DA team to help with this effort, and for them to carry the message back to the Army Staff in advance. The DA team was led by MG Huntoon. BG Goedkoop of FORSCOM also accompanied the team. Finally, I reported I was going to Arifjan 28 May to present a briefing to the C4, MG Christianson, and the 377th TSC Staff on the force generation conferences and expected arrival of forces from other nations this summer.

Reports from around the country indicated a range of Ba'ath Party activity, and a corresponding re-energizing of dormant political parties intending to re-enter Iraqi politics. This was good news, as we heard of SCIRI setting up free medical clinics near Tal Afar and SCIRI/Badr Corps taking action to rein in the black market of weapons. On the downside, in the Sunni area of An Bar governate, 3rd Cavalry faced a number of direct fire incidents. In Baghdad, our intelligence reporting indicated planned attacks on Coalition forces, and the reporting came from local intelligence. I recorded this in my journal, "The situation is getting better. So, are these planned attacks desperation or reminders?" We were to take as much risk in leaving as we had coming in, and we'd not yet captured Saddam, his sons, or any of the other fifty high-ranking members of Saddam's regime. It was an amazing day.

In the C5 Plans Update for 28 May, D+70, I reported to LTG McKiernan that we continued to focus on CFLCC priorities, coordinating the integration of Coalition forces and monitoring the order of redeployment. We also monitored the CENTCOM J3 and J5 actions on the new Iraqi Corps and the CPA/ORHA. As in the preceding reports, this report reflected the depth of the planning efforts on near-, mid-, and long-term efforts in theater.

In our force package work, I acknowledged receipt of the task to develop a course of action on force structure for the transition period, along with a personal for message to GEN Franks and RFF (if required). I started the plans group on the development process immediately. I wrote we'd have a draft for MGs Thurman and Webster's review the evening of 29 May, with a final draft on 30 May, and that we would be ready to present to LTG McKiernan on 31 May, as directed.

I ensured that V Corps and I MEF planners were aware of and involved in the process. This effort looked into the future as we crafted the correct size of our CJTF-7 forces for sustained operations in Iraq, ultimately setting conditions for the series of tasks which would be handed over to the Iraqi government. We continued to coordinate with civil affairs, C7, in the form of a warning order for I MEF, the Koreans, the UK, and V Corps command-and-control arrangements for South Korean engineers in the current I MEF zone, and the transition to the UK expanded zone. In our plans activities, we released the transfer of authority order on 28 May. Happily, we received word of an extension on the CENTCOM J5 tasking for a month-by-month schedule of forces withdrawing from theater. I reported my team would pick this task up after the DA Team departed.

Along those lines, I reported we had a superb day of briefings with the DA G3 Team. I sent the most pertinent briefing charts to the Command Group Secretary for placement in the daily briefing book for review. The DA G3 was completely on board with the CFLCC vision of the future theater posture and view on APS.

I offered my opinion the cost of two, two armor and two mechanized infantry battalion, brigade combat team sets of equipment at Arifjan, Kuwait was pretty steep, and required review with a more formal decision to be taken. I confirmed to LTG McKiernan all was set for continuing discussions with DA G3 Team on 29 May.

I let LTG McKiernan know my C5 Team had presented a briefing on the Polish MND to C4 and 377th. We also covered the force generation conferences and expected arrival of forces from other nations that summer. Finally, I reported the C5 Team involved in NIC planning had submitted a cost estimate to Mr. Slocombe in time for his presentations to the chairman, Joint Chiefs of Staff, and Secretary Rumsfeld. We had no word yet on the outcome of the presentations.

Iraq was simmering across all of our zones of operation. In the south, Grand Ayatollah Sistani was working behind the scenes to build Shia consensus and coalesce Shia political power. The Marines also reported a possible Ba'ath Party training camp near al Hillah, and they were working to confirm or deny the report.

There were multiple reports of Ba'ath Party activity in the north, near Mosul, some of which suggested the preparation of insurgency operations to take place in late June and early July. From my journal I recorded "Ba'ath Party still operating so we are still unsuccessful in removing the regime." Al Jazeera reported that Ba'ath Party activity was a popular uprising against the US LTC Frank Jones, our representative at the CPA, let us know that COL Mulholland, the Special Forces Group Commander, had reported on SCIRI activity in the north, and that he wanted to know about a policy on dealing with the Shia SCIRI and Badr Corps. LTG McKiernan needed to write to Ambassador Bremer about policy. Finally, in Baghdad, former Iraqi Army officers were protesting the dissolution of the Iraqi Army and there were reports of former Iraqi Intelligence Service officers organizing groups to resist the Coalition.

We were planning on the transfer of authority of CJTF-7 from CFLCC to V Corps. V Corps was changing command, which was to switch from LTG Wallace to soon-to-be LTG Sanchez. My planners were engaged in "right-sizing" the force, and handing over loosely controlled areas to Coalition divisions. All of this work done with Iraq simmering in the background.

I wrote my report to LTG McKiernan late on the night of 29 May, D+71. My planners' work remained split between a focus on force package work and the planning activities associated with the transfer of authority between CFLCC and V Corps as CJTF-7. I also indicated my thoughts on the long-term presence of our Army in Iraq. I was becoming more unsettled by the building unrest in Iraq, and the lack of forward progress in setting up an Iraqi Government.

Our force package work remained focused on the task of developing a force structure course of action for the transition period. We were trying to convey the dangers to the mission inherent during the TOA, as well as that the range of adversary forces could not fail to observe the withdrawal of US troops and replacement with other Coalition forces. Our OPG worked on the development process that night, and received some timely guidance from our DCG (O), MG Webster. My target was to complete the final draft by the late evening of 29 May for LTG McKiernan's review. I reported that V Corps and I MEF remained involved in the process. Our plans activities were related to the nuts and bolts of the TOA.

The TOA work aimed at continued refinement of the staff update/transfer presentations. Our deputy chief of staff and senior staff went to Baghdad on 29 May for more talks with the V Corps Staff. The transfer included the full range of command-and-control issues, from current operations to sustainment, as well as the reports which CENTCOM needed. This was painstaking work.

I informed LTG McKiernan of the month-by-month review of forces withdrawing, directed by CENTCOM, and which now included the forces we had in Saudi Arabia. Our Army forces in Saudi Arabia consisted of Patriot air defense battalions. The Saudis were purchasing their own Patriot systems, and were pressing for our units to depart as theirs came online. My planners put this effort on the back burner while the Department of the Army team visited us.

Our staff talks with the DA G3 team concluded on 29 May. We covered DA G3 topics. The department-level planners were concerned about the long-term nature of the Iraq mission and how the Army could continue to provide trained and ready forces over an expected long term. My C5 planners focused on the redeployment of forces and rotation period for sustainment of a force in Iraq. This was sobering work too, since none of us really had an idea of how long the mission would go on for. The DA G3 team conducted final presentation reviews the morning of 30 May, and would outbrief LTG McKiernan the evening of 30 May. The DA G3 team departed for Washington at midnight on 30 May. The series of meetings I'd had with the planners from Washington put me in tune with views from the capital, and I was concerned.

I let LTG McKiernan know I intended to write a short paper on a proposal for using a time limit as the criterion for the decision on retrograde and withdrawal of the force from Iraq. I was increasingly convinced our Army could not sustain a large force in Iraq for a long period of time. I was also more and more convinced that the military needed to set an end date for the mission, as this would spur efforts from other agencies of our government to assist the efforts in Iraq. Setting a date would also serve to tell the Iraqis we were not interested in occupying their country, but rather were more interested in the Iraqis reestablishing governance so we could engage in business and trade. This might have been somewhat naïve on my part, but I felt we could not remain in the country for long given my sense of a lack of US interest in a long term, on the ground, forces commitment. I also did not think our Coalition was interested in remaining in Iraq for very long either.

I recorded the increasing levels of unrest in my journal. In the south, tribal elders near the Iraq–Iran border were growing concerned over increasing Iranian influence. These elders wanted Coalition presence to counter this influence, and soon. In the north, Mosul, pensioners and ex-military demonstrated for back pay. The demonstrations grew and became better organized. We had reports of a larger demonstration planned for 8–9 June. In the center of the country, between Ar Ramadi and Fallujah, a Jordanian fuel resupply convoy was attacked. The Jordanians established a pattern; a single, soft convoy every four to five days. The ambush, according to reports, was well organized. Ramadi and the west of Iraq was growing more and more dangerous. Baghdad sources reported growing planning efforts for attacks within the city.

On a happier note, I concluded my report to LTG McKiernan by letting him know one of our C5 troopers had reenlisted on 29 May. Specialist Takela Simeton had reenlisted to become a military police officer. I also reported that we had said goodbye to our comrade-in-arms, LTC Chris Field, on the evening of 29 May. Field had returned to Australia to take command of 1st Battalion, Royal Australian Regiment in December.

30 May, D+72, and my report to LTG McKiernan was little different than for the preceding days. The force package work concentrated solely on completing the details of the process to hand over the CJTF-7 authority to V Corps. The other planning activities ranged from planning redeployment of forces in theater to reviews of new plans for the CENTCOM area of operations. Of course, in the background Iraq continued to seethe.

Our work with V Corps continued as well. In my report, I stressed the V Corps planners' thoughts on "right sizing," and future combat operations to destroy pockets of resurgent enemy cells in the zone. I felt this was prudent, and although I knew LTG McKiernan was deeply involved in this effort, I wanted to let him know I too was working in that direction. I also recalled the email BG Vince Brooks had sent me months earlier.

Brooks pointed out Washington was impatient. We had not yet captured Saddam, or any of the top Ba'ath leaders, but we were still being pressed to bring troops home. This effort was slipping from senior leader attention, given what was going on in theater. I felt I needed to point out we must continue the work on redeployment, especially in regard to the scheduling of ships and planes for redeployment. We were nearing the window in which it would be difficult to impossible to redeploy forces in June, given ship and plane ordering times with TRANSCOM.

Our plans activities reflected all the other tasks my planners received. Planners never had easy days in Kuwait. We continued a review of the month-by-month schedule of forces withdrawing from Saudi Arabia. I let LTG McKiernan know that my C5 team would depart for the next conference with the Polish MND staff on 31 May. I reported on the conclusion of the DA G3 team visit which had addressed some of our major Army concerns about: rotation policy, major command status, Army Prepositioned Stocks reconstitution, communications modernization, and general officer positions.

McKiernan told the departing G3 team two important things; he felt there was a continuing long-term need for a CFLCC function in Third US Army. He also stressed our Army needed to rotate entire units into theater; he said, "We can't keep the 377th TSC here forever. We must rotate entire units even if this breaks the wartrace."[2] I asked myself, *Do we want to have the most active theater be 90 percent reliant on the RC, or do we break the paradigm?* I was thinking in line with LTG McKiernan. Iraq was not quiet while my planners worked.

In my journal, I noted that our C2 had reported no change in the indicators of a growing Ba'ath Party resurgence. Our intelligence section and the British were working on developing human intelligence sources to reinforce technical means. MG Marks was clear: "HUMINT is the most important factor in this fight." In the north of Iraq, the Turks told us they were beginning "small ambush-like operations against KADEK." We also received reports of the Muslim Brotherhood attempting to form a cell in Tal Afar. In the west of Iraq, we received reports of groups, ranging from Saddam Fedayeen to Palestinian mercenaries, preparing to attack American forces. Many of the reports were unconfirmed, and indeed never panned out, but it was enough to keep us all busy.

My report of 31 May, D+73, to LTG McKiernan again reflected the mundane yet necessary work of the planners. We continued our focus on CFLCC/CJTF-7 priorities, coordinating the integration of Coalition forces, monitoring the order of redeployment and the NIC and the CPA/ORHA. I reported on our work developing the task for a presentation for Ambassador Bremer and GEN Franks which conveyed McKiernan's views on the changing nature of force requirements in Iraq. The latter had directed us to focus on assessment, stance, and forming/sustaining the force over time. I coordinated the effort with both V Corps and I MEF planners. I let McKiernan know we would complete the work by the morning of 1 June.

The other plans activities ranged from supporting the logisticians in setting up a two-day effort to produce the required theater-wide concept of support to informing LTG McKiernan of the departure of the C5 team for the next conference with the Polish MND Staff. We also continued work on Coalition integration. Most of the current Coalition units were battalion sized or smaller. I recalled GEN Shinseki's testimony in February wherein he offered that we needed two hundred and fifty thousand troops to establish security and stability in Iraq. The Polish multi-national division, MND numbered around eight thousand five hundred Soldiers. The UK division totaled nearly ten thousand. Washington was pressing us to get down to two US divisions in country by September, so CJTF-7's total strength would be

2 The wartrace is a method by which Army Reserve units are linked to active headquarters for planning, as well as a reflection on how the reserve is apportioned for actual war plans. In so many words McKiernan was telling the Army G3 officers he thought the war was going to take longer than we all thought.

around fifty thousand troops, with an uncertain number of newly formed Iraqi security forces. We wondered if this would be sufficient, and based on intelligence reports, we did not think it would be.

In the south of Iraq, Bakir al Hakim conducted Friday prayers while carrying a rifle. He preached that the UN Security Council resolution legitimized the occupation of Iraq. The Marines reported renewed Ba'ath Party activity in and around Karbala. In the north, the 101st Air Assault conducted operations against reemerging Ba'ath Party remnants. There was activity all across the center part of the country, from Badr Corps training tribal fighters in small unit tactics and weapons handling to the Muslim Brotherhood operating in Fallujah. We were looking for links between Sunni groups, the Ba'ath, and Wahabi extremists, while also looking for links between Shia elements and Iran. It was not clear if the groups were preparing to attack us and the Coalition forces, each other, or both. The military activity competed with political activity in Baghdad. All our analysis led to the observation that the parties were seeking legitimacy with the people and standing to compete in planned elections.

CHAPTER NINE

My Last Month in Theater, June 2003

The reports from 1 June through 14 June reflected a pace of operations and a focus on the transfer of authority for CJTF-7 from Third Army to V Corps. We were aware of the activity in theater, but my focus and that of my planners was drawn to the handover briefing, continued planning for the retrograde of US forces, coupled with the arrival of replacement US and Coalition forces. The plans update to LTG McKiernan on 1 June, D+74, set the basis for my continued reports. We monitored work done by others on developing the new Iraqi Corps, but really could not do anything to affect the work. We continued to focus on CJTF-7 priorities, coordinating the integration of Coalition forces, and monitoring the order of redeployment, but only for our situational awareness.

I used this day, 1 June, to prepare for a trip to Qatar with LTG McKiernan, who was to deliver a proposed presentation for Ambassador Bremer to GEN Franks. My planners and I completed the briefing and sent the presentation to V Corps and I MEF to ensure all commanders knew what McKiernan intended to say. I was scheduled to depart for Qatar on 2 June with the C35 and C2. While I was in Qatar, my planners worked on developing the RFFs for the light infantry forces we felt we needed to establish security conditions in Iraq, and for the 3rd Brigade, 2nd Infantry Division, a Stryker equipped brigade combat team. We believed the Stryker brigade could conduct security operations in a wider area, given the breadth of the command and control systems within the brigade.[1] These forces reflected McKiernan's thinking on the types of forces CJTF-7 was going to need to conduct operations and establish security conditions, given the growing range of adversaries we faced.

The major plans activity was our continuing work on Coalition integration. The British handled the reception and integration of the Italian brigade with no US assistance required, as planned thus far. My C5 Plans team would speak to the British PJHQ (COL Everard) while in Warsaw about the rest of the inbound

1 Stryker brigades were equipped with wheeled armored vehicles and an advanced command control system that enabled a shared common operating picture through the sharing of information and displays on computer screens.

Coalition countries for the UK area of operations. This was important given the fact we all depended upon the use of Kuwaiti port facilities to enter the Iraq theater of operations.

I reported that on 29 May I learned Secretary Rumsfeld had approved the NIC plan briefed by Mr. Slocombe. We received a copy of the presentation Slocombe actually used to brief Rumsfeld. It was disappointing, as CJTF-7 was going to be responsible for pulling the corps together, yet had no real authority to make things happen to accomplish this task. My view was there would be a wrestling match between CJTF-7 and Ambassador Bremer's CPA.

I ended my report on a positive note. I let LTG McKiernan know we had the great privilege of promoting our administrative NCO, SGT Teltoe, to Staff Sergeant. Command Sergeant Major Sparks assisted in the promotion. Once again, Sergeant Teltoe took great delight in telling me I was the lowest-ranking person she'd ever worked for, as her first post in the Army was in the office of the Supreme Allied Commander, Europe, General Wes Clark. Sergeant Teltoe was a superb non-commissioned officer.

I rendered my C5 Plans Update for 2 June, D+75, to LTG McKiernan from Qatar. We were both in Qatar for a visit to CENTCOM forward headquarters. My planners were monitoring our CFLCC/CJTF-7 priorities, but our focus of effort was clearly with CENTCOM efforts in preparing for a visit by President Bush and General Pace, the vice chairman of the Joint Chiefs of Staff. We endured a bomb scare at CENTCOM headquarters during our visit. We waited in the Qatar heat until the headquarters was cleared. We never received any other information on this threat.

LTG McKiernan delivered the Bremer presentation to GEN Franks. I did not get to attend the briefing. While LTG McKiernan was engaged, I went through the Operation *Iraqi Freedom* update presentation with the CENTCOM J5 planners. The focus of our discussions was on how to use this information, as well as anything else we could provide to help CENTCOM J5 prepare a response for GEN Franks to a chairman, of the Joint Chiefs personal for, P4, message. The CENTCOM J5 planners shared the message with me. The chairman wanted to know GEN Franks's assessment of the campaign to date, in terms of expectations for establishment of security conditions which would allow for a reduction of US forces, and a handover of the mission to NATO and other Coalition forces. I informed LTG McKiernan that the CENTCOM planners' deadline for a response presentation was 3 June, for GEN Franks review prior to a VTC briefing sometime on 4 June. I also affirmed him that I would remain engaged with the CENTCOM J5 on the effort. My best guess was we could influence the presentation but might not get to see it before it went to the chairman given the press of activities in Qatar with the impending presidential visit.

I pressed LTG McKiernan a bit, writing I would stand by to receive an update on what happened inside the room with GEN Franks, and any new thoughts or guidance on the proposed briefing to Ambassador Bremer from GEN Franks. I informed him I would continue to work with CENTCOM in support of the effort to prepare for the briefing to the President. I would coordinate with Moran on our input to the CENTCOM J5. Lastly, I informed LTG McKiernan that a C5 team would participate in reconnaissance of potential NIC training locations in the coming week. One team focused on the north, and the other would travel in the south with I MEF.

What struck me about our visit to CENTCOM was there was no daily J2 intelligence and J3 current operations update for either theater of war: Iraq or Afghanistan. I noted in my journal, "we have zip → KADEK policy, POTUS briefing and CJCS P4." I could not get a hard copy or electronic version of the baseline presentation for the President, nor the personal for message from the chairman to GEN Franks. It was tough to craft input to either without being able to study the drafts.

The C5 Plans Update for 3 June, D+76. The major event of this day was a report on missing US Army engineers. The engineers had been conducting a water reconnaissance of the Shatt-al-Arab waterways to Umm Qasr. We learned the Iranian Navy took the engineers and watercraft to Iran. The Iranians questioned our engineers, then released them. The Iranians retained custody of the watercraft captains and first mates. These were Kuwaiti citizens, but they had been born in Iran. The Iranians had questions over their country of origin. The Kuwaiti Foreign Ministry took charge of negotiations. Aside from this excitement, it was another day of a broad range of efforts on CFLCC/CJTF-7 priorities. Our efforts ranged from an array of presentations and input to CENTCOM presentations to coordinating the integration of Coalition forces. We also continued monitoring actions on the NIC.

I went over the Bremer briefing with our OPG to ensure the group had an appreciation of the way ahead. Nudging LTG McKiernan again, I stated I would "coordinate with Terry [Moran] for a precise read-out of what was said during the briefing to COMCENT." Regarding two other briefing efforts—General Pace and the President—I wrote that I'd learned Pace arrived in Qatar early, so briefings were not required, but I wanted to see what was on the charts. I coordinated with the CENTCOM J5 on the President's briefing preparation and learned no slides were required. MG Renuart was working only on talking points for GEN Franks. I said I would get a set of these from the CENTCOM planners for review and pass them on to our command group.

Our other plans activities ranged from completing a draft of the work on the month-by-month schedule of forces withdrawing from Saudi Arabia to completing a review of UNSCR 1438. Passed on 14 October 2002, the resolution concerned the bombings in Bali, Indonesia. It reaffirmed UNSCR 1373, passed after 9/11, and called on all states to cooperate with Indonesian authorities. Both of the Security Council resolutions were counter-terrorism resolutions. I sent the information review to the command group. There was no impact on CFLCC/CJTF-7 tasks based on our review. The major event in our plans activities regarded a report from the C5 team in Poland.

The C5 team called us from Poland and reported that the Poles were making the assumption US units would be available to meet unfilled key capabilities on the Polish statement of requirements. Specific capabilities in question were: military police, civil affairs, psychological & information operations, and MEDEVAC helicopter units. MEDEVAC remained the highest medical issue. Neither the Poles nor any other nation were offering this capability. The current Polish MoD and General Staff's assumption was that these forces would remain in place, because the Poles had not been instructed otherwise for over three weeks and their requirements still existed. The team reported it was impossible to continue detailed planning without finalizing the force structure within the Polish sector. In my journal I noted:

> The Polish General Staff are very proactive and are considering a request today to the Minister of Defense to increase Polish forces to fulfill the requirement for a third Bde HQ. The team is not sure how this will be accepted and is only provided to communicate the Polish Staff's understanding of the overall requirements to be successful.

Our team also reported that the CENTCOM J5 position on US troops was we would not offer any troops to the Poles unless directed. This was all a question of money. Our Coalition partners knew we, the US, wanted other flags to play a role in Iraq. They used this knowledge to get as much as possible from US resources to avoid covering costs for vital needs. It was a clever approach.

In other Coalition integration work, I reported earlier on the status of the Jordanian civil police. I spoke with MG Renuart and RADM Robb, CENTCOM J3 and J5. Both C3 and C5 believed we, CJTF-7, should send a message to GEN Franks formally requesting this type of assistance. This would get CENTCOM engaged in talking to the Jordanians about which type of assistance the Jordanians were offering, informally, via special forces channels. I told LTG McKiernan I would work on the draft message with MG Thurman. I also reported that reconnaissance of potential NIC training locations continued.

The CPA announced a weapons policy late in May. The intent of the policy was to control the amount of firearms families could retain. From north to south, there was confusion and growing opposition to Ambassador Bremer's policy.

We observed the Turks conducting company- and battalion-level operations against KADEK. We also learned the Iranian Ministry of Intelligence and Security was working in As Sulaymanieh, and was being guarded by Kurdish Peshmerga. This was most interesting, and we continued to watch this activity. We were unsure of what this meant in so far as relations across the Iraq–Iran border. We were developing intelligence and sources on efforts to attack US forces, but thus far there had been no hard and actionable intelligence on just who was responsible for the series of small-scale attacks. Iraq continued to simmer.

Now the C5 Plans Update for 4 June, D+77. This report to LTG McKiernan continued to reflect the split focus of myself and my planners. We continued to focus on CFLCC/CJTF-7 priorities, but these became more and more centered on upcoming events, the President's visit, and the mission handover in 11 days. I was still trying to pry a draft of the CENTCOM proposed talking points for GEN Franks's use when he spoke with the President, with no luck. The big event for my planners was news on Coalition building from Poland and India.

The C5 team called from Poland. I passed word on to MAJ Innocenti to hold our line on not committing US forces to the Poles. Innocenti reported that it appeared the Poles would go back to their MoD and ask for two vice one brigade headquarters for their division. The Polish General Staff had major concerns over the retention of US MPs in zone to assist the Poles in sector security and situational awareness. The Poles remained very concerned over the availability of dedicated MEDEVAC support from CJTF 7 if they were unable to convince another NATO nation to provide this support. We were all continuing to work on getting this support for the Poles. Time was not our ally in this effort, as the Poles were getting close to their deployment timeline.

We did get some good news on the Coalition front from the CENTCOM VTC, although it later turned out to be a "first report." MG Renuart announced that the Indians would contribute a division to the Coalition. I called COL Fitzgerald immediately after the VTC. He could not confirm this announcement, but did say a very high-level, presidential, vice presidential or secretary of defense note had gone to the Indian government requesting this support. Fitzgerald also reported that the Spanish had reconsidered their stance on providing troops and would provide a brigade under command of the Poles. This was very good news.

We worked with V Corps planners on a draft message to CENTCOM J5 requesting assistance in the form of Arab civil police to both train Iraqi police forces and to patrol the cities in Iraq. We were trying very hard to get visible Arab support for Iraq. I also reported the NIC garrison recon team had returned late this evening. I would provide a detailed recon report on 5 June.

Iraq was growing more dangerous, or at least giving the appearance of being so to Coalition forces. In the south, in An Nasiriyah, retired and former Iraqi military were demonstrating against the CPA order disbanding the Army. In the north of Iraq and in Baghdad we continued receiving reports of former Ba'ath Party loyalists and regime members working to organize resistance. The Turks told us that Ansar al Islam was planning attacks on US forces, as well as the Kurdish PUK and KDP. Reports from Baghdad indicated the same, with a goal of an attack by mid-June. In the west, the 3rd Armored Cavalry Regiment continued to have firefights and we were getting reports of even more attacks to come.

I noted in my journal that I needed to follow up on what type of division the Indians would send, logistical arrangements, and rules of engagement. The Indians never did send a division of troops to Iraq.

Onto the C5 Plans Update for 5 June, D+78. We neared the handover of the CJTF-7 mission. My planners and I continued our efforts to look to the mid- and long term regarding the mission in Iraq and returning our Third Army headquarters to a theater-wide focus. We were also monitoring CCJ3 and -5 actions on the NIC and the CPA/ORHA.

Our redeployment and force structure work ranged from trying to get a copy of the CENTCOM talking points raised to the President, to dealing with notes from our liaison officer to Ambassador Bremer. I never did get a set of the CENTCOM talking point papers, and I let LTG McKiernan know I was pursuing an after-action report. I sent a briefing shell on CJTF-7 plans to our forward headquarters in Baghdad in support of MG Webster's talks with the Japanese. We continued to support broadening the Coalition, but we understood the Japanese offered nothing of substance for the Coalition.

On 4 June, the forward headquarters operations section briefed Ambassador Bremer on the state of the Coalition: who was on the ground and, who was expected, when. Ambassador Bremer offered the opinion that Coalition contributions (sans the Brits) were not as capable as US forces. He wanted to ensure that we factored this into our redeployment plans and stance. I was glad MG Blackman directed that I put LTC Frank Jones with the CPA. I trusted Frank Jones to reassure the ambassador.

Our plans activities revolved around building the Coalition. I reported we'd received a series of C5 team reports from Poland. The reports contained Polish requests for information which we passed on to our operational plans group and the CENTCOM J3 and J5. The conference was going well, all in all. The team did report with the prospect of the Spanish providing a brigade headquarters and a battalion, plus necessary engineer and logistical support. Also, there would be another conference in Poland prior to the deployment of the Polish headquarters to theater. The CENTCOM J5 representative suggested CJTF-7 and the Joint Movement Center send a team to remain with the Poles through deployment to theater. I told LTG McKiernan I needed to study the feasibility of the suggestion.

In other Coalition-building efforts, I reported I could not confirm the report of the contribution of an Indian Division. I would continue to press CENTCOM for information. I reported completion of a draft message for MG Thurman's release regarding Arab police. Action officers and senior staff were all working hard to get an "Arab" face on the Iraqi "Arab" street. This included working on getting the NIC operational as quickly as possible.

Our NIC garrison reconnaissance team wrote a superb report. The essence of the report was that while there were several locations in the south which could accommodate a battalion, there were none larger than one-battalion posts which could be refurbished without considerable expense. The locals were using the former garrisons in the south as "Home Depots" for building material. The British also had their own ideas on establishing the NIC. They wanted to use an Iraqi military consultative council of former officers. I suggested that LTG McKiernan use MG Whitley to get more details on this proposal.

Finally, I reported I had reviewed a "Hunting Saddam" document from CENTCOM J3. Essentially, it was a recap of the security procedures underway in Iraq to capture/kill high-value targets. There was nothing in the document that was objectionable. This was timely, as our reports from the north of the country indicated Ba'ath Party diehards preparing a series of attacks at the end of June.

There were rumblings in the center of the country about new groups of regime loyalists forming and acquiring arms and munitions. From Baghdad, we learned the KDP was considering not participating in the Interim Iraqi Council which Ambassador Bremer was forming. Barzani intended to go to Najaf to talk to clerics. We interpreted this as an attempt to establish a broad political base. It was an interesting move on his part. I imagined that in Iraq, all politics was local as well.

The C5 Plans Update for 6 June, D+79, covered the same efforts as previous reports, with two exceptions. First, I kept LTG McKiernan informed of the news from Poland on the development of the Polish-led multinational division. Second, I highlighted a development on the future use of Ali al Salem Air Base as a staging base for our future Persian Gulf theater security and engagement strategy.

I informed LTG McKiernan that we had received a series of C5 team reports from Poland. These reports contained Polish RFIs which we passed on to the operational plans group and future operations section for answers. The conference went well, based on the reports. The team further recommended CFLCC and the 377th TSC participate in the next planning conference, and CFLCC/377th TSC plan on supporting a CENTCOM-led movement/coordination cell embedded in the Polish General Staff for this operation. I recommended that we think about this suggestion.

I used my report to make a proposal for the future of Ali Al Salem Air Base, since we had a chance to step into existing CFACC contracts. GEN Franks's proposed posture of US forces in the region, following the conclusion of operations in Iraq, called for a rotating brigade combat team in Kuwait as the combatant commander's ready brigade in theater, stationing another reinforced brigade combat team set of combat vehicles and equipment at our base at Arifjan, with Army watercraft (and possibly high-speed vessels in the future) at the Kuwait Naval Base. This force posture, coupled with a US and Kuwaiti desire to reduce our visible footprint in Kuwait City, led me to offer that Third Army should consider establishing Ali al Salem Air Base as our aerial port of debarkation. My rationale was this would take advantage of the good road network, the straight route to the desert training areas, the base capable of expanding to accommodate incoming troops, and the assured power, water, and fuel, all of which supported this course of action. I suggested we should present this proposal to GEN Franks. If he concurred, we could make this a part of the 18 June presentation to the Kuwaiti MoD and the Kuwaiti chief of defense staff. I told LTG McKiernan I would present this to our plans group on 7 June and get started on fleshing out a proposal.

Lastly, I reported I completed a review of the Joint Forces Command "quick look" at the campaign thus far, and on the lessons learned from the results of the campaign. I sent my review to the chief of staff through MG Thurman. Personally, I believed the trouble with the "quick" look was just that: it was quick, and tended to form based opinions on the euphoria or gloom of the moment. I offered that this would be the only report anyone would bother reading, while the more thorough reports would be buried, as the authors knew.

Iraq continued to simmer. In the south, SCIRI and its militia, the Badr Corps, was changing its message to the Shia from armed resistance to rebuilding, which was a somewhat positive indicator. There was also a report of the assassination of a Sunni tribal leader, our first indication of more Shia–Sunni violence. We received reports of a potential shipment of man-portable antiaircraft missiles coming to Ansar al Islam, although this was a first report. We worked to establish a database of these activities as we prepared for our battle handover of the mission in Iraq to V Corps.

The focus of our efforts in the days up to our handover remained on refining the V Corps staff's understanding of operations in theater, from intelligence gathering to Coalition force arrival. There were other events which affected our planning and execution efforts.

The C5 Plans Update for 7 June, D+80, covered one such event, among the many which happened. I learned this day the Civil Reserve Air Fleet had been ordered released from TRANSCOM. This meant our maximum capacity for redeployment went from four thousand to two thousand personnel per day, at most. I also learned that the DoD was slowly depleting the number of Military Sealift Command ships holding at Diego Garcia. The consequence of this was that we would need to request ships and planes for redeploying units 50 days prior to any departure date we might want, which meant we needed to submit the request for redeployment for our units, especially the 3ID, immediately if we wished to avoid delays in Kuwait.

Plans activities ranged from reporting the return of our C5 team from Poland on 8 June, to still being unable to confirm the report of the contribution of an Indian division for Coalition duty. We were also continuing to press State Department contacts for information to confirm/deny rumored State reluctance to ask for Arab police to support our efforts to secure Iraqi cities.

We conducted a VTC with LTG Cody, the Army G3, and what appeared to be the entire Army staff. The major topic of discussion was our request for infantry units, light and Stryker, to assist in furthering our efforts to control Iraqi cities and other areas near the borders. Cody relayed that he understood our request, and told us his challenge was finding enough infantry to meet our requests and those coming from Afghanistan. He was also keeping an eye on Korea. LTG McKiernan shared with LTG Cody Ambassador Bremer's concern over the quality and constraints on inbound Coalition forces, which led the ambassador to be concerned over the pace of redeployment of US divisions. We spoke of the so called "way ahead" CJTF-7 stance message we sent to Bremer.

The Iraq theater continued to roil with overt and covert movements. In the south in and around Basrah, SCIRI leaders and religious leaders from Iran were crossing into Iraq. We interpreted this move to Najaf as an attempt to establish a religious center to counter al-Sadr's growing influence. The Kurdish leader, Barzani, met with Grand Ayatollah Sistani. This was a political meeting focusing on how long US and Coalition forces would remain in Iraq. At the joint press conference, both men called for no clashes with Coalition forces, but did call for resistance to Ambassador Bremer's authority. These men wanted an Iraqi Government in place at a much faster pace than was scheduled at the time.

In the center of the country, a new party, al-Awda, the party of return, offered $100 bounties for each American killed. The group was hiring snipers for action in Basrah, as well as indicating it intended to build a nation-wide effort against us. There was nothing really conclusive from our reporting, but it quickly became an area of concern for the J2. All of this contributed to the urgency of ensuring V Corps was completely read into everything we had about the current threat situation.

The day of our mission handover to V Corps continued to loom closer. Looking at my reports from 8 June until the handover, one can see that while this was a major event, it was still but one event out of many we dealt with in these final days of being in charge in Iraq. The C5 Plans Update for 8 June, D+81, continued our focus on redeployment, force structure work, and activities related to planning. We also monitored our staff actions on the NIC and the CPA/ORHA.

I reported I'd coordinate with V Corps on the effective date and time group for the TOA order. I suggested the evening of 15 June 2003 to the V Corps G3 Plans. Along with coordinating with the CFLCC staff for input into the order, my officers and I continued refining our developing RFFs for forces based on the CJTF-7 stance message to include the appropriate combat support and combat service support units for echelon above-division support. Ensuring this support was present in theater became especially important as we envisioned the deployment and employment of a Stryker brigade combat team relieving the 3rd Cavalry Regiment in the north and west of Iraq. We could not allow this new unit to fail.

I learned the UK multinational division projected it would be fully set in its expanded zone, with all national contingents set in zone, by 15 July. The British 3rd Mechanized Division expected to complete the relief in place of the British 1st Armoured Division on 12 July.

The final item in force structure dealt with the completion of our report/presentation on the Warsaw planning conference. I let LTG McKiernan know that

CFLCC would bring the Polish and associated forces into theater conducting the reception, staging, and onward movement portions of the overall process. CJTF-7 would then integrate the Polish MND into its battle rhythm. The Poles' base plan did not include the Spanish brigade, as there was still no concrete offer from Spain to contribute troops. Time was moving on this, although CENTCOM, the Defense and State Departments, and European Command were pressing the Spanish for such a decision. Our plans activities also demanded focus and effort.

I reported on my continued efforts to try to confirm the report of the contribution of an Indian division to the Coalition. I told LTG McKiernan that I had spoken with CCJ5 Tampa. Colonel Halverson reported that the military-to-military talks had gone well, but as usual the holdup was in the policy area. The Indian government still had to act. Until then, we had no firm offer of support. I continued to coordinate with CENTCOM J5 on a review of our Kuwaiti Ministry of Defense presentation. I let LTG McKiernan know I would keep the key folks in the CENTCOM J5 informed on the proposed content, and send the final proposed briefing to them for a higher headquarters' review. I knew LTG McKiernan was doing the same with GEN Franks, and I assured McKiernan that our work would be done for the 18 June presentation to the Kuwaiti chief of defense staff and key people in their MoD.

We continued to reach out to former members of the Iraqi senior military. I acknowledged a task to develop a short, simple, graphically oriented presentation on the new Iraqi Army for LTG McKiernan's use at a 13 June meeting with former Iraqi senior military. The presentation covered 1) a summary of prospective new Iraqi Army sites, 2) consolidated information on weapons, vehicles, equipment, and, 3) where the ex-military population centers were located. We needed the involvement of these men to set conditions for success of the re-building task, which was a part of the handover of authority to V Corps.

In my journal, I recorded LTG McKiernan's intense focus on a smooth mission handover. McKiernan directed me to think through any potential points of friction with the handover and let him know what I thought these might be, and how they should be dealt with. He directed there would be no ceremony, just the final handover briefing. MG Thurman was charged with reviewing the headquarters task organization, supported by our personnel director. McKiernan wanted to ensure V Corps retained enough of our late-arriving staff augmentees to tide V Corps over until its own replacement flow began. As the old Army saying went, I was spinning a large number of plates, and some of them were getting a bit wobbly. Handover was approaching and we still had not captured Saddam, his sons, or any of the major regime individuals on the blacklist.

The days were rushing by, and mission handover was closing on us. The main thrust of my C5 Plans Update for 9 June, D+82, remained on the efforts to ensure V Corps was as prepared as possible to take over the role as controlling headquarters in theater.

I worked on the details of the battle handover between my C5 and V Corps G3 Plans. I reported to LTG McKiernan that we had no major issues in plans. In the remaining days, our focus was on Coalition integration and the new Iraqi Army efforts as major points for information handover. I reminded McKiernan I intended taking LTC E. J. Degen, the V Corps G3 Plans chief, to Qatar to work with CENTCOM J5 on a smooth Coalition integration and overall theater information handover.

I shared with LTC Degen the reports from the members of the CENTCOM J5 team who had remained in Poland. The Poles requested an order which focused their deployment and answers questions on payments, supply requisitions, and other national-level memorandum of record items. Developing this order took an effort between CENTCOM J5, CFLCC, and V Corps/CJTF-7. While we were working on handover, our talks with the Kuwaitis also demanded our time and effort.

I reported to LTG McKiernan that my lead planner on the Kuwaiti MoD presentation worked with MG Stratman. Of our CFLCC general officers, MG Stratman knew the Kuwaitis the best. I acknowledged receipt of guidance to send the presentation to LTG McKiernan for review prior to clearing it with CENTCOM J5. McKiernan wanted to keep the presentation short. He also directed I would give the presentation to the chief of defense staff while he sat next to the Kuwaiti chief.

My final report note of 9 June let LTG McKiernan know we had received a presentation to review from MG Renuart. GEN Franks intended to take the theater overview presentation to Washington for presentation to the chairman, Joint Chiefs of Staff, and Secretary Rumsfeld. McKiernan was in Baghdad that day, so I let him know I had sent the draft to Terry Moran as well. I would coordinate our response and send it to Baghdad for his review.

As I was focusing on these operational- and strategic-level details, the war continued. In the south, the various Shia leaders were contending for power among themselves. Al Sadr went to Qom, Iran, ostensibly for a religious retreat. In the center and north we received reports on various regime loyalist groups trying to recruit people for a fight, although whether against our Coalition or the Shia was not really clear.

US units in the west were developing intelligence on enemy training camps and planning on operations to kill them. In the north, the 173rd Airborne Brigade began execution of Operation *Peninsula Strike*. The operation was against remnants of Ansar al Islam. While Baghdad was momentarily quiet, there was fighting at the tactical level across the country. Our conventional and special operations forces were fighting very hard.

Ambassador Bremer directed us to look into reports of sabotage against the southern oil fields. Of course, these were key to Iraqi economic recovery, thus a focus for Bremer. The British, who controlled the south, were not reporting widespread sabotage. LTG McKiernan directed our civil affairs and intelligence sections to get a solid picture on the extent of the damage so he could talk to Ambassador Bremer.

In my journal, I recorded a prescient comment from LTG Abizaid, who had said we should all focus our intelligence efforts on the so-called "Sunni triangle" of Tikrit, Baqubah, and ar-Ramadi. At the time, I wondered if LTG Abizaid was thinking about a possible insurgency forming against us and a future Iraqi government.

The C5 Plans Update for LTG McKiernan of 10 June, D+83, reflected the urgency of our mission handover of CJTF-7 to V Corps, as well as a refocusing of effort on longer-range planning tasks. My planners were working diligently on tying up loose ends in the handover of plans tasks. Our redeployment and force structure work centered on the completion of the RFF in accord with the proposed forces we projected would be needed over time. I worked with the V Corps G3 Plans and sent it to Baghdad for review. The RFF, as LTG McKiernan told LTG Wallace and LTG Sanchez, included combat, combat support, and combat service support units for the smooth continuation of the mission in Iraq. I told LTG McKiernan that I would execute a right-seat, left-seat ride with V Corps G3 Plans which focused on the new Iraqi Army project. This included a trip to Qatar to ensure the key officers in CENTCOM J5 knew the key officers in V Corps G3 Plans.

The focus of the information exchange and trip to Qatar was Coalition integration. My planners transferred all files on Coalition building to V Corps G3 Plans. I assured LTG McKiernan my planners and I would continue to keep V Corps planners informed on this, and would remain engaged after the mission handover. During our force structure work, an issue of mobilization arose.

I informed McKiernan that I had learned of a nuance in mobilization of various reserve infantry units. A battalion of infantry from the National Guard, tasked initially to guard Patriot sites in Saudi Arabia and now being used as a security force in Baghdad, had been mobilized under Operation *Desert Storm* rules in October 2002. The duration of the mobilization was set for only 270 days, per the existing presidential selective reserve call-up at the time. This discovery triggered a complete review of the call-up authorizations of all National Guard and Army Reserve units within theater. I made this a priority effort in the redeployment group to ensure we met the redeployment timelines for this battalion as the timelines were mandated, as we understood it, by law. Our Third Army Reserve Affairs section was involved, as well as our FORSCOM support team. We had to develop a swift understanding of the nuances of calls to active duty as the duration of time, later on called "Boots-on-the-ground" time, a called-up reserve unit could spend in theater materially affected our operational plans.

My planners and I also continued to balance work on the impending GEN Franks presentation for the chairman and secretary of defense, the presentation for the Kuwaiti chief of defense staff, and LTG McKiernan's 13 June meeting with Iraqi general officers on the new Iraqi Army. We also received reports of a mission handover update briefing held in Baghdad for LTG Wallace. The presentation grew "testy," as LTG Wallace, who would depart theater on 14 June, viewed the handover, in his words as "leaving a bucket of shit" for LTG Sanchez to deal with. There was not much he or anyone could do about this fact. The enemy was learning and continuing to fight.

The C5 Plans Update for 11 June, D+83, four days till mission handover, focused on a range of topics, some of which were related to the handover and others to the multitude of activities my planners were dealing with at the time. We were working with the increasingly frantic CENTCOM planners who were under pressure to hone to perfection GEN Franks's upcoming briefing to the chairman and Secretary Rumsfeld. The major point of the update dealt with Coalition integration. The Poles sent us some relatively good news.

We received word from Poland that "unofficially," Spain had communicated to the Polish MoD its intent to participate in the MND operation. The Spanish, however, requested they be more involved in the command of the division, and they wanted a dual Polish/Spanish command. They also requested the post of MND Deputy Commander be held by a Spanish officer for this initial force. and a Spanish general officer be designated as the MND Commander for the next rotation (anticipated to occur after approximately six months). The Polish indicated it would be difficult for this to occur in time for the initial force, due to the late date of the request and the fact a Deputy Commander had already been already designated. The Poles also pointed out some of the other national contingents might question this position since: a) Spain was not the largest troop contributor, and b) they were latecomers to the planning process. General Tysczkiewicz asked for the US position concerning this request from the defense attaché in Warsaw. I told LTG McKiernan we did not know if the request was made to the Defense Department or the State Department. Liaison officers in Warsaw believed they would have some clarity on this situation over the next 24 hours. The Poles handled this situation very deftly.

While I was still engaged in operational and strategic issues, Iraq simmered. From my journal, I recorded reports of a meeting in the north hosted by the Kurdish leader, Barzani. Ambassador Bremer had not been invited. The focus of the meeting was Kurd–Arab unity. The consensus was that Barzani was moving to increase the influence of the Iraqi Senior Leader Council vis-à-vis Ambassador Bremer.

We were also watching the Turkish task force in Dahuk, which was conducting a relief in place and—as per the usual pattern—the force was being probed by Turkey-based Kurdish insurgents. McKiernan asked me to press CENTCOM J5 for a policy regarding the Turkish presence. In the center and west of the country, V Corps was tracking the establishment of a base camp by some unidentified enemy force, al Qaeda or regime loyalist. There was a great deal of traffic from Syria. V Corps wanted to fire ATACMS at the camp. CENTCOM favored a special operations attack on the camp to gather intelligence as well as kill enemy operatives. Baghdad was rife with rumors of retribution committees set up to kill Ba'athists, and fedayeen attack planning against US and Iraqi government targets. McKiernan stressed no action would be conducted against the range of our opponents without positive intelligence. Our special operating forces attacked the enemy base camp in the west on the evening of 11/12 June. It was a complete success, and the enemy force there was destroyed.

The C5 Plans Update for 12 June, D+84, reflected our continuing focus on preparations for the mission handover of CJTF-7 to V Corps. My planners and I worked on coordinating the integration of Coalition forces, monitoring the order of redeployment and handover of responsibilities to V Corps, and the establishment of bases and sustaining structures for the continuing mission, as well as retrograde and redeployment of units being relieved. Indicative of the complexity of war, however, there were also two other events this day which took up my time. There was a snowflake from Washington, and yet another reminder that war is an extension of policy.

General Franks departed for Washington this day. I reported to LTG McKiernan just prior to his scheduled departure that I had a fast request from COL Halverson to answer a snowflake from Secretary Rumsfeld. The Rumsfeld snowflake said:

> I would like a projection on how we are going to be pulling down Kuwait and remaining Gulf states over the next three months… We have some 80,600 in Kuwait and another 15,800 in the remaining gulf states… I would think that at this point you might be able to give me a fix as to what your projection is between now and 1 Oct 03.

I replied:

> Our retrograde from Kuwait is conditions based, the primary condition being a frank assessment of the security situation in Iraq by CJTF-7 and CPA and the ability of the forces to sustain that security. These forces are coalition and Iraqi. As we come to our series of decision points in the upcoming months if conditions allow we will retrograde combat units and supporting combat support and combat service support units, divisional, EAD [echelon above division] and EAC [echelon above corps]. We will leave in place, in Kuwait and Iraq, a theater support structure appropriate to supporting the force that remains in Kuwait. This structure will meet both US and coalition support requirements (as needed). The drawdown of forces in Kuwait will be proportionate to the draw down of forces in Iraq.

I sent this to LTG McKiernan to ensure he knew my reply to COL Halverson and GEN Franks. I was certain that I had answered as he too would have responded. McKiernan did not reply, and I took this to mean I hit the mark in my reply.

We continued to try to nail down whether or not the Indian government would join the Coalition and send a division of troops to support the efforts to build and sustain security in Iraq. We were also trying to understand the CPA's stance on bringing other Arab nations' police forces into Iraq. I reported that I had spoken with planners in the CENTCOM J5 on our Arab police message feedback. Our message was with Ambassador Crocker at the Office of the CPA. The planners in the CENTCOM J5 were under the impression there was a difference of opinion about whether or not to have Arab civil police assist in the effort in Iraq. Ambassador Crocker was reportedly strongly against the proposal, although no one knew why.

In my talks with the J5 planners, I learned the Indian Ambassador would visit CPA either 13 or 14 June. I reported this to LTG McKiernan as I did not know if he knew of this impending visit. I told him I'd learned our folks in the State Department and JCS J5 believed this visit was critical in convincing the Indians to join the Coalition. I learned the J5 wanted CENTCOM to provide a general officer to accompany the Joint Staff team going to New Delhi in the upcoming week. The J5 preferred to have a general officer with current experience in Iraq was assigned to be a member of the team. McKiernan sent BG "E.J." Sinclair, Assistant Division Commander of the 101st Air Assault, on the trip. The Indians appeared to have three issues: 1) command and control, however from the US Ambassador to India, this issue was mostly cosmetic as the Indians did realize they would answer to US commanders, 2) peace keeping vice peacemaking; the Indians expressed concern about which role Indian soldiers would serve, and about the possibility of a scenario in which Indian soldiers were shooting into Muslim crowds—given there are over one hundred and twenty million Muslims in India, and 3) which sector Indian troops would serve in, as we also learned from the US Ambassador that both Secretary Rumsfeld and the President had told the Indian leaders their troops would serve in the north of Iraq. The Indians never did send troops to support the Coalition.

The fight continued across the country. We lost an F-16 on 12 June due to mechanical troubles. The pilot ejected safely and had been recovered. Shia groups in the south and center of the country were vying for power. There were continuing reports of groups planning to infiltrate the Syrian–Iraq border, which triggered more intensive patrolling in the area. On an ominous note, a C-130 coming in for a landing at BIA had been fired at with a man-portable air defense missile.

The C5 Plans Update to LTG McKiernan for 13 June, D+85, was almost mundane. The work on the mission handover was done. My planners' focus was now on coordinating the integration of Coalition forces, monitoring the order of redeployment, and completion of the handover of responsibilities to V Corps. We started to focus efforts on longer-range planning tasks; we completed a draft of the RFF for follow-on forces, and the draft copy for review to the Forces Command G3, the Army G3, and CENTCOM J5, as well as V Corps G3 Plans. We continued to refine the RFF and sent it to forward command post for review. I was departing for Baghdad on 14 June at 0800hrs, where I would link-up with V Corps G3 Plans.

I reported I'd learned from COL Jeong that the ROK Minister of Construction and Transportation was coming to the region for a visit, with a party of 30, on 8–10 July. The ROKs wanted us to provide C-130 transport for the Minister and party from Kuwait to Tallil, where he intended to visit Korean troops and projects in An Nasiriyah and remain overnight. Next, a trip to Baghdad where he wanted to pay a call on the CPA, Ambassador Bremer, and LTG Sanchez, CG, CJTF-7.

He intended to inquire about potential work projects for ROK construction firms before returning to Kuwait. I informed V Corps.

The Iraqi religious and political leaders held a series of meetings across the country. Grand Ayatollah Sistani stated he was suspicious of Sunni Wahabi influence in Iraq. Bakr al Hakim gave an interview on Lebanese television stating Coalition actions were endangering the Iraqi people. A cleric in Fallujah issued a fatwa to kill Ba'ath Party members. In the north, in Mosul, we noticed an emerging arms market. There was also a demonstration conducted by former Iraqi military members who had been angered by the loss of their pensions and the disbanding of the Army. Iraqi police fired on the demonstrators and killed two people. The violence in the country continued.

I flew to Baghdad on the morning of 14 June, D+86. I missed the V Corps change of command ceremony, thus I did not get to say goodbye to LTG Wallace, but I would see him again at Fort Leavenworth. I learned our presentation to the Kuwaiti chief of defense staff was scheduled for 18 June. This was the same day as the change of command of the 2nd Cavalry Regiment, so I would miss another ceremony and another friend, COL Terry Wolff, departing the theater.

The highlight of the day, and night, was a patrol. I accompanied COL Marty Stanton on a patrol through Baghdad. Going outside the wire, Stanton was all business. We loaded and locked our weapons, made radio checks, and coordinated immediate response actions, just in case. We went to the parade ground made famous by the arch of swords, the arms of which were supposed to be modeled on Saddam's. We drove through the downtown area of the city. The markets were coming back. There were fruit sellers and vegetable markets on every corner. Electrical power was coming back to the city, and Jordanian entrepreneurs were in the city in force, selling window air conditioning units, satellite televisions, and satellite dishes. This of course would contribute to a drain on the ancient power grid, but for the moment there was power in the city.

We saw children playing. While I also saw sullen looks on the faces of young men at this moment, Baghdad was not on the edge of social disorder. I recognized a smell I first encountered in Port-au-Prince, and later in Tuzla, Bosnia. It was the smell of leaded gasoline, sewerage, and a crowd of humanity. It was hot. I imagined how tough it was to patrol on foot wearing the "concrete suits" of body armor. Sweating was better than a sucking chest wound, one of Stanton's Soldiers told me. It was good to go outside the wire, as I felt like a Soldier again, if only briefly. We returned to the palace, and I went over my part of the briefing.

The commanders of I MEF and every division in country assembled at Al Faw Palace on 15 June 2003, for the handover of command briefing. LTGs McKiernan, Sanchez, and Conway sat at the head of the table. The division commanders—MGs Petraeus, Blount, Odierno, Mattis, Amos, and BG Marty Dempsey—were all seated around the large conference table. A day earlier, newly promoted LTG Sanchez had taken command of V Corps. He was now going to receive the responsibility of commanding Joint Task Force 7 and all US operations in the Iraq theater of war. The palace ballroom was packed with commanders and key staff officers. Sanchez sat at the head of the table, beaming and very proud of the three stars on his collar. His good mood would not outlast the presentation.

I opened the presentation by stating its purpose, the briefing order, and the presenters. I also outlined the current plan under execution: Eclipse II. MG Marks followed me, and gave a truly insightful and almost prophetic appreciation of the current operational conditions. He mainly spoke from one chart, shown below (see Chart 7). Marks skillfully outlined the lines of operation and the main points of frictions, and how these would influence accomplishment of the major tasks facing JTF-7. He was followed by MG Thurman, who gave an operations overview, and MG Christianson, who gave the state of the supply situation, the expected departure sequence of 3rd ID, and the arrival of follow-on forces, including the array of international forces that would comprise the Polish and British international divisions. LTG McKiernan concluded the handover presentation from his seat at the head of the table.

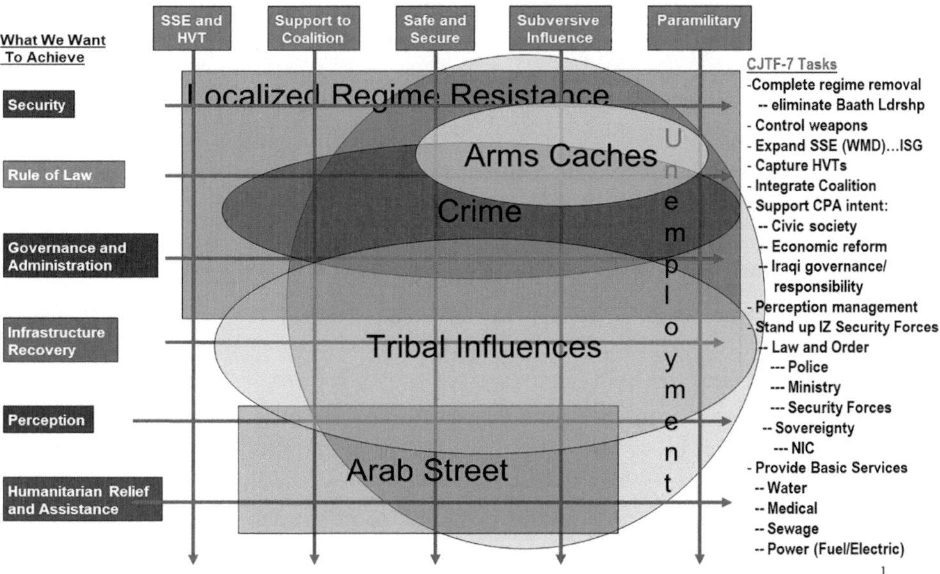

Chart 7. This chart was produced during the wargaming effort to develop operations plan Eclipse II. The purpose was to inform the commander and senior staff of CJTF-7 how the C2 planners saw potential friction points between the CJTF lines of operation and the array of threats we would face. The chart was presented during the handover briefing to LTG Sanchez in June 2003. (From the author's personal files, and prepared in 2003 by officers working for the author.)

Throughout the presentation, I observed LTG Sanchez. When it began he had been sitting upright in his chair and looking at each presenter with a keen eye, leaning forward and occasionally taking notes. As the presentation went on, he began sitting further back in his chair and then sinking lower in his seat. By the end of the presentation, he was slumped in his chair. I believed that, up until the handover briefing, he really had no idea what he was getting into by commanding the forces in Iraq. He had the look of a man who was stunned. When the briefing concluded, LTG Sanchez did not say anything, and the conference broke up as the division commanders assembled around LTG Sanchez and the CFLCC staff cleared out to head south to Kuwait. Before I left for the airport, I went to visit LTC E. J. Degen, the chief of plans for V Corps, now JTF-7.

I found LTCs Degen, Chuck Eassa, and MAJ Kevin Marcus in a whirl of activity. The newly established plans office was almost frenetic with movement and shouts for various papers and curses over inoperative computers. I waited to talk to Degen. From listening to the conversation among the V Corps SAMS guys, I learned that LTG Sanchez had decided our plan, Eclipse II, was not good enough for the current situation. He wanted to put his own stamp on JTF operations, so he directed his planners to start a new mission analysis and give him an initial briefing the next morning.

Every commander has the right to put his stamp on operations, just as LTG McKiernan did when he took command of Third Army/CFLCC. At that time, I was not burned out from fighting my way north to Baghdad, and had a wealth of knowledge available as well as a relatively fresh staff. LTC Degen was not in good shape physically, nor were the officers working for him. They were tired, and now faced learning the style of a new commander. E. J. Degen looked up at me with tired, red eyes.

LTC Degen is a very good man, and while I think he was trying to be somewhat funny, he snarled at me and said, "Kevin, Sanchez just threw out the plan and we are starting over … and you, you bastard, are leaving!" He then turned back to directing the effort of putting together a new look at mission analysis for LTG Sanchez. I could not do anything to help him, save get out of his way.

With E. J. Degen's words still ringing in my ears, MGs Blackman, Marks, Thurman, Christianson, and I boarded the C-130 cargo plane at Baghdad International Airport and flew south to Kuwait. We flew with the tail ramp of the plane open slightly, and as we banked away from the city we could see Baghdad stretch out below us. The plane suddenly twisted and turned in flight, giving all of us a few exciting moments. Once the plane reached level flight, the crew chief came back and spoke with MG Blackman. I saw Blackman shake his head, and then he motioned for all of us to gather about him. He said the crew chief asked if any of us had seen the small arms fire coming at the plane, and then joked that the crew was looking to get an Air Medal. The remainder of the flight was uneventful.

When we returned to Camp Doha, the exodus of the staff began. I started preparing the handover plan for within the C/J-5. I was departing the command, and wanted to ensure I left as few loose ends as possible for my successor. The "Dream Team" of general officers quickly departed.[2] My final planning effort at Third Army to develop and present a proposal to the Kuwaiti Joint Staff on how US operations would be done in the "post-Saddam" era.

The Kuwaitis were anxious to find a "peace dividend," as the Kuwaiti Armed Forces was funding our operations in Kuwait as well as allowing us to use their ports and airfields, military and civilian. They wanted the Camp Doha facility back so it could return to its former use as a light industrial and warehouse complex. McKiernan and I made the case that while Saddam was gone there were other actors in the gulf who would require close coordination between US and Kuwaiti forces, and the geographic location of Kuwait was ideal for the rotation of a US brigade for joint training exercises with Kuwaiti Land Forces. We discussed the reestablishment of a brigade set of equipment in Kuwait, training for Kuwaiti Patriot missile crews, and other stationing plans.

The Kuwaitis were polite, and LTG McKiernan and I left knowing that this was just the first in what would likely be a series of meetings our successors at Third Army would have to undertake before getting a decision from the Kuwait Joint Staff. As the plans team left the country, I continued to think about the situation in Iraq. I spoke with COL Fitzgerald, who was still in Qatar, and CENTCOM headquarters. I tried to make a case for a prolonged withdrawal from theater. The war, I thought, was far from "won."

---

2 Major General Thurman returned to the Army staff as deputy G3. He went on to four stars and command of US Army Forces Command, then US Forces Korea. Major General Christianson served as the G4 of the Army and retired as a three-star general. Major General Webster went on to command Third Army and retired as a three-star general. Major General Blackman retired as a Lieutenant General of Marines. Major General Marks retired as a major general. Major General Stratman, the only flag officer at CFLCC who served under both LTG Mikolashek and LTG McKiernan, retired as a major general. Lieutenant General McKiernan's story is widely known, and he retired as a four-star general.

CHAPTER TEN

Final Thoughts

Shortly after I returned from Baghdad, I made a case, colonel-to-colonel, with COL Fitzgerald: no one should go home until the end of September 2003, the projected end date of Phase III in the original campaign plan. I argued we had not yet captured Saddam, his sons Uday and Qusay, or any prominent member of the deck of 52 BG Brooks made famous. Once again, I erred in not making this an official position, as I never wrote this out or sent it through the chain of command.

I left the region with mixed feelings. My team had written two terrific plans, although the plan for Phase IV had been thrown out at the direction of LTG Sanchez. I felt our headquarters should not have left Iraq, but I was as anxious to go home as everyone else. I left Kuwait on the evening of 4 July. Arnold Schwarzenegger debuted his new Terminator movie at Camp Doha. It was interesting, but I was more interested in heading home. I was going home and on to Fort Leavenworth, where I had the honor of serving as the Director of the School of Advanced Military Studies. I never thought I would return to Baghdad. I put my thoughts in order as a basis from which to put SAMS on a war footing.

Based on my experiences at the operational/strategic level, however, my take—starting with the handover of CJTF-7 from CFLCC to V Corps—was that what contributed to the confusion in method was an absence of orders and commanders' guidance from the headquarters directing operations in Iraq. LTG Sanchez and crew never issued a campaign plan until they were relieved by III Corps. Eclipse II, our Phase IV-focused plan, might not have been perfect—what plan is?—but it did contain commander's guidance and, I am proud to state, did articulate the range of enemy forces we expected to face. We discounted an insurgency as the most likely enemy course of action, preferring to describe the array of threats CJTF-7 would face.

I thought the tactical methods being embraced in 2003 would have dealt with the growing array of threats. In SAMS, we had learned that tactics without strategy, the essential link of tactical success to attaining strategic and policy goals, is the path to defeat. We were certainly on that path for a while. I kept coming back to my failure to persuade LTGs McKiernan and Wallace to place the 101st Air Assault in

Baghdad. My thinking at the time was that the larger presence of infantry, combined with the mobility differential of the helicopters, and a combined arms team of armor and mechanized infantry, would allow a tactical solution to defeat any elements of the threat array I felt we would face. This tactical success would allow us the time to deal with the challenges of rebuilding the political infrastructure needed to re-establish a government. The enormity of that challenge, no government in exile to step in, was undermined by Ambassador Bremer's decision to 1) disband the Iraqi Army and 2) favor de-Ba'athification. At the time I had made the recommendation, Ambassador Bremer was unknown to me.

Frankly, the strategic dysfunction bugged the hell out of me, but I fell back upon the only constant bits of strategic and policy guidance that were available to me from the 1003V campaign plan to wit:

> US Strategic Objectives. Operations in the ITO will support the following US strategic objectives:
>
> A stable IRAQ, with its territorial integrity intact and a broad- based government that renounces WMD development and use and no longer supports terrorism or threatens its neighbors.
>
> Success in IRAQ leveraged to convince or compel other countries to cease support to terrorists and to deny them access to WMD.
>
> Military Objectives. Operations in the ITO will accomplish the following strategic military objectives:
>
> Destabilize, isolate, and overthrow the IRAQI regime and provide support to a new, broad-based government.
>
> Destroy IRAQI WMD capability and infrastructure.
>
> Protect allies and supporters from IRAQI threats and attacks.
>
> Destroy terrorist networks in IRAQ. Gather intelligence on global terrorism, detain terrorists and war criminals and free individuals unjustly detained under the IRAQI regime.
>
> Support international efforts to set conditions for long-term stability in IRAQ and the region.

When in doubt, fall back on the last known guidance, don't ask for anymore guidance, and press on with planning was the line I took. Aside from a few, infrequent, sessions I never engaged LTG McKiernan in a lengthy discussion on what he wanted to get done in Baghdad after we took it so, again, I fell back on my earlier learned behavior as a planner: never ask a question without providing what you think the answer should be. I took on a lot in that regard, crafting the Eclipse plan with my own made-up guidance (and here the team of planners I had on this plan might disagree, because they wanted a lot more than I could give them). In the back of my mind, I also felt this was the ultimate compliment from LTG McKiernan. He trusted me to do what I thought was the correct thing. It was a huge vote of confidence.

Why did I seek an operational solution for a larger problem of strategic dysfunction? Because I felt it was my duty. I was a SAMS guy, and I felt I had to figure it out. In the face of continuous questions on particular facets of the campaign, the serious work of thinking through potential decision points, transitions, branches, and sequels continued. The key result of the continuous questioning was that the senior leadership at CFLCC and CENTCOM, despite their best efforts, were drawn into the current fight and the effort to keep Washington informed. It is a planner's job to think about the "how" and "what if" of unfolding plans, but planners are not empowered to take decisions. That privilege is reserved for commanders.

Commanders at CFLCC and CENTCOM, from my point of view, were caught up in approving what was sent back to Washington. McKiernan repeatedly told me to remain at the operational level while he was drawn more and more into short-term decisions on what to send to Washington through CENTCOM and, once the fighting started, on corps-level tactical decisions in an effort to sequence and sustain the battles en route to Baghdad.

Linking the tactical successes V Corps and I MEF gained en route to Baghdad was important, and while it was well done, this success was gained at the expense of time spent on addressing what to do after we seized Baghdad. LTG McKiernan directed me and the planners to work with MG Whitley so he could focus on getting to Baghdad. MG Whitley, as the deputy commander for Phase IV, would shape the work we were doing on envisioning the future.

Our future was outlined, at first, by the CENTCOM campaign plan. CENTCOM defined Phase IV in three sub-phases: A, B, and C. The CFLCC role in the campaign concluded at the end of Phase IVA. Phase IVA was focused on establishing security conditions and completing emergency repairs to vital infrastructure. The campaign plan envisioned CFLCC handing over responsibility for continuing the Phase IV effort to another headquarters once these conditions had been met.

It has been acknowledged that there was controversy over the differing opinions a range of people held on the number of troops necessary to provide a secure environment in Iraq. This table (below) represents what the CFLCC C5 was asked to produce: the minimum number of combat troops, US, Coalition, etc., we felt were needed to establish a secure environment for the restoration of Iraqi control and free operation of non-governmental organizations such as the UN, etc. We had fewer troops in Iraq than Governor Schwarzenegger had police in California.

Lieutenant General Sanchez assumed command of V US Corps on 14 June 2003, and became Commander, CJTF-7, on 15 June 2003. The CFLCC staff worked with the V Corps staff 1–14 June 2003, on the handover of tasks to ensure as smooth a handover as possible. The CFLCC C2, under the direction of MG James "Spider" Marks, prepared the intelligence situation portion of the handover briefing.

In what I thought was my final analysis of the situation in Iraq, I felt I was leaving too soon. My impression was that LTG Sanchez was out of his depth in dealing with the tactical through to strategic and policy level of command and the echelons of war. Our army was not doing him any favors by leaving him with a very tired corps staff and a dangerous and rapidly changing enemy situation. He did not know about any of the planning efforts completed by my J5 section, or

This table was developed during the wargaming effort to develop operations plan Eclipse II. The purpose was to display the anticipated number of Coalition troops required to sustain the desired level of security in Iraq that would be needed to begin the handover from military to Coalition civil control, and ultimately to Iraqi civil control. The table was presented to the CENTCOM staff in May 2003. A brigade combat team, or BCT, had a strength of five thousand Soldiers. Twenty BCTs would require a similar amount of logistical sustainment units, another 150,000 Soldiers. (From the author's personal files, and prepared in 2003 by officers working for the author.)

Governate	*Units required*	*Comments*
Baghdad	6 BCTs	Capital city, score settling, large population, SSE
Al Basrah/Maysan	2 BCTs	Rumaillah oil fields, score settling, border crossing with Iran, SCIRI
Al Tamim/Irbil	3 BCTs	Kirkuk oil field, KDP/PUK intentions, border crossing with Iran
Salah ad Din	2 BCTs	Tikrit, SSE sites
Ninawa	1 BCT	Mosul, KDP/PUK intentions, border crossing with Syria
As Sulaymaniyah	1 BCT	Al-Qaeda enclave, PUK
Al Anbar	1 BCT	Border crossing with Jordan/Syria, SSE sites, LSA Copperhead
Babil	2 Battalions	Population merge with Baghdad, SSE sites
An Najaf	1 BCT	Shia holy city, LSA Bushmaster
Karbala	2 Battalions	Shia holy city
Dhi Qar	1 BCT	An Nasiriyah, SCIRI, LSA Adder
Wasit	2 Battalions	MeK, border crossing with Iran
Diyala	1 Battalion	MeK, border crossing with Iran, SSE sites
Dahuk	1 Battalion	Border crossing with Turkey
Al Qadasiyah	1 Battalion	
Muthanna		
Total	20 BCTs	

those of the planners at I MEF and V Corps. I also felt that he made a mistake by throwing out the plan in place and starting over, as he would be playing catch up for the duration of his command.

My impression was the prevailing opinion in Washington and Tampa was that the war was over, and it was simply a matter of finding the correct Iraqis to whom we could turn over control of the country and bring the troops home. Simply put, it felt wrong. I was tired of pointing this out and having my thoughts dismissed out of hand, or more often just ignored. I erred in not formally putting my thoughts and recommendations on paper and forwarding them up the chain of command. I was also physically tired when I got back to Atlanta and faced the move across the country to Fort Leavenworth and the School of Advanced Military Studies. I knew I'd retire from that position, so I accepted the challenge of putting the school on a war footing and contributing to our efforts in Iraq and Afghanistan as best I could. I thought I knew I'd never go back to Iraq. I was wrong. I returned to Baghdad in October 2010, at the request of GEN Lloyd Austin, to assist in developing the plan for the handover of security to Iraqi forces, and the operational maneuver of US forces to Kuwait and then back to the US I departed Baghdad in January 2011.

The final word I offer on our attempt at Phase IV planning is from testimony given by MG Whitley. He said:

> ECLIPSE II was named after the comprehensive plan for Post Hostilities in Germany after WWII. There the similarity stops. It was an attempt to produce some coherence for the military aspects of Post Hostilities and give subordinate commands, responsibilities, direction and tasks. Col (now Maj Gen) Colin Boag and the tiny planning team within ORHA produced the civil mirror image. I am not sure this was ever read by anyone in authority. Both plans attempted to bring coherence to chaos. Eclipse II had some local practical effect: military teams and locals working on sanitation plants, jury rigging the national power grid, recommissioning power stations, repairing and opening the Baghdad–Umm Qasr–Basra railway (essential to bring bottled gas from Kuwait into the country so people could cook), hospitals and so on. ECLIPSE II was inadequate and so were the resources available but it did achieve something.[1]

I did not write this book seeking any vindication or praise. My purpose was to write an "unofficial history" from my perspective on the planning efforts that went into the opening of our eight-year campaign in Iraq. The men and women who worked for me from 2002–03 put in their very best effort to craft a complete major operations plan. We did plan for what to do after we got to Baghdad, despite the myth suggesting otherwise which continues to be sustained. Some have recognized the planning that went on: Dr. Gordon Rudd and Dr. Fred Kagan to name but two. While GEN Odierno said (in February 2011) that, at the start of the war, planners were "ill-informed," I am proud to note that in 2006 Kagan thought otherwise, writing:

> Central Command did not entirely ignore the problem of post-war planning, nevertheless. On the contrary, a team headed by Colonel Kevin Benson worked hard to develop a sophisticated plan for the transition from hostilities to peace. It has become common wisdom that this team received the less capable officers, less support, and much less interest than the teams developing the plans for combat operations, and the "Phase IV" plan suffered from important flaws. But

1 From the statement of MG Whitley, CMG, to the United Kingdom Iraq Commission, 2010, undated and unpaginated. Found at https://www.google.com/url?sa=t&rct=j&q=&esrc=s&source=web&cd=&ved=2ahUKEwiCjLm1xsuAAxXdlGoFHRdMD-JcQFnoECBgQAQ&url=https%3A%2F%2Fhumanities-research.exeter.ac.uk%2Fwarn-ingsfromthearchive%2Ffiles%2Foriginal%2F3f60c38294bb67a966676c9584129965.pdf&usg=AOvVaw2qL6UvDSFojRpZrfDomju-&opi=89978449.

> the work Colonel Benson and his team did would have provided Franks and Rumsfeld with a good basis for thinking about establishing the conditions for a successful transition period, had they heeded it.[2]

President Obama announced the end of the Iraq War on 21 October 2011.

2 Frederick W. Kagan, *Finding the Target The Transformation of American Military Policy*, New York: Encounter Books, 2006, p. 335.

Bibliography

Books

Bush, George W. *Decision Points*. New York: Crown Publishers, 2010.

Clausewitz, Carl. *On War*. Edited and translated by Michael Howard and Peter. Princeton, NJ: Princeton University Press, 1976.

Cohen, Eliot. *Supreme Command: Soldiers, Statesmen and Leadership in Wartime*. New York: Free Press, 2002.

Draper, Robert. *To Start A War: How the Bush Administration took America into Iraq*. New York: Penguin Press, 2020.

Fontenot, Gregory, E. J. Degen, and Sohn, David. *ON POINT: The United States Army in Operation* Iraqi Freedom *Through 01 May 2003*. Fort Leavenworth, KS: Combat Studies Institute Press, 2004.

Gordon, Michael and Bernard Trainor. *COBRA II: The Inside Story of the Invasion and Occupation of Iraq*. New York: Pantheon Books, 2006.

Issikoff, Michael and Corn, David. *HUBRIS: The Inside Scandal of Spin, Scandal, and the Selling of the Iraq War*. New York: Crown Publishers, 2006.

Kagan, Frederick W. *Finding the Target: The Transformation of American Military Policy*. New York: Encounter Books, 2006.

Rayburn, Joel D. and Frank K. Sobchak, ed. *The US Army in the Iraq War, Volume 1, 2003–2006 Invasion—Insurgency—Civil War*. Carlisle Barracks, PA: US Army War College Press, January 2019.

Ricks, Thomas E. *FIASCO: The American Military Adventure in Iraq*. New York: The Penguin Press, 2006.

Rudd, Gordon W. *Reconstructing Iraq Regime Change, Jay Garner, and the ORHA Story*. Lawrence, KS: University Press of Kansas, 2011.

Oral Histories

Douglas Feith. Accessed at https://millercenter.org/the-presidency/presidential-oral-histories/douglas-j-feith-oral-history, February 20, 2024.

Index

Abizaid, John, 52, 55, 67, 72–74, 76, 80, 98, 99, 118, 145, 150–153, 159, 161, 162, 164, 169, 184, 232
Agoglia, John, xix, 160
Amos, James, 13, 14, 236
Arnold, Steven, xvii
Blackman, Robert R. "Rusty," 39, 57, 64, 65, 73, 80, 93, 97, 106–108, 111, 115, 117, 119, 121, 129, 139, 145, 148, 151–154, 156, 157, 160, 166, 168, 172, 176, 179, 187, 189, 191, 196, 197, 199, 200, 210, 211, 226, 238, 239
Blount, Buford "Buff," 173, 236
Boag, Colin, 91, 245
Boltz, Steven, 81
Bonham, Gordon, 35
Bradshaw, Adrian, 18, 18n, 33
Bremer, Paul AMB, xx, 157, 184, 185, 187, 193, 197, 198, 204, 212, 213, 215, 218, 221–224, 226, 227, 229, 231, 233, 235, 242
Brims, Robin, 33
Bromberg, Howard, 48, 61, 125–26
Brooks, Vincent, vi, vii, 1, 217, 241
Brown, Heidi, 82
Cagan, Debra, 206, 207
Cambone, Steven, xviii, xxi, 102–104, 106, 108, 110, 117, 119, 120, 122
Chalabi, Ahmed, xix, xx, 129, 148, 150, 152, 169, 174, 177, 191, 212
Chiarelli, Peter, 37, 74–76
Christianson, Claude "Chris," 26, 42, 48, 68, 69, 95, 182, 186, 214, 237, 238, 239n
Cody, Richard, 32, 74, 75, 94, 189, 228, 229
Cohen, Eliot, 5
Coleman, John, 81
Conway, James, 49, 67, 71, 72, 77, 79, 85, 105, 173, 236
Davis, Willie, 6, 38, 45, 137, 176
De Rita, Larry, 131, 135, 137, 145, 150, 167
Degen, E. J., 231, 238
Delbianco, Gene, 153, 154
Dellajocano, John, 132, 148, 151
Dreby, Andy, 44
Drumm, Robert, xix, xx
Elliot, Nick, 74
Eshelmann, Mark, 97, 127, 133, 135, 143, 166–168
Feith, Douglas, xviii, xxi, 98, 115, 118, 119, 122, 128, 135, 145, 167
Field, Chris, 13, 13n4, 43n3, 217
Fitzgerald, Michael, xix, 20, 22, 24, 25, 34, 91, 93, 96, 118, 124, 130, 136, 144–146, 155, 158, 161, 162, 165, 166, 176, 185, 186, 193, 197, 203, 225, 239, 241
Franks, Fred, 49, 50
Franks, Tommy, xvii, xviii, xix, 5, 7, 8, 11–13, 16n7, 19, 22–24, 27, 30–32, 34, 35, 37, 43–45, 52, 56, 60, 62, 66, 69, 73, 75, 77, 79, 80, 83, 89, 91–93, 100, 102–106, 112, 126, 130, 136, 139, 141, 142, 144, 145, 147, 150, 151, 153–155, 160–163, 165–169, 171, 175, 176, 183, 187, 193, 211–214, 218, 221–225, 227, 228, 230–234, 246
Freakley, Ben, 81
Gaines, Winston, 6, 38, 137, 143
Garner, Jay, 46, 52, 56, 83, 84, 88, 90, 91, 93, 97, 98, 101, 103, 106, 115, 119, 122, 127–129, 131, 132, 141, 145, 147, 148, 157, 159, 167, 177
Gingrich, Newt, xix
Goedkoop, Thomas, 36, 213
Gordon, Michael, 73, 74, 96
Greer, James, 51
Grieme, Wayne, 45, 74, 90n
Guenther, Chris, 136
Halverson, David, xix, 161, 166, 203, 230, 234
Hamm, Candi, 38
Hawkins, Steven, 45, 46, 88,
Hawrylak, Michael, 7–9, 51,
Hendricks, Michael, 6, 19, 38, 39, 46, 68, 144, 158, 183, 210, 211
Hildenbrand, Mark, 81
Huelfer, Evan, 18, 37, 38, 43, 45, 64, 163, 183, 194
Innocenti, William, 45, 68, 74, 90n3, 163, 202, 209, 225

Irons, Richard, 32, 33
Jeong, COL, 135, 183–187, 189, 204, 235
Jette, Bruce, 109
Jones, Frank, 30, 38, 43, 44, 156–158, 197, 198, 215, 226
Keane, Jack, 14, 32, 72, 146, 147, 151, 154
Kern, BG, 160
Kratzer, David, 79, 173
Luck, Gary, 49–51
Marcus, Kevin, 165, 238
Marks, James "Spider," 26, 29, 29n2, 42, 47–49, 78, 134, 148, 182, 218, 237, 238, 239n, 243,
Mattis, James, 13, 14, 236
McKiernan, David, 6, 12–14, 18–21, 24, 26–38, 40–47, 50, 52, 53, 55–62, 64, 65, 67, 69–80, 82–86, 88–90, 94, 95, 97–99, 101, 105–107, 111, 112, 120, 127–136, 141–145, 148, 150, 151, 153–155, 159–161, 163–169, 171–173, 176–179, 182, 184, 185, 188, 189, 191–194, 196–201, 206, 208–218n2, 221–239n, 242–244
Mikolashek, P. T., xviii, xix, 4, 6–9, 26, 28, 31, 32, 88, 239n
Moseley, Michael, 7–9, 13, 27, 169
Odierno, Ray, 98, 236, 245
Parasiliti, Andrew, 153
Patten, Glenn, 6, 38, 45
Penor, Joseph, 74, 81, 94
Petraeus, David, 172, 173, 236
Reilly, Thomas, 4, 19, 20, 38, 39, 43, 44, 56, 66, 68, 69, 90, 101, 133, 134, 151, 184
Reith, John, 63, 178–180
Renuart, Gene, 10, 22, 23, 26, 30, 57, 59, 83, 91, 126, 141, 142, 147, 161, 162, 177, 223–225, 231
Robb, James, 55, 101, 117, 122, 128, 147, 161, 164, 166, 189, 211, 224
Rotkoff, Steven, 21, 29
Rumsfeld, Donald, xviii, xxi, 1, 2, 10, 12, 17, 23, 30–32, 50, 56, 68, 73, 75, 78, 83, 85, 91, 93, 94, 97, 98, 101, 102, 105, 107, 116, 118, 119, 121–124, 126–128, 132, 135–137, 140, 141, 145, 147, 148, 150, 151, 155, 160–164, 166–169, 174, 184, 203, 211, 213, 215, 222, 231, 233–235, 246
Sadr, Moqtada al, 134, 150, 157, 174, 190, 229, 231
Sanchez, Ricardo, 215, 232, 233, 235–238, 241, 243
Schneider, James, 17, 151
Sharp, Walter, xvii, xix, 99, 118, 124, 128, 135, 145, 167
Shinseki, Eric, 36, 56–57, 66–67, 78, 137, 178, 230
Sinclair, "E.J.", 81, 235
Sistani, Grand Ayatollah Ali al, 79, 157, 195, 201, 215, 229, 236
Slocombe, Walt, 157, 159, 187, 189, 197–201
Snowflake, 1, 4, 5, 9, 12, 50, 73, 75, 76, 85, 144, 155, 234
Sparks, John, CSM, 47, 82, 222
Sparling, Bryan, 45, 74, 90n
Spiller, Roger, 87, 88, 88n
Stanton, Marty, 123, 165, 236
Stewart, Stan, 38, 139, 163
Sterling, Jack, 81
Stratman, Henry, 3, 4, 29–31, 42, 64, 65, 69, 93, 97, 115, 128, 129, 139, 145, 146, 151, 156, 168, 191, 196, 210, 231, 239n
Sutherland, Thomas, 45, 163
Swannack, Charles, 172, 173
Talwar, Puneet, 153
Teltoe, Trinket, 43n4, 91, 222
Thurman, J. D., 10, 26–29, 37, 38, 42, 48, 50, 59, 65, 69, 70, 78, 112, 125, 127, 130, 143, 145, 147, 148, 159, 174, 177, 182, 189, 199, 200, 211–214, 224, 226, 228, 230, 237–239n
Tysczkiewicz, Andrzej, 196, 197, 200, 201, 203–205, 208–210, 213, 233
Wallace, W. Scott, 13, 48, 49, 70, 77, 78, 81, 85, 86, 91, 104, 105, 173, 215, 232, 236, 241
Weber, Bill, 81
Webster, William G., 21, 26, 27, 39, 42, 46, 50, 57, 59, 64, 65, 68, 69, 78, 83, 93, 97, 102, 103, 115, 129, 130, 135, 139, 143, 145, 147, 151, 156, 167, 168, 170, 191, 196, 214, 216, 226, 239n
Whitcomb, Steven, 161, 162
Whitley, Albert, 45, 46, 55-59, 61–63, 73, 76, 84, 89–91, 97, 100, 108–110, 112, 117–120, 123, 125, 136, 140–142, 144, 148, 227, 243, 245, 245n
Whitlock, Joseph, 36–38, 43n4, 108, 176
Wickman, Al, 8, 9
Wolff, Terry, 106, 118, 236
Wolfowitz, Paul, xviii, xxi, 4, 64, 76, 98, 109, 144, 145, 167, 169
Workman, Marc, 82